TRUST IN SOCIETY

TRUST IN SOCIETY

KAREN S. COOK

EDITOR

VOLUME II IN THE RUSSELL SAGE FOUNDATION SERIES ON TRUST

Russell Sage Foundation • New York

The Russell Sage Foundation

The Russell Sage Foundation, one of the oldest of America's general purpose foundations, was established in 1907 by Mrs. Margaret Olivia Sage for "the improvement of social and living conditions in the United States." The Foundation seeks to fulfill this mandate by fostering the development and dissemination of knowledge about the country's political, social, and economic problems. While the Foundation endeavors to assure the accuracy and objectivity of each book it publishes, the conclusions and interpretations in Russell Sage Foundation publications are those of the authors and not of the Foundation, its Trustees, or its staff. Publication by Russell Sage, therefore, does not imply Foundation endorsement.

Library of Congress Cataloging-in-Publication Data
Trust in society / Karen S. Cook, editor.
    p. cm.—Russell Sage Foundation series on trust; v. 2)
  Includes bibliographical references and index.
  ISBN 0-87154-248-X
    1. Interpersonal relations. 2. Trust. I. Cook, Karen S. II. Series.
HM1106.T78 2001
302—dc21

                                                  00-050998

Text design by Suzanne Nichols

RUSSELL SAGE FOUNDATION
112 East 64th Street, New York, New York 10021
10 9 8 7 6 5 4 3 2 1

The Russell Sage Foundation Series on Trust

T HE RUSSELL SAGE Foundation Series on Trust examines the conceptual structure and the empirical basis of claims concerning the role of trust and trustworthiness in establishing and maintaining cooperative behavior in a wide variety of social, economic, and political contexts. The focus is on concepts, methods, and findings that will enrich social science and inform public policy.

The books in the series raise questions about how trust can be distinguished from other means of promoting cooperation and explore those analytic and empirical issues that advance our comprehension of the roles and limits of trust in social, political, and economic life. Because trust is at the core of understandings of social order from varied disciplinary perspectives, the series offers the best work of scholars from diverse backgrounds and, through the edited volumes, encourages engagement across disciplines and orientations. The goal of the series is to improve the current state of trust research by providing a clear theoretical account of the causal role of trust within given institutional, organizational, and interpersonal situations, developing sound measures of trust to test theoretical claims within relevant settings, and establishing some common ground among concerned scholars and policymakers.

Previous Volume in the Series

Contents

Contributors

Karen S. Cook is the Ray Lyman Wilbur Professor of Sociology at Stanford University.

Michael Bacharach is professor of economics and director of the Bounded Rationality in Economic Behaviour Research Unit at the University of Oxford, and fellow of Christ Church, Oxford.

Jean Ensminger is professor of anthropology at the California Institute of Technology.

Diego Gambetta is reader in sociology at the University of Oxford, and fellow of All Souls College, Oxford.

Robert Gibbons is Sloan Distinguished Professor of Management at the Massachusetts Institute of Technology.

Russell Hardin is professor of politics at New York University and professor of political science at Stanford University.

Carol A. Heimer is professor of sociology and chair of the Department of Sociology at Northwestern University and senior research fellow at the American Bar Association.

Jack Knight is the Sidney W. Souers Professor of Government at Washington University in St. Louis.

Roderick M. Kramer is professor in the Graduate School of Business at Stanford University.

Gerry Mackie is research fellow in the Social and Political Theory Group within the Research School of Social Sciences at the Australian National University, Canberra, Australia.

David M. Messick is Morris and Alice Kaplan Professor of Ethics and Decision in Management at the Kellogg Graduate School of Management at Northwestern University.

Gary Miller is professor of political science at Washington University in St. Louis.

Victor Nee is Goldwin Smith Professor of Sociology at Cornell University.

Jimy Sanders is professor of sociology at the University of South Carolina.

Dietlind Stolle is assistant professor of political science at the University of Pittsburgh.

Tom R. Tyler is professor of psychology at New York University.

Toshio Yamagishi is professor of social psychology at Hokkaido University in Japan.

Trust in Society

KAREN S. COOK

W E ARE concerned as a nation about declining trust in doctors, lawyers, merchants, and priests, as well as in politicians, teachers, and scientists. Recent explorations of the topic of trust extend over a wide range of phenomena, including trust in teams, families, organizations, the professions, and various other social, political, and economic institutions. The chapters of this volume were written by scholars from a variety of disciplines who were brought together at a conference in Seattle and subsequently at various workshops in New York City to begin to identify the fundamental concerns of both the social scientists writing about trust and those in the society at large who seemed to be worried about matters of trust. Though work on the topic dates back several decades (if not earlier), its reemergence as a central topic of discussion across the social sciences in the 1990s can be argued to reflect the political, social, and economic realities of an increasingly interdependent, global world. This renewed interest also comes on the heels of massive, somewhat cataclysmic social and political upheavals in the world political scene, two of the most significant being the "fall of the Wall" in 1989 and the largely unanticipated demise of the Soviet Union. Such periods of uncertainty understandably occasion reflections on the breakdown of trust.

Our conferences and workshops focused on identifying the various forms of trust that are discussed in the social science literature and analyzing the functions of trust in society. We also focused on alternatives to trust. What social institutions and social customs emerge in the absence of trust or to handle new problems and contexts in which trust might be hard to establish? How effective are these institutions and customs? What link do they have to the decline in trust, and how is trust fostered where it does not exist? What mechanisms replace trust, and at what cost? Other questions were also addressed in our discussions. These are identified more fully as we lay out the framework for this volume and discuss its contents.

This is the second volume in our series on trust sponsored by the Russell Sage Foundation, which funded the conferences and workshops that produced the papers we include here. The first volume is *Trust and Governance*, edited by Valerie Braithwaite and Margaret Levi (1998). It focuses more exclusively on the role of trust in good government and evaluates the ways in which trust and distrust form the basis for effective governing arrangements. That volume addresses some key questions: Is trust really essential to good governance, or are strong laws more important? What leads people either to trust or to distrust government, and what makes officials trustworthy? Can trusting too easily render the public vulnerable to government corruption, and if so, what safeguards are necessary? Many of the essays in this volume assume that regulatory institutions are necessary to protect citizens from the worst effects of misplaced trust. Too much trust in government may not be a good thing in democratic societies.

The Structure of the Book

This volume takes a broader sweep, moving from the psychology of trust to much more macro claims about the organizational, institutional, and cultural causes and consequences of trust. The book is divided into three parts. The three chapters in part I, "Conceptions of Trust," lay out several overlapping and sometimes competing orientations to trust. This part begins with a chapter by Russell Hardin, who compares his own view of trust as "encapsulated interest" with other conceptions of trust, including some of the formulations presented in this volume. Carol Heimer's chapter on solving the problem of trust focuses on two primary determinants of the degree to which trust is required in any social situation: the nature of the uncertainty in the situation and the degree of the actor's vulnerability. She provides a complex theory of the trust-related mechanisms used in differing social settings to reduce vulnerability and uncertainty. Her essay is followed by a chapter by David Messick and Roderick Kramer, who lay out the foundations for treating trust as a "shallow form of morality." Unlike the formulation outlined by Hardin (and developed more fully in his forthcoming book *Trust and Trustworthiness*), these authors view trust as the result of a specific decision often based on the presumed honesty and perceived morality (not the interests) of the trustee. Heimer's argument includes aspects of both Hardin's and Messick and Kramer's theoretical formulations.

The second part of the book, "Trust: Social Bases and Social Consequences," includes five chapters that focus on different bases of trust and the significance of these bases of trust in various social settings. Toshio Yamagishi, for example, treats trust as based on social intelligence—a kind of intelligence that allows individuals to assess the degree of risk they may face in social situations when confronted with the possibility of interacting with strangers who might be the path to new and beneficial outcomes. He compares standard conceptions of differences between high and low trusters in their capacities for social intelligence and examines the implications of these differences for social interactions. Michael Bacharach and Diego Gambetta shift the focus to trustworthiness and our capacity (possibly based on social intelligence) to detect it in those we decide to trust. For Bacharach and Gambetta, the "secondary problem of trust," that is, whether we can trust the signs of trustworthiness we are confronted with prior to our decision to trust, is the *central* problem of trust. They highlight the analysis of signals, mimicry, and identity in an attempt to specify the precise conditions under which trust is justified.

Jean Ensminger's chapter also focuses on the determination of trustworthiness. She examines the use of "fictive kin" relations as a basis for social trust among East African herders. Hers is an interesting story (examined in more depth later in this introduction) about the use of pseudo-kin relations to solve a principal-agent problem among the nomadic pastoralists along the Kenyan coast near Somalia. Dietlind Stolle's chapter moves us from Africa to Europe, where she investigates involvement in social associations as a basis for the development of generalized trust in society. Stolle tests an argument made popular by Robert Putnam (1995) in the context of Germany, Sweden, and the United States. Her results are discussed in relation to the link between social capital and the emergence of general trust. Part II concludes with a chapter by Gerry Mackie, who argues that differing patterns of family formation may have been a significant basis for the development of different types of trust in different societies in Europe, moving from high-trust societies in the northwest to lower-trust societies in the southeast of Europe. It is an intriguing idea that needs further examination.

The third and final part of the book, "Trust: Network, Organizational, and Institutional Bases," comprises five essays that investigate the specific role of trust in the broader social context. Tom Tyler's chapter examines the role of trust in authorities in the production of voluntary deference in society. Gary Miller presents a theory and some evidence concerning the importance of trust inside organizations, particularly with respect to motivating productivity and cooperation apart from other forms of incentives. Robert Gibbons extends some of the work in Miller's essay to the larger society, using a repeated-game analysis of relational contracting within and between firms. Gibbons also investigates the role of the "self-enforcing institutions of political economy," the state being among the most prominent. The final two chapters look beyond organizations and the economy to examine the role of trust in socially diverse societies characterized by high rates of immigration. Jack Knight compares the effectiveness of social norms and the rule of law as mechanisms for building trust in socially diverse societies. Victor Nee and Jimy Sanders look empirically at how new immigrants to states like California (the Los Angeles area, for example) find access to needed social and economic capital and how they use trust relations, initially based directly or indirectly on kinship and ethnic ties, as the basis for economic and social advancement.

I describe the contribution of each chapter to the analysis of the role of trust in society more completely before drawing a few conclusions based on the work presented in this book. I begin with the more conceptual pieces.

Conceptions of Trust

In the first chapter Hardin lays out a framework for analyzing current conceptions of trust. A major contribution of this chapter is that it also makes clear the distinction between trust and related concepts of trustworthiness, confidence, and the act of entrusting something to someone. In clarifying the conceptual ground he identifies several major confusions in the work on trust. Perhaps the most common flaw in much of the literature on trust is the failure to distinguish discussions of trust from discussions of trustworthiness. If everyone we interact with were trustworthy, there would be no problem of trust. Much of the concern with trust in the popular literature can best be understood as concern over the lack of trustworthiness in society. When we attempt to produce mechanisms for making people more trustworthy, we are trying to solve the problem of trust by creating conditions under which it is much less risky to trust. At the extremes, if you are 100 percent trustworthy, I would be taking no risk in leaving my valuables in your possession; the act of "trusting" in this context is thus not at all problematic. In fact, for Hardin this kind of act would not fit well under the rubric of trust. For him it is simply the class of actions in which we choose to take or not take risks. For Heimer (chapter 2) I would not be particularly vulnerable in such a situation, given your high degree of trustworthiness; thus trust would not be much at stake in the interaction. For her trust comes into play in situations involving both the vulnerability of one party to the other and uncertainty.

Hardin develops briefly what he calls the encapsulated-interest conception of trust. He defines trust as a three-part relation: A trusts B to do X. It is a dyadic conception, focused on specific actions. All three parts are necessary. It does not make much sense in his formulation to state that A trusts B. Implied in this statement is a list of specifics that A trusts B to do. A might trust B to do X, Y, and Z, but not S and T. So I might trust you to manage my money while I am away on vacation and to handle my mail, perhaps even to feed and take care of my cat, but I might not trust you with my car or my child. Understanding trust, Hardin argues, entails clarifying the underlying logic of the trust relation and being precise about what we mean.

"Encapsulated interest" refers to the idea that A trusts B with respect to X when A believes that B has some reason to act in A's best interest or to take A's interests fully into account. This can occur through B's close identification with A, such that A's welfare is highly valued by B. Or more simply in many cases, perhaps B has good reason to take A's interest into account because B wants to maintain the relationship with A. Though some will object to Hardin's use of the term "interest," it is important to note that the definition fits many of the cases we would want to include under a definition of a trust relationship, including mother-child relations and relations between intimates. Excluded from the definition are acts of "pure" altruism in which an action is taken on behalf of another for purely moral reasons—that is, it was the "right thing to do." In practice, however, many of the situations we might at first wish to identify as pure acts of altruism often have, on closer analysis, more affinity with the encapsulated-interest account.

Heimer provides a more general framework for the analysis of problems of trust. From her perspective, the core elements in trust relations are uncertainty and vulnerability. In solving problems of trust, she argues, actors select strategies that reduce uncertainty or decrease vulnerability depending on the particular social context in which the problems emerge. In more traditional societies people attempt to reduce uncertainty about the intentions and competence of others. In modern societies, she argues, efforts to reduce vulnerability are more common. Mechanisms for reducing vulnerability in the face of increased contact with strangers include enforceable contracts and insurance schemes, among others. Reducing uncertainty entails reputational effects and efforts in traditional communities—for example, a by-product of controlling behavior normatively is to shift the uncertainty to relations between communities rather than within communities.

Heimer identifies the characteristics of four types of trust relations: faith, confidence, legal trust, and trust/distrust. Trust problems, for her, encompass a broad array of dimensions. For Hardin trust issues are to be distinguished from problems of faith, confidence, and regulatory control (legal mechanisms). Heimer's perspective places trust issues firmly under a broad umbrella of concepts linked closely to her underlying notions of uncertainty and vulnerability. Insurance, she claims, is a particularly effective technique for managing vulnerability under uncertainty.

She suggests that such strategies—ones fundamentally based on distrust (or the lack of trust)—can lay the foundation eventually for the formation of trust relations: "Distrust is in important ways a minimax solution in which people try to control losses." Mechanisms put in place to limit loss from distrust based on the lack of information regarding intentions and competence may generate the conditions under which trust can emerge if they allow people to collect information and take tentative steps toward establishing trust where none previously existed.

Woven throughout Heimer's chapter is the story of the "Jane" organization, set up a few years before the *Roe v. Wade* decision in 1973 to help women terminate unwanted pregnancies at a time when abortions were not legal. The case is interesting precisely because trust was a central element in the relations involved. The organization established a network of ties between physicians willing to perform abortions and those women who wanted them. Women in support of the "right to choose" were the agents for the women in need. All of the participants in this informal network were concerned about trust. Could the physicians trust their clients not to reveal their identity? Could the women who received abortions trust the physicians to deliver high-quality care? Could the women who connected the clients with physicians trust that they would not be betrayed in their efforts to offer an illegal service at some risk? In various respects all of the parties involved had to deal with both uncertainty and vulnerability, the key elements in Heimer's analysis of trust relations. Understanding how the parties dealt with uncertainty and vulnerability allows her to make interesting generalizations about the kinds of behavior and social structures that are likely to emerge under such conditions. For example, good information on the reputations of the physicians was crucial to the survival of the organization. The women who used Jane's abortion services were debriefed after the event by members of the organization in order to determine their perceptions of the competence and trustworthiness of the physicians involved. Since many unqualified physicians were also offering such services underground, it was critical for Jane to protect itself by establishing its own assessment of the competence of physicians serving its clients. Other strategies were also adopted that helped the participants deal with both the uncertainty of the times and their own vulnerabilities. Trust is certainly a central element in this story, but even more important in many respects is the establishment of the trustworthiness of others, a theme present in many chapters in this volume, especially Tom Tyler's chapter on trust and social identity (chapter 9).

In this volume Messick and Kramer (chapter 3) come closest to including morally motivated actions in their account of trust, though they define trust in terms of a "shallow" form of morality. Using this term, they imply that acts of trust are decisions in situations of interdependence in which the potential costs involved in the interaction depend on another person's actions. In an interesting twist to the standard decisionmaking literature, they treat the decision to place trust in someone as based on an assessment of the degree to which that person will abide by "ordinary ethical rules," or what they refer to as a "shallow" form of morality. Will the person act honestly? Will she abide by her promise? The failure of trust thus becomes a violation of these simple ethical rules, generating a moral tone to the failure to be trustworthy that is reflected in much of the extant literature on trust.

The underlying argument made by Messick and Kramer is that the decision to trust follows many of the same principles of cognitive miserliness that other decisions do. For example, decisionmaking heuristics are often applied in complex decision situations in order to help us "satisfice" in arriving at an acceptable decision. Given information limits, we often satisfice. One way in which we cut corners in such situations is to use as proxies for more complete information ascriptive characteristics of individuals as the basis for our assessments of trustworthiness. As argued by Messick (1991), Messick and Kramer (this volume), and Tyler (this volume), common group membership is invoked in order to provide relevant information about the probable trustworthiness of the other party. Marilynn Brewer (1981) refers to this as "depersonalized trust"—trust based on category, not personal information or experience. Messick and Kramer explore the implications of their view of trust for embedded relations in different organizational settings, including in temporary work groups (on "swift trust," see also Meyerson, Weick, and Kramer 1996).

The Social Bases and Consequences of Trust

The chapters by Bacharach and Gambetta and by Yamagishi deal more directly with how we decide whom to trust and what the differences are between high trusters and low trusters in society. What signs or signals allow us to determine who is trustworthy, and how do we sort out mimicry from truth-telling in this context? Bacharach and Gambetta set out to examine how people solve the primary problem of trust—that is, answering the question "Can I trust this person to do X?" They locate the source of the uncertainty in the truster's lack of knowledge concerning the payoffs of the trustee and the extent to which the trustee will in fact turn out to be trustworthy. They label this latter problem the "secondary problem of trust"—the problem of determining whether to "trust" the signs that someone is trustworthy.

Bacharach and Gambetta analyze in detail the significance of signs of trustworthiness for the "primary problem of trust"—deciding when and whom to trust about what. Using signaling theory and game theory, they work out some of the specific conditions under which trustworthiness is accurately communicated and trust therefore justified. The problem to be resolved in this analysis is the potential for opportunism and mimicry of trustworthiness. While Hardin's approach addresses the question "When is it rational to trust someone to do something?," Bacharach and Gambetta deal with the related problem: "How can I, who am trustworthy, convince the truster that I am?" Much of the game-theoretic literature on trust actually deals more successfully with the latter concern. The focus on credible commitments (such as "hostage posting") is only one example.

Signaling theory proves to be a powerful tool enabling Bacharach and Gambetta not only to frame the problem of trustworthiness more precisely but also to answer questions concerning when, and how much, false signaling will occur. They develop a more in-depth analysis of the role of identity signaling in situations in which the actors must decide whom to trust. In this way their work is closely linked to the approach taken by Messick and Kramer, who also treat the primary trust problem as falling within the domain of more general decisionmaking principles. Another commonality in these chapters is the focus on understanding something about the person to be trusted. Is he or she trustworthy? Answers to this question can hinge on assessments of the extent to which the truster either believes the trustee will follow simple ethical rules (like honesty) or makes a direct assessment of the trustee's trustworthiness based on the truster's own belief, derived from experience, that the trustee's qualities make him or her a good bet. Identity, both sets of authors argue, often "signals" trustworthiness since it is a sign of a more mundane quality that is known to be correlated with trustworthiness (for example, same clan, hometown, gender, or ethnicity).

Yamagishi's chapter on trust as a form of social intelligence develops the argument that high trusters are not more gullible, as some have argued, but in fact more discerning in their attitudes toward others. Contrary to popular wisdom, the experimental evidence that Yamagishi presents suggests that high trusters are more capable of detecting and processing proper signs of risk in social interaction, whereas low trusters tend to avoid such risks. This argument, while interesting at the individual level, is even more intriguing in its implication for groups or societies generally characterized by high and low trust (see, for example, Fukuyama 1995). Yamagishi speculates that the people in societies that are generally distrustful are less likely to enter into risky social interactions and more likely to interact in relatively closed circles, even at the risk of giving up new opportunities. Development of generalized trust under these circumstances, he goes on to argue, is not easy: not only does distrust breed distrust, but individuals in these societies must make conscious efforts to develop the social intelligence required for detecting risks and taking risks when appropriate. For Bacharach and

Gambetta the person making such an effort would need to increase his attention to sign detection and develop mechanisms for detecting mimicry or false signals of trustworthiness. Yamagishi and his collaborators have demonstrated that high trusters in various settings are more accurate in discerning which partners are likely to defect and which are likely to cooperate. A natural extension of this work would be to explore further the specific mechanisms by which high trusters come to develop this cognitive capacity (which may well be what Bacharach and Gambetta refer to as "sign detection"). What about those who are low in trust? Here the picture is more dismal. The evidence suggests that they are more likely to make mistakes in sign detection; it is thus more prudent for them to assume the worst about human nature to avoid being victimized. Breaking out of this equilibrium state is difficult, since these individuals take fewer and fewer risks, and then only to discover that the costs of misplaced trust are often high.

When the costs of misplaced trust are high, individuals often try to solve the problem of trust by relying on family members or other kin, assuming them to be more trustworthy than strangers. Embedding the act of trust in a network of social relations is a move that often reduces both uncertainty and vulnerability. It also increases the extent to which the trusted has an incentive to fulfill the trust. The use of family relations to "solve" the problem of trust is so common that in some cultures it has been extended by creating kinlike relations as the basis for trust in significant economic endeavors. Ensminger provides a particularly compelling example. The Orma of northeastern Kenya, where Ensminger does fieldwork, have evolved a "fictive kin" system for treating some hired herders as if they were sons. Ensminger argues that this system has evolved to solve a problem of trust that involves both uncertainty and vulnerability, to use Heimer's terms. In the cattle-dependent Orma economy, cattle are one of the most significant family resources. The cattle in this area are often herded on remote camps to take advantage of lush lands for grazing and watering. The practice has grown with economic changes in the country, necessitating further concern over securing the livelihood of the herd owner, who must entrust his herd to those in the camps. In the past the herders were sons of the herd owner, but sons are now being educated and are less available for labor. To reduce "agency costs" the Orma develop very close personal ties with their non-kin herders, even to the extent that some are treated as "adopted" sons. This allows them to generate trust relations that reduce the necessity for monitoring.

The puzzle that Ensminger sets out to solve is how this mechanism for solving the problem of trust evolves and how effective it is as a substitute for supervision. She also attempts to clarify within the context of economic agency theory precisely how kin relations (or kinlike relations) reduce transaction costs, a key argument in the work of Robert Pollak (1985) and others. Reciprocity (and what some theorists have called generalized exchange) comes to characterize the relations between Orma herd owners and herders. This entails looser accounting over time and development of a sense of loyalty or commitment to the relation itself (see also Lawler and Yoon 1998). Ensminger's fairly detailed account of the Orma herding relationships in the end fits in well, she argues, with Hardin's encapsulated-interest account. The primary mechanism by which trust is generated is the practice of employing herders at above-market wage (or at what is called an efficiency wage by Shapiro and Stiglitz 1984). This practice not only signals to the herders the value of their relation to the owner but also increases for them the cost of obtaining other employment (giving up a higher-than-average wage). The workers, Ensminger argues, are also less likely to risk job loss by engaging in shirking or other forms of opportunism. She goes on to argue that it is this practice (and various reputation effects) that puts the parties to the relation on the "escalator of increasing trust." Other cases in which trust eventually replaces the need for close supervision and monitoring are common in the interpersonal and organizational literatures, but few have empirically documented the precise nature of the transformation of an economic relation into a social relation. The Orma case is paradigmatic in this respect.

In the absence of kinlike relations or access to family members, people often turn to close associates or fellow group members for assistance. Political scientists have recently argued that trust is a kind of social capital that facilitates cooperation and civic-mindedness and makes democracy work (Putnam 1993). Arguably one source of this kind of generalized trust is the voluntary association. Membership in such associations, in which we exercise our civic spirit, forms the bedrock of cooperation in society, in part because it extends beyond the confines of the family. The general social capital framework developed and advanced in the work of Robert Putnam (1993, 1995) is now being examined in even greater empirical detail by many scholars in the social sciences. Each is attempting to evaluate not only the theoretical message but also the adequacy of the empirical evidence for the claims about the role of social capital in modern democratic societies. Dietlind Stolle, in her chapter for this volume on the benefits of joining an association, takes a closer look at the causal mechanisms that may underlie the claim that association membership is good for society at large because it generates a kind of generalized trust that then facilitates even more positive cooperative interactions. However, if this "generalized" trust is based primarily on the membership networks formed through social association, the question remains: How does this network-based trust become generalized to strangers in the society?

The empirical research on which Stolle reports comes from a survey she conducted in Stockholm, Berlin, and Philadelphia of one thousand members of various voluntary associations, including bowling leagues and choral groups, to address some of Putnam's claims concerning the role of group membership in fostering generalized trust and civicness in the society at large. Stolle examines the extent to which voluntary group membership affects civic values and behavior at both the group level and the societal level.

To examine the effects of membership in voluntary groups on civicness, Stolle compares the values and behaviors of relatively new members with those of longtime members. This comparison is her proxy for longitudinal analysis of these effects over time. What complicates the picture is that there are potential selection effects that cannot be ruled out, and they confound the results as well as the interpretations of the results. One selection effect is the possibility that those who join such groups in the first place are more civic-minded. Without longitudinal data (studying the same people over time in these groups and organizations) there is no way of fully investigating the additional impact of years of membership or of evaluating the extent to which there are selection effects in the findings. In this chapter Stolle examines both private (group-related commitments and ingroup trust) and public social capital—that is, the impact of membership on behaviors and attitudes that benefit the society at large (such as voting in local elections and involvement in community projects as well as rating high on generalized trust and openness to strangers).

The actual results that Stolle reports are quite interesting since they challenge some of the assumptions of the social capital perspective on the role of voluntary association involvement in fostering the mobilization of civic spirit in democratic countries. In general, the findings suggest that length of membership is associated with greater participation, commitment, and socializing with group members outside of group events in all three countries, but it is less clear that such participation extends to life in the larger society as indicated by voting in local elections and community involvement. In the United States and even in Germany there is some positive association, but it is quite weak in Sweden, where there is a negative association between length of membership in voluntary associations and community engagement outside of the group. In addition, the results suggest that generalized trust and openness to strangers do not increase with longevity of group membership. Rather, generalized trust appears to be affected more by personal resources and characteristics (for example, age, income, personal experiences of betrayal). The findings raise interesting questions about the more general claims of social capital theorists and, in particular, the specific nature of voluntary association membership in fostering civic-mindedness and generalized trust. Additional empirical work, most likely including panel data, will be required in various cultural contexts to evaluate such claims fully.

Taking a broad sweep, Gerry Mackie attempts to explain differences in the patterns of declining social trust in the countries of Western Europe. In a provocative essay he links patterns of trust to differing styles of family formation. Mackie presents *Eurobarometer* data on trust levels from 1980 to 1996 for twelve Western European nations. Despite some variation in the overall pattern of results, in general trust levels are lower for the countries in the southeastern quadrant than in the northwestern quadrant. In addition, trust levels are somewhat stable across countries as well as time. Mackie attempts to explain this pattern of trust results, or what he calls the "social trust gradient," across Europe.

Mackie argues that different marriage strategies and styles of family formation are the primary explanatory factor. He draws on various forms of evidence to support the hypothesis that fundamental differences in family structure account for differences in social trust at the macro level. In particular, he compares the tendency for neolocal residence, nuclear households, and late age at marriage (especially for the first marriage of women) in the northwestern countries (Switzerland, the Netherlands, Sweden, Denmark, Belgium, and Norway) with the tendency for patrilocal residence, joint households, and early age of female marriage in the southeastern countries (Spain, Portugal, Greece, and Italy). Drawing loosely on game theory, Mackie presents these dominant modes of marriage strategy as social conventions (to use the term employed by Schelling 1960) that solve particular coordination problems in the society. Institutions and traditions are viewed as stable within this framework when they serve as useful coordinating mechanisms. Aspects of family structure, Mackie argues, are conventions of the same sort: they coordinate the interdependent interests of the parties involved. Regulation of access to reproduction (through age of marriage) is the main focus of convention. Neolocality and patrilocality are alternative modes of establishing residence that tend not to coexist and in Mackie's terms represent different Schelling conventions or equilibria for societies. Mackie ventures additional evolutionary arguments for these conventions. Social conventions often become institutionalized.

Network, Organizational, and Institutional Bases of Trust

Other ways in which specific social institutions, organizational arrangements, and social networks form the background for the development of trust relations are examined in part III of the book, beginning with Tyler's analysis of authority relations.

What work does trust do in society? Tyler argues that one of its central roles in any society is to foster the willingness of citizens to obey the authorities they trust. Tyler presents data from surveys in several settings, including various organizations in different cultures, that indicate that trust in the benign motives of authorities encourages voluntary deference to their decisions and also increases the extent to which citizens feel obligated to obey social rules. Tyler focuses especially on the trustworthiness of officials, and it is this factor that leads to his results. Belief in the trustworthiness of others yields trust in this account.

The identification with groups in society and the desire to maintain affiliations with group members form the basis for what Tyler calls "social trust," a kind of trust that is non-instrumental in character. Social identity and the treatment one receives from the group or an authority who represents the group are viewed as critical in the emergence of social trust. Group members trust those who are respectful, caring, benevolent, fair, and trustworthy. This is the kind of information, Tyler argues, that individuals infer from their treatment by authorities, especially when those authorities are members of their own group or represent groups relevant to their social identities. For Tyler group identification represents a form of "social capital" that facilitates the functioning of social groups.

While Tyler attempts to link the emergence of generalized trust at the societal level with interpersonal and group-level trust, Miller takes a closer look at the work done by trust in organizations. In addressing this question, Miller reveals the moral hazard of profit maximization in the context of organizations. Taking on standard conceptions in economic theory, he challenges the notion that rational self-interest generally replaces trust or that trust can be reduced to a set of rational expectations, as well as the idea that contractual solutions to the principal-agent problem eliminate the need for trust. Miller argues more generally that there is reason to take the concept of trust more seriously in the context of organizations (see also Kramer and Tyler 1996) and to attempt to understand how mutual expectations of what he calls "self-denying" behavior can bridge hierarchical differences between superiors and subordinates. Reviewing the standard literature on principal-agent problems, team production, the role of ownership, and theories of incentives, he explains how research on trust can help us address questions in organizational behavior literature that strictly economic notions of behavior fail to answer. With interesting examples he provides insights into how businesses run more smoothly and productively when trust is part of the human equation. Citing Southwest Airlines CEO Herbert Kelleher's clever leadership techniques that build loyalty, Miller argues that, "with a leader they trust, employees provide enormous levels of nonmonitorable, noncompensated effort." Southwest, he notes, is the most consistently profitable airline in the nation.

Instilling trust of the employer in the employees is partly a function of leadership, as the Southwest Airlines example demonstrates; it is also a result of various strategies related to implicit contracts, long-term employment, and commitment mechanisms that bind workers to their organizations. The problem for employers who seek to obtain significant efficiency improvements over the long haul but who also engage in deferred compensation schemes (paying workers low wages during their early years and higher wages as they attain seniority in the firm) is employee suspicion. As Miller points out, "Employees must be willing to trust the owners not to renege on an implicit contract—one that is not enforceable in courts." He goes on to discuss evidence regarding the kinds of firms that are more likely to be viewed by their employees as making credible commitments to them over their career in the firm and the kinds of mechanisms that work to constrain the profit-maximizing orientation of the owners. Miller sides with those, such as Kenneth Arrow (1974), who argue that trust has real, practical economic value in the form of increased efficiency. His conclusion is that the interdependent technology typical of many modern organizations "requires cooperation by a variety of stakeholders—cooperation that is inhibited by the unilateral commitment of the firm to shareholder profits." Constitutional development of the firm must be guided by more factors than the simple maximization of shareholder influence. Trust is essential for efficiency purposes in the long run and for the continued development of human capital—the kind that is increasingly critical to the overall success of firms in a complex, technologically interdependent economic and political world.

Gibbons reexamines the role of trust in what have traditionally been viewed as strictly economic transactions. Acknowledging that many transactions do not fit neatly into the simple one-shot or spot-market conception, Gibbons explores the ways in which repeated-game models are being used across the social sciences as a representation of economic reality. In particular he uses repeated games to investigate relational contracts both within and between firms. Social structure affects relational contracts in his model depending on whether the parties involved are integrated (for example, vertically integrated). In the "spot" social structure or one-shot game the parties will not see each other again. In what Gibbons calls the "relational" social structure the parties will continue to interact into the foreseeable future; hence, repeated-game models are appropriate. Extending Oliver Williamson's earlier work on markets and hierarchy, Baker, Murphy, and Gibbons (1999) develop a typology of governance regimes based on whether asset ownership is integrated and whether the social structure involved is a one-shot interaction (i.e. "shot") or relational. These two dimensions combine to produce four types of regimes: spot and relational outsourcing versus spot and relational employment.

Following the lead of theorists such as Douglass North and Avner Greif, Gibbons moves beyond the focus on economic transactions to examine self-enforcing institutions in addition to the state as the ultimate producers of social order. This analysis also draws on repeated-game models of the underlying processes. One obvious role of the state is in the enforcement of contracts, since individuals are likely to prefer relational contracts that are backed by law. In his chapter Knight, however, notes some of the limitations of reliance on law. Gibbons sets up the framework for future analytical work on the provision of social order, comparing models of the role of the state with models of the role of other institutions that emerge, are self-enforcing, and produce cooperation. In this account trust plays a minimal role, unless it is equated with repeated interaction and the "calculation" that in a repeated game you might "trust" me not to yield to short-run temptations. Although this calculation might indeed involve trust, it need not.

The role of norms and other institutions in fostering trust at the societal level is the focus of the chapter by Jack Knight, who challenges the reader to examine more carefully the nature of the linkages between norms, trust, and the law. If trust is essential to political and economic performance in society, as Robert Putnam (1993, 1995) and Francis Fukuyama (1995) argue, then we must begin to understand more fully just how it is produced and what work it does in the production of social cooperation. In Knight's view, the confounding of trust and cooperation in much of the existing literature makes the claim that trust produces cooperation vacuous. Knight reviews trust's potential roles as an explanatory concept, differentiates trust from cooperation, clarifies the basis of generalized trust in society, and examines the relations between formal mechanisms imposed by law and informal mechanisms for producing cooperation, including trust. He addresses three questions: Is trust independent of cooperation? What are the factors that make trust more or less possible in society? Can we foster trust through formal, legal institutions, and what is the precise nature of the link between trust and the rule of law?

Knight takes as the problematic case the role of trust in a socially heterogeneous society in which there are intergroup conflicts of interest. He treats this case as paradigmatic of the future. Analyzing the role of social norms in producing generalized expectations of behavior, he anticipates that achieving consensus across groups will be complicated, especially in settings in which the different groups have asymmetric access to valued resources (that is, settings in which there is what he calls distributional inequality). Without consensus, the expectations of the likelihood of cooperation across group boundaries will be low; the basis for trust is therefore also low. In such situations Knight presumes that the intervention of formal institutions—in particular the law—will be required to establish the grounds for cooperation. Despite the rather pessimistic conclusion, that informal mechanisms such as trust across group boundaries will be ineffective, he takes a very pragmatic approach to legal solutions. While recognizing the potential downside to legal solutions—that they may actually spoil the seeds of cooperation (see, for example, Taylor 1982)—he develops the more positive theme that the cooperation of diverse groups in the formation of law and other types of dispute resolution procedures may provide the basis for mutually beneficial cooperation at more informal levels, a kind of translation of skills from one arena to another. Knight acknowledges that this will entail a balance of power and the willingness to resolve complex political problems regarding fundamental conflicts of interest. The key empirical question is whether the rule of law can produce as a "by-product" informal mechanisms of social cooperation and the basis for generalized trust in a large, socially diverse society.

One of the major consequences of increasing economic interdependence in the global economy is the migration of people to the more advanced capitalist societies. Nee and Sanders look at this flow of human capital across national boundaries as one of the major social movements of our time. Problems of trust arise in the host societies as a by-product of this flow of labor, mainly into the urban centers. In this chapter the incorporation of recent immigrants into the United States is viewed as a major determinant of the economic trajectory and evolution of the society. Analyzing the incorporation of immigrants, Nee and Sanders move beyond assimilation theory to present a more comprehensive look at the diverse paths taken by immigrants to establish economic viability. They view the family as the key institution that provides a basis for trust and for collective action among contemporary immigrants.

The family becomes a source of social capital by making available to kin a multidimensional array of resources to facilitate their incorporation into the larger society. In an empirical investigation of samples of Chinese, Filipino, and Korean immigrants in the Los Angeles area, Nee and Sanders demonstrate how different modes of incorporation tend to be adopted by the various immigrant groups. These differences are a function of the differential access of these groups to social, financial, cultural, and human capital. Although the samples are not large enough for the authors to study each immigrant group extensively, they do examine overall patterns in access to resources and its effects on the extent of incorporation into the larger society. They use event history analysis to examine the residential and job histories obtained from extensive interviews with the three groups of immigrants. Specifically, they examine the transition of immigrants into ethnic entrepreneurship and self-employment.

One major reason immigrants rely on family capital is that for them these relations form the basis of both interdependence and trust in a world of strangers where, at least initially, they have no access to the resources they need to enter the mainstream.

Conclusion

Because trust relationships are fundamental to the stability of democratic societies and to the orderly conduct of social and economic affairs, they have become a central topic of concern in the social sciences. The contributors to this volume come from a wide array of disciplines: social psychology, sociology, anthropology, organizational studies, economics, and political science. Although there is no clear consensus among them on the precise meaning of the term "trust," all would agree that trust plays a significant role in the functioning of social groups and societies. In the absence of trust, what are often fairly complex systems must be put in place to protect against exploitation and opportunism and to produce close monitoring and effective sanctioning. Even the law is a blunt instrument that cannot efficiently produce the kind of social order that comes from the existence of trusting relations in a group or society. The chapters in this volume provide a broad overview of the many ways in which trust works in society to provide the bedrock for social cooperation.

References

Arrow, Kenneth J. 1974. *The Limits of Organization.* New York: Oxford University Press.

Baker, George, Robert Gibbons, and Kevin J. Murphy. 1999. *Relational Contracts and the Theory of the Firm.* Unpublished manuscript, Sloan School of Management, Massachusetts Institute of Technology.

Braithwaite, Valerie, and Margaret Levi, eds. 1998. *Trust and Governance.* New York: Russell Sage Foundation.

Brewer, Marilynn B. 1981. "Ethnocentrism and Its Role in Interpersonal Trust." In *Scientific Inquiry in the Social Sciences,* edited by Marilynn B. Brewer and Barry E. Collins. San Francisco: Jossey-Bass.

Fukuyama, Francis. 1995. *Trust.* New York: Basic Books.

Kramer, Roderick M., and Tom R. Tyler, eds. 1996. *Trust in Organizations: Frontiers of Theory and Research.* Thousand Oaks, Calif.: Sage Publications.

Lawler, Edward J., and Jeongkoo Yoon. 1998. "Network Structure and Emotion in Exchange Relations." *American Sociological Review* 63(6): 871–95.

Messick, David M. 1991. "On the Evolution of Group-Based Altruism." In *Game Equilibrium Models,* Vol. I, edited by Reinhard Selten. Berlin: Springer Verlag.

Meyerson, Debra, Karl E. Weick, and Roderick M. Kramer. 1996. "Swift Trust and 'Temporary Groups.'" In *Trust in Organizations: Frontiers of Theory and Research,* edited by Roderick M. Kramer and Tom R. Tyler. Thousand Oaks, Calif.: Sage Publications.

Pollak, Robert. 1985. "A Transaction Cost Approach to Families and Households." *Journal of Economic Literature* 23(2): 581–608.

Putnam, Robert D. 1993. *Making Democracy Work.* Princeton, N.J.: Princeton University Press.

———. 1995. "Tuning In, Tuning Out: The Strange Disappearance of Social Capital in America." *PS: Political Science and Politics* 28(4): 664–83.

Schelling, Thomas C. 1960. *The Strategy of Conflict.* Cambridge, Mass.: Harvard University Press.

Shapiro, Carl, and Joseph Stiglitz. 1984. "Equilibrium Unemployment as a Worker Discipline Device." *American Economic Review* 74(3): 433–44.

Taylor, Michael. 1982. *Community, Anarchy, and Liberty.* Cambridge: Cambridge University Press.

PART I

CONCEPTIONS OF TRUST

Chapter 1

Conceptions and Explanations of Trust

RUSSELL HARDIN

I N MODAL trust relationships, the trusted party has an incentive to be trustworthy, an incentive grounded in the value of maintaining the relationship into the future. That is, *my trust of you is encapsulated in your interest in fulfilling the trust.* It is this fact that makes my trust more than merely expectations about your behavior. My expectations are grounded in an understanding (perhaps mistaken) of your interests specifically with respect to me. Although one might object superficially to bringing interests into trusting relationships, such as those between close relatives or friends, they are clearly there much, and perhaps most, of the time. Indeed, the whole point for many other trusting relationships is likely to be interests. For example, I have an ongoing commercial relationship with a local merchant that becomes a trust relationship. This is not the place to make the full case for such a view of trust, but part of the case is that it fits a remarkable array of trust relationships. It is primarily those with whom we have ongoing relationships that we trust. And the richer the ongoing relationship and the more valuable it is to us, the more trusting and trustworthy we are likely to be.[1]

The encapsulated-interest account of trust suggests at least two other forms that might characterize trustworthiness that would give us reason to trust. The first is in a sense a special case of the encapsulated-interest account. I might trust you because I know that you love me or are my close friend and that you genuinely take my interests to heart to some extent. You genuinely encapsulate my interests. But you do so for arguably different reasons from those of a mere acquaintance with whom I have an ongoing relationship that is beneficial to that acquaintance. Love or friendship may be an important aspect of relationships in the lives of most of us, but it is not the form of many of our trust relationships, in which there need not be a genuine adoption of the interests of another as such. Commonly we merely share interests through causal connections in our ongoing interaction or through the reputational effects of our interaction, not through strong value commitments to one another.

The second form is distinctively different from the encapsulated-interest account and is very important in certain cases, but it also cannot be characteristic of the bulk of our trust relationships. I may trust you because I know that you have strong moral commitments to fulfill certain kinds of trust placed in you, such as those in which you go so far as to make a promise to fulfill (a view held in this volume by Messick and Kramer and by Tyler). There might be reasons for you to fail to fulfill, but I might generally expect that in the circumstances most likely to obtain you will fulfill, and I therefore trust you. I have known people with extremely strong moral commitments of relevant kinds for trust, but most of my trust relationships are not grounded in such commitments of others, and it seems unlikely that overriding moral commitments make much of the social order or most ongoing relationships work.

Returning briefly to reputational effects, I might trust you not because you and I have an ongoing relationship, but rather because you have relationships with others that may be damaged by your failure to fulfill certain trusts with me. Carol Heimer's account in this volume of the organization Jane suggests that it achieved its purposes (in counseling women on options for abortion) largely by establishing a reputation for reliability, particularly with respect to confidentiality. Hence, women who might interact with the organization only once in their lives could probably be said to trust it. The trustworthiness of various actors in the organization and those dealing with it as clients was clearly very important. Indeed, one might suppose that the doctors whom it recommended to its clients were at risk, as were the clients themselves. Few of our trusting relationships are more critical than those of the kind typical in this organization with its constantly changing clientele. (On reputational issues, see also Messick and Kramer, this volume.)

As an objection to the encapsulated-interest account, one might suppose it perverse to say, "I trust you to do Y," when it is in your interest to do Y. For example, consider an extreme case: I am confident that you will do what I want only because a gun is pointed at your head. (I have grasped the wisdom of Al Capone, who is supposed to have said, "You can get so much farther with a kind word and a gun than with a kind word alone" [quoted in McKean 1975, 42n].)

Part of what is wrong when I coerce you to do what I "trust" you to do is that such an act violates the sense that trust as a concept has no meaning in a fully deterministic setting. I do not trust the sun to rise each day, and if people were fully programmed robots I would not in our usual sense trust them. This is presumably the reason some writers think trust is inherently embedded in uncertainty. "For trust to be relevant," Diego Gambetta (1988, 218–19) says, "there must be the possibility of *exit*, betrayal, defection," by the trusted (see also Yamagishi and Yamagishi 1994, 133; and Luhmann 1979). More generally, one might say trust is embedded in the capacity or even need for choice. Giving people overwhelmingly strong incentives seems to move them toward being deterministic actors with respect to the matters at issue. (That is one reason romantics detest rationality.) At the other extreme, leaving them with no imputable reasons for action makes it impossible to trust them in many contexts. Trust as well as choice and rationality are at issue just because we are in the murky in-between land that is neither deterministic nor fully indeterminate.

Part of the issue in the gun case is that your compliance with my request is not motivated by your concern with my interest at all. It is motivated purely by your concern with your own interests. That is to say, the gun case fails to fit the encapsulated-interest account of trust.

I wish to establish a vision of trust that helps us to explain—and perhaps evaluate—behavior. The same concerns have driven many writers on trust to elucidate quite different visions of it. I canvass many of these visions to see how they differ in their implications for understanding behavior and, in some cases, to query their conceptual coherence. Many of these visions, especially those of philosophers, are essentially definitional or conceptual. Others, especially those of social scientists, are explanatory. The encapsulated-interest account of trust is *both a definitional and an explanatory account.*

One important view not canvassed here is the view that trust is essentially noncognitive, that it is simply a disposition of the truster to trust. This is the view of some philosophical accounts (Becker 1996; Jones 1996) as well as of the economist Oliver Williamson (1993). It also seems to be implicit in discussions of social or generalized trust (as discussed later in the chapter). To some extent, any view that takes cognitive learning of who is or is not trustworthy into account could be read as a dispositional view, because, for example, it becomes my disposition not to trust you after I have been betrayed by you. In fact, some of the claims of dispositional theorists are plausibly little more than claims that my trusting now is a disposition, although it was previously based on cognitive assessments of your behavior and apparent commitments. In the actual lives of real people, the noncognitive dispositional view can be only part of the story of trusting; cognitive elements must play another part. The alternative is for trust to be blind and ungrounded, and often self-destructive. The high truster's disposition (see Yamagishi, this volume; Rotter 1980) might be little more than a simple learning model. If your experience with others—perhaps especially in your earliest years (Hardin 1992; Yamagishi, this volume)—has been good and cooperative, then you may tend to be optimistic about the prospects of cooperation with new people; if not, you may be pessimistic.

Again, even in my daily interactions, if our relationship is ongoing, I now may have a disposition to trust you rather than to give a lot of calculative thought to whether you are trustworthy. I already know without having to think it through anew. But this cannot be what the noncognitive theorists have in mind, because in this kind of case the fact of my trust builds entirely on a cognitive past history, as in Heimer's (this volume) account of how a trust relationship might develop. As Alfred North Whitehead quipped, civilization advances by the reduction of more and more to habit. That is, we have to outgrow the need to calculate if we are to have time for other things, and we do.[2] One might have some trust relationships that are substantially more dispositional and noncognitive than others. But if so, one is most likely to have first made a cognitive selection of *whom* to trust in that way. For example, my relationship with a close friend may have been built from relatively conscious choices to take risks (most likely minor risks at first). By now, however, the relationship simply works, and neither of us might be pressed to make such conscious choices—although we might if novel circumstances arise. A very strong anticognitive position therefore seems implausible.

All of the contributors to this volume include strong cognitive elements in their accounts when, for example, they suppose that it matters whom one trusts. They therefore do not build their claims from a strong noncognitive view. Most explicit are Heimer, Ensminger, Gibbons, and Yamagishi, although those, such as Tom Tyler and David Messick and Roderick Kramer, who define trust as based on the moral commitments of the trusted are also cognitive. There are, however, noncognitive tendencies in many of the contributions—for example, in discussions of the one-way trust game, in which one has to take a risk without even knowing who one's partner is (see Messick and Kramer, Gibbons, and Miller, who present the one-way trust game of Kreps 1990), and perhaps in some discussions of so-called generalized or social trust, which is trust in unknown others.

Before turning to alternative visions of trust, I discuss five conceptual moves that undercut many discussions of trust and in fact can infect virtually any discussion of trust. After clearing the conceptual ground, I turn to various visions of trust. The account moves from essentially individual-level issues and conceptions to increasingly socialized conceptions. It is a compelling characteristic of the encapsulated-interest theory that it works at all levels without conceptual change (Hardin, forthcoming–a). Some of the accounts are compatible with each other, others not. For example, an evolutionary account—which is explanatory—might fit well with the encapsulated-interest account, perhaps by augmenting it in various ways. The chief alternatives to the encapsulated-interest account in the contributions to this volume are a somewhat vaguely articulated view of trust as noncognitive or as a psychological disposition and the view that trust is grounded in the moral commitments of the trusted. Much of the following discussion relates the noncognitive dispositional and the cognitive encapsulated-interest views and addresses ways in which the two views might be distinguished empirically.

Conceptual Confusions

Consider five conceptual slippages that are especially pervasive and worthy of brief discussion. These slippages are not themselves alternative theories of trust or even inherent in any specific theory of trust. Rather, they can often vitiate conclusions in any such theory. All of these slippages evidently require vigilance to avoid. Two of them involve somewhat misleading inferences from the ordinary language of trust.

The first slippage is an instance of a common conceptual presumption in the social sciences: assuming that some notion of trust is an epistemological primitive and not subject to analysis. In many Russell Sage Foundation workshops on trust, it is astonishing how often prestigious scholars have responded to a presentation by retorting, roughly, "But that's not what trust is."

Second, most accounts of trust are essentially expectations accounts. That is to say, they build on the expectations that a potential truster has. Trust is thus inherently a matter of knowledge or belief. Many ordinary-language statements about trust, however, seem to conceive it as a matter of behavior, at least in part. Messick and Kramer include behavior in their definition of trust for seemingly methodological rather than conceptual reasons, and several others here explicitly or implicitly include behavior in trust.

Third, trust is a three-part relation: I trust you to do Y. This view is commonplace (see Luhmann 1979, 92; Baier 1986, 236).[3] For example, I might ordinarily trust you to keep even the most damaging gossip confidential, but not with the price of today's lunch (you always—conveniently?—forget such debts), while I trust another with the price of lunch but not with any gossip. A very few people I might trust with almost anything, and very many others with almost nothing. Even for a particular three-part relationship, the trust commonly depends on the context. For example, although I normally trust you with gossip, if you are under great duress and my piece of gossip would help you out of a bad situation, I might no longer trust you with it.

Fourth, there is an oddly commonplace slippage between trust and trustworthiness in what many authors present as accounts of trust. This is especially true of normative accounts, but it is also true of evolutionary accounts. Surprisingly, this slippage is pervasive in academic discussions of trust, as we see later in the chapter.

And a final sort of slippage is the transposition of claims about entrusting something to someone into claims, which make less sense, about trusting someone.

One might choose to put forward a theory of trust built on one of the slippages by taking it as a principle. One could then attempt to keep the theory coherently fitted to that principle. I do not think any such theory would be of interest because it would be so thoroughly inapplicable to actual experiences of trust. One of the moves that is commonly a slippage, however, is basic to some theories of trust in which it is deliberately asserted, as noted later in the discussion of trust as a two-part relation. The large literature on generalized trust often conceives it as a two-part relation, although for survey respondents the third part, even if unstated, might be elliptically assumed.

Because all of these conceptual slips are standard parts of vernacular discussions and invocations of trust, they are very hard to avoid even for careful writers. Although I cite some instances of such conceptual confusions in many writers, I suspect that many or even most of these writers would happily expunge the confusions.

Trust as a Primitive Term

In many accounts, trust seems to be a primitive, unanalyzed term. As in foundationalist epistemology, we just know it when we see it. This supposition is a constant problem in serious discussions of anything in the social sciences. We often tend to suppose that our quick, even sloppy intuitions or insights are foundational, not merely casual. Casual accounts might not even distinguish between trust in another person, trust in a fact of nature, and trust in an institution, such as money or government. These are all simple primitives that cannot be unpacked into the elements of a model of trust. Perhaps they are different primitives that, by convention, happen to have the same label. Or perhaps they are all the same primitive and there are no real distinctions to be drawn between them. In general, however, we should not indulge a so-called social science or philosophy that depends on no more than a whimsical personal intuition that X must be so if that notion cannot be spelled out for others to question, test, and understand.

In discussions of trust, people regularly say, in effect, "When we say 'trust,' what we mean is X." Unfortunately, X is a variable with radically different meanings for different people. Ordinary-language analysis can exclude some meanings perhaps, but it typically cannot promote one meaning above all other contenders. Trust is, not surprisingly, a messy, even confused notion in the vernacular. Quarrels about what it really means sound like the worst of platonic debates about the "true" meaning of something. No matter how enticing it may sometimes be, to engage in that debate is foolish. I do not put forward the "true" meaning of trust. Rather, *I put forward a workable notion that can be used to cover much of our experience of relying on others in that it can be used to help explain variations in our behavior and beliefs about the reliability of others, including collective others.* My central concern is such explanation.

Finally, note a peculiar implication of an ordinary-language analysis of trust. Anyone who wishes to make trust a simple primitive or who wishes to take it as a deontological normative concept, that is, one that is universally applicable and derivable from pure reason, should have trouble with real-world experience, which has often lacked any such notion. Even today there is no direct, perspicuous translation of the term into many languages, such as French. In French, one says, I have confidence in someone—or oddly, in something (*j'ai confiance en quelqu'un ou quelque chose*). As Fredrik Barth noted at the Russell Sage Foundation-New York University conference on trust held 25–26 February 1995, there is no noun for "trust" in Norwegian. The Japanese terms were deliberately invented about a century ago (Toshio Yamagishi, private communication, March 31, 1998). Translations from other languages into English often use the term "trust" where it is not clearly apt and thereby add significantly to and distort what is being translated. And even in English, with its root in the word *tryst*, the word *trust* has an ambiguous history.

Trust as Behavior Versus Trust as Knowledge

One of the most interesting problems in our relations with others is that of taking a risk on them when we have no ground for trusting them. One might think that this is really what trust is about. Under this view—call it the scant-expectations view—I have greater trust the less I expect you to fulfill my trust. Superficially this might sound right, for the reason that my motivations are especially sharply focused in a case that is very different from my normal experience dealing with close associates, about whom I have very clear and grounded expectations. But the scant-expectations view is implausible even as an ordinary-language notion.

If it is trust only when I have little reason to expect you to fulfill and not when I have substantial reason to expect you to do so, then I never trusted my mother and do not trust my son, my best friends, or any of the other people I am most likely to say—in ordinary language—I trust. It seems extremely unlikely that anyone really means by trust what the scant-expectations view entails. On that view, I can trust a complete stranger or Hitler, but not my mother. (For an experiential account of trust that likens it to infant "trust" in one's mother, see Baier 1986.) Although there can be many contradictory notions of trust in our messy ordinary language, the scant-expectations view cannot stand even the beginnings of ordinary-language analysis.

Virginia Held (1968, 157) has proposed an intermediate position that is still odd. She supposes that "trust is most required exactly when we least know whether a person will or will not do an action." This statement is ambiguous, and it may not imply a definition of trust. But suppose she means it definitionally. It is true that where there is no room for choice on the part of another, trust cannot be at issue. Yet it can be at issue when I am quite confident of your choice of action. In a particular context, it makes sense to say I trust most the person I think most likely to act in a certain way and I trust least the person I think least likely to act that way.

In the scant-expectations view, what seems to strike us is the act of "trusting" despite the lack of adequate expectations of fulfillment to justify taking the relevant risk. The act could follow from many motivations. For example, one might act as if one did expect fulfillment in order to give the "trusted" a moral impulse or to give her a chance to establish a cooperative relationship. Or, if one holds that trusting is a good thing in its own right, one might conclude that trusting in such a case is an especially strong case of such goodness. One who insists that this is one of the ways we use the term "trust" is surely right. But unfortunately, this way of speaking of trust blurs any distinction between the assessment of trustworthiness and the act of "trusting" someone. Such blurring is typical of ordinary language. But it gets in the way of explanation of behavior. I therefore keep trust in the category of knowledge and belief rather than in the category of action and behavior.

Annette Baier (1985, 61) says that trusting someone is always a risk "given the partial opaqueness to us of the reasoning and motivation of those we trust and with whom we cooperate." There is an "expected gain which comes from a climate of trust"—hence, in trusting we give up security for greater security. But again, it is not trusting that is risky, *it is acting on trust that is risky.* Trusting is merely a bit of knowledge, and of course, knowledge is fallible. Fallible trust can give us grounds for acting when the acting will turn out to be harmful to our interests.

That trusting someone and acting on that trust are clearly different is trivially evident. For example, I may trust you in various ways but never have reason to act on that trust. Against this distinction, Jane Mansbridge (1999) argues for "altruistic trust," which implicitly runs trust into action. To speak of altruistic trust is implicitly to say that it is not trust, that one acts cooperatively beyond what one would do if one acted only from the degree of trust one had in another. One *acts* altruistically despite lack of sufficient trust to justify the action. Hence, to speak of altruistic trust is to make trust a term of action rather than of knowledge. That seems rather odd, because I could trust you very much without having occasion to act on that trust. And I can easily act cooperatively toward others whom I do not expect to reciprocate and whom I do not trust.

Another way to frame this issue is to imagine that we use behavioral indicators or measures of trust. With a behavioral measure, we might tend to confound the behavior with the trust, but this would be an error that vitiates the principle of using the behavioral measure for determining the level of trust (rather than defining it). Moreover, if we use behavioral measures, we want measures *in a particular context* so that we can relatively meaningfully claim that the issues are similar for all the subjects we are studying. For example, I might trust a close friend and yet display no behavior over a long period of time that reflects the extent of my trust in her. To say that I trust her more than I trust someone else makes little sense if the only measure is behavior that has not been elicited. Again, the measures must be context-dependent if they are to make sense.

We can choose to put ourselves in a position to come to know something. But we cannot look at the evidence and then *decide* to know. The evidence might compel us or it might not, but we do not choose the degree to which it does compel us. The recognition of this point *and* its denial are in contest in Niklas Luhmann's (1979, 43) claim that it "is not possible to demand trust of others; trust can only be offered and accepted." My trust of you can be neither offered nor withheld. It just is. I cannot withhold it from you—and it would make no sense to do so even if I could because it would be contrary to my interest as I understand it. And you can neither accept nor refuse it. But both of us can choose not to act on it in various contexts. Moreover, you might be able to act on it to the extent of getting me to do something for you—because I trust you—and then violating my trust, all to your advantage. Trust is in the category of knowledge; acting on trust is in the category of action. Yet, as Luhmann correctly, if metaphorically, notes, it is "not possible to demand" trust. That is to say, if I do not trust you, your demand that I trust you cannot be honored merely on the ground of your demand plus the knowledge I already have of you, because that knowledge was insufficient for me to trust you. Your mere demand adds little or nothing to my knowledge of you and therefore cannot lead me to trust you if I do not.

Commonplace claims that one *chooses* to trust mistakenly imply that trusting is a matter of acting. Kenneth Arrow (1974, 26) speaks of the "agreement to trust each other." John Dunn (1988, 73, 80) says that trust is "a more or less consciously chosen policy for handling the freedom of other human agents or agencies" (see also Miller, this volume). Baier (1986, 244) speaks of "conscious trust the truster has chosen to endorse and cultivate." Luhmann (1979, 24) speaks, as do many others, including Baier and Held (1984, 65), of trust as a gamble, a risky investment.

Held (1968, 158) also says that one may be obligated to trust.[4] Messick and Kramer (this volume) and many others speak of deciding to trust someone.[5] All of this is wrong. Usually I just do or do not trust to some degree, depending on the evidence I have. I do not, in an immediate instance, choose to trust, I do not take a risk. Only actions are chosen—for example, to act as I would *if I did in fact trust*, to take a chance on your being trustworthy beyond any evidence I have that your incentive is to be trustworthy.[6] And when I am not confident of your motivations toward me or of your likely actions, I clearly cannot be obligated to trust, which would be to know what the evidence denies. That way leads the Inquisition—to be obligated to believe what one does not and cannot believe. Plausibly none of these writers would maintain that we choose to trust or distrust rather than that we just do trust or distrust after relevant experience. Luhmann (1979, 88), for example, says elsewhere that trust "is not a means that can be chosen for particular ends." Apparent claims to the contrary are merely slippages into looser vernacular usage.

Trust as a Two-Part Relation

In the vernacular, it is common to say, simply, "I trust her." We do not add the condition "with respect to matters X." But vernacular speech is commonly elliptical in this way, and it does not follow that people generally mean they literally trust a particular person with respect to any and everything. There is almost no one of whom anyone would fully say, "I trust you independently of the content of the phrase 'to do Y' or 'with respect to matters X' and entirely independently of the larger context." Unfortunately, however, this vernacular usage sometimes pervades analytical, explanatory, and theoretical discussions of trust. That is an inherent problem with the use of ordinary notions in such discussions. It often requires deliberate effort to avoid falling into vernacular usage and, hence, into drawing the wrong implications.

There are, however, theories of trust based on the assumption that trust is (or at least can be) a two-part relation of the form: A trusts B, without any conditional constraint on the scope of the trust. If, as some writers sometimes suppose, trust is unfounded faith such as Abraham evidently had in his god, it could be as simple as this two-part relation, without any limits. It should be superficially evident that the field of play for a theory of trust restricted to such cases is very limited. It is not relevant to the trust that most of us sometimes have in others, few of whom are gods. But the assumption that trust is merely this two-part relation is itself commonly smuggled into discussions of other theories in which it is a conceptual slippage that should be avoided.

The assumption that trust is a rather different two-part relation is also basic to some theories or definitions of trust that do not make it a sibling of knowledge. In noncognitive dispositional views of trust, it is sometimes even suggested that there is no second part: I simply trust. I think such a view is incoherent and utterly implausible. At most, someone's claim to trust in general might be elliptical. Pushed to act on that trust, however, they would not turn their infant over to the care of a random stranger or lend large sums to anyone who asks. At best, my disposition to trust can merely be a relatively more optimistic stance than that of many others. It cannot be stupidly one-part if I am to prosper in the world. Nevertheless, so-called generalized trust is sometimes cast as such a one-part view. Let us turn to it.

The bulk of the fast-growing literature on the value of trust in society seems to focus on the possibilities for social exchange that follow from *generally* trusting others (for example, Luhmann 1979; see also Knight, this volume, and Yamagishi, this volume). So-called generalized or social trust is trust in random others or in social institutions without grounding in specific prior or subsequent relationships with those others and, as is often argued or implied, without taking into account the variable grounds for trusting particular others to different degrees. Such "trust" might seem to be a two-part or even a one-part relation. There is a substantial literature on such generalized trust, which is loosely seen as unspecific trust in general others, including strangers.

This literature is based primarily on standard survey questions; for example, "Would you think that one can trust other people, or should one be careful with others?" (For other, even less well framed questions, see the appendix of Stolle's contribution to this volume.) People commonly answer that they can or, on a multilevel scale, they choose a relatively high level. Some researchers read such responses far too loosely. If I say I can trust most people most of the time, I may merely be saying I trust most of those I deal with most of the time. Of course, that is partly why I deal with them in particular and not with lots of other people whom I would not trust most of the time. Moreover, even if I trust most of those I deal with most of the time, that is because most of the time there is little at stake in my dealings with them. Ask anyone instead whether they would lend a hundred dollars to a random stranger on the street, and they will presumably say no. Ask them whether they would lend even a moderately good friend thousands of dollars without a legally enforceable contract for repayment, and again they would probably say no.

Therefore, it is implausible that the standard survey results are merely one-part or two-part. It is virtually inconceivable to suppose that trust in such results is one-part if we pay even slight attention to what it could mean: I trust, period, everyone and with respect to everything. Those who assert that trust can be a one-part relation should introduce us to the person who actually has such trust. We could say that our trust is only two-part in two different ways. First, to say the two parts are the truster and the trusted is to say that the trust is utterly open-ended with respect to all possible matters. To say that the two parts are the truster and the matter at issue is to say we trust literally everyone equally. The first of these is implausible for any but the very closest relationships. We trust only certain others with respect to some things, maybe an even more inclusive set of people with respect to somewhat less demanding things, perhaps a disjoint set of people with respect to certain other things, and so forth. This is not genuinely generalized trust. The second of these possibilities is openly absurd. It is the survey interpreters and not the respondents who misdescribe what is at stake when survey responses are taken to entail such simplistic views of trust. The respondents are forced by the vagueness of the questions to give vague answers.

At best, in any case, so-called generalized trust must be a matter of relatively positive expectations of others' trustworthiness, cooperativeness, or helpfulness. It is the stance of, for example, the child who has grown up in a very benign environment in which virtually everyone has always been trustworthy. By inductive generalization, that former child now faces others with relatively positive expectations. The value of generalized trust is the value of such an upbringing: it gives us the sense of running little risk in cooperating with others, so that we may more readily enter relationships with others. Of course, this is, again, a value only if others are relatively trustworthy.

One might say that generalized trust is more than merely expectations about the trustworthiness of others, that it is genuine trust in others. But it is very hard to say who is the B and what is the X in the relation "A trusts B to do X" if A's trust is truly generalized and not, as usual, heavily limited and conditional. Hence, generalized or social trust seems to violate this paradigm of trust. But if generalized trust is, in a perhaps very complicated way, limited and conditional, what could it mean to call it generalized? In any real-world context, I trust some more than others, and I trust any given person more in some contexts than in others. I may be more optimistic in my expectations of others' trustworthiness than you are, but apart from such a general fact, I do not have generalized trust. I might also typecast many people and suppose some of the types are very likely to be trustworthy and therefore worth the risk of cooperating with them, other types less so, and still others not at all. But such typecasting falls far short of generalized trust. It is merely optimism about certain others (Hardin 1992). Such optimism from typecasting makes rational sense just as typecasting of those one might employ makes rational sense as a first, crude indicator of competence or commitment (as in the analysis of discrimination in hiring in Becker 1957/1971).

Many, maybe even most, claims for generalized trust can readily be restated as claims that, in contexts in which trust generally pays off, it makes sense to risk entering into exchanges even with those whom one cannot claim to trust in the encapsulated-interest sense because one does not yet have either an ongoing relationship with them or reasons of reputation to trust them.[7] This is not a claim that one trusts those others, but only that one has relatively optimistic expectations of being able to build successful relationships with certain, perhaps numerous, others (although surely not with everyone). If the context is even slightly altered, this conclusion may be wrong, as it is in dealings with con artists who propose quick-profit schemes or, often, with sellers in tourist traps. Hence, generalized trust seems likely to be nothing more than optimistic assessment of trustworthiness and willingness therefore to take small risks on dealing with others whom one does not yet trust and whom one might not even have grounds to trust. That assessment would quickly be corrected if the optimism proved to be unwarranted because people and agencies in the relevant context proved not to be generally trustworthy.

One reading of the apparently varied levels of so-called generalized trust is that some people have a greater psychological disposition to trust than others do. Studies of trust therefore often divide subjects into those who are high trusters and those who are low trusters (Yamagishi, this volume). I do not discuss this issue extensively here but note that variant levels of seeming trust might simply be variant degrees of risk-taking or of learning about others (Hardin 1992). As noted earlier, several of the contributions to this volume (Bacharach and Gambetta; Messick and Kramer; Yamagishi) sometimes treat trust as essentially or partially dispositional, although not always explicitly. If it is grounded in a moral commitment (as in Messick and Kramer and in Tyler), *trustworthiness* would, of course, be dispositional in large part. Another way in which I might read your dispositions is to assess whether you are likely to be sufficiently future-oriented as to be cooperative now in part for reasons of future prospects of cooperation with me. But this disposition also has to do with psychological propensities to be trustworthy rather than a psychological propensity to trust.

Yamagishi's (this volume) high trusters are clearly cognitive—they correct their assessments of another's trustworthiness as evidence becomes available. Hence, he finds that generalized trust matters less in dyadic interactions. Why? Because we typically have and gain evidence in dyadic interactions. Generalized trusters might be thought to be noncognitive, but when they turn to dyadic relations, they become cognitive.

Tyler (this volume) speaks of noninstrumental "social" trust. This is not strictly the social—or generalized—trust that has become a standard notion in the literature (as discussed earlier in this section). His "social trust" arises in contexts of group identity (or identification; see Hardin 1995, 6–10) and validation. Because even the standard notion of social trust is implausible as an absolute category of always trusting everyone, Tyler's restriction of his social trust to a particular ethnic or other group is similar to what must happen in standard social trust that is supposedly generalized. Just as is true in many ordinary relationships, such as choices of marriage or dating partners, we must often suppose that we are more likely to understand and be understood by someone from a background similar to our own and that such a person is more likely to share our own values, tastes, and so forth. Conceivably, if we could measure Tyler's social trust, we would find that it is defined by something like this epistemological issue of, essentially, the comfort of dealing with a relatively familiar type of person.

Trust and Trustworthiness

Perhaps the oddest conceptual slippage in the large and growing literature on trust is to make claims ostensibly about trust that make sense only if they are really about trustworthiness. Much of the literature that moralizes trust, for example, makes easy sense in at least some contexts if the point is to moralize trustworthiness, but essentially no sense if the purpose is to moralize trust. Many of the accounts of trust discussed later make this slippage—so many in fact that one might suppose there is something more to the move than merely conceptual slippage or error. Perhaps "trust" is the term loosely used to refer to the entire relationship, both the trusting and the trustworthiness. Although plausible, this move then evidently sets us up for facile, and wrong, specific arguments that are ostensibly about merely the trusting and not about the whole relationship.

For example, Bernard Barber (1983, 170) says that "we need to discover . . . how to foster trust and make it more effective." His concern is with general social relations. Surely what we need for making these go better is trustworthiness. This is the inference to be drawn from Barber's study of professionalism and the problems of getting professionals to behave well on behalf of their clients, who need professional help because they do not know enough to handle their own problems of health care, legal advocacy, and so forth. Resolving this problem, in Barber's account, was the reason professional norms were created in the first place. Teaching potential patients merely to trust their doctors would have been perverse if the doctors were not trustworthy.

In the discussions later in the chapter of several conceptions and explanatory models of trust, the slippage from trust to trustworthiness is evident. This is true of both the genetic and the social evolutionary explanations for the rise of trust, which actually make sense rather of the rise of trustworthiness. It infects discussions of trust as a commodity and of trust as social capital. It might even infect functional accounts, such as Barber's and, less clearly, Luhmann's. (It is true also of moralized accounts, with the possible exception of that of Lars Hertzberg [1988], who seems genuinely to insist that it is trust that is morally demanded of us. But I will not discuss these accounts here.)

Perhaps the most compelling reason for the frequent slippage, or at least for why it is not recognized immediately as such, is that *trustworthiness commonly begets trust.* My trustworthiness potentially rewards your trusting me (if you act on your trust). Hence, if something conceptually entails or causes trustworthiness, then indirectly it tends to cause trust. This point is clarified in various later discussions.

Trusting and Entrusting

Finally, consider a conceptual slippage that might be included under the confusion of behavior with knowledge or belief. A family of related concepts includes entrusting, accepting a promise, and contracting. I entrust something to you; I accept your promise that you will do something in the future; I contract with you to do something for me later. I might be forced to entrust something to you even though I do not trust you, just as I might have no better move than to "accept" your promise or to put myself at risk in a contractual dealing with you even though I do not trust you. Or I might say to you that I entrust some matter to you as a challenge to get you to live up to my trust, as a parent might do with a child or a therapist with a recovering alcoholic. Moreover, I can trust you to do something that I have not (even could not have) entrusted to you. Entrusting, accepting a promise, agreeing to a contract, are actions. Trust is not an action.

Hence, trusting and entrusting are not equivalent or even parallel, although we might use the two terms as though they were interchangeable, especially in contexts in which both might apply. We will not often go very far wrong even if we interchange them when they do not both apply.

In actions that come under any of these terms, our purpose is commonly to bring the future into the present in some sense, as in presentiation in contract law. We may be unable to complete some joint project or exchange in this moment but wish to secure our expectations about its future before we expend effort or resources or make commitments in the future whose value will turn on completion. As Luhmann (1979, 13) says, "Managing complex futures means corresponding performances by people in the continuous present." He adds, "Trust is one of the ways of bringing this about." The addition is not quite right. We hope to bring it about by entrusting, contracting, or accepting a promise, by turning over some future part of our project to another or others. It is the turning over—an action—that fits that hope. Even then, of course, we may fail to control the relevant future because the others may fail to do their part—they may be untrustworthy.

Within the family of terms, note a strangely deceptive parallel between the pair promising/promise-keeping, on the one hand, and the pair trusting/being trustworthy, on the other. The moral burden, if there is one, is typically on promise-keeping and being trustworthy, not on either promising or trusting. That is because the incentives in relationships of promising and trusting are on the side of failing to fulfill the promise or the trust. But the potential promise-keeper is first the promiser. *I make a promise to you, and I am expected to keep it.* On standard understandings of obligation, I impose my own obligation on myself when I promise. The trust relationship is very different. The one who faces the burden of trustworthiness is not the one who trusts. *I trust you, and you are the one who is expected to fulfill the trust.* But I cannot impose an obligation on you. Moreover, it would be odd to moralize promising, as opposed to promise-keeping; similarly, it should be seen as odd to moralize trusting as opposed to trustworthiness (but see Hertzberg 1988).

Trust as Dependent on Characteristics of the Trusted

A natural and common account of trust is that certain people are trustworthy and can therefore be trusted. Hence, in the view taken by, for example, Messick and Kramer (this volume) and Yamagishi (this volume), it is characteristics of the trusted—characteristics not dependent on my trusting of her or even on my relationship with her—that make me trust her. For Yamagishi and his colleagues in various experiments on trust, "trust" is defined by its dependence on such characteristics rather than on the kinds of reasons implicit in the encapsulated-interest view of trust. Indeed, Toshio Yamagishi and Midori Yamagishi (1994) call the latter merely "assurance," on analogy with game theorists' assurance games. Unfortunately, this is a confusing term here. Trust as encapsulated interest commonly grows out of an ongoing exchange or iterated prisoners' dilemma interaction. Although an iterated prisoners' dilemma is not technically equivalent to an assurance game, it can lead to mutual trust.

Against the view that trust *typically* turns on such independent characteristics of the trusted, note that I might trust you while others do not. Somehow, something other than your characteristics must be in play. Most people in their professional lives can probably count some of their colleagues as untrustworthy and others as trustworthy. They might even be able to do this with fine gradations, but let us simplify to the two extreme types. Often, those whom you trust tend to trust each other, and those whom you distrust tend to be distrusted by those you trust. Yet many of those you distrust may trust each other. Such patterns make sense if trusting is a matter of shared interests that make for the reliability of the trusted. They do not fit an account of trust as based on bald characteristics of the trusted. Studies to determine whether there typically are disjoint networks of trust and distrust would address the variant claims.

An extreme version of the supposition that trust is merely a matter of the characteristics of the trusted—characteristics that are not grounded in the relationship between the truster and the trusted—is what might be called one-way, one-shot trust (Bacharach and Gambetta, this volume; Hardin, forthcoming–b; see also Kreps 1990; and the one-way trust game in Gibbons, this volume, and Miller, this volume).[8] Consider a lovely example of this extreme view. At the February 1995 Russell Sage Foundation–New York University conference on trust, Fredrik Barth told the story of dealing with a rug dealer in a Middle Eastern bazaar. Barth liked a rug that he had no way of paying for at the time. The dealer told him to take the rug and send the money later. Many of us have been similarly trusted by an utter stranger who would probably never see us again and could not compel our trustworthiness. The experience seems striking and inexplicable in its virtual uniqueness.

What is the role of trust in this interaction? Let us first consider its one-way character. Barth took no risk in walking away with his rug and a debt that probably could not be enforced; only the rug dealer faced a risk of loss. Such one-way trust relationships, while not rare, are arguably relatively unusual in the mass of all trust relationships.[9] For very good reason, the more stable and compelling trust relationships are likely to be mutual. Why? Because a good way to get me to be trustworthy in my dealings with you, when you risk trusting me, is to make me reciprocally depend on your trustworthiness. As James Coleman (1990, 177) notes, a reciprocal trusting relationship is mutually reinforcing for each truster, because each person then has built-in incentive to be trustworthy. I trust you because it is in your interest to do what I trust you to do and you trust me for the reciprocal reason. I want to be trustworthy in part to induce you to be trustworthy. If there is some residue beyond rational expectations from relevant incentives in one-way trust, there is less role for that residue in this straight, probably mutually self-interested exchange. If, as subjectively seems to be true, trust relationships are typically reciprocal, we have reason to suppose they are not typically grounded in particular characteristics of the trusted. They are more likely to be grounded in incentives for trustworthiness, as in the encapsulated-interest account. If this is true, then unfortunately experiments with one-way trust games and other games that do not allow for richer ongoing relationships may not be able to mimic standard trust relations.

Now consider the one-shot character of Barth's relationship with his rug dealer. In particular, consider the case from the perspective of the one who seems to trust us. For the rug dealer in the bazaar, the difficulty of selling to customers unable to pay on the spot might be commonplace. If experience shows that those customers are reasonably reliable, then the rug dealer might profit substantially from increasing total sales by "trusting" people to send the money later. Barth's rug dealer might have had some sense from experience or from guessing, right or wrong, that some types of people (those who struggle to speak the local language, women, men, the well-dressed, the friendly, those who seem to be knowledgeable about rugs or who praise the workmanship and artistry) often enough send the money to make it worth the risk of parting with rugs on expectations—perhaps with less willingness to bargain down to the lowest price.

For many cases of supposedly one-way, one-shot trust, such as those canvassed by Michael Bacharach and Diego Gambetta (this volume), it is hard to see why trust is at issue at all. Some of these cases are purely calculative in a very ordinary way. Williamson (1993, 473) notes, for example, that "cab drivers need to decide whether to pick up a fare or not. Although the probability assessment out of which they work is highly subjective . . . , this is an altogether calculative exercise. There is no obvious conceptual or explanatory value added by describing a decision to accept a risk (pick up a fare) as one of trust." Williamson is hostile to the use of the term "trust" for even more complex relationships in which calculation of risks seems to be at stake. But for this simple case his hostility seems clearly right. Similarly, my decision whether to give money to a beggar on the street does not turn on whether I trust this person I have never met, will probably never meet again, and can judge only from appearances this moment. It turns on whether I think my donation is likely to be beneficial and what my stance on such altruistic actions is. Reading the beggar's signs as signals about whether his plea is a scam may affect my altruistic decision, but it does not elevate my choice to a matter of whether I trust him.

The master of scam at the center of the play and movie *Six Degrees of Separation* worked his magic on his targets by coming to know enough about them and their family to persuade them to think of their relationship with him as one involving trust and trustworthiness. The trustworthiness was of the form of the encapsulated-interest account in that it was reputational, because it was grounded in what they thought to be the relationships of their own children to the scam artist. They fell for the scam, did trust, and were burned, although they evidently enjoyed the ride enough not to feel too burned. My relation with the beggar on the street has none of the qualities of that mistaken trust, although the beggar might also be trying to scam me.

Trust as a Good

In many discussions, trust is treated not merely as a matter of the assessment of others but as a good in itself—not in the normative sense of being a virtue but in the economic sense of being a good like the goods we buy in the market. In these discussions, trust seems almost palpable, something we can create and destroy, use or not use, just as we create and destroy capital and other goods of various kinds. The first way trust is deemed to be a good is that it is a commodity. (Messick and Kramer call it "a scarce resource.") The second way is that, in a remarkably large and growing literature, trust is treated as a good that is a kind of social capital that enables groups and whole societies to accomplish various purposes (in this volume see Stolle, Tyler, and Knight).

In both these discussions, *the actual concern is trustworthiness, not trust.* It is trustworthiness that may be a commodity, and trustworthiness within relevant social networks that is at least the background of social capital. If there were no trustworthiness, it would, of course, be absurd to suppose that trust is a good morally, and it would be a commodity only to others who might exploit it, not to the truster. If there were no trustworthiness, trust would not constitute any part of social capital because it would not enable larger social purposes but only opportunities for exploitation of the misplaced trust.

More generally, if trust were a commodity, we would invest in it for ourselves. But that would be absurd in many contexts. If trust were a form of social capital, it would have the character of a public good, and each of us would have incentive to "free-ride" by not doing our share of trusting. That too is absurd. If others are trustworthy, I typically have incentive to trust, not to free-ride by not trusting. Hence, in the two following discussions I am concerned with whether trustworthiness, not trust, is a commodity or an element of social capital.

Trustworthiness as a Commodity

Partha Dasgupta (1988) argues that trust is a commodity, something that can be produced if there is adequate demand. In this claim, it is clear that he is directly concerned with trustworthiness and only indirectly with trust. He treats the general issue as an analog of the business firm's problem of generating a reputation for trustworthiness. In such an analysis, of course, we must look at costs and benefits that give people incentive to be trustworthy. Typically, we might expect that we need enforcement and punishment that are credible. My trust in you will be a function of my confidence in institutional enforcement. You trust persons (or agencies) to do something only if you expect them to choose to do it (Dasgupta 1988, 50–51, 60). Hence, Dasgupta says, you must think of the trusted's position and probable incentives at the time of the need for fulfillment. Dasgupta's view is one of the class of *expectations theories* of trust; it is an incentive-to-be-trustworthy theory. Gambetta has a similar view (1988, 217).

If trustworthiness is a commodity comparable to the reputation in which a firm might invest, then we should economize on it, using more formal devices when economically feasible. And we should invest in it, or rather, in the reputation for trustworthiness (not trust). But if trustworthiness (not trust) is a collective good, we may tend to underinvest in it, just as we may tend to underinvest in reputation. For example, an auto dealer's reputation is partly a function of the general reputation of all auto dealers, and any single auto dealer's investments in its own reputation have little or no impact on that general reputation (Dasgupta 1988, 51, 64).

In general, it seems plausible that, in the end, all that one can invest in is reputation, which is not necessarily correlated with trustworthiness. The only way to affect trustworthiness is by changing one's incentives, for example, by entering into long-term relationships with those whose trust one would like to have. Hence, trustworthiness is *not* a commodity, even though perceived trustworthiness (that is, reputation) is.

When Tyler (this volume) says that his social trust is noninstrumental, what he means is that, although trust sometimes arises in instrumental relationships, such as exchange relationships, his social trust does not. If trust is cognitive, then, of course, trust is itself virtually by definition noninstrumental. I may have instrumental motivation to learn something that could be useful to me, and this motivation and my use of knowledge may both be instrumental. But the knowledge per se is not instrumental. I do not trust you in order to do something. I merely do or do not trust on the evidence of your apparent actions and incentives. Again, however, *trustworthiness* might be instrumental, as when one works to establish a reputation for reliability or creates institutional devices to give oneself incentive to fulfill a trust.

Trustworthiness as Social Capital

Kenneth Arrow (1974, 23) implicitly and Dasgupta (1988, 64) explicitly, among others, characterize trust as a public good. (See also Hardin 1999, on which this discussion draws.) Sissela Bok (1978, 28) says that trust is a "social good . . . and when it is destroyed, societies falter and collapse." Luhmann (1979, 64) says that trust "accumulates as a kind of capital." These seem to be nascent claims that trust is, or is an element in, what is now widely called "social capital." Although he is not the inventor of this term, it is now especially associated with James Coleman, whose compelling overview of the idea of social capital has had great influence (see also Knight, this volume). In his applications of that idea, Coleman considers the lower-level structures of ongoing relationships, with family, work groups, and so forth (Coleman 1990, 300–21, 361–63, 590–93, 595–96). These structures enable us, as individuals or corporate actors, to do many things, including cooperate successfully with each other in manifold ways. Hence, as is true of other forms of capital, social capital is enabling.

Other recent users of the term typically do not define it specifically but rather refer to instances of it or give very general characterizations of it. By social capital Robert Putnam (1995, 665–66) means "social connections and the attendant norms and trust," which are "features of social life . . . that enable participants to act together more effectively to pursue shared objectives." John Brehm and Wendy Rahn (1997, 999) define social capital as "the web of cooperative relationships between citizens that facilitates resolution of collective action problems." Francis Fukuyama (1995, 10) shares this general view with Putnam and Brehm and Rahn. Of these scholars, he gives the most general statement of what social capital is: "the ability of people to work together for common purposes in groups and organizations." What is the nature of the relationship between social capital and trust? Although Coleman, Putnam, and others say that trust is social capital, or an element of social capital, it appears that the core of the meaning of social capital in the work of these scholars is not trust but rather the social relationships, or the networks of such relationships (as emphasized by Brehm and Rahn), that enable us to undertake cooperative endeavors. These relationships, of course, ground trust in those participating in them: we are trustworthy to each other in our networks, therefore making it beneficial to us to trust each other in various undertakings. Hence, it seems confusing to think of the trust itself as an element of social capital. Gambetta (1988, 225) says, trust is "a result rather than a precondition of cooperation"; Bacharach and Gambetta (this volume) hold a contrary view. It is actually both, as is not surprising in an iterated interaction in which there can be feedback between the parties. But Gambetta's point may be modally correct. I risk cooperating, and if it pays off, I begin to trust you. Thomas Hobbes (1651/1968) requires an all-powerful sovereign to establish the conditions for cooperation, from which trust can then flow.

There might be some feedback between trust and further development of trust. I cooperate with you, discover your trustworthiness, and therefore cooperate even more or on even more important matters with you. And if I trust most of the people with whom I interact, I might begin to take the risk of cooperating with almost anyone I meet, at least if they are likely to remain in my ambit. Hence, my general optimism about others is a benefit to those others when they wish to cooperate with me (or even to abuse my optimistic expectations). Again, however, it is the high level of trustworthiness of people in my network that generates this benefit. And their trustworthiness is, on the encapsulated-interest account, the result of their having an interest in being trustworthy toward those with whom they have ongoing interactions that are beneficial and likely to continue to be. Hence, again, it is the network of exchangers that is the social capital that enables us, not our trust. More generally, what concerns most of the writers on social capital seems to be such networks of relationships, so that one might sooner call their social capital "interpersonal" or "network" capital (Hardin 1999a).

Dietlind Stolle (this volume) studies the relationship of generalized trust to strong membership in social organizations. One might suppose that such membership is facilitative for various things, so that it is a form of social capital. Our social networks enable us to accomplish things and thereby reduce the risks we might otherwise have to take to accomplish those things. Stolle finds that generalized trust (that is, trust in random others in the society) is not enhanced by strong group membership, evidently because such membership reduces exposure to the larger society and substitutes for relations in that society. This finding is similar to that of Yamagishi and Yamagishi (1994) for Japan in their comparison of Japanese and American trust relations (see also Cook and Hardin 2001). Gerald Mackie (this volume) similarly finds that differences in family patterns in northwestern and southeastern Europe lead to strong intragroup trust in the southeast. This intragroup trust reduces extragroup trust, again partly by substituting intragroup for extragroup interactions and partly through biased learning about the two groups.

Developmental Accounts of Trust

Several of the discussions suggest that there is a developmental path to trust and trustworthiness. The capacity to trust and the understanding to be trustworthy might develop through experience or learning, as they surely do to some extent. On an ethological account, one might even suppose that I can trust at all only if I had relevant experiences at formative moments in my life. Or there might be evolutionary mechanisms that lead us to trust or to be trustworthy. These could be genetic or social evolutionary mechanisms. Models of learning or of evolutionary mechanisms are clearly explanatory rather than conceptual. What is explained might be dispositions, or behavior, or both.

Psychological Development

The bulk of the psychological literature on trust is concerned with psychological correlates of trusting, or rather of being a high truster as opposed to a low truster (see, for example, Rotter 1980; Yamagishi, this volume). But some of it is about the development of a capacity or propensity to trust. The simplest psychological path for such development might merely be a learning model. The more I encounter people who reciprocate my cooperative gestures, the more I come to understand the nature of our potentially beneficial interaction, so that I become trustworthy in the sense that I begin to take others' interests into account in deciding what I do. When furthering their interests furthers mine and I recognize this fact, they have reason to judge me to be trustworthy.

Elsewhere I have proposed a simple learning model that would explain why some people grow up with optimistic expectations of the trustworthiness of others while other people grow up with pessimistic expectations (Hardin 1992). One may call what is learned a disposition, but it entails action or inaction in relevant contexts. If I have optimistic expectations, I more readily take risks that depend on the trustworthiness of others, and if others in the context are relatively trustworthy, I may benefit greatly from the cooperation that we can achieve. If, however, others are not trustworthy in the context, I quickly learn that fact and thereafter protect myself against betrayal by them (see also Yamagishi, this volume).

If, on the contrary, I have pessimistic expectations, I do not readily take risks that depend on others. Hence, I may not even gain the experience needed to revise my expectations when I come into a context in which others would commonly be trustworthy—if only I would take a risk on them.

A behavioral learning account, such as that of Erik Erikson (1963, 249), supplies an essential part of an economic or rational account of trust. In this account, particular expectations develop from experience. Such expectations are, of course, central to the rational account. "The firm establishment of enduring patterns for the solution of the nuclear conflict of basic trust versus basic mistrust in mere existence is the first task of the ego, and thus first of all a task of maternal care." What is needed is not simply quantities of food and so forth, but the quality of the maternal relationship. "Mothers create a sense of trust in their children by that kind of administration which in its quality combines sensitive care of the baby's individual needs and a firm sense of personal trustworthiness."

Baier (1986) and Hertzberg (1988) discuss infant trust to try to establish the *conceptual* nature of trust. One might think, however, that the infant instinct for holding the mouth open to let good things fall in might be an important *learning* or *developmental* experience. John Bowlby and his colleagues have assumed that the child faces ethological constraints during development. For example, if language is not learned before a certain young age, it cannot be learned thereafter. So too there might be developmental stages in attachment (Bretherton 1992, 762)—and, one might suppose, in trusting and in grasping the value of trustworthiness over time.

Yamagishi (this volume) argues that, de facto, some people are better able to recognize who has the disposition to be trustworthy. This is his "social intelligence." He reports that high trusters are better at discerning who is trustworthy. This fits with a simple learning model, which implies that those who are optimistic about the trustworthiness of others take the risk of cooperating more often and therefore expose themselves to more opportunities to learn about others. After such learning, one might conclude, what is commonly called generalized or social trust is a matter of optimism about the competence of others to recognize the value to themselves of trustworthiness. It might help to determine which of these motors—generalized trust or learning plus optimism—is at work if we could have real-world or experimental accounts of how both high and low trusters respond to both high and low levels of trustworthiness in their societies or their experimental groups.

Evolutionary Development

For Robert Frank (1988), trust and trustworthiness often involve the commitment problem, which is very hard to resolve. An absurd resolution of it is that of Wagner's *The Ring of the Nibelung:* Alberich adopts celibacy and forswears love forever in order to gain the power of the Rheingold (Wagner 1853–1854/1977, 16; see also Hardin, forthcoming–a, ch. 2). The sniveling Alberich has impossibly great willpower (as perhaps befit the ego of Wagner). A somewhat less absurd resolution is offered by David Gauthier (1986) as a matter simply of adopting a relevant disposition to be cooperative with others who are cooperative. This is a less extravagant demand on willpower, but it is still no more than such a demand.

One non-absurd way to resolve the commitment problem is genetically. One who blushes when lying may be able to establish credibility very easily without any willful commitment or manufactured disposition. One who does not blush when lying may have to create a reputation for honesty that is worth more to her than any gain she might make from cheating on that reputation. Sentiments such as vengeance and guilt often incur substantial avoidable costs—hence, Frank (1988, 54, 57) supposes, they must also confer some sort of compensating gain in order to have persisted socially or genetically. But these sentiments are most effective if they can be properly communicated to deter or encourage relevant actions from others. If devices for communicating, such as blushing, are genetic, we may then explain the genetic selection as the result of interests—it may even develop through intensive cultural conditioning.

Frank has a tendency to conflate the language of self-interest with shortsightedness (as perhaps does Miller, this volume). He says that defectors are pure opportunists who "always make whatever choice will maximize their personal payoff." But the choice that maximizes personal payoff in the longer run is the one the self-interested person wants to make, and that is not defection, as he assumes it is, in Frank's iterated prisoners' dilemmas. Frank (1988, 57, 11) poses his "commitment model" as counter to the "self-interest model." But in any case, his account is a resolution of the problem of my capacity to be trustworthy; *it is not an account of trust.* If there is an evolutionary account of trust, it is presumably roughly that of the infant trust argument of Baier and others. The infant must accept offered sustenance or die. Hence, infants of species that survive tend to accept it. They at least act as if they trusted, although it would be perverse to say that a cognitively undeveloped infant human or bird actually does trust.

Frank's model of trustworthiness is merely his model of cooperativeness more generally. (Indeed, experimental work that not long ago was characterized as being about cooperation is increasingly described as being about trust. I return to this point later in the chapter.) The conclusions of Frank's model are if cooperators and defectors look alike, then cooperators will be extinguished; if cooperators and defectors are easily identified, defectors will be extinguished; if mimicry has no cost or delay, cooperators will be extinguished; if mimicry entails fixed costs of detection, there will be a stable mix of cooperators and defectors.[10]

Albert Breton and Ronald Wintrobe (1982, 69–70; see also Hardin, forthcoming–a, ch. 8) suppose that, if they are to prosper, individuals must develop reasonably good instincts for assessing indicators of others' trustworthiness even absent institutions and reputations to certify them. Hence, we might suppose Frank's fourth state is that of human societies. Most of us are reasonably trustworthy, and the costs of mimicry are not negligible for most of us. Hence, we have reason to be confident to at least some extent.

If sentiments for vengeance, generosity, trustworthiness, and so forth have developed genetically, one may act from them even when it is not in one's interest to do so. Hence, there may be something left over from the rational choice account. But generally, a person with observable character traits for trustworthiness "will benefit by being able to solve important commitment problems. He will be trustworthy in situations where the purely self-interested person would not, and will therefore be much sought-after as a partner in situations that require trust" (Frank 1988, 14–16).[11]

Robert Axelrod's (1984) model of cooperation is a social rather than a genetic evolutionary model. Axelrod supposes that people in a large society use various kinds of strategy when they face an opportunity for beneficial cooperation with another. They can do relatively well only if they can take advantage of the cooperativeness of others or if they can selectively cooperate only with others who are contingently cooperative. In particular, he proposes following a strategy of tit-for-tat: one tries initial cooperation and then continues to cooperate if the other also cooperates but stops cooperating if the other does not initially cooperate. Players who follow this strategy prosper, and those who defect instead of cooperating are excluded from relations with the cooperators.

One might call this a model of the rise of cooperativeness. One might also call it a model of trustworthiness, because those who reliably cooperate fit the encapsulated-interest account of trust in being trustworthy with respect to other cooperators. Because they do so, they are enabled to cooperate beneficially with others who are trustworthy. Axelrod's social evolutionary model is a model of trustworthiness and not directly a model of trust, although trustworthiness begets trust by giving others the incentive to trust. Similarly, in one of Dasgupta's (1988, 58) evolutionarily stable models of reputation, if everyone assumes everyone is trustworthy, then it is in the interest of everyone to be trustworthy. What evolves socially, then, is trustworthiness, which begets trust and, increasingly, actual instances of cooperation. It is perhaps this close causal connection between trustworthiness and the possibilities of cooperation that makes it seem easy to label these experiments as about either cooperation or trustworthiness.

Functional Accounts of Trust

Carol Heimer (this volume) sees trust as one way in which actors in social relationships can cope with the "uncertainty and vulnerability" that pervade relationships. Luhmann (1979, 5, 8, 15) wishes to explain the existence of trust by its value to us in causing good things. "Where there is trust," he says, "there are increased possibilities for experience and action." In this view, the function of trust is that it gives us the present sense of understanding and reducing complexity. It increases tolerance for ambiguity. Complexity is the central problem, because the individual cannot know enough to handle everything and must therefore rely on others as agents for some matters. At least casually, these claims sound like a functional explanation for the existence, rise, or maintenance of trust. Such explanations are often shallow metaphors without genuine explanatory content. Let us unpack this one to see what content it has.

In a functional explanation, *an institution or a behavioral pattern X is explained by its function F for group G* if and only if:

1. F is an *effect* of X;
2. F is *beneficial* for G;
3. F maintains X by a causal *feedback* loop passing through G (Elster 1979, 28).[12]

The pattern X is trust; its function F is that it leads to beneficial interaction; G is the society. Let us fill in this paradigm, *with a strong condition* (in *italics*):

1. *If enough others are trustworthy,* beneficial interaction (F) is an effect of trust (X), that is, interaction is enhanced by trust.

2. Beneficial interaction (F) is good for the members of the society (G).

3. Beneficial interaction (F) maintains trust (X) by a feedback loop passing through the members of the society (G). Why? Because beneficial interaction leads to ongoing relationships and institutions that induce and support trust (as in the encapsulated-interest account).

Hence, Luhmann's theory is a functional explanation, *given the condition that enough people are trustworthy.*

What does this tell us? It does not say that, because trust is functional, it will happen. Rather, it says that, if the causal chain producing trust gets under way, it tends to be sustained by the feedback mechanism of the explanation. It would be sloppy reasoning to suppose that this functional account necessitates or automatically leads to trust in a complex world. *It is only an account of the maintenance of trust in such a world.* This comment raises an important additional question. How does the causal chain get under way? This might not be easy because, if others are generally untrustworthy, we can generally expect all to learn not to trust (Hardin 1992).

We could imagine that trusting is a result of social evolution from a prior, less complex world in which ongoing interactions are dense enough to ground trust. This would work because many of us might see that trustworthiness is in our interest, and our trustworthiness would then beget trust from others. Moreover, in a small community in which everyone's actions are relatively public, noncooperators might be shunned until they learn that their cooperation is beneficial not merely to others but also to themselves. We might then imagine that a more complex society could rise from such a well-regulated society to produce people who, perhaps only instinctively, understand that they must be trustworthy if they are to benefit from relationships with others.

Note, incidentally, that trustworthiness would fit this account without a strong caveat parallel to the one required for the functional account of trust. I do not automatically have incentive to trust when I enter a relationship, but I often have incentive to be trustworthy in order to make that relationship beneficial over the longer run. Hence, the condition required for Luhmann's functional explanation of trust to work may be fulfilled through a functional explanation of the rise of trustworthiness. It is not a morally grounded trustworthiness that is required or explained here. Rather, it is merely the trustworthiness of anyone who understands the implications of being reliable in various interactions that are likely to be repeated or continued if they work out beneficially to both (or all) parties.

Here is the quick functional account of trustworthiness (X is now trustworthiness rather than trust, but F and G remain the same):

1. Beneficial interaction (F) is an effect of trustworthiness (X), that is, interaction is enhanced by trustworthiness.
2. Beneficial interaction (F) is good for the members of the society (G).
3. Beneficial interaction (F) maintains trustworthiness (X) by a feedback loop passing through the members of the society (G). Why? Because beneficial interaction leads to ongoing relationships and institutions that *give incentive for trustworthiness* (as in the encapsulated-interest account).

Acting on the incentive for trustworthiness just is to be trustworthy on the encapsulated-interest account of trust. In his functional explanation of the maintenance of trust in complex society, Luhmann does not make the direct mistake, discussed earlier, of confusing trust and trustworthiness. Nevertheless, it is much easier to account directly for trustworthiness, which then begets trust. It begets trust because trust is essentially in the category of knowledge, and evidence of trustworthiness ultimately defines trust.

Luhmann does not confuse trust and trustworthiness conceptually because it is genuinely his interest to explain trust, which is the individual's device for dealing with complexity. Trustworthiness does not directly help to deal with complexity, although it does so indirectly by begetting trust. On this account, trustworthiness is in a sense prior. Hence, there is reason to suppose *it is the rise of trustworthiness that allows for the development of complexity, which actually results from successful trust.* In other words, trust enables us not only to handle complexity when we have it but therefore to develop complexity. This would make sense, in a way that his own general argument does not, of Luhmann's claim (1979, 7) that the "increase and reduction of complexity belong together as complementary aspects of the structure of human response to the world." Indeed, for Locke, trustworthiness is arguably the fundament of social order. The duty to be trustworthy is for him, John Dunn (1994, 287) says, "more fundamental than the moral conventions or positive laws of any society, because none of the latter is necessarily morally valid and because, without [trustworthiness] human society would not be possible at all." Against this claim, the anthropologist Fredrik Barth claimed in discussion at the Russell Sage Foundation–New York University conference on trust that in two of the societies he has studied—the Swat Pathan of northern Pakistan and the traditional Omani of Oman—distrust is endemic and yet these societies historically achieved stable social order.

Also note that, while trust fits the paradigm of functional explanation on the encapsulated-interest theory of trust, it might not under some other theories or definitions of trust. Indeed, it cannot fit a functional explanation under some of the noncognitive or ungrounded definitions because trust under these definitions cannot be affected by its effects; feedback plays no role for it. Inherently normative trust is also unlikely to fit an analogous functional explanation. It is an oddity of Luhmann's account that one cannot be sure what conception of trust he has in mind, although he does rule out some conceptions. For example, although he is not consistent in his claims, he generally holds that trust is in the cognitive category with knowledge, as when he supposes that trust is dependent on expectations and when he writes that it has to be learned, just like any other kind of "generalization" (Luhmann 1979, 27). Plausibly, his conception is essentially the encapsulated-interest view. Evolutionary accounts typically are functional, and the account of trustworthiness as social capital might be constructed as functional, although these need not suppose that the problem to be resolved is complexity.

Luhmann's functional account works if there are enough people who are trustworthy. In Barber's (1983) account of professionalism, trustworthiness is achieved by indoctrinating the professionals. I, a patient with limited medical understanding, trust a doctor to take my interests to heart and to serve me well. In this account, there is a functional relationship between trust and the trustworthiness of doctors.[13] Alternatively, one might suppose that the reliability of doctors is secured by a strong institution that stands on its own and does not depend on feedback from patients and doctors in the form of actions that support it any more than the institutions of justice, which secure compliance with the law, are dependent on feedback from citizens and criminals.

In general, functional explanation fits especially well with rational choice understandings because the feedback can work through the creation of incentives for acting according to the pattern of behavior that is to be explained.[14] The relevant functional pattern of behavior is commonly no more than a response to incentives. No one need know the general implications of everyone acting from those incentives. Robert Merton (1949/1968, 103) notes that the requirements of functional explanation in the biological sciences "come to be met almost as a matter of course." Elster (1979, 29) supposes that it is nearly impossible to find cases of functional explanation in sociology that meet the conditions of his paradigm. The correct claim would be that few extant accounts that are called functional meet these conditions. But sociology and the social world are rife with cases that do fit it.

Concluding Remarks

The great importance of trust in ordinary life can be read in the massive role it plays in great literature—or rather, the role played by betrayal of trust. Trust may be second only to love as a plot line and motivator, and even half of the power of love as a plot line is in the eventual betrayal of it. Betrayal is, of course, not a failure of trust but a failure of trustworthiness. It is odd therefore that academic writings—both philosophical and social scientific—focus heavily on trust rather than on trustworthiness. Indeed, most writings on trust tend to say things that, as noted earlier, would make easy sense if applied to trustworthiness but that make less sense when applied to trust. If such statements make sense for trust at all, it is only indirectly through the causal connection that trustworthiness begets trust.

This conclusion is forcefully underlined by the discussion of the functional explanation of trust in the previous section. That explanation works specifically for the encapsulated-interest account of trust and trustworthiness. Many of the discussions of trust canvassed in this chapter are really about trustworthiness, and some of the conclusions of those discussions are therefore misguided. But Luhmann's functional account of trust is merely a causal step away from a more fully correct account, which is a functional account of trustworthiness.

How far wrong may some other accounts go in focusing on trust rather than trustworthiness? Consider the largest recent body of speculative thought on trust. The causal fact that trustworthiness begets trust allows and perhaps encourages fretting about the ostensible decline in trust in modern societies, or at least in contemporary America. If the decline is real, it must be *a decline in perceived trustworthiness.* Or, of course, it might be a decline in faith or some attitude that is labeled trust in the vernacular (see Hardin 1998). Declining faith in religion has historically followed increased understanding of the nature of the world. Declining faith in government, its agents, and various others may similarly be the result of increased understanding or, more plausibly, increased knowledge.

For a trivial example, the kinds of information we have about President Bill Clinton go far beyond what was popularly known about any previous president, including some whose actions as president were far more scurrilous than any of Clinton's. The knowledge we have about many governmental actions is also astonishing in comparison to past times. The civil rights movement may well have been so successful largely because of instant television coverage of the brutality and stupidity of many southern officials, such as Sheriff Jim Clark in Selma, Alabama (Garrow 1978).[15] The White House tapes drove Richard Nixon out of office when mere testimony probably could not have done so. Comparable events in earlier times could not have been so vividly grasped by much of the populace. Even though it was massively manipulated by the military, televised coverage of the Gulf War in 1991 similarly brought it to the sharp attention of people who a generation earlier would only curiously have read a bit about it.

Recent students of declining trust try to discover what is wrong with *citizens* that they are so increasingly distrustful of government. Because he defines generalized trust as part of social capital, Putnam asks why there has been a decline in such capital. For reasons argued earlier, labeling trust as social capital is misleading. Putnam's thesis still stands, however, as an argument about declining trust (in some sense) in government. He looks at many factors, but not generally at the evidence on the trustworthiness of the *officials* and others whom the citizens supposedly distrust.[16] Putnam (1995, 677) cites in particular the amount of time people now spend watching television as a cause of their reduced group activity, which, he speculates, leads to reduced attachment to the political system.[17] This has the sound of an apparently functional explanation that is not spelled out articulately, but it does not appear to fit such an explanation. The functional explanation of the rise of trustworthiness in Luhmann's work, as discussed earlier, probably often fits the claim that participation in groups leads to *trustworthiness of the group members toward each other* and hence to trust of each other. But the arguments of Putnam and company require further that there be some kind of *spillover* from local group participation and the trust it engenders in those participating with each other to trust in general others, including government (see Stolle, this volume).

Spillover arguments here are often essentially arguments about the creation of a disposition, on which people then act even without direct reasoning. This is roughly Williamson's (1993) view that trust is not generally calculative. There is calculation or at least solid reasoning somewhere in the past, but not in this moment when I am dealing with you. This raises the question of whether there is calculation when I first meet someone or whether my disposition is very generally applied to virtually anyone, including those newly met and those never to be met again. To assess whether the dispositional (or spillover) thesis is correct would require psychological data that go beyond the correlations between measures over time of generalized trust and participation in group activities. This is a fundamentally important issue on which we have inadequate knowledge.

Suppose the decline in supposed trust of government is merely a decline in the disposition to trust without much thought about the trustworthiness of the other. Is that a bad thing? It would probably be bad for a person never to be willing to take a risk on anyone. But it would probably not be bad for a person to withhold trust unless there is reason for, or until there is evidence of trustworthiness. Is it bad for others? The claims of Putnam and company are, essentially, that such not-trusting is bad for the larger society. In a sense, the typical person today is individually less likely to have ungrounded faith in government. To treat this as a worry is to suggest that the world would work better for us if people did have such ungrounded faith. Indeed, two decades ago a *New York Times* editorial on "the age of suspicion" (cited by Rotter 1980, 1) speculated on the political costs of distrust of government and wondered whether citizens would be better off trusting more. Given that such trust may be cognitively unwarranted, let us try out such a thesis.

If you have ungrounded trust in me, that might benefit me (but not you) by getting you to do things for me out of misplaced trust. If you have ungrounded faith in our government, that would benefit me only if that government happens to serve my interests fairly well and if, as we may assume, your faith in the government helps to license its actions and reduces the chance of its being successfully challenged. Hence, in the United States ungrounded faith by the upper-middle-class might be okay for that class (it would not harm their interests to license the government's continuation of its policies). But since the government might actually be thought to do a good job of serving their interests anyway, that class might have correct, grounded expectations that it will do so. Ungrounded faith by other groups, such as the poor, might enable the government to support the upper-middle-class even better. It is hard to imagine how any group could serve its own interests *better* by having ungrounded faith rather than grounded expectations. Our interests might be served better by having ungrounded faith rather than maintaining *mistaken* distrust.

One might suppose that the first and last steps of Putnam's argument are right: watching television and declining trust (or faith) in government are causally related. But the cause might not be Putnam's indirect one: time before the television screen displaces group activities, leading to fewer trusting relationships in group activities; less trust in government is the spillover effect of having fewer of these types of trusting relationships. The intervening step need not be this claim of spillover but the claim that citizens, in part because of the visual power of television, now know too much to trust (or have faith in) many officials. Citizens may now know less about the substance of government but more about its character, because television can convey the latter better than it conveys the former.

Indeed, one need not even think contemporary leaders are less committed to caring for our interests than earlier leaders, many of whom were venal, avaricious, and grievously biased in favor of certain narrow interests, or all of these. One need only have the sense, which may be widely shared, that the world is much harder to manage than was thought earlier. The fact that we now can understand more of the world raises the bar on how much we might suppose should be done by government, professionals, and more or less everyone. But competence may not have increased in tandem with understanding, so that we now see people in roles of many and varied kinds fail to achieve what we demand of them. Our trust or faith declines because our expectations rise and we increasingly judge our leaders incompetent (Hardin 2000).

It is striking that, retrospectively, Harry Truman is seen as a paragon of competence, not because we have forgotten how limited he was but because we now know that others are at least as limited but, being perhaps less self-aware than Truman, expect to be judged competent.[18] William Butler Yeats (1956, 185) spoke as a profoundly committed conservative when he wrote that "the centre cannot hold." Even liberals today might add that little or nothing else holds either. The economic progress that not long ago seemed like a nearly unmitigated good now seems sour to many—at least when it is happening to people other than themselves.

To see the decline in faith in government as a result of, in a sense, the decline of citizens is to treat it as (the analog of) a problem of trusting when it might more cogently be seen as (the analog of) a problem of trustworthiness. The differences in what we must explain in these very different visions of the problem are categorical. For the Putnam thesis of a deficit of trust, we would need data on psychological dispositions toward trust and an account of how these work for the Putnam thesis of a deficit of trust. And for the thesis that trust is primarily dependent on trustworthiness, we would need data on the evidence people have to trust or not trust government officials—or to have or not have faith in them.

Some of the contributors to this volume use the terms "trust" and, implicitly, "trustworthiness" in ways quite different from how I use them. One might say that they disagree, and sometimes they have said that, often quite forcefully. But I think it pointless to say we disagree about concepts until we first have a theory or theories—or at least explanations—in which the concepts gain meaning. It will be evident to readers that either there are no theories or there are manifold theories implicit in various discussions of this book. Unfortunately, very few theories are explicitly articulated, although many, often novel, explanations of important social phenomena are offered.

Trust as encapsulated interest is a theoretical conception because it is grounded in an explanatory account of *why* people trust or distrust relevant others. That account leads to a further account of how trust and distrust work. Varied conceptions of trust—if they are explanatory or grounded in explanatory theory—are what we probably want at this stage of research. Alternatives to the encapsulated-interest view of trust in the contributions to this book include the view that trust is a disposition (as in the various accounts of generalized trust in some of the contributions and in the discussion of trust from social identity in Tyler) and the view that it is grounded in the strictly moral commitments of the trusted.

Probably everyone would agree that trust is sometimes grounded in encapsulated interest and sometimes in a belief in the moral commitment of the trusted. Many would disagree that there is any significant incidence of full-blown generalized trust, because such trusters must be too gullible to prosper in most societies in which studies of trust have been done. But there must still be some incidence of trust as partially dispositional. Interesting next moves would be to find experimental and real-world contexts in which these three views could be differentiated, and to assess the incidence of the different forms in our actual lives.

I am grateful to John Brehm, Karen Cook, and an anonymous referee for comments on this chapter. I am also grateful to many participants in Russell Sage Foundation conferences and workshops for debates on these issues. It has been enlightening to discover the number and diversity of views of trust.

Notes

1. There is a fuller argument in Hardin (1991), from which some of this discussion is drawn.

2. Early critics of utilitarianism asserted that we cannot be utilitarian because, if we were, we would spend so much time calculating that we would have no time left over for doing and enjoying. John Stuart Mill retorted that rationality does not require calculation anew every time, say, a sailor goes to sea and navigates by past experience any more than it requires calculation in many other utilitarian choices.

3. In the so-called trust game used in many experiments, trust is clearly a three-part relation: two players and a limited range of potential payoffs (see also Hardin, forthcoming–a, ch. 1; and Hardin, forthcoming–b).

4. Presumably Held means that one might be obligated to act in certain ways contrary to one's degree of trust.

5. Their concern with cognitive miserliness, however, fits well with the view that trust is itself a cognitive rather than a behavioral concept.

6. For noncognitive dispositional views, some writers (for example, Gauthier 1986) suppose that one can choose to have a disposition. None of the contributors to this volume seem to make this claim, but perhaps some of them would accept such a claim and therefore defend their assertions that one can choose to trust. Perhaps they should say that one can choose to be trusting in general rather than that one chooses to trust a particular person. This is Gauthier's claim: that I choose to be a cooperative person as a matter of general character or disposition. Until a whole-cloth dispositional theory of trust is laid out for us, rather than merely assumed, we might not be able to settle the issue of whether the claims of choosing to trust someone are coherent with such a theory.

7. The reputational effect at issue is potential damage to one's future possibilities for interaction with others who may learn of one's default on a trust now. The reputational effect for the potential cheater is incentive-based and therefore future-oriented.

8. If there are no characteristics of the trusted in evidence, as is commonly true in experimental plays of the one-way, one-shot trust game, then the putative truster must be acting on some hope, perhaps from learned experience, for cooperation or must be acting from a mere disposition to trust.

9. For another case, see the tale of duplicity that drives Dostoevski's *The Brothers Karamazov*, which is discussed in Hardin (1991).

10. This result contrasts with the standard sociobiological claim that only defectors survive. Robert Axelrod (1984) shows that, in competition with a relatively large set of alternative strategies, tit-for-tat cooperators survive quite well.

11. In addition, Frank (1988, 18) notes that behavior influences character: "Few people can maintain a predisposition to behave honestly while at the same time frequently engaging in transparently opportunistic behavior"—as argued by Pascal.

12. Elster adds two other considerations that seem unnecessary. See also Hardin (1995, 82–86), Merton (1949/1968, 104–9), and Stinchcombe (1968, 80–101).

13. Because this relationship is fully understood and deliberately secured through indoctrination and monitoring of doctors, Elster (1979, 28) would reject it as not fitting a functional explanation. For him, a functional explanation is valid only if the feedback is not understood.

14. See also Hardin 1980. The title of this article should be "functional explanation" rather than "functionalist explanation"; the latter suggests the blind assumption that whatever is good for a society must have happened and whatever behaviors a society develops must be good for it.

15. The words *stupidity and brutality* were used by the *Alabama Journal* at the time (Chong 1991, 26).

16. They are mentioned as a period effect on those who came of political age during the era of the revelations of governmental duplicities in the Vietnam War, the Watergate scandal, and, one might add, the practices of J. Edgar Hoover's FBI (Putnam 1995, 674).

17. Just how important television viewing seems to Putnam is suggested by his title, "Tuning In, Tuning Out."

18. I once stood on line at the stand of a German street vendor who dispensed wurst, sandwiches, drinks, and many other things with seemingly choreographed efficiency of movement that was remarkably graceful. When complimented for his efficiency by the person before me, he said, no doubt truthfully, "I know my limits."

References

Arrow, Kenneth J. 1974. *The Limits of Organization*. New York: Norton.

Axelrod, Robert. 1984. *The Evolution of Cooperation*. New York: Basic Books.

Baier, Annette. 1986. "Trust and Antitrust." *Ethics* 96(2): 231–60.

———. 1985. "What Do Women Want in a Moral Theory?" *Nous* 19(1): 53–64.

Barber, Bernard. 1983. *The Logic and Limits of Trust.* New Brunswick, N.J.: Rutgers University Press.

Becker, Gary. 1971. *The Economics of Discrimination.* 2d ed. Chicago: University of Chicago Press. (Originally published in 1957)

Becker, Lawrence C. 1996. "Trust as Noncognitive Security About Motives." *Ethics* 107(1): 43–61.

Bok, Sissela. 1978. *Lying: Moral Choice in Public and Private Life.* New York: Pantheon. Reprint, New York: Vintage Books, 1979.

Brehm, John, and Wendy Rahn. 1997. "Individual-Level Evidence for the Causes and Consequences of Social Capital." *American Journal of Political Science* 41(3): 999–1023.

Bretherton, Inge. 1992. "The Origins of Attachment Theory: John Bowlby and Mary Ainsworth." *Developmental Psychology* 28(5): 759–75.

Breton, Albert, and Ronald Wintrobe. 1982. *The Logic of Bureaucratic Conduct: An Economic Analysis of Competition, Exchange, and Efficiency in Private and Public Organizations.* Cambridge: Cambridge University Press.

Chong, Dennis. 1991. *Collective Action and the Civil Rights Movement.* Chicago: University of Chicago Press.

Coleman, James S. 1990. *Foundations of Social Theory.* Cambridge, Mass.: Harvard University Press.

Cook, Karen S., and Russell Hardin. 2001. "Networks, Norms, and Trustworthiness." In *Social Norms,* edited by Karl-Dieter Opp and Michael Hechter. New York: Russell Sage Foundation.

Dasgupta, Partha. 1988. "Trust as a Commodity." In *Trust: Making and Breaking Cooperative Relations,* edited by Diego Gambetta. Oxford: Blackwell.

Dunn, John. 1988. "Trust and Political Agency." In *Trust: Making and Breaking Cooperative Relations,* edited by Diego Gambetta. Oxford: Blackwell.

———. 1994. "The Concept of 'Trust' in the Politics of John Locke." In *Philosophy in History,* edited by Richard Rorty, J. B. Schneewind, and Quentin Skinner. Cambridge: Cambridge University Press.

Elster, Jon. 1979. *Ulysses and the Sirens.* Cambridge: Cambridge University Press.

Erikson, Erik H. 1963. *Childhood and Society.* 2d ed. New York: Norton.

Frank, Robert. 1988. *Passions Within Reason: The Strategic Role of the Emotions.* New York: Norton.

Fukuyama, Francis. 1995. *The Social Virtues and the Creation of Prosperity.* New York: Free Press.

Gambetta, Diego, ed. 1988. *Trust: Making and Breaking Cooperative Relations.* Oxford: Blackwell.

Garrow, David J. 1978. *Protest at Selma.* New Haven, Conn.: Yale University Press.

Gauthier, David. 1986. *Morals by Agreement.* Oxford: Oxford University Press.

———. 1980. "Rationality, Irrationality, and Functionalist Explanation." *Social Science Information* 19 (September): 755–72.

———. 1991. "Trusting Persons, Trusting Institutions." In *The Strategy of Choice,* edited by Richard J. Zeckhauser. Cambridge, Mass.: MIT Press.

———. 1992. "The Street-Level Epistemology of Trust." *Analyse und Kritik* 14 (December): 152–76. Reprint, *Politics and Society* 21 (4, 1993): 505–29.

———. 1995. *One for All: The Logic of Group Conflict.* Princeton, N.J.: Princeton University Press.

———. 1998. "Trust in Government." In *Trust and Governance,* edited by Valerie Braithwaite and Margaret Levi. New York: Russell Sage Foundation.

———. 1999. "Social Capital." In *Competition and Cooperation: Conversations with Nobelists About Economics and Political Science,* edited by James Alt, Margaret Levi, and Elinor Ostrom. New York: Russell Sage Foundation.

———. 2000. "Public Trust." In *What's Troubling the Trilateral Democracies,* edited by Susan J. Pharr and Robert D. Putnam. Princeton, N.J.: Princeton University Press.

Hardin, Russell. Forthcoming–a. *Trust and Trustworthiness.* New York: Russell Sage Foundation.

———. Forthcoming–b. "Gaming Trust." In *Trust and Reciprocity: Interdisciplinary Lessons from Experimental Work,* edited by Elinor Ostrom and James Walker. New York: Russell Sage Foundation.

Held, Virginia. 1968. "On the Meaning of Trust." *Ethics* 78(2): 156–59.

———. 1984. *Rights and Goods: Justifying Social Action.* New York: Free Press. Reprint, Chicago: University of Chicago Press.

Hertzberg, Lars. 1988. "On the Attitude of Trust." *Inquiry* 31: 307–22.

Hobbes, Thomas. 1968. *Leviathan.* Edited by C. B. Macpherson. Harmondsworth, Eng.: Penguin. (Originally published in 1651)

Jones, Karen. 1996. "Trust as an Affective Attitude." *Ethics* 107(1): 4–25.

Kreps, David. 1990. "Corporate Culture and Economic Theory." In *Perspectives on Positive Political Economy,* edited by James Alt and Kenneth Shepsle. Cambridge: Cambridge University Press.

Luhmann, Niklas. 1979. "Trust: A Mechanism for the Reduction of Social Complexity." In *Trust and Power,* edited by Niklas Luhmann. New York: Wiley.

Mansbridge, Jane J. 1999. "Altruistic Trust." In *Democracy and Trust,* edited by Mark E. Warren. Cambridge: Cambridge University Press.

McKean, Roland N. 1975. "Economics of Trust, Altruism, and Corporate Responsibility." In *Altruism, Morality, and Economic Theory,* edited by Edmund S. Phelps. New York: Russell Sage Foundation.

Merton, Robert K. 1968. *Social Theory and Social Structure.* Enlarged ed. New York: Free Press. (Originally published in 1949)

Putnam, Robert. 1995. "Tuning In, Tuning Out: The Strange Disappearance of Social Capital in America." *PS: Political Science and Politics* 24(4): 664–83.

Rotter, Julian B. 1980. "Interpersonal Trust, Trustworthiness, and Gullibility." *American Psychologist* 35(January): 1–7.

Stinchcombe, Arthur L. 1968. *Constructing Social Theories.* New York: Harcourt, Brace.

Wagner, Richard. 1977. *Das Rheingold.* In Richard Wagner, *The Ring of the Nibelung,* translated by Andrew Porter. New York: Norton. (Composed 1853–1854)

Williamson, Oliver. 1993. "Calculativeness, Trust, and Economic Organization." *Journal of Law and Economics* 36(1): 453–86.

Yamagishi, Toshio, and Midori Yamagishi. 1994. "Trust and Commitment in the United States and Japan." *Motivation and Emotion* 18(2): 129–66.

Yeats, William Butler. 1956. "The Second Coming." In *The Collected Poems of W. B. Yeats.* Definitive ed. New York: Macmillan.

Chapter 2

Solving the Problem of Trust

CAROL A. HEIMER

PEOPLE seeking medical care or engaging in sexual relations often are intensely aware of their vulnerability and very uncertain about the wisdom of trusting others (on medical care, see Barber 1983, Freidson 1970/1988, Heimer and Staffen 1998, and Rothman 1991; on sexuality, see Blumstein and Schwartz 1983, Heimer 1985, 220–26, Horowitz 1983, and Vaughan 1986). For a woman wishing to terminate a pregnancy, the ordinary trust problems of medical care and sexual relations are multiplied when abortion is illegal. A pregnant woman has only a few weeks to make a decision, obtain whatever funds are necessary, and locate someone she can trust with her secrets and her health (Lee 1969). As Leslie Reagan (1997) shows, however, the practice, policing, and politics of abortion varied a good deal between 1867 and 1973, the period "when abortion was a crime." The early, relatively open practice of abortion gave way to restrictions on abortion in the 1940s and then to repression and secrecy in the 1950s and 1960s, with increasing police intervention.

During the four years just before the 1973 U.S. Supreme Court decision that legalized abortion, a remarkable Chicago-area feminist abortion service helped about eleven thousand women terminate their pregnancies. At the beginning, the group counseled the women and made referrals to others who would perform the abortions. But soon they came to believe that they could ensure safe, inexpensive, and empowering abortions only by learning to perform abortions themselves. Something like one hundred women worked as members of Jane (the group's pseudonym) at one time or another, and dozens more were involved in other ways—a pharmacist, physicians for advice and follow-up, lawyers, and the abortionists who performed the procedures before group members took over the task.

Questions about who could be trusted crop up repeatedly in Laura Kaplan's (1995) account of Jane's activities (see also Reagan 1997, 223–27, 243–44). In the early days, when Jane only made referrals, members worried about whether they could trust the abortionists. Some abortionists were occasionally drunk, asked for sexual favors or additional payments from the pregnant women, were arrogant with Jane members or treated the pregnant women disrespectfully, were incompetent or careless, or refused to make themselves available by telephone to help manage complications. Jane slowly acquired information about abortionists by debriefing the women who received abortions. Because they had so little information, Jane members tried to limit their own vulnerability and that of their clients. Gradually the work was shifted to abortionists who were willing to help manage trust problems, either by supplying more information to Jane or by allowing a Jane member to be present during the procedure. Abortionists who seemed incompetent, unreliable, likely to have connections with organized crime, too greedy, or unwilling to negotiate about price or conditions received less work or were dropped entirely.

Operating outside the law, abortionists in turn worried about whether they could trust Jane members and clients. Many used street-corner pickups, blindfolds, and false names so that no one could identify them or their location. Even Jane members were not permitted to meet the abortionists. Nick, who ultimately trained Jane members to perform abortions, was by far the most cooperative of the abortionists. But even he had to be pushed. He initially concealed his identity, pretending to be the "doctor's" middleman. Jenny, one of the leaders and the first to perform abortions, eventually discovered that Nick was actually the abortionist but that he was not a licensed physician. While keeping Nick's secrets, Jenny simultaneously attempted to win his trust by becoming his friend rather than just his business associate. This strategy seemed to work—Nick trusted women he met as Jenny's friends more than women who were Jane members (even when Jenny vouched for them).

Jane members also worried about whether they could trust each other and the women for whom they arranged abortions. Members shared information only on a "need-to-know" basis. The division of labor in contacting women, arranging appointments and payment, counseling, ferrying women to and from abortions, and ultimately doing abortions was as much a division of *information* as a division of *work*. Some members had information about the abortionists, others about how to contact particular pregnant women, and still others about women's medical histories. Most members were unaware that Jane members were performing abortions. Rather than keeping records on the women who went through their service, Jane destroyed information as quickly as possible. At the extreme, after their arrest three Jane members spent their time in the paddy wagon eating portions of client index cards.

The women who received abortions had the most serious trust problems. Others involved faced legal sanctions such as prison terms and threats to their jobs and reputations, but the pregnant women faced these costs and more. Their lives and health were at risk. The reputation of a medical care provider could not be investigated in the usual ways, and women could not protect themselves by asking a friend or family member to accompany them. No friendly face waited in the recovery room, and sometimes no one even knew that a woman had gone to an abortionist. In her study of how women located abortionists, Nancy Howell Lee (1969, 95) finds that about one-third of the women had gone for their illegal abortion alone; about 9 percent said that no one had sufficient information to locate them if something went wrong. Unfortunately, we know relatively little about how such women reassured or protected themselves. One-third of the women Lee interviewed felt they had no choice but to use the abortionist they happened to locate, and another 29 percent said they chose a particular abortionist because they trusted the recommendations and reassurances they had received from others (Lee 1969, 76; see also 63, 64, 159). We also have poignant accounts of women's desperation and fear in historical documents, in interviews with women who had illegal abortions in the 1960s, and in Jane members' recollections of their clients (Reagan 1997, Lee 1969, and Kaplan 1995, respectively). We cannot really know whether the women who sought illegal abortions were satisfied that the abortionists were competent and trustworthy or whether they simply accepted the risks they faced. Although most women survived their abortions, we do know that illegal abortions were risky. As Reagan (1997, 22) points out, many of the documents she used were from coroners' inquests—records available because women died.

Arrangements for illegal abortions are an apt illustration for introducing a discussion of trust because they display with particular clarity the key ingredients of all trust problems and the canonical strategies that can be used to solve them. Participants are uncertain and vulnerable—they lack information about what others can and will do, but they also have a stake in the interaction because some of their objectives cannot be achieved without the cooperation of others. When the alternative is as unpalatable as bearing an unwanted child, women may decide to go ahead with an abortion even if they do not trust the abortionist. Abortionists may likewise be willing to accept a good deal of risk to gain the high income that can sometimes be earned from participation in an illegal activity. But the participants in such a situation may nevertheless attempt to assuage their anxiety or increase the predictability of outcomes by collecting what information they can about each other. When abortionists ask pregnant women who referred them, they are not collecting information on the success of their marketing campaign but attempting to assess the women's trustworthiness. When information is especially scarce (and so uncertainty cannot be reduced), participants may attempt to reduce their vulnerability. When information about abortionists was unavailable, Jane decreased its vulnerability by using the services of several abortionists. If one practitioner proved unreliable or incompetent or was raided by the police, only a proportion of Jane's clients suffered. Unable to trust the abortionists about whom it had so little information, Jane and its clients initially adopted distrusting, vulnerability-reducing strategies. Yet such strategies were not uniformly employed; as some Jane members slowly and cautiously developed relationships with abortionists and other service providers, trusting strategies dynamically supplanted distrusting ones in small enclaves of this otherwise high-risk, distrusting environment.

I argue that uncertainty and vulnerability are the core elements of trust relations. What form uncertainty and vulnerability take varies a good deal with the substance of the relationship. And although the canonical strategies involve decreasing uncertainty or reducing vulnerability, participants' choices about which strategy or mix of strategies to adopt typically are constrained by the features of their social worlds.[1] Moreover, it is crucial to recognize that trust is dynamic. Even though participants may opt for distrusting strategies at one point in time, by facilitating interactions that would otherwise be too costly, distrusting strategies permit the first tentative moves from which relationships, exchanges of information, mutual adaptation, and sometimes eventually trust develop.

In all social life actors are vulnerable to each other. Although some social interactions yield rewards for all participants, many involve rewards for some at a cost to others. To the extent that the interests of all parties do not coincide perfectly (and social norms are unable to correct the misalignment), people may be motivated, both consciously and unconsciously, to take advantage of each other. Social interaction is risky, and people have ample cause to be uncertain about each other's intentions and the probable outcomes of their encounters. Beyond some irreducible minimal level, however, interaction is optional. When it is not possible to trust others, those who have no effective way to reduce uncertainty or vulnerability may conclude that the costs of interaction outweigh the benefits. As Luhmann comments (1988, 103), sometimes a "lack of trust means that behaviour which presupposes trust will be ruled out." Although misplaced trust can lead to large losses, Russell Hardin (1993, 507) reminds us that the costs of forgone interactions can also be formidable.

From this brief discussion it is possible to abstract more rigorous definitions of uncertainty and vulnerability that apply to a wide variety of social situations. By uncertainty I mean the inability of an actor to predict the outcome of an event because he or she lacks information about the intentions and competence of another actor who directly controls this outcome. Vulnerability has to do with the amount of risk an actor incurs by engaging in a particular interaction and is a function (nonlinear and increasing) of the proportion of the actor's total assets that are at stake in the interaction.

Uncertainty and vulnerability can be managed in numerous ways. I argue that whereas in traditional societies people often can manage trust problems by reducing their uncertainty about the intentions and competence of others, reducing vulnerability becomes more important in modern societies. Traditional communities, by controlling the behavior of people, reduce the uncertainty of interaction, concentrating uncertainty instead in relations between communities. This solution remains important in modern life, although it is sometimes ineffective. But urban society also brings increased contact with strangers. Because it is difficult to reduce uncertainty in contacts with strangers, people often find it necessary to reduce their vulnerability instead. Institutions like insurance supplement less formal methods for decreasing vulnerability to any single person. Growth in the number and power of corporate actors has brought other changes. Uncertainty cannot easily be reduced through personal relations, and power differences between individuals and corporate actors often prevent the reduction of vulnerability. Individuals have to accept their uncertainty and vulnerability and decide whether to interact without resolving either issue. Decisions often are based on needing what corporate actors have.

The remainder of this essay is divided into four parts. I begin by discussing the components of trust relations and how they combine to yield different forms of trust relations. Next I explain the link between forms of trust and strategies for managing trust. Choices of strategy are also affected by social structure; these structural influences are the subject of a third section. Finally I discuss historical changes in the mix of strategies used in managing trust relations and the implications of basing interaction on particular strategies. I focus particularly on changes brought by the rise of corporations and the development of insurance.

Forms of Trust Relations

First a note on terminology. In this essay, I use the word *entrustor* rather than the more common *truster*. I do this for two reasons. The first concerns the topic of the essay: following Messick and Kramer (this volume), one might argue that to "trust" means to accept the hypothesis that another actor (a person, group, or organization) will follow ordinary ethical rules about such matters as truth-telling and avoiding harm to others. This much is consistent with Hardin's assertion in this volume that "trust is not an action." In a very important subset of situations, however, trustworthiness matters because there is something at stake in the relation between interaction partners. One is especially concerned about the trustworthiness of others when one is vulnerable to them. This essay focuses on those situations in which trust has action implications—in which "trust" and "entrusting" overlap. At the same time, however, I emphasize that entrusting may not be fully voluntary. I may be forced to entrust something even when I do not feel I can trust my interaction partner. The second reason to eschew the word *truster*, then, is because an "entrustor" may or may not trust the trustee on whom he or she is dependent. As I discuss later, the category "entrustors" encompasses the subset "trusters"— those who are employing a trusting rather than a distrusting strategy.

Trust relations, such as those between the members of the women's collective, the abortionists, and the pregnant women discussed earlier, can be characterized by the presence or absence of four factors.[2]

1. In many situations in which people have to decide whether they can trust each other, they are objectively vulnerable to one another. As Hardin (1993, 507) puts it, "Trust involves giving discretion to another to affect one's interests." The entrustor has something (such as a possession or a prerogative) that could be entrusted to the control of someone else (an individual, an organization, a network), here referred to as the "trustee." Alternatively, the trustee may be able to deprive the entrustor of something he or she currently has.[3]

2. In many situations, entrustors are uncertain about the intentions and competence of trustees and therefore also about the outcome of their interactions.[4] The objective amounts of uncertainty and vulnerability vary across social situations—people may be more or less well intentioned and competent, and people's interests diverge to different degrees. Perhaps equally important, situations vary in whether it is legitimate for people to perceive and acknowledge their uncertainty and vulnerability. Unless everyone agrees that it is normal and legitimate for an entrustor to feel anxious or doubtful, information and side bets to reduce uncertainty and vulnerability are unlikely to become topics of negotiation.

3. In some situations, there is a particular person to whom this uncertainty and vulnerability, once acknowledged, can be directed. A customer service representative or ombudsman may serve this function in an organization, for instance. But an entrustor may not always be able to locate someone to whom an appeal may be directed. Individual entrustors dependent on trustees that are either groups or organizations may be especially likely to find themselves in this situation.

4. An entrustor sometimes has the right to attempt to influence the intentions and behavior of the trustee. In other cases, trustees have neither an obligation nor a need to negotiate. A customer service

Table 2.1   The Forms of Trust Relations

	Faith	Confidence	Legal Trust	Trust/Distrust
Characteristic				
1. Vulnerability—entrustors have something of value that can or must be entrusted	X	X	X	X
2. Uncertainty—entrustors recognize their vulnerability and the disparity between their interests and those of trustees/and see that outcomes of interactions are uncertain	—	X	X	X
3. Trustees or trustees' agents acknowledge obligation to listen to complaints about entrustors' uncertainty and vulnerability	—	—	X	X
4. Entrustors have right to try to influence trustees or alter situation	—	—	—	X

Source: Author's compilation.

representative may or may not be empowered to make concessions, for instance. Powerful actors may conclude that they have little need to reassure anxious and vulnerable interaction partners.

We can distinguish four fundamental types of trust relations on the basis of the presence or absence of these four characteristics (see table 2.1). These forms are faith, confidence, legal trust, and trust/distrust.[5] In each instance, the first characteristic is present—in all forms of trust relations, people are vulnerable to each other. To the extent that a person believes that the trustee is certain to act in his or her interest and continues to believe this, despite information about conflicts of interest or evidence of the hostility or indifference of the trustee, he or she is acting on the basis of faith. Such people either do not experience uncertainty about the intentions and competence of the trustee or cannot acknowledge it (characteristic 2), do not appeal their uncertainty and vulnerability to another person (3), and do not try to influence the intentions and behavior of the trustee (4).

An example may clarify the point. Some parents seem to have faith in the physicians caring for their hospitalized, critically ill infant (Heimer and Staffen 1998, 249–51). One mother puts it this way: "I put my faith in the doctors, and what the doctors say is necessary, I'll go along with that" (227). Parents do not face the hospitalization of their newborn with equanimity—they know that their child may die or be disabled or chronically ill. They are also acutely aware that their child is fatefully dependent on skilled physicians, nurses, therapists, and technicians. Yet despite their vulnerability, the parents who have faith in physicians seem oblivious to conflicts of interest, competition for scarce medical resources, and caregiver indifference, incompetence, or inattention. They are more likely to attribute setbacks and bad outcomes to uncontrollable factors (for example, preexisting medical conditions) than to variations in the skill or devotion of the medical staff.

Such faith seems more characteristic of our grandparents and is surprising in an era when opinion polls show a steady decline of public confidence in the people running a wide variety of institutions. (See, for example, the discussion of these polls in Coleman 1990, 95.) In truth, only a minority of parents (the parents of about 16 percent of infants) had faith in their infant's care providers (Heimer and Staffen 1998, 261), and their faith was sometimes undermined over a long hospital stay. But in the late 1960s and early 1970s, even though confidence in those running medicine was still high, we can be sure that the women seeking illegal abortions did not extend this view of medical practitioners to the unknown abortionists from whom they were forced to seek care.

If people perceive their vulnerability and feel uncertain about trustees' intentions but cannot direct these feelings to any particular person, their choices are rather limited. They need the cooperation of the trustee or some agent of the trustee to gain the information to resolve the dilemma. When this is not an option, entrustors must draw their own conclusions about the likelihood of their interests being violated and decide for themselves whether to interact or withdraw. I refer to such interactions, grounded in perceptions of vulnerability and uncertainty, as interactions based on confidence (rather than faith). Entrustors act on the basis of confidence when they can legitimately perceive vulnerability and feel uncertain (characteristic 2), but can neither share these concerns with trustees or the trustees' representatives (3), nor negotiate with trustees about their intentions or behavior (4).

Many women seeking illegal abortions were in just this situation—they felt vulnerable and were painfully aware that they could not assess the trustworthiness or competence of the abortionist. At the same time, the abortionists typically did not offer information about their training and track record, nor did they hire public relations firms to reassure anxious pregnant women. It was exactly these problems that Jane hoped to address. Maybe abortionists wouldn't listen to women discuss their fears, but abortion counselors could. And maybe abortionists wouldn't turn over information even to Jane members, but Jane members could gather some data by debriefing their patients. Jane members were also sometimes able to negotiate with abortionists about the costs and conditions of abortions. Such interactions grounded in confidence (or mistrust, when the entrustors suspect that the trustees' intentions are not benevolent) are rather common for relatively powerless people interacting with stronger people or organizations.

Trust relations that fall into the category of legal trust rather than confidence are only a small improvement from the point of view of the entrustor. A person may feel vulnerable and uncertain about the trustee's intentions and competence (characteristic 2), know that a specific person (the trustee or the trustee's representative) is supposed to listen to complaints on these subjects (3), but discover that no one will do more than listen (4). Such a situation resembles the legal arrangement of a trust, where a trustee's obligations are legally fixed and not subject to negotiation. The pure form of legal trust is exceptional in that the parameters in the interaction are specified and not subject to change, so any losses accrue largely or solely to the entrustor or beneficiary. Often trustees also have something at stake in the interaction and so are motivated to negotiate should uncertainty and vulnerability be perceived, acknowledged as normal, and communicated.[6]

This form of trust is important because relations between individuals and corporate bodies, a fixture of contemporary life, often are similar in form to legal trust. For instance, in designing structures that resemble legal trust, corporations may confront vulnerable interaction partners with a corporate representative, such as a customer service representative, who is empowered only to listen and politely stonewall or at most to offer a limited range of solutions to common problems. In some states, the legal system exacerbates the inequality between corporate actors and individuals. Arizona, for example, has strongly pro-landlord real estate laws; management companies require information and deposits from tenants but make no commitments in return. Jane members' relation with abortionists, particularly in the early phases, closely resembled legal trust.

Only select members of the group could contact abortionists (or their representatives), and although abortionists would listen to Jane's pleas, they typically refused to negotiate. Abortion was illegal and abortionists were hard to find. Given such a strong market position, why should they negotiate? Even Nick, the abortionist, initially took the position that abortions were like mink coats—a lot of women wanted them, but not everyone could afford one (Kaplan 1995, 85).

Finally, when people see that they are vulnerable and feel uncertain (characteristic 2), can identify someone to whom concerns can be directed (3), and have the right to negotiate with their trustees (4), they act on the basis of trust or distrust. In these cases, the interaction occurs either when entrustors are reasonably satisfied that trustees are unlikely to violate their interests (trust) or when they have safeguarded those interests to the point where they need not worry as much about others' intentions or competence (distrust).

Once the parties to an exchange agree to negotiate about the entrustor's uncertainty and vulnerability, there are four logically possible ways to proceed: maintain both uncertainty and vulnerability; maintain uncertainty but reduce vulnerability; reduce uncertainty but maintain vulnerability; or reduce both uncertainty and vulnerability. Logical possibility and psychological and social realism are not the same thing, of course. When trustees acknowledge entrustors' uncertainty and vulnerability and seem willing to negotiate, such a show of goodwill may well decrease anxiety about the trustees' intentions. Thus, although the first alternative is logically possible, it is factually improbable. Nevertheless, one can imagine scenarios such as illegal abortion where desperate entrustors agree to proceed despite both parties' dissatisfaction with what the other can offer.

The second, third, and fourth alternatives are more socially and psychologically realistic. The second and third are pure strategies, the former based on distrust, the latter on trust. The fourth is a mixed strategy of trusting or distrusting on a contingent basis. If information is available and inexpensive, people probably reduce uncertainty before deciding whether it is necessary or desirable to reduce vulnerability. If information suggests that the trustee is competent and benevolent, no further reduction of vulnerability is necessary because the probability of the loss is small. When entrustors cannot easily get information about trustees, they may instead opt to reduce their vulnerability, for instance, by spreading their dependence across a series of trustees or by arranging insurance to cover any losses. When entrustors safeguard their interests, the probability of loss drops. Entrustors then get a different form of certainty—certainty about the outcomes of interactions—even though they were unable to reduce their uncertainty about the trustee.

Vulnerability and uncertainty thus turn out not to be completely independent, and this is particularly true when entrustors and trustees have an ongoing relationship. Entrustors may use early distrusting exchanges to gather information, as Jane members did by debriefing women after their abortions. Entrustors may not feel comfortable moving from distrusting to trusting strategies, but they may feel they have sufficient information to move to a mixed strategy that combines continuing (but perhaps more moderate) reduction of vulnerability with further attempts to gather information and reduce uncertainty. In the long run, if a trustee demonstrates competence and proves trustworthy, an entrustor may move from this watchful stance to a strategy of pure trust. This transition from distrust, to contingent trust and distrust, and finally to trust is exactly what occurred in Jane's relationship with Nick.

Strategies for Managing Trust Problems

Because voluntary interaction will not occur until the problem of trust has been dealt with, we would expect to find numerous strategies to cope with uncertainty and vulnerability. Five variables are involved in the choice of strategies, following the previous discussion: the legitimacy of feelings of uncertainty about the trustee's intentions; the existence of an actor to whom uncertainty and vulnerability can be directed; the right to negotiate with the trustee or the trustee's agent; uncertainty about the intentions of the trustee and the outcome of the interaction; and vulnerability to the trustee. Five strategies arise from attempts to manipulate these variables.

1. Trustees deny the legitimacy of feelings of uncertainty; they try to transform confidence into faith.

2. Trustees obscure or eliminate the actor to whom appeals can be directed; they try to transform legal trust into confidence.

3. Trustees deny the right of entrustors to attempt to influence trustees; they try to transform trust into legal trust.

4. Entrustors try to alter the situation or influence trustees by reducing their uncertainty about trustees' intentions or competence (trust).

5. Entrustors try to alter the situation or influence trustees by reducing their vulnerability to the trustees (distrust).

These strategies are related to the forms of trust relations shown in table 2.1. Because the variables are not completely independent, the order of the strategies is meaningful. Strategies 1, 2, and 3 are less expensive for trustees and more likely to be used when trustees are powerful and entrustors relatively weak. Stronger entrustors can insist that trustees negotiate with them, supply information, or accept limits on the inter-action. Strategies 4 and 5 are more likely to be employed by stronger entrustors.

Creating or Shoring up Faith by Denying the Legitimacy of Uncertainty

Trustees need not cope with entrustors' uncertainty and vulnerability if that uncertainty is defined as abnormal, paranoid, or illegitimate. Manipulating the legitimacy of perceptions of vulnerability and feelings of uncertainty may therefore be a particularly efficient way for trustees to manage trust relations. Drawing on charismatic, traditional, and rational-legal sources of legitimacy (see Weber 1978, 215–45), trustees can deny the legitimacy of entrustors' uncertainty by a variety of assertions. They can claim to be constrained by religious bodies. They can claim expertise certified by disinterested institutions such as professions. Or they can offer legally based guarantees backed by a legitimate government.

Religious and charitable institutions, and those associated with them, inspire faith because they are not motivated to profit at the expense of others. Conflicts of interest are reduced and ethical behavior is reinforced by the authority of the religious beliefs and the supervision of the religious community. But the authority of religious guarantees probably does not penetrate as far into social life as it once did, and at any rate it does not now govern most social relations. Much religion itself relies on interpre-tation and leaves many matters to individual discretion. The proliferation of religious bodies, each challenging the validity of others' beliefs, has probably undermined religious authority (as has the rise of secular authorities such as science). Pastoral counseling focuses on problems of social relations rather than religious legitimation of submission to authority and collective purposes. When Hare Krishnas, Children of God, Branch Davidians, fundamentalist televangelists, and charis-matic branches of traditional churches join mainstream religious bodies in proclaiming the virtue of their members, entrustors may wonder whether a trustee's religious affiliation is sufficient reason to set aside doubts.

The claim of expertise undermines the legitimacy of feelings of uncer-tainty and vulnerability partly by eliminating alternatives. Unable to per-form the task or service themselves, people are dependent on the expert; faith is necessary. The claim of expertise draws on the charisma of scien-tific knowledge, which seems to have retained its cachet. The more scien-tific the specialty in question, and the more the science is organized as a profession with internal peer review, the stronger its claim that feelings of uncertainty and vulnerability on the part of entrustors (clients, patients) are inappropriate. Professional organizations not only legitimate this claim to expertise but also offer assurances that a professional community is keeping tabs on its members, making sure they stay abreast of new developments and research, and generally safeguarding public interests.

But claims of disinterested expertise are just as precarious as claims of religious virtue. The monopoly benefits that professions create (Larson 1977) inevitably invite competition, and in the professions, as in religion, doubts are fueled by competitors' challenges. As Paul Starr (1982) amply documents, medical practitioners have struggled to convince others that their medical knowledge is based on legitimate complexity, not mere obfuscation. Starr also shows that physicians have long enlisted governments in disputes over who can legally practice medicine, attempting to limit competition and threats to legitimacy with requirements that practitioners be licensed. Other professions have employed parallel strategies (Abbott 1988; Halpern 1992). Competing professionals have not been the only ones, however, to threaten professional legitimacy. Administrators have been eager to discipline willful professionals and substitute the cheaper labor of paraprofessionals, technicians, and even clerical workers for the labor of more expensive workers. In "how-to" books, consumer specialists have pointed out how to bypass professionals entirely. And insurance coverage for professional malpractice and the publicity surrounding malpractice suits have heightened awareness of the fallibility of professionals. In such a climate, doubts about professionals' goodwill and expertise are considered anything but paranoid.

The intervention of a stable and legitimate government can sometimes restore declining faith.[7] The government is probably more effective in undermining the legitimacy of feelings of uncertainty and vulnerability directed toward other trustees when it acts as an insurer than when it legislates or enforces laws. Susan Shapiro (1987), for instance, notes that the advertisements of financial service providers often feature combinations of letters that resemble the acronyms of federal guarantors (such as "FDIC"). Presumably their objective is to suggest to unsuspecting clients that their investments are protected by government bodies. Government guarantees of the banking system, for instance, were crucial in shoring up faith in the financial system after the Great Depression and in averting other major financial crises. Clients' faith in the system of regulations and guarantees saves banks the trouble of convincing individual depositors of their trustworthiness. Likewise, insurers are regulated by state governments and to some degree protected by federal reinsurance programs.

Faith without evidence has probably declined in social legitimacy, in the regulation of human affairs, and even in religious bodies. This is perhaps the core correct observation of the extensive literature on secularization. This literature, and the previous discussion here, imply that strategies based on bolstering faith by denying the legitimacy of feelings of uncertainty are currently rather ineffective. We should not, however, be deluded about the significance of this change. It does not herald the end of trust relations. It only means that one strategy, which often worked well in the past and sometimes works now, often is abandoned in favor of other options.

Creating Confidence by Making Appeal Difficult

Trustees who are unable to inspire faith may nevertheless be able to avoid negotiating with potential entrustors. Organizational trustees often raise the costs of negotiation substantially for individual entrustors and make it difficult to locate the proper recipient of an appeal. Obscure titles and complex divisions of labor make it hard to find the appropriate person; gatekeepers such as receptionists deny access; telephone answering systems contain only irrelevant options; letters, phone calls, or electronic mail go unanswered. Although such phenomena may arise as much from the pattern of growth of organizations as from conscious planning, powerful trustees may not adjust organizational routines to make them more satisfactory to weak entrustors. The problems of communicating uncertainty and vulnerability may become increasingly acute particularly when increases in organizational size and complexity are correlated with decreased dependence on particular entrustors (because they are interchangeable with other members of a large class of clients, customers, or suppliers). Trustees may become immune to dissatisfaction, except perhaps the dissatisfaction of stockholders. Shifts in power with changes in economic circumstances, the collective action of entrustors, or the sheer burden of misdirected complaints may then lead to the creation of a grievance procedure or a specialized position to which uncertainty and vulnerability can be directed. Confidence—remaining uncertain and vulnerable but keeping one's eyes open—depends on inequalities between entrustor and trustee. When the power balance shifts, confidence becomes an unstable mode of interaction and, depending on which party has gained strength, is transformed into faith, legal trust, trust, or distrust. As I have argued earlier, however, confidence is unlikely to give way to faith given that faith is currently so difficult to create and maintain.

Creating Legal Trust by Refusing to Negotiate

When Jane members made contact with abortionists or their representatives, they discovered that many abortionists were unwilling to negotiate. Abortionists knew they were in a seller's market. Powerful trustees or their agents may refuse to offer evidence of goodwill or competence and instead hide behind bland statements about organizational policy. Ultimately the issues are evaded and the entrustor must either accept the situation or forgo the potential benefits of interaction.

As the number and power of corporate actors have grown in contemporary societies (Coleman 1974), the proportion of people's interactions that are with corporations rather than other people has also increased. These last two strategies (making it hard for entrustors to locate appropriate recipients for their complaints and refusing to negotiate with entrustors) are especially favored by corporate actors interacting with less powerful individuals. That people are dissatisfied with confidence and legal trust as solutions to trust problems is quite clear—witness, for instance, the popularity of newspaper columns about businesses that are unresponsive to consumer complaints.

James Coleman (1974, 57–84) discusses methods for shifting power from corporations back to individuals, emphasizing mechanisms to restrict corporations' capacity to mold their markets into noncompetitive forms. As the power of a weak entrustor increases, we might expect to find a move from confidence to legal trust. An agreement to listen to entrustors' views—for instance, by creating a new customer service representative or ombudsman position—may be the move of an actor who senses a shift in the balance of power. Such a token step serves, first, to give the trustee information about the character and extent of entrustor dissatisfaction and, second, to give the illusion that actual bargaining will occur.

Reducing Uncertainty: Interactions Grounded in Trust

The fourth variable that can be manipulated in trust relations is uncertainty itself. In an effort to promote an anticipated interaction, actors may seek or offer information that will reduce the entrustor's uncertainty about the goodwill and competence of the trustee.[8] Trust can be grounded in either the past or the future. An entrustor's own experiences with a trustee or class of trustees may lead him or her to believe that the trustee's intentions are benevolent. Alternatively a trustee may support claims of trustworthiness with references or credentials—evidence about others' experiences. Trust is grounded in the future when the entrustor can make future outcomes of the trustee contingent on trustworthiness in the situation at hand. A person may threaten to ruin the trustee's reputation or deny the trustee future business if the trustee proves untrustworthy. When uncertainty is reduced, entrustors really do become "trusters."

These points are well illustrated by Jean Ensminger's account (this volume) of the creation of fictive kin relationships among herders in northeastern Kenya. Understanding that "one trusts those whom one can control," Omra herd owners preferred to entrust their herds to relatives who stood to lose a great deal if they mismanaged the herd. When no kin were available, herd owners increased supervision by visiting cattle camps more frequently and structured contracts to increase herders' dependence on herd owners. Herders who performed well received far more than the contracted payments in clothing, food, and stock; they sometimes received bride payments, so that they could marry, as well as the status and privileges of an adopted (but non-inheriting) son.

Trust is intimately related to the involvement of truster and trustee in a network of relationships. If we think of communities as networks some of whose links are important to all the people or corporate bodies they comprise, it would not be an overstatement to say that people cannot trust each other without some form of community. We trust other community members because we have multiple channels for pursuing trustees who have violated our trust. The absence of such a community worried Jane members and the women seeking abortions. Employers may believe that the need for a stable income makes married people with children reliable employees. But whatever their financial situation, parents are more likely to have regularized contacts with in-laws, the parents of their children's playmates, and educational institutions, and it is these commitments that make deviance more costly. As Howard Becker (1960, 1964) argues, stability is a product of social life, not a personality trait. He also stresses (Becker 1973) that rules are enforced only when someone has an interest in enforcing them. When interdependent members of a network have a common stake in an actor's trustworthiness, pressure to conform comes from multiple sources, lessening the burden on any one entrustor.

The relationship between trustworthiness and community membership also has a positive aspect. Peter Blau (1964) distinguishes between economic exchange, focused on a one-shot exchange of goods of approximately equal value, and social exchange, whose main purpose is to create continuity in social interaction. Karl Polanyi (1944) similarly argues that until the advent of the modern market, economic systems were grounded in non-economic motives. People embedded in communities are more trustworthy precisely because they are committed to continuity in relationships and to social as opposed to economic exchange, a point developed more fully by Mark Granovetter (1985).[9] Michael Hechter (1987) makes a parallel argument that group solidarity—and, I would argue, the trustworthiness of group members—is produced jointly by members' dependence on the group and the group's capacity to monitor and sanction. But if trustworthiness is a social product rather than a personality trait, people may be trustworthy in their interactions with community members and unscrupulous, even larcenous or violent, in their dealings with strangers.

When people are involved in social exchange, then, the calculation of self-interest necessarily involves consideration of the interests of others. We can trust people whose trustworthiness is motivated by religious beliefs, community ties, or the desire for future exchange more than we can trust those seeking only one of these benefits. We might also expect that internalized patterns of trustworthy behavior and identification with groups would supplement calculation of long-term interest. Because they are subject to scrutiny and sanction and dependent on the group for a variety of rewards, people behave in more trustworthy ways within their own ethnic or racial group, within their college fraternity or sorority, and within organized crime families. But such groups may continue to function as reference groups long after direct contact ceases, and episodic contact with members may elicit trustworthy behavior by reinvigorating lapsed identities long after dependence on the group has declined and the group has lost its capacity to exert control.

Max Weber's (1946, 305–6) discussion of the Protestant sects in the United States illustrates these points. Sects, he argues, are more effective than churches in creating trust:

> It is crucial that sect membership meant a certificate of moral qualification and especially of business morals for the individual. This stands in contrast to membership in a "church" into which one is "born" and which lets grace shine over the righteous and unrighteous alike. Indeed, a church is a corporation which organizes grace and administers religious gifts of grace, like an endowed foundation. Affiliation with the church is, in principle, obligatory and hence proves nothing with regard to the member's qualities. A sect, however, is a voluntary association of only those who, according to the principle, are religiously and morally qualified. If one finds voluntary reception of his membership, by virtue of religious *probation*, he joins the sect voluntarily.

These sects were voluntary only for those permitted to join; people with suspect reputations were excluded, whatever their wishes. Because religion was so important and because sect and community were so entwined, exclusion from the sect meant exclusion from the community. In this sense, the sect was not a voluntary association. The sect was a community whose strong boundaries created extraordinary capacities for social control.

It is also important that the "certificate of business morals" was a byproduct of community. Economic exchange is more likely than social exchange to be zero-sum. In a community with a reputation for ethical business relations, the single person who violates the norm may gain an advantage. Such free riding is less advantageous when the reward is contingent (or thought to be contingent) on the fact rather than the reputation of trustworthiness. In Weber's example, the possibility of benefit from the violation of trust was all but eliminated by the fusion of moral and religious goals. The purity of members had to be ascertained before they were permitted to participate in the communion service. The participation of an untrustworthy person defiled the sacrament for all.[10] Because the success of the collective act depended on the morality of each participant, individuals had to be trustworthy. General trustworthiness was thus a by-product of community members' dependence on the group and their joint responsibility for the achievement of collective and individual religious goals. Weber notes that religious organizations were less effective in generating and guaranteeing trust after the early American sects became more like churches.[11] Because church members can achieve religious goals without the cooperation of other members, a lesser premium is placed on trustworthiness and churches are less able than sects to guarantee the morality of their members.

Reducing Vulnerability:
Interactions Grounded in Distrust

Rather than gathering information about trustees, people may try to reduce their vulnerability. Large, complex societies have been innovators here. Two common techniques for reducing vulnerability are compensating for the losses if trust is violated and spreading vulnerability over a series of trustees.

Should trust be violated, an entrustor can be compensated for losses in a variety of ways. A damaged or destroyed object might be replaced, a person might receive financial compensation for a lost investment in an anticipated exchange, or a victim of a botched abortion might be helped to get medical care. Personal suretyship and guarantees from sponsors, once the preferred mechanisms for arranging such compensation, have largely been displaced by commercial insurance covering everything from nonperformance of contracts (surety bonds) to thefts by employees (fidelity bonding). Warranties and guarantees, reinforced by product liability laws, give consumers some alternative to trusting those from whom they make purchases.

All of these forms of compensation require commensuration. Compensation depends on being able to assess the value of the entrusted object and to compare it with the value of similar objects or other stakes. Such an assessment often requires that the object's money value be determined, although in principle some other metric or standard of comparison could be used. But commensuration has its limits. Not all objects are culturally defined as having a cash value. Some things cannot be replaced or returned. Some stakes are not really subject to guarantees. Children and original artworks are defined as irreplaceable, but works of art have monetary equivalents whereas children do not.

People may disagree about whether commensuration is possible and appropriate (Espeland 1998; Espeland and Stevens 1998). The Yavapai, for instance, were unwilling to leave their ancestral lands and couldn't understand how the bureaucrats of the Bureau of Reclamation could believe that they would yield if the price went high enough (Espeland 1998). Cultural definitions change, however. Children were somewhat replaceable during the feudal ages, and spouses were more replaceable than brothers (Bloch 1961). Viviana Rotman Zelizer (1985), for instance, shows how our understanding of the value of children has changed. Although we do not now regard spouses or children as directly replaceable or as having monetary equivalents, the courts do seem willing to make partial evaluations—for instance, by placing a value on a husband's contribution as breadwinner and occasionally awarding compensation for pain and suffering.

In the types of compensation described earlier, trust is not created, although vulnerability and uncertainty about some kinds of loss are reduced. Trust violators usually are not punished or fined, although courts sometimes assess punitive damages and insurers may raise premiums. Trust violators (or their insurers) are merely compensating for losses experienced by entrustors. These assessments of value often are legally questions of fact: How much is a painting worth? How much is physical pain worth? How much earning power has been lost? How much emotional suffering has occurred and what is its money value? The intent of the trustee, whether benevolent or malevolent, is not relevant in these calculations. The point of such calculations is to create certainty about particular types of loss when information about the trustworthiness of the trustee and the outcome of a specific event are unavailable. Obviously, uncertainty and vulnerability are not truly eliminated—irreplaceable objects remain irreplaceable; losses are merely compensated.

Modern societies have institutions such as banks and insurance companies that specialize in assessing vulnerability. Uncertainty is statistically defined, and economic vulnerability is reduced or eliminated. Actors thus enter into exchanges with the aid of intermediaries who administer and control transactions, dictate the range of acceptable prices, and specify what collateral is required. Risk from malevolent interaction partners becomes essentially identical to risk from natural disasters, accidents, war, and impersonal criminal acts.

Vulnerability can also be reduced by entrusting parts of the object to several trustees. If we assume that each trustee violates the entrustor's interests with probability p (≤ 1) and that the entrustor breaks the object into n pieces that he or she distributes to n different trustees, the entrustor loses everything with only probability $p^n \leq p \leq 1$. Thus, in the absence of information about differences in the trustworthiness of a number of potential trustees, the entrustor is less vulnerable, or at worst equally vulnerable, when he or she entrusts parts of the object to n different trustees than when the entire object is entrusted to a single trustee.[12] In the sphere of interpersonal relations, for instance, a person with little information would be less vulnerable if he or she commuted with one person, attended concerts with a second, confided in a third, worked with a fourth, and listed a fifth as the person to be notified in an emergency. If any one of these "friends" defaulted (for example, by quitting the relationship without warning), the entrustor would experience only limited losses; not all of his or her life would be empty at once. Those who keep work and personal friendships separate or distinguish carefully between friends and lovers are following just such a strategy of limited liability relationships.[13] Similar strategies may arise in the temporary groups (juries, construction teams, commissions, film crews, and so on) that Messick and Kramer (this volume) suggest are characterized by a thin form of trust.

Norman Mailer (1968, 107) illustrates this type of strategy in *Miami and the Siege of Chicago:*

> So the true political animal is cautious—he never, except in the most revolutionary of times, permits himself to get into a position where he will have to dare his political stake on one issue, one bet, no, to avoid that, he will even give up small pieces of his stuff for nothing, he will pay tribute, which is how raids are sometimes made, and how Barry Goldwater won his nomination.

While other strategies may have become less feasible in modern urban societies, strategies based on the reduction of vulnerability have probably become cheaper, more effective, and more socially acceptable than they once were. Distrust is the stopgap when faith and trust are not possible.[14]

Matching Strategies with Situations

What determines which strategy will be employed? I argue that the choice of strategy depends on the social structure of a society or group, which in turn affects the resources available to people and the cost of using one strategy rather than another. These structural variables may describe the relationships between the members of the group (for example, network density or the distribution of power), the relationship of individuals or subgroups to the larger group (such as norms about individual contributions to collective goals), or features of the group or society as an entity (for example, social technologies for managing risk or cultural definitions of particular objects as interchangeable). Figure 2.1 depicts the relationship between the structural characteristics of groups and forms of trust relations. It also shows how historical factors work through these structural properties to shape the mix of strategies employed in any given society, the topic of the next section.

We begin by asking about the nature of the tie between entrustor and trustee, because the interactional structure of the group affects the solution of trust problems. Perceived trustworthiness (others' certainty about

Figure 2.1   Historical Change, Structural Factors and Forms of Trust Relations

HISTORICAL FACTORS ⟶	STRUCTURAL FACTORS ───────	⟶ FORMS OF TRUST RELATIONS
population density	1. variables describing relationship among group members	proportions of all interactions based on each form
differentiation and specialization	a. interactional—networks of multi-purpose relationships carry information and facilitate social control	
legal changes	b. relational—power differences between interacting parties; particularly crucial in inter- actions between people and corporate actors	
general economic development		
rise of corporate actors	2. variables describing relationship of individual or subgroup to larger group, such as normative orientation to individual versus collective goals, norms about trustworthiness, orientation to intermittent or continuous exchange	
	3. variables describing global features of group or society	
	a. cultural definitions of replaceability of objects	
	b. technology to handle various forms of trust relations—development of money, credit and insurance	
	c. legal mechanisms to handle trust problems	

Source: Author's compilation.

one's intentions and competence) depends on the implicit possibility of recourse, and threats of recourse are most convincing in a dense network. Numerous others will have a stake in and be willing to help secure a trustee's conformity, decreasing the cost that any one person must pay to enforce an agreement. Further, information about trustee misbehavior can be transmitted quickly throughout the network. A trustee who derives a large proportion of his or her rewards from interacting with other group members has much to lose by violating trust.

The relevant variables here are the frequency of interaction, the scope of the interaction, and the degree of overlap of functionally distinct networks. Overlapping networks characterized by frequent interaction and rather diffuse involvement should be characteristic of smaller communities, sects, communities with low geographic and occupational mobility, societies with low divorce rates, and families with children. Whatever variables lead to regularized interaction and close community ties make for high predictability and therefore reduce uncertainty in social interaction. All other things being equal, actors in such groups or networks tend to operate on the basis of trust or faith.

Power distributions also affect the solution of trust problems. Actors grossly unequal in power are unlikely to negotiate about the uncertainty and vulnerability of the weaker party. When an entrustor's power significantly exceeds the trustee's, the entrustor may insist on reducing vulnerability with guarantees, deposits, or carefully crafted contracts. When the trustee is more powerful, the interaction is more likely to be based on confidence or legal trust. For example, a policyholder entrusts premiums to an insurer so as to be compensated if an accident or death occurs. Usually insurer trustees are more powerful than their policyholder entrustors, and policyholders are forced to accept whatever conditions insurers offer. The balance of power is somewhat different, however, in mutuals. Mutual insurers are somewhat more responsive to their policyholders, who are also members.[15] Unequal relationships are especially characteristic of interactions between corporations and individuals, although (as the example of illegal abortions shows) they can also arise between individuals when one actor is especially dependent on another to supply a scarce and valuable good or service.

In addition to measures of network density or inequalities in power, the normative structure of a group is important in predicting the form of trust relations. The relevant norms are those about trustworthiness itself, orientation to individual or collective goals, and orientation to continuous or intermittent, and to social or economic, exchange. As noted in the discussion of religious sects, we would expect trustworthiness to rise when the attainment of a group's goals requires ethical behavior and when individuals cannot achieve their goals independently. Norms emphasizing contributions to the collective and concern about the group's future also are found in familial relationships, which are expected to endure over a lifetime. But in contrast to sects, which in Weber's view foster general trustworthiness, strong familial ties sometimes require trustworthiness only in interactions between family members. The families studied by Edward Banfield (1958) certainly did not expect to be able to trust anyone outside their family circle.[16] A similar sharp differentiation in norms about how one should treat family members and outsiders was found in the organized crime families discussed later in the chapter.

Finally, certain properties of the group as a whole may predispose actors to choose some solutions to trust problems over others. Among such global characteristics would be a general cultural climate of suspicion or trust, cultural definitions of the replaceability of certain objects, technological devices that undergird particular forms of trust relations, and legal codes permitting some solutions while proscribing others. The inclination of most group members to accept assertions of good faith becomes a group property that encourages and legitimates the adoption of such an orientation by individuals.[17] Uncertainty cannot be negotiated if everyone else is inclined to trust a specific person or the occupants of a particular position. Under such circumstances, one has little choice but to have faith. Before charges of sexual abuse and sexual harassment became part of our cultural repertoire, victims faced an up-hill battle, particularly when bringing charges against especially trusted people such as clergy. Likewise others' doubts about the incumbents of particular roles (for example, used-car salesmen) legitimate uncertainty and encourage demands for proof of trustworthiness or a reduction of vulnerability.

The culture of commensuration has changed too, mostly in the direc-tion of defining objects as comparable with others, although some objects and relationships have gradually come to be seen as priceless or unique. For instance, giving one's children as hostages in an alliance is no longer customary or even legal. The development of money, credit practices, and insurance has been crucial to the widespread use of distrusting strategies, as have the legal forms that authorize and support these modes of interaction. After such initial innovations, the diffusion of an "insurance ethic" has undoubtedly accelerated the spread and acceptance of monetary evaluation of social objects and relationships. Although there is no logically necessary relation between cultural repertoires and levels of trustworthiness, people who live in an environment in which the re-duction of vulnerability is inexpensive and effective may be more likely to employ a vulnerability-reducing strategy than those with similar personal traits and problems living in a context less permeated by in-surance and similar institutions. Ironically, insurance itself rests on a modicum of trust in insurers. History and folklore about insurance salespeople and adjusters suggest that such trust may sometimes have been misplaced.

The striking variations in the ways different racial and ethnic groups in the United States handle the problems of trust illustrate the relation-ship between these structural factors and the tendency to solve trust problems in particular ways. These differences are especially visible in organized crime. When one's own life (which is neither replaceable nor partitionable) is at stake, strategies based on the reduction of vulnera-bility are not very useful. With no analog to the Geneva Convention to protect prisoners of war in turf battles in organized crime, people want to be completely certain about others' trustworthiness.[18]

Scholars seem to take it for granted that because members of an eth-nic group are at roughly equal status positions they will climb the American occupational ladder together, including collectively passing through a stage of participation in organized crime. Yet the process of racial or ethnic group mobility does not explain why any given crime ring tends to be dominated by a single racial or ethnic group when other groups occupy approximately the same social status. Rather, the domination of crime rings or gangs by a single racial or ethnic group indicates the importance of common race and ethnicity as a basis for trust. This bond adds a common language, common religious and familial patterns, common cultural understandings, and common orientations to trust and collective goals.

Francis Ianni (1974) documents the harsh reaction of Italian Mafia families when one family incorporated African Americans into its activities.[19] The Italian system was based on loyalty to extended families and the Catholic Church. Because of the strong emphasis on the group rather than the individual (individuals moved up with the aid of the collectivity or were hindered by it if they failed to obey), on absolute trustworthiness within the group, and on continuous interaction and familial domination of other spheres, the Italian organized crime sector tended to solve its problems through trust. Uncertainty was legitimate because of the nature of the objects entrusted and could therefore be discussed; there was a clear recipient of such appeals; that actor would negotiate issues of uncertainty and vulnerability. Thus, the problem of trust was resolved by reducing uncertainty about the actor's intentions and competence.

From what one can discern from Ianni's (1974) account of the transitions of the 1960s, methods for managing uncertainty and vulnerability changed when Hispanics and African Americans moved into organized crime. One might expect that Hispanics, who share Italians' strong familial and religious culture, would solve trust problems through the reduction of uncertainty. Cuban gangs followed Italian patterns much more closely than Puerto Rican gangs did. The movement of family members between the mainland and Puerto Rico and the predominance of common-law rather than legalized marriages meant that Puerto Rican family relationships were both less continuous and less extensive, tending more toward a nuclear family pattern. An interesting note here is that both African Americans and Puerto Ricans involved their wives and lovers as partners in criminal activities whereas Italians and Cubans did not. The African American groups that Ianni discussed relied most heavily on the childhood gang as a solidary unit. Both African Americans and Puerto Ricans also relied on networks composed of people who had proven their loyalty by helping each other in prison. In addition to reducing uncertainty through nonfamilial links (lovers, childhood gangs, prison friends), African Americans and Puerto Ricans sometimes based exchanges on distrust. Business transactions, in which rights and obligations were clearly specified, retained their character as intermittent or one-shot economic exchanges.

A second example shows how the management of trust relations shapes economic outcomes. Actors in economically and socially deprived groups lack easy access to credit and insurance, the institutionally mediated reduction of vulnerability. When people cannot reduce vulnerability, one common alternative is to rely on trust. (They may also opt to accept the risks or to forgo interaction.) But such functional problems are not always solved. Coleman (1971) argues that differences in managing uncertainty and vulnerability help explain the different economic outcomes of Jews and African Americans in the United States.[20] Although both groups experienced considerable economic deprivation, they differed in the extent to which individual resources were available as resources for other community members (for example, through extensions of credit, apprenticeships, or sponsorship and recommendations for jobs). According to Coleman, the limited resources of African Americans benefited individuals without benefiting the entire community. In contrast, Jews were able to translate relative poverty into a strong economic position partly because their close families and tightly knit communities enabled resources to flow relatively freely through the entire community, creating a multiplier effect. Black power and black consciousness groups may have improved the economic circumstances of African Americans by creating an orientation toward collective goals and providing a foundation for trust. With such changes, scarce resources would be more likely to be pooled and circulated throughout the group.

A variety of scholars have examined the contribution of trust to the efficient use of economic resources. Tom Tyler (this volume) extends this argument to the creation of non-economic resources. If, as he contends, our willingness to defer to organizational or governmental authorities depends as much or more on whether we trust them as on whether we approve of their decisions, trust in leaders and officials should lead to efficiencies in government and law enforcement that parallel those possible in the economy. In pointing out the "fundamentally political nature of social groupings," Gary Miller (this volume) shows why Tyler's claims about trust and compliance are equally as important to firms as to governments. Just as supervisors and owners worry about whether workers can be trusted to put in the honest day's work that ultimately generates the firm's profits, so workers worry about whether owners can be trusted to keep their bargains about the share of that surplus workers will receive. Workers who are not worried about the opportunism of their bosses will be more willing to help create the surplus. What can be accomplished by leaders of governments or firms thus depends partly on whether their subordinates perceive them to be trustworthy.

Historical Changes

Modernization has been associated with three fundamental changes in the way trust problems are managed: the reduction of uncertainty (trust), especially by communities, has become less feasible; the reduction of vulnerability (distrust) has become more feasible; and entrustors are less likely to have practical rights to negotiate about uncertainty and vulnerability. Thus, trust has probably become less common while confidence, legal trust, and distrust have all become more common.

Because of both changes in patterns of interaction (more contact with strangers, more differentiation and specialization of roles) and the cultural changes associated with urbanization and modernization, the average contact is probably briefer and more specific and therefore less likely to carry the information necessary to evaluate trustworthiness or competence.[21] Early statements bemoaning the loss of community (for example, Wirth 1938; Tönnies 1957) received salutary correction by those observing that such institutions as the community press maintain important neighborhood ties (Janowitz 1967), that territorial ties and neighborhoods remain important in creating and sustaining trust (Suttles 1972), and that even modern mass societies are held together by "an infinity of personal attachments" (Shils 1957; see also Shils 1962). Still, urban society has brought the expansion of a sphere of interaction with strangers in which trust is out of the question without some formal certification of trustworthiness. Even in relatively continuous and multistranded interactions such as those between coworkers and family members it may be difficult to accumulate sufficient information to reduce uncertainty. These changes create a need for techniques to reduce vulnerability. The development of insurance and related techniques for assessing and comparing value and shifting risks from one party to another have been particularly important in encouraging the use of distrusting, vulnerability-reducing strategies when reduction in uncertainty is not feasible. At the same time, the growth in the number and power of corporate actors often has forced people to accept interactions grounded in confidence and legal trust when they might prefer to reduce vulnerability.

Insurance as a Technology of Distrust

Insurance is an especially useful technique for the management of vulnerability in the absence of certainty. Insurance has developed as an organized business in four (overlapping) stages. In its earliest forms, insurance covered only losses attributable to natural, physical hazards such as storms at sea, earthquakes, hurricanes, and floods. Human beings could neither predict nor control the events that caused losses, although they might be expected to try to reduce losses when an accident occurred. For instance, although bottomry (the early name for marine insurance) covered losses from perils such as storms, it also required that cargo owners, the captain, and the crew "sue and labor" to reduce damages. Further, insurers would not cover losses that occurred because a vessel was not well maintained. Socially caused catastrophes were not insurable.

Later, insurers covered environmental perils and losses attributable to the acts of persons who were not members of the same social system as the policyholder. Thus, insurers were willing to treat piracy and war as perils similar to the storms that vessels routinely encountered, reasoning that ship and cargo owners, captains, and crews had precious little control over these causes of loss. Losses arising from riots and impersonal crimes such as theft and arson fell into the same category. But control over loss-causing events is a continuous variable, and a policyholder may have little control over another person's behavior even if that person is neither an outlaw nor an enemy. Social or physical distance and organizational boundaries are sufficient to decrease control. Reasoning that the key question was whether a policyholder had any influence over loss-causing events, insurers eventually extended coverage to losses attributable to acts of people in the same social system as the policyholder so long as they were not in positions of trust with respect to the insured. Because cargo owners could not control stevedores, for instance, insurers were willing to cover losses caused by their actions.

Finally, insurance companies developed ways of handling risks arising from violations of trust. Initially insurers contended that fidelity bonds (covering the behavior of dishonest employees or guaranteeing the trustworthiness of government officials) and surety bonds (guaranteeing specific performances) were really "loans" to be repaid by dishonest or incompetent employees or contractual partners. This fiction was subsequently abandoned as insurers learned how to estimate the potential losses in different lines of business and for various categories of employees. For instance, they learned to set premium rates higher for banks and liquor stores than for churches. But they also became aware that in large businesses, policyholders had relatively little control over the loss-causing events. If policyholders could do little to decrease losses, then moral hazard (and fraud) were less important than insurers had initially thought. Any decrease in policyholder vigilance once an insurer had promised to compensate losses was relatively unimportant if the policyholder was too distant from the "accident" to have any effect.[22] To summarize, then, insurance is now both more and less "social." Insurance now often covers the risks of social life as well as losses from physical perils, but that coverage is now a monetary compensation supplied by a business organization rather than a guarantee given by a family, friends, or community members.

But what does insurance actually accomplish here? Why is it important in a discussion of trust? To see this we must look at human behavior and relationships as sources of risk—perils comparable to a storm, earthquake, or fire that might cause unpredictable losses. As Coleman (1990, 91) points out, "Situations involving trust constitute a subclass of those involving risk. They are situations in which the risk one takes depends on the performance of another actor." Thinking this way, insurers and policyholders might categorize employee theft as a peril, a cause of loss appropriately covered by an insurance policy. But that's not the end of the story. Insurers and their policyholders also worry about hazards, factors that increase the likelihood of loss from a covered peril. Physical hazards such as the presence of combustibles or an industrial process that generates sparks would increase the odds of loss from the peril of fire. Likewise we can imagine hazards that might increase the probability of loss from human relationships and behavior. For instance, dispersal of work to several sites, as occurs in branch banking, might make supervision more difficult and so increase the likelihood of employee theft.

But while other kinds of hazards (insurers discuss physical and legal hazards) increase the likelihood of loss only through their effects on the direct causes of loss (perils), the hazards associated with human behavior have their effects on all points in the causal chain. Physical hazards that modify the likelihood of loss from covered perils can themselves be shaped by human behavior. Policyholders might, for instance, decrease the effects of physical hazards through loss prevention. A policyholder might construct a firewall to decrease the likelihood of loss from fire. Human behavior can have more direct effects, however. The odds of loss from the peril of fire rise dramatically with intentionally set fires. At the final stage, insurance losses can be inflated when people make false claims. Insurers have referred to these perils and hazards that arise directly from human action and human relationships as "moral hazards."

Both insurers and social scientists have worried about moral hazard.[23] The connection between moral hazard and trust is more apparent when we note that the core of moral hazard, as it is usually conceived by insurers and social scientists, is trustworthiness. The key question is, when can people be expected ("trusted") to keep a bargain and when will they instead use the bargain as a starting point for further strategizing? The problem of moral hazard is ubiquitous. Social scientists and insurers usually write about relations between employers and employees or between insurers and policyholders, but the same principles apply to any parties who have entered into any agreement, whether formalized in a contract or not. Further, the techniques that insurers use for securing trustworthiness from policyholders are used in modified form in ordinary social life. I elsewhere show how parallel strategies are employed in used-car sales, bargaining about sexual relations, and product liability law (Heimer 1985, 218–37).

As insurers began to cover losses from human actions such as theft or failure to meet contractual obligations, a key challenge was to untangle the effects of moral hazard in different stages in the causal chain linking insurance contract and insurance losses and to devise solutions appropriate to these distinct problems.[24] Moral hazard in the relation between insurer and policyholder is a problem somewhat different from other behavioral perils, including moral hazard in the relation between a policyholder and his or her employees or other interaction partners. It should therefore be managed differently. Insurers needed to be certain that the insurance contract did not substantially modify relations between policyholders and those whose behavior might be the direct cause of loss. For instance, insurers worried that a policyholder with fidelity bonds covering employee theft might be less careful about supervision and perhaps would even hint to midlevel employees that with the new insurance policy theft was no longer a concern. In such a scenario, insurance, originally intended as a tool for managing uncertainty about employees, would increase the likelihood of dishonesty. Insurers therefore devised techniques to help policyholders cope with their uncertainty about the trustworthiness or competence of interaction partners without simultaneously increasing insurance losses by altering the incentives of policyholders or, indirectly, their employees and partners.

Only a portion of the risks arising from human behavior and human relationships are managed through insurance coverage. Insurance decreases the effects of uncertainty by spreading the costs of disastrous events over a large group. By charging a relatively small fee (an insurance premium) to a large number of people, insurance reduces the losses to the small number who experience a catastrophe. But while insurance itself is a *distrusting* technique that reduces vulnerability (through guarantees of compensation should losses occur), it incorporates some elements of a *trusting* strategy. In particular, insurers use a variety of techniques to reduce their own uncertainty about policyholders' intentions. They collect some information about the policyholder and those (such as employees) whose actions create the losses covered by the insurance contract. They also collect information about the temptations and opportunities for dishonesty in the situation covered by the insurance policy.

In addition, however, insurers try to design a contract that encourages and supports honest behavior. By insisting that policyholders participate in losses (for example, through deductibles) rather than shifting the full cost to the insurer, insurers attempt to create a community of fate in which both policyholder and insurer have an interest in preventing and minimizing losses. By insisting on a separation between production processes and loss prevention activities (for example, safety inspections by outsiders or the creation of an internal position for a risk manager or safety expert), insurers increase the odds that the client or its agents will take the insurer's perspective and that loss prevention will not be sacrificed when production pressures are high.

Episodic comparisons of the insured value and the market value of the insured object help insurers assess the appropriateness of the insurance bargain. If the market value has dropped while the insured value has remained high, some policyholders may be less scrupulous about averting losses and others may even attempt to defraud their insurer by trading a worthless piece of property or a failing business for insurance compensation. Insurance, the distrusting, vulnerability-reducing solution to the trust problems of policyholders and their interaction partners, is possible only because the trust problems in the relationship between insurer and policyholder are managed partly by trusting, uncertainty-reducing devices.

The reduction of vulnerability with distrusting strategies such as insurance makes possible exchanges that would otherwise be too risky. Thus, distrust perhaps even more than trust acts as a multiplier in the exchange system, encouraging the circulation of resources on a scale inconceivable if we had to rely on trust alone.[25] Trust, because it is embedded in social relationships, is not amenable to wide diffusion throughout a society. A religious sect may guarantee a person's trust-worthiness, as Weber argues, but this guarantee can be spread only as far as the reputation of the sect extends, and only as far as the sect guar-antees trustworthiness. South African Boer sects were not much good in guaranteeing bargains with blacks, for example. Because the reduction of vulnerability depends less on personal ties and reputation and may take a more tangible form (such as a clearly specified offer of compensation for losses), its effects reach further. Some clearly specified agent, the insurer, is always responsible, and its accountability is clearly demarcated. For this reason we can be approved for loans based on life insurance but not on our membership in a tightly knit family that pulls together in times of disaster. (Family ties are taken into consideration in the issuing of credit cards, for example, but only when the member applying for the card has already passed the tests necessary to reduce the vulnerability of the credit card company.)

To say that insurance makes it possible for us to take risks (and make investments) we would otherwise avoid does not mean that these risks should be taken.[26] Insurance eliminates some incentives to reduce risk rather than compensate losses. Risk sometimes can be reduced by alter-ing the characteristics of a situation, but easy access to insurance cover-age may lead people to overlook this option. Although some organized groups (such as consumer groups and some mutual insurers) do supply information about efficient and practical ways to reduce risk, and gov-ernment regulators such as the Food and Drug Administration do sometimes substitute for or complement organized groups, insurers themselves have been less motivated to reduce losses than spread the cost of losses. Insurer profits derive more from investment of large pre-miums than from the "underwriting profit" that results when careful loss prevention programs keep losses low. But the fine points of these distinctions are not emphasized in insurers' advertisements and are ob-scured further when compensation of loss and reduction of risk are both presented in monetary terms. Policyholders may forget that reducing risk means designing safer cars and streets so that traffic accidents are less often fatal, making surgery safer, and getting contractors to do the work and do it correctly the first time. When insurers offer compensation for employee theft, employers may be lulled into overlooking the uncompensated costs of sloppy work, high turnover, and the high absentee rates that come with "shrinkage."

Further, qualitative differences between distinct types of losses disappear. When expressed in monetary terms, loss of life is not so sharply distinguished from damage to plate glass windows. Karl Marx (1964, 169) notes this transformational character in his discussion of money:

> He who can buy bravery is brave, though he be a coward. As money is not *exchanged* for any specific quality, for any one specific thing, or for any particular human essential power, but for the entire objective world of man and nature, from the standpoint of its possessor it therefore serves to exchange every property for every other, even contradictory, property and object: it is the fraternalization of impossibilities. It makes contradictions embrace.

This transformational property is carried to an extreme in the insurance business. In this case, "contradictions embrace" when the insurance business facilitates the compensation of losses that by their very nature cannot be compensated. Monetary evaluation permits us to include in a cost calculus factors that may not belong there and encourages us to believe that the insurance value is the "real" value. Because organized businesses benefit from such practices, we too often compensate losses when we should be trying to reduce risks. Efficient compensation of loss is important in facilitating interaction in a complex and interdependent society, of course, but difficulties arise when insurers become too zealous in carrying out this function and cease to distinguish between reparable and irreparable loss.

The distinction between objects or relationships that can be replaced and those that cannot, obscured by insurance, undergirds Émile Durkheim's (1933) contrast between repressive and restitutive law. Repressive law (including most criminal law) punishes a person who has committed a crime, but restitutive law (including most civil law) does not impose on the perpetrator any costs beyond those necessary to make the victim whole. It is easy to overstate the distinction, and easy to overlook the repressive elements in legal regimes whose emphasis is largely restitutive. For instance, although modern tort law is primarily restitutive, it has always included a repressive element. Restitution often involved a severe drain on the resources of the negligent party and was required only when blame could be assigned.[27] Because the negligent party suffered in making restitution, restitution was partly a punishment.

Insurance, particularly no-fault insurance, implies a fundamental change in the application of tort law. The repressive element once present is now largely removed. An insurance premium paid in advance by offenders and non-offenders alike is too dissociated from the offense to be construed as a punishment. Even when tort cases are brought against individuals, their character is much altered by the participation of insurers and other organizations. Although one might argue that a premium increase following the commission of a tortious act would serve as a punishment, the punitive effect of an increase in insurance premiums is unlikely to be substantial when a time lag separates the commission of the act and the "punishment" and when the "punishment" is identical in form to the precautionary payment. No distinction is made between the blameless and the guilty, between punishment and routine activity. Any punitive effect is further diminished in no-fault regimes. Thus, we have statistical punishment rather than punishment based on guilt. And because this punishment takes an economic form, it falls more heavily on the poor than on the rich, exacerbating the bias of most systems of justice. With insurance, negligence becomes essentially indistinguishable from any other hazard or peril. The sin no longer lies in the commission of a tortious act but in the omission of coverage.

We are now sufficiently interdependent that we cannot afford the fluctuations associated with punishment, reintegration, and badly managed restitution. Our vulnerability is now social, and hence risk taking has been socialized. Instead of assigning blame and trying to reform deviants, we compensate victims because this is the more manageable task. While handling restitution efficiently, insurance largely eliminates the repressive aspect of law, the part that Durkheim (1933) suggests is crucial to defining and reinforcing distinctions between acceptable and deviant behavior. When negligence is not met with repressive sanctions, it may be harder to define and reinforce a contrasting norm of responsibility.

Although insurance is the quintessential distrusting strategy, it is well to keep in mind that there are other distrusting strategies. Insurance reduces vulnerability by spreading risk (including uncertainty about the intentions and competence of others) over a larger group. What is insidious about insurance is that it discourages policyholders from collecting information about interaction partners and switching to other strategies when their experience suggests that they could trust rather than distrust.[28] Other strategies reduce risk by decreasing the losses that might be sustained in any single interaction rather than by arranging for compensation should losses occur. Because these strategies do not require the creation and management of a reserve out of which losses can be compensated, no one benefits from locking people into a distrusting strategy. When chain stores, branch banks, or franchises reduce vulnerability to any single group of customers by operating in several locations, they also use the information they amass to decide where to invest in the future. Businesses at some locations are expanded, those at others closed. Eggs are moved to safe baskets rather than remaining scattered. Although the insurance ethic encourages continued skepticism about others' intentions, other vulnerability-reducing strategies incorporate knowledge gained from experience and so can evolve into trusting strategies. This is true both for strategies that rely on replaceability and compensation and for those that spread vulnerability over a group of trustees.

Strategies that spread vulnerability over a group of trustees are useful in interpersonal relations as well as in other kinds of interactions. If they will be interacting with trustees repeatedly, entrustors who initially have reduced vulnerability by taking smaller risks with a number of trustees can consolidate their investments, shifting them to a few trustees who prove trustworthy.[29] Trust is gradually built up and the overall probability of loss simultaneously reduced. Although this strategy was not available to individual women seeking illegal abortions, Jane's contribution was to be a repeat player initially using the services of a larger number of abortionists, amassing information about women's experiences, and using this information to winnow the pool to those who proved reliable. With this combined strategy of distrust followed by trust, implemented on behalf of individual women by a collective that could function as a repeat player, illegal abortions were almost certainly made safer for Chicago-area women who went through Jane than for those who sought abortions on their own.[30]

Here I would differ with Toshio Yamagishi (this volume), who suggests that distrust prevents people from engaging in potentially rewarding social interactions and therefore from improving their capacity to judge others' trustworthiness. The social technologies of distrust outlined earlier make interaction possible even for those who do not trust their interaction partners. These strategies thus reduce the risks people must face as they acquire the information and skills that ultimately may make trust possible.

Although it seems clear that both people and organizations sometimes benefit by switching from distrusting to trusting strategies once they amass sufficient information, it is also apparent that both individuals and organizations sometimes stick with distrusting strategies. Actors may not collect the information that would permit a transition from distrust to trust. They may find it easier to employ a single routine for all interaction partners rather than follow a distrusting strategy with some and a trusting strategy with others. When interaction partners are unequal, the stronger partner may find distrusting strategies efficient because most of the cost of such strategies can be imposed on the weaker partner. And how costly a distrusting strategy is depends on both *what* is being entrusted (and so whether insurance, guarantees, or diversified portfolios of investments reduce vulnerability) and how adequate the technology is. Changes in the need for and availability of distrusting strategies have surely altered the mix of strategies used. The historical trend toward reducing vulnerability through insurance may reduce the pressure to motivate trustworthy behavior, thus reducing total societal trust and the social capital trustworthiness creates. If we can trust only insurance companies, and can trust even them only some of the time, we will all be socially poorer, although perhaps not economically worse off.

Inequality Between Corporate Actors and Individuals: Confidence and Legal Trust

Ironically, although corporations have been instrumental in originating techniques for reducing vulnerability and employ some of these techniques when they act as mediators in relations between individuals, the interactions between corporations and individuals are often based on confidence or legal trust. Figure 2.2 shows how trust relations are typically managed in the relations between these two kinds of actors.[31] The interactions between two natural persons are likely to be based on either trust or distrust. Those between two corporations likewise can be based on either distrust or trust. When a corporate actor is entrusting some object to a natural person, the interaction is likely to be based on distrust (with the stronger corporation insisting on deposits, for example). However, when an individual entrusts something to a corporate actor (money for a mail-order product, confidential information on an application form), he or she often must interact on the basis of confidence or legal trust. As I have suggested, a key question is whether one interaction partner is more powerful than the other; inequalities reach their peak in interactions between corporations and individuals.

Strong corporations tend to use power differences to their advantage in bargaining. Corporate interests often are better represented in the law than the interests of people. Because natural persons and corporate actors often are formally equal under the law, the power and resources of corporate actors give them a marked advantage over most people. De jure equality creates de facto inequality. This means that, in the context of an exchange, corporate actors can violate at least some of the entrustor's interests with impunity. Because corporations are likely to be repeat

Figure 2.2   Trust Relations Between Different Types of Actors

	TRUSTEE	
ENTRUSTOR	Natural Person	Corporate Actor
Natural person	Trust or distrust	Confidence or legal trust
Corporate actor	Distrust	Trust or distrust

Source: Author's compilation.

players interacting with many individuals, they usually are the ones to mold markets, setting the conditions for exchange. For instance, patients have little capacity to design their own contracts with hospitals or medical teams; they cannot build in the guarantees that would make them feel safe before undergoing surgery.

Corporations also can insist that individuals supply them with information while supplying relatively little data in exchange. Differences between corporations and individuals in information collection, storage, and processing capacities, which are especially important in managing trust relations, magnify the already substantial inequalities. Because a corporation stores and retrieves information differently than an individual, it can successfully manage far more interactions than an individual can. Thus, the stimulus overload that individuals experience in dense, urban societies is foreign to many corporations. Given these differences, corporations may have information that permits them to pick and choose among potential interaction partners when individuals do not. Hospitals can press patients for information about insurance coverage or other evidence of capacity to pay the bill without offering any information about their own capacity to provide good health care. Corporations may even use their resources to supply misleading information, advertising to create a reputation that overlooks or distorts key facts. Lacking good information and facing a small array of choices among corporate interaction partners, people who need the goods and services available only through corporations—health care, telephone service, electricity, home mortgages, education for children, to name only a few—have little choice but to accept their own uncertainty and vulnerability and interact on the corporation's terms. Confidence and legal trust have become increasingly important modes of interaction simply because the number of corporations and the proportion of our total interactions that involve them have increased.

Further, it is hard to hold corporations accountable when they break contracts, supply shoddy goods, make mistakes, or overcharge for their services. The component parts of corporate actors are positions, not the people who occupy those positions. This separation of actor from position results in a corporate capacity to evade responsibility and makes it difficult to punish corporations (and the people who work in them) for their misdeeds. This slippage between role and role incumbent exacerbates (from the perspective of individual entrustors) or facilitates (from the point of view of the corporate actor) the shell game of interactions based on confidence or legal trust. People who have been badly served by a corporate actor cannot appeal to the corporate body but must appeal to a human occupant of some particular position. But that person can easily claim "not me" (on the grounds that the fault lay with some previous occupant of the position) or "not my job" (on the grounds that appeal must be made to some other position). In combination, the resource discrepancy between people and corporate actors, the legal advantage of corporations, and the difficulties of pinpointing responsibility create significant impediments to holding corporate bodies accountable. Despite the popular conception (promoted by groups like the American Tort Reform Association) that businesses are beleaguered victims in endless disputes with individuals, Terence Dunworth and Joel Rogers (1996, 562) find that

> businesses win overwhelmingly, both as plaintiffs and defendants, against other parties. . . . Large business firms are spirited defenders of what they take to be their legal rights; they are highly successful in simply removing challenges to them very early in legal proceedings; they show no greater reluctance than other parties to proceed to trial if need be. And again, somewhere along the line, they generally win.

Nevertheless, we should not ignore evidence that corporations, like people, sometimes choose trusting strategies over distrusting ones. Writing about business groups such as the Korean chaebol and the Japanese kigyo shudan or keiretsu, sociologists have argued that some organizations benefit from interacting with a few partners who have proven trustworthy, have a stake in each other's success, are willing to invest in adjusting to each other's peculiar needs, and wish to settle disputes without court intervention (Gerlach 1992; Gerlach and Lincoln 1992; Granovetter 1994). Nicole Woolsey Biggart and Gary Hamilton (1992, 488) offer a salutary reminder that the neoclassical economic paradigm, with its assumption of autonomous actors (whether they be individuals or firms), draws on a Western institutional tradition and should not be expected to fit as well in Asian societies with a different legal, religious, economic, and cultural heritage. Networks "form the building blocks" of the social order and "the presence of networks—of kin, of friends, of fellow regionals—is institutionalized in business and other social practices." "It is networks that have the stability," they conclude.

Although organization theorists have made this argument forcefully about Asian business practices, scholars also have noted that American firms do not always fit the stereotype.[32] Before the explosion of interest in Asian business patterns, Stewart Macaulay (1963), for instance, argued that American businesses often avoided litigation in the interest of preserving good working relations with interaction partners, a point that has been explored more fully in recent scholarship on business disputing (see, for example, Dunworth and Rogers 1996; Esser 1996; and Kenworthy, Macaulay, and Rogers 1996). A related point is made by Joseph Rees (1994), who argues that organizations police each others' compliance with regulations when they believe that they share a joint fate. Because nuclear power companies believe that their common fate depends on public confidence in their devotion to safety, they are deeply concerned with ensuring the trustworthiness of other nuclear utilities.

A balanced assessment is in order. Although some organizations are interested in their own and others' reputations for trustworthiness, other entrustor organizations prefer distrusting strategies because some trustee organizations are not trustworthy. Recognizing the diversity of organizational practices, Ian Ayres and John Braithwaite (1992; see also J. Braithwaite 1998) advocate a regulatory pyramid in which regulatory approaches are matched to organizational stances. In essence they are arguing that trustworthy organizational behavior should be met with trusting regulatory strategies and untrustworthy behavior with regulatory distrust. The question is not *whether* organizations employ trusting strategies, but *when* and *with whom* they use them.

Conclusion

Questions about trustworthiness have always plagued human societies and always will. Trust is efficient, but those situations in which it seems safest to trust are also those in which betrayal is most tempting. The desire for trust and anxieties about the wisdom of trusting necessarily coexist.

It is clear that many truisms about trust are simply false. Premodern societies may have contained some of the prerequisites for trust more abundantly than contemporary societies. But they also provided fertile ground for intrigue, dishonesty, and betrayal. A contrast between traditional and contemporary societies that suggests that faith and trust flourished in the one but not the other is just too simple, as sociological work has amply demonstrated. Likewise we can reject as too facile suggestions that business organizations provide especially poor soil for trust because they are unusually likely to conform to assumptions about rational, autonomous, economic actors. At first blush, organizations with a strong moral order, such as families and kinship groups or religious bodies, may appear to be likely sites for trust. Closer inspection suggests that we must at least distinguish between the treatment of insiders and outsiders rather than expect that close ties always support general trustworthiness.

Granovetter (1985, 1992) is surely correct, then, in asserting that neither the undersocialized view (that mistrust and malfeasance are kept in check by various clever institutional arrangements that simply make them too costly) nor the oversocialized view (that antisocial behavior such as cheating is controlled by the inculcation of a generalized morality that makes malfeasance unthinkable) is a sufficient explanation for why trust is possible some of the time. And he is also surely correct that one's ties with transaction partners form an important part of the equation. That is, people behave in a trustworthy manner because it is in their interest to do so, because they believe that is the morally correct thing to do, and because that is how they behave in their personal relationship with a particular transaction partner. This argument leads us to look at variations in economic incentives (and the institutional arrangements that shape incentives), in moral principles (and the social arrangements that inculcate and reinforce such principles), and in the ongoing ties that make trust and trustworthiness important and meaningful in particular, concrete relationships.

Nevertheless, several elements are missing from Granovetter's account. First, the account is too static both in according too little importance to the transformations of social life that came with urbanization and industrialization and in failing to acknowledge that particular relationships are themselves anything but static. The single-church towns of early colonial America are different from the same towns in the late twentieth century. Strong, multiplex networks may start as single-stranded, sparser networks; new participants in a network are usually not tightly connected from the outset.

Second, too little attention is paid to how interactions differ depending on how the three causes of trustworthiness combine and in what quantities they are present. Granovetter (1992) notes that institutional arrangements and moral principles are themselves embedded in social structure and should be seen as social constructions. To the extent that they are partially independent of one another, then, we can imagine situations strongly shaped by one or another but not all of these causal factors. Levels of trustworthiness surely vary with the mix of moral, economic, and personal supports for honesty. But what do people do when they are unsure whether institutional arrangements, moral principles, and personal relationships will be sufficient to induce trustworthiness? Do they simply not interact with one another?

Finally, we need to ask about the dynamic properties of strategies for managing trust relations. That is, we need to ask not just whether trust is possible, but how it *comes to be possible.* If people have some reason to interact with one another but are unable to trust each other at the outset, are they able to employ inefficient strategies at the outset and move to more efficient ones later?

My account of trust relations addresses these three points. I have suggested that trust problems arise from our vulnerability to others and our uncertainty about their intentions and competence, and that trust problems are solved by manipulating one or the other of these components. Distrusting strategies work primarily by reducing vulnerability, trusting ones by reducing uncertainty. I have tried to show what historical changes have done to our capacity to solve trust problems, what solutions (besides faith and trust) are available, and how distrust can in fact lay the foundation for trust. Although we may be as vulnerable to our fellows as we always have been, we are probably more often profoundly ignorant about their intentions and competence. In such circumstances, the distrusting strategies of contemporary societies (insurance, guarantees, deposits, diversified portfolios of goods and relationships) nevertheless make high levels of interaction possible. Distrust should not be confused with trust. Distrust is in important ways a minimax solution in which people try to control losses. They may hope that others will behave honorably, but they have no reason to expect that to be the case. But distrust does something more than permit people to interact without losing too much. Distrusting strategies are also mechanisms that allow people to begin in tentative and relatively safe ways to collect information, construct appropriate institutions and norms, and build social relationships with enough past and history so that they can trust one another. Distrust is the first tentative step toward trust.

I thank Per and Kai Stinchcombe for transforming an ancient typescript into a usable word processing file and catching a few errors along the way. I am grateful to Arthur Stinchcombe, whose paper "Norms of Exchange" (1986) stimulated this essay, for comments on a draft twenty some years ago as well as more recently. I am indebted to Valerie Braithwaite, Susan Shapiro, and Lisa Staffen for many invaluable discussions as well as for lending me their libraries and notes. I thank Karen Cook for encouraging me to revisit and rework the manuscript and two anonymous reviewers for their helpful comments on the piece. Finally, I thank the Lochinvar Society for creating a warm working environment. This chapter is a revision of my unpublished master's thesis (Heimer 1976). I have kept the core ideas from the original paper but added new examples and attempted to make some connections with the voluminous literature published in the intervening period. Nevertheless, because of the way the essay evolved, readers may find that my ideas are juxtaposed to, rather than influenced by, subsequent work.

Notes

1. In asserting that there are canonical strategies, I am disagreeing with Niklas Luhmann (1979, 84), who argues that it is not useful to search for general formulas given the multitude of ways that trust can be created.

2. In this discussion, I draw heavily on Klatzky and Teitler (1973).

3. See Baier (1986, 233–40) for a careful discussion of the relation between trust and vulnerability and the variety of forms that vulnerability can take. Edward Lorenz (1988) also ties trust to vulnerability. In addition, he distinguishes between risks that arise from the behavior of others (when they act opportunistically) and those associated with acts of nature or other exogenous factors (for example, market forces).

4. Others have discussed the importance of such information shortages and uncertainty to trust. Bernard Williams (1988), for instance, suggests that cooperation might be ensured by interacting only with others whose character and disposition one knows well (this he calls "thick trust"). David Good (1988) thinks of trust as a theory that helps people predict future actions. Likewise, Partha Dasgupta (1988) discusses trust as expectations about others' actions, and Bernard Barber (1983, 19) writes about "cognitive and moral expectational maps." Niklas Luhmann (1979) argues that because trust is based partly on history, it is riskier in the modern world, where the past is of less use in predicting the future.

5. My use of the terms "faith," "confidence," "legal trust," "trust," and "distrust" does not correspond exactly to general usage. For instance, in this essay "distrust" is a method of handling trust problems by reducing vulnerability and is not necessarily correlated with feelings of suspicion. Distrust is not a psychological state or an attribution of bad faith by others. My task here is less to elucidate the *essence* of faith, confidence, and trust than to describe a set of problems commonly encountered in social relations, the strategies for handling these problems, and the constraints on choices of strategies.

    One could distinguish three additional forms of trust relations by attending to the perceived benevolence or malevolence of the trustee's intentions. I have not made these distinctions because the strategies for the positive and negative forms are identical. I have, however, retained the contrast between trust and distrust because it entails a difference in strategy. Trust involves reducing uncertainty, distrust reducing vulnerability. But even though people may be especially likely to employ distrusting strategies when they believe others' intentions are malevolent, they may also choose such strategies when they are simply uncertain about others' intentions and have no way to reduce their uncertainty.

6. Klatzky and Teitler (1973) treat legal trust as a residual category, perhaps because they focus on relations between natural persons. Legal trust and confidence are more common in relations between corporate actors and natural persons than between either two corporate actors or two people. Given that little negotiation takes place in either case, the distinction between confidence and legal trust may seem unimportant. As I explain later, however, shifts in power often bring with them attempts to shift from legal trust to confidence or vice versa.

7. For a deeper look at the institutional arrangements that foster and support trust (in some cases by institutionalizing skepticism and scrutiny), the importance of trust to effective governance, and the additional payoffs for maintaining high levels of trust, see the essays in Braithwaite and Levi (1998).

8. As savvy entrustors will understand, trustees sometimes employ the techniques of impression management outlined and illustrated by Erving Goffman (1959, 1969) to feign trustworthiness. See David Shulman's (1997) illuminating account of the routinization of deception in workplaces.

9. For a different perspective on the connection between trust and social bonds, see V. Braithwaite (1998) and Blackburn (1998).

10. Making a similar point about a contemporary evangelical congregation, Stephen Warner (1988, 227) comments that it was "a group mobilized for the purpose of social control . . . preventing the spread of bad leaven was more important than simply saving the soul of the sinner."

11. This deterioration in a sect's capacity to create and maintain trust as it becomes more like a church may well be critical to the ongoing process of sect formation. Because outsiders are suspicious of its members, a young sect is able to guarantee trust only within the group. Assuming it endures, the sect becomes more socially acceptable and acquires a reputation for supervising its members. A mature sect is able to guarantee trust both within and outside the group. Later, as the sect becomes more churchlike, with children of members granted membership regardless of their qualifications, its capacity to guarantee trust either within or outside the group erodes. New sects or subgroups with adult recruitment may then begin to take over the functions of creating and maintaining trust.

12. This observation depends on an assumption that the probability of losing is independent across actors—for instance, because there is no communication among the n actors.

13. Not all objects (relationships, prerogatives, and so on) are partitionable in this manner. When people disagree about the partitionability of objects, entrustors who attempt to reduce their vulnerability by spreading risk over a series of trustees may discover unexpected costs. Thus, married people who attempt to reduce their vulnerability to their spouses by seeking sexual or emotional gratification elsewhere may find that the probability of trust violation by the spouse increases. If the object is not truly partitionable, the probabilities are not constant or independent and p^n may no longer be less than or equal to p.

14. Luhmann (1979, 71) makes a similar observation: "It would hardly be worthwhile paying particular attention to distrust if it were simply a lack of trust. Distrust, however, is not just the opposite of trust; as such, it is also a functional equivalent for trust. For this reason only is a choice between trust and distrust possible (and necessary)." Because Luhmann defines distrust differently than I do, he means that both negative and positive expectations reduce complexity.

15. Insurers are also vulnerable to policyholders, however, because policyholder behavior affects the likelihood of the losses that insurers must compensate. Insurers therefore worry about whether they can trust policyholders to remain vigilant once the insurance contract is signed. From this perspective, insurers are entrustors, and policyholders are trustees with some control over the future costs to be borne by their insurers. As trustees, insurers have made only limited use of evidence about the trustworthiness of policyholders. Insurers deny coverage to applicants about whom they have doubts but have traditionally been unwilling to adjust premiums to take account of evidence that some policyholders are especially careful. Instead, insurers have preferred to charge large premiums on the assumption that policyholders cannot be trusted to engage in loss prevention. The "factory

mutuals" were formed by policyholders who knew they were working hard at loss prevention and wanted credit (lower premiums and more favorable contract provisions) for their successes. The difference between mutuals and stock companies is no longer so great. Responding to the competition, stock companies adopted some of the practices of mutuals, and state insurance regulations and provisions of insurance contracts both now substitute for some of the "community" functions of mutuals (see Heimer 1985).

16. See Pagden (1988) on the historical conditions under which it is possible to extend trust beyond the immediate family.

17. When Hardin (1993, 507) suggests that "we require a theory that focuses on the individual and on the ways the individual comes to know or believe relevant things, such as how trustworthy another person is," he is arguing that the traits of the entrustor matter as much as those of the trustee. For instance, we need to know whether the entrustor's history predisposes him or her to be trusting. Some variations among individuals in their disposition to trust probably come from a general cultural climate of trust or distrust, but some derive from more idiosyncratic experiences.

18. In situations of rampant malfeasance, Diego Gambetta (1988) notes, organizations like the Mafia step in to supply trust at a premium price. In such situations, it is also in the interest of those selling trust to control the supply and keep the price high.

19. In discussing the importance of trust-warranting properties and how potential entrustors can gain information about them, Michael Bacharach and Diego Gambetta (this volume) comment that American Mafia boss Vincent Teresa decided not to deal with African Americans. Their reaction to threats of punishment apparently was a factor in his reasoning. Ordinarily, with some information about a trustee, an entrustor can devise a system of punishments and rewards sufficient to control the trustee. Teresa concluded, however, that there were no punishments sufficiently severe that threats to use them would keep black people under control. To his way of thinking, then, such nonresponse to the prospect of punishment made blackness a sign of untrustworthiness.

20. For a more general treatment of this public goods problems and similar issues about the expansion and contraction of trust, see Coleman (1990, 115–16, 175–240).

21. Keith Hart (1988, 188) argues that without the constraints of kinship or legal contract, others have the freedom to act against our interests. He would "situate the notion [of trust] in a set of belief concepts bounded at the extremes by faith and confidence, where the variable significance of evidence or proof is matched by a compensating level of affectivity. As such, trust is located in the no man's land between status and contract, the poles of primitive and modern society in evolutionary theory." See also Luhmann (1988) for comments on the impact of historical changes on the possibilities for confidence and trust, which he too defines somewhat differently than I do.

22. These paragraphs summarize material presented in Heimer (1985) on the history of insurance and insurers' thinking about incentives, trust-

worthiness, and human control over losses. Readers are reminded that this abbreviated account collapses the histories of several lines of insurance, suggesting (inappropriately) a monotonic development. For instance, long after marine insurers had gained a sophisticated understanding of incentives and control over losses, fire insurers made grave errors in thinking of fires as acts of God, completely ignoring the human capacity to set fires and overlooking the incentives created by excessive face values. On the increasing sophistication of insurers' thinking about moral hazard, see also Baker (1996).

Readers should also note that I do not here discuss the very substantial technical and legal developments, as well as more general cultural changes, that undergird these innovations in insurance. Insurers had to devise techniques for assessing losses; statistical techniques for estimating the probability of loss from a variety of perils; methods for collecting and processing information; and administrative routines for collecting, investing, and disbursing funds over a long period of time. In England, insurers needed permission, in the form of a charter, to start selling a new form of insurance. In the United States, state regulation put insurers on a more stable financial footing and changes in tort law went hand in hand with new changes in insurance practices. Lawrence Friedman (1973), for instance, argues that decisions about what constituted negligence closely tracked the capacity of the negligent party to make restitution, and the availability of insurance had a substantial effect on that. For insurance to become commonplace, people also had to be willing to accept monetary evaluations in situations in which they would once have been unthinkable. See Friedman (1973) on the assignment of money values by juries. See Zelizer (1979, 1985) on changes in the acceptability of monetary evaluations of human life and changing valuations of children in particular.

23.   Usage varies somewhat, with insurers sometimes using the plural and distinguishing between morale hazards—relatively permanent personality or character traits—and moral hazard—the tendency to be especially responsive to modifications in incentive systems particularly when such modifications create an advantage to cheating on a contract. For social science treatments of moral hazard, see Arrow (1971, 1985), Fama (1980), Fama and Jensen (1983), Heimer (1985), and Holmstrom (1979, 1982).

24.   Tom Baker (1996) reminds us that insurer incentives as well as policyholder incentives are altered by the signing of insurance contracts. Insurers have some interest in defining perils narrowly, looking for reasons to refuse compensation, and delaying compensation. And insurers are not always able to control the behavior of their employees. For instance, earlier generations of fire insurance salesmen sometimes collected larger commissions by encouraging property owners to exaggerate the value of their property, knowing full well that if a loss occurred the policyholder would not receive the full face value.

25.   This move from trusting to distrusting strategies has also occurred in capital markets. In the past, investments seemed safe because the investor could rely on a trustworthy and knowledgeable stockbroker; now investor confidence

depends much more heavily on risk-spreading and the use of portfolio management tools. In a regime based on distrusting, risk-spreading mechanisms, investors are as willing to dabble in foreign markets as domestic ones and invest in products they can't understand as well ones with which they are familiar. This elaborate risk-spreading and the profound changes it has wrought in the nature of capitalism depend in fundamental ways on the social, technical, and legal innovations (discussed in Carruthers and Stinchcombe 1999) that undergird liquidity.

26. In fact, one might argue that, just as health and life insurers worry about adverse selection among their applicants, one should be wary of an interaction partner who seems too eager to purchase insurance. Especially in a high-trust setting, a suggestion that the transaction be guaranteed by a bond, deposit, or some other form of insurance may be read as a sign that a breach of trust is likely. Where insurance has been thoroughly institutionalized and the purchase of insurance coverage has become a standard practice, however, a failure to insure might instead be read as evidence of sloppiness or irresponsibility.

27. In theory, restitution was not required unless blame could be assigned. In practice, requirements for restitution have varied with the power of the groups involved, the sympathies of the public, the intervention of legislatures, and the legal interpretations made by the judges. Friedman (1973) states that initial definitions of negligence were quite strict and followed common sense. During the period of the development of railroads, negligence was so strictly defined that employees and clients rarely recovered losses. Further, the responsibilities of the negligent party extended only to the wronged individual, so relatives were unable to recover losses when negligence contributed to accidental deaths. More recently, definitions of negligence have become looser. Friedman argues that because corporations are more financially secure, legal practice no longer favors corporations over the individuals who sue them. In many cases, negligence is no longer a precondition for the recovery of losses. No-fault auto insurance is thus simply one more step in the long-term trend.

28. Rather than decreasing the total cost of risk management by combining trusting and distrusting strategies, policyholders and insurers economize on their own bargains by playing moral hazard games. Insurers and policyholders defraud each other in minor ways, insurers by undercompensating and policyholders by neglecting loss prevention and overclaiming.

29. Note the similarity here to Messick and Kramer's (this volume) account of the behavior of "conditional trusters."

30. The only information available on the safety of Jane abortions was collected during a period when Jane members were performing the abortions themselves. They show that Jane members were as skilled as the physicians performing legal abortions. But these data about the competence of Jane members as medical practitioners do not speak to the question of whether in the earlier period Jane increased safety by reducing uncertainty about the trustworthiness and competence of other abortionists (see Kaplan 1995, 264–67).

31. Of course, one could also inquire about trust relations *within* organizations, as many of the papers in Kramer and Tyler (1996) do.

32. In a similar vein, I argue (Heimer 1992, 158) that we cannot ignore the "continuity and particularity of networks" because at most, "organizations are islands of universalism in a particularistic sea." Although organizations employ a universalistic language in many of their policy statements, continuing ties with others depend on convincing them that, in addition to treating them fairly, the organization has their (particular) best interests at heart.

References

Abbott, Andrew. 1988. *The System of Professions.* Chicago: University of Chicago Press.

Arrow, Kenneth J. 1971. *Essays in the Theory of Risk Bearing.* Chicago: Markham.

———. 1985. "The Economics of Agency" In *Principals and Agents: The Structure of Business,* edited by John W. Pratt and Richard J. Zeckhauser. Boston: Harvard Business School Press.

Ayres, Ian, and John B. Braithwaite. 1992. *Responsive Regulation: Transcending the Deregulation Debate.* New York: Oxford University Press.

Baier, Annette. 1986. "Trust and Antitrust." *Ethics* 96(2): 231–60.

Baker, Tom. 1996. "On the Genealogy of Moral Hazard." *Texas Law Review* 75(2): 237–92.

Banfield, Edward C. 1958. *The Moral Basis of a Backward Society.* Glencoe, Ill.: Free Press.

Barber, Bernard. 1983. *The Logic and Limits of Trust.* New Brunswick, N.J.: Rutgers University Press.

Becker, Howard S. 1960. "Notes on the Concept of Commitment." *American Sociological Review* 66(1): 32–40.

———. 1964. "Personal Changes in Adult Life." *Sociometry* 27(March): 40–53.

———. 1973. *Outsiders: Studies in the Sociology of Deviance.* Expanded ed. New York: Free Press.

Biggart, Nicole Woolsey, and Gary G. Hamilton. 1992. "On the Limits of a Firm-Based Theory to Explain Business Networks: The Western Bias of Neoclassical Economics." In *Networks and Organizations: Structure, Form, and Action,* edited by Nitin Nohria and Robert G. Eccles. Boston: Harvard Business School Press.

Blackburn, Simon. 1998. "Trust, Cooperation, and Human Psychology." In *Trust and Governance,* edited by Valerie Braithwaite and Margaret Levi. New York: Russell Sage Foundation.

Blau, Peter M. 1964. *Exchange and Power in Social Life.* New York: Wiley.

Bloch, Marc. 1961. *Feudal Society.* Chicago: University of Chicago Press.

Blumstein, Philip, and Pepper Schwartz. 1983. *American Couples: Money, Work, Sex.* New York: Morrow.

Braithwaite, John. 1998. "Institutionalizing Distrust, Enculturating Trust." In *Trust and Governance,* edited by Valerie Braithwaite and Margaret Levi. New York: Russell Sage Foundation.

Braithwaite, Valerie. 1998. "Communal and Exchange Trust Norms, Their Value Base and Relevance to Institutional Trust." In *Trust and Governance*, edited by Valerie Braithwaite and Margaret Levi. New York: Russell Sage Foundation.

Braithwaite, Valerie, and Margaret Levi, eds. 1998. *Trust and Governance.* New York: Russell Sage Foundation.

Carruthers, Bruce G., and Arthur L. Stinchcombe. 1999. "The Social Structure of Liquidity: Flexibility, Markets, and States." *Theory and Society* 28: 353–82.

Coleman, James S. 1971. *Resources for Social Change: Race in the United States.* New York: Wiley-Interscience.

———. 1974. *Power and the Structure of Society.* New York: Norton.

———. 1990. *Foundations of Social Theory.* Cambridge, Mass.: Harvard University Press.

Dasgupta, Partha. 1988. "Trust as a Commodity." In *Trust: Making and Breaking Cooperative Relations*, edited by Diego Gambetta. Oxford: Blackwell.

Dunworth, Terence, and Joel Rogers. 1996. "Corporations in Court: Big Business Litigation in U.S. Federal Courts, 1971–1991." *Law and Social Inquiry* 21: 497–592.

Durkheim, Émile. 1933. *The Division of Labor in Society.* Translated by George Simpson. New York: Free Press.

Espeland, Wendy Nelson. 1998. *The Struggle for Water: Politics, Identity, and Rationality in the American Southwest.* Chicago: University of Chicago Press.

Espeland, Wendy Nelson, and Mitchell L. Stevens. 1998. "Commensuration as a Social Process." *Annual Review of Sociology* 24: 313–43.

Esser, John P. 1996. "Institutionalizing Industry: The Changing Forms of Contract." *Law and Social Inquiry* 21: 593–629.

Fama, Eugene F. 1980. "Agency Problems and the Theory of the Firm." *Journal of Political Economy* 88(2): 288–307.

Fama, Eugene F., and Michael C. Jensen. 1983. "Agency Problems and Residual Claims." *Journal of Law and Economics* 26: 327–49.

Freidson, Eliot. 1988. *Profession of Medicine: A Study in the Sociology of Applied Knowledge.* Chicago: University of Chicago Press. (Originally published in 1970)

Friedman, Lawrence M. 1973. *A History of American Law.* New York: Simon & Schuster.

Gambetta, Diego. 1988. "Mafia: The Price of Distrust." In *Trust: Making and Breaking Cooperative Relations*, edited by Diego Gambetta. Oxford: Blackwell.

Gerlach, Michael L. 1992. *Alliance Capitalism: The Social Organization of Japanese Business.* Berkeley: University of California Press.

Gerlach, Michael L., and James R. Lincoln. 1992. "The Organization of Business Networks in the United States and Japan." In *Networks and Organizations: Structure, Form, and Action*, edited by Nitin Nohria and Robert G. Eccles. Boston: Harvard Business School Press.

Goffman, Erving. 1959. *The Presentation of Self in Everyday Life.* Garden City, N.Y.: Doubleday.

———. 1969. *Strategic Interaction.* Philadelphia: University of Pennsylvania Press.

Good, David. 1988. "Individuals, Interpersonal Relations, and Trust." In *Trust: Making and Breaking Cooperative Relations*, edited by Diego Gambetta. Oxford: Blackwell.

Granovetter, Mark. 1985. "Economic Action and Social Structure: The Problem of Embeddedness." *American Journal of Sociology* 91(3): 481–510.

———. 1992. "Problems of Explanation in Economic Sociology." In *Networks and Organizations: Structure, Form, and Action,* edited by Nitin Nohria and Robert G. Eccles. Boston: Harvard Business School Press.

———. 1994. "Business Groups." In *Handbook of Economic Sociology,* edited by Neil Smelser and Richard Swedberg. Princeton, N.J.: Princeton University Press.

Halpern, Sydney. 1992. "Dynamics of Professional Control: Internal Coalitions and Cross-Professional Boundaries." *American Journal of Sociology* 97(4): 994–1021.

Hardin, Russell. 1993. "The Street-Level Epistemology of Trust." *Politics and Society* 21: 505–29.

Hart, Keith. 1988. "Kinship, Contract, and Trust: The Economic Organization of Migrants in an African City." In *Trust: Making and Breaking Cooperative Relations,* edited by Diego Gambetta. Oxford: Blackwell.

Hechter, Michael. 1987. *Principles of Group Solidarity.* Berkeley: University of California Press.

Heimer, Carol A. 1976. "Uncertainty and Vulnerability in Social Life." Master's thesis, University of Chicago.

———. 1985. *Reactive Risk and Rational Action: Managing Moral Hazard in Insurance Contracts.* Berkeley: University of California Press.

———. 1992. "Doing Your Job *and* Helping Your Friends: Universalistic Norms About Obligations to Particular Others in Networks." In *Networks and Organizations: Structure, Form, and Action,* edited by Nitin Nohria and Robert G. Eccles. Boston: Harvard Business School Press.

Heimer, Carol A., and Lisa R. Staffen. 1998. *For the Sake of the Children: The Social Organization of Responsibility in the Hospital and the Home.* Chicago: University of Chicago Press.

Holmstrøm, Bengt. 1979. "Moral Hazard and Observability." *Bell Journal of Economics* 10: 74–91.

———. 1982. "Moral Hazard in Teams." *Bell Journal of Economics* 13: 324–40.

Horowitz, Ruth. 1983. *Honor and the American Dream: Culture and Identity in a Chicano Community.* New Brunswick, N.J.: Rutgers University Press.

Ianni, Francis A. J. 1974. *Black Mafia: Ethnic Succession in Organized Crime.* New York: Simon & Schuster.

Janowitz, Morris. 1967. *The Community Press in an Urban Setting: The Social Elements of Urbanism.* 2d ed. Chicago: University of Chicago Press.

Kaplan, Laura. 1995. *The Story of Jane: The Legendary Underground Feminist Abortion Service.* Chicago: University of Chicago Press.

Kenworthy, Lane, Stewart Macaulay, and Joel Rogers. 1996. "'The More Things Change . . .': Business Litigation and Governance in the American Automobile Industry." *Law and Social Inquiry* 21: 631–78.

Klatzky, Sheila, and Marcel Teitler. 1973. "On Trust." Working paper 73–9. Madison: Center for Demography and Ecology, University of Wisconsin.

Kramer, Roderick M., and Tom R. Tyler, eds. 1996. *Trust in Organizations: Frontiers of Theory and Research.* Thousand Oaks, Calif.: Sage Publications.

Larson, Magali Sarfatti. 1977. *The Rise of Professionalism: A Sociological Analysis.* Berkeley: University of California Press.

Lee, Nancy Howell. 1969. *The Search for an Abortionist.* Chicago: University of Chicago Press.

Lorenz, Edward H. 1988. "Neither Friend's nor Strangers: Informal Networks of Subcontracting in French Industry." In *Trust: Making and Breaking Cooperative Relations*, edited by Diego Gambetta. Oxford: Blackwell.

Luhmann, Niklas. 1979. *Trust and Power*. Chichester, Eng.: Wiley.

———. 1988. "Familiarity, Confidence, Trust: Problems and Alternatives." In *Trust: Making and Breaking Cooperative Relations*, edited by Diego Gambetta. Oxford: Blackwell.

Macaulay, Stewart. 1963. "Non-contractual Relations in Business: A Preliminary Study." *American Sociological Review* 28(1): 55–66.

Mailer, Norman. 1968. *Miami and the Siege of Chicago*. New York: World Publication.

Marx, Karl. 1964. *Economic and Philosophic Manuscripts of 1844*. New York: International Publishers.

Pagden, Anthony. 1988. "The Destruction of Trust and Its Economic Consequences in the Case of Eighteenth-Century Naples." In *Trust: Making and Breaking Cooperative Relations*, edited by Diego Gambetta. Oxford: Blackwell.

Polanyi, Karl. 1944. *The Great Transformation: The Political and Economic Origins of Our Time*. Boston: Beacon Press.

Reagan, Leslie J. 1997. *When Abortion Was a Crime: Women, Medicine, and Law in the United States, 1867–1973*. Berkeley: University of California Press.

Rees, Joseph V. 1994. *Hostages of Each Other: The Transformation of Nuclear Safety Since Three Mile Island*. Chicago: University of Chicago Press.

Rothman, David J. 1991. *Strangers at the Bedside: A History of How Law and Bioethics Transformed Medical Decision Making*. New York: Basic Books.

Shapiro, Susan P. 1987. "The Social Control of Impersonal Trust." *American Journal of Sociology* 93(3): 623–58.

Shils, Edward. 1957. "Primordial, Personal, Sacred, and Civil Ties." *British Journal of Sociology* 8: 130–45.

———. 1962. "The Theory of Mass Society." *Diogenes* 39: 45–66.

Shulman, David. 1997. "The Social Organization of Workplace Deception." Ph.D. diss., Northwestern University.

Starr, Paul. 1982. *The Social Transformation of American Medicine*. New York: Basic Books.

Stinchcombe, Arthur L. 1986. "Norms of Exchange." In Arthur L. Stinchcombe, *Stratification and Organizations: Selected Papers*. Cambridge: Cambridge University Press.

Suttles, Gerald D. 1972. *The Social Construction of Communities*. Chicago: University of Chicago Press.

Tönnies, Ferdinand. 1957. Community and Society. Translated and edited by Charles P. Loomis. East Lansing: Michigan State University Press.

Vaughan, Diane. 1986. *Uncoupling: Turning Points in Intimate Relationships*. New York: Oxford University Press.

Warner, R. Stephen. 1988. *New Wine in Old Wineskins: Evangelicals and Liberals in a Small-Town Church*. Berkeley: University of California Press.

Weber, Max. 1946. "The Protestant Sects and Capitalism." In *From Max Weber: Essays in Sociology*, edited by H. H. Gerth and C. Wright Mills. New York: Oxford University Press.

———. 1978. *Economy and Society: An Outline of Interpretive Sociology*, edited by Guenther Roth and Claus Wittich. Berkeley: University of California Press.

Williams, Bernard. 1988. "Formal Structures and Social Reality." In *Trust: Making and Breaking Cooperative Relations,* edited by Diego Gambetta. Oxford: Blackwell.

Wirth, Louis. 1938. "Urbanism as a Way of Life." American Journal of Sociology 44(1): 3–24.

Zelizer, Viviana A. Rotman. 1979. *Morals and Markets: The Development of Life Insurance in the United States.* New York: Columbia University Press.

———. 1985. *Pricing the Priceless Child: The Changing Social Value of Children.* New York: Basic Books.

Chapter 3

Trust as a Form of Shallow Morality

David M. Messick and Roderick M. Kramer

I N THIS CHAPTER, we consider trust as a type of social dilemma. By providing some background on principles that apply to these types of decisions, we can identify classes of variables that should be relevant. However, behavior is notoriously context-dependent—details matter—making it necessary to examine the proximal, simple, and heuristic features of situations that manifest the more general principles.

What is trust? Let us start by offering three illustrations.

1. Late on a cold snowy night, a stranger rings your doorbell and explains that he and his wife—who is in the car around the corner, were on their way home when their car stalled. He cannot get it started. He says that the cab they hailed will take them home for ten dollars, but that he does not have cash with him and the cabby wants to be paid in advance. He asks you to loan him ten dollars to get him and his wife home. He will repay you within the next day or two after he can get to the bank. You must decide whether to give the man ten dollars.

2. You and a colleague, who is also a friend, have been nominated to chair your academic department. Both you and your friend, who is also about your age, would like to have the job since you both are interested in pursuing college administration in your careers. You would like to be able to win the support of your colleagues, but you would not like to see your relationship with your friend damaged in the process. The problem is that your friend knows you went through a scratchy patch a couple of years ago that left you in a hospital diagnosed as suffering from depression. None of

your other colleagues know of this episode, and if they did they would probably support your friend for the chair. If you decide to pursue the candidacy, you create an incentive for your friend to divulge her knowledge of your illness. She says that she will not mention your past illness. You must decide whether to withdraw your name from candidacy.

3. You and your family have been staying in your summer home, and you are preparing to leave in the next couple of days. You have noticed that you need to have some tree work done, and while you are examining the trees a young man with a pickup truck on whose door is painted "Ralph's Tree Service" stops to ask whether you need help. You explain what you need to have done, and Ralph says that he can easily do it and gives you a price that seems a bit high but in the ballpark. You verbally agree to have him do the work for you. Ralph shows up the following day with a crew of a couple of young chaps and starts the job. They have a problem with their chain saw in the morning, and it takes a couple of hours to get it repaired. Ralph tells you that he can finish the job the following day. The problem is you have to leave very early in the morning and have no convenient way to verify that the job was finished. Ralph would like you to pay for the whole job now so that he can pay his crew tomorrow when the job is done. The bill will be four hundred dollars, and he asks you to go to the bank with him so that he can cash your check immediately. You must decide whether to go to the bank and pay him now or to make some other arrangement.

What these examples have in common, and what they reveal about our working definition of trust, is that they involve a decision whose potential costs depend on the actions of another person. Trust involves taking the risk that the other person will follow more or less simple moral rules. If the other follows the rules, you stand to profit; if he or she does not, the costs can be great. The other, moreover, has an incentive to break the rules. The first example involves at least two issues. Is the person telling the truth about his situation—is his wife in a stalled car around the corner?—or is this encounter a form of panhandling in which the "victim" can earn several hundred dollars by telling his tale at many doors in the course of an evening? The second issue is whether he has any intent to repay the ten dollars if it is given to him, even if his story is true. However, this is a case where the worst outcome of the trust decision is that you are duped and ten dollars poorer. By deciding to give him the ten dollars even though you do not believe the story, you can just be out the ten bucks. The stakes here are not high.

The second example invokes different issues. First, the person whose behavior is at stake is not a stranger but a friend. Your decision to go forward with your candidacy makes her intimate knowledge of your past a potential danger. The worst outcome here is quite serious. You could fail in your effort to become department chair, have your medical problem made public, and lose a friend. If your friend does not reveal your treatment for depression, you may only fail in your effort to achieve the chair, but since you would not know the reason for your failure you may harbor the suspicion that she did reveal that information, at least to enough people to make the difference. Could you believe her assurances that she kept your secret?

In the final example, you have entered into an agreement with Ralph, and your question is whether he will honor the agreement when he knows that it will be difficult and expensive for you to enforce it. You would be willing to pay Ralph now if you had assurances that he would complete the job tomorrow, but you do not want to be euchred out of four hundred dollars with the job only partly done.

We will define *trust* in these situations as making the decision *as if* the other person or persons will abide by ordinary ethical rules that are involved in the situation. Our definition of trust is similar to LaRue Hosmer's (1995, 399) recent attempt to integrate organizational and ethical conceptions of trust. He defines trust as "the expectation by one person, group, or firm of ethically justifiable behavior—that is, morally correct decisions and actions based upon ethical principles of analysis—on the part of the other person, group, or firm in a joint endeavor or economic exchange." The two most important of those rules involve truth-telling and the avoidance of harming others, but there may be other rules as well in different contexts. Truth-telling is involved in all of the examples, and a trusting response is one that is consistent with the hypothesis that what you are told is true: that the stranger on your doorstep really has a stalled car and a cold wife, that your friend will not disclose your illness, and that Ralph will come tomorrow and finish the job. This definition of trust does not require that you actually believe these things. You may not know, or you may be pretty sure that what you are being told is false. But trust is to act *as if* the accounts are true.

The avoidance of harm, broadly defined, concerns whether the man on your doorstep would harm you by taking your money with no intention of returning it, whether your friend would harm you and your reputation in order to win the chair, and whether Ralph would take your money and not finish the work. (The last example thus also invokes the ethical rule of keeping promises.)

Defining trust as a decision rather than an attitude, belief, or judgment is compatible with the approach that others have taken, notably Roderick Kramer, Marilynn Brewer, and Benjamin Hanna (1996). An advantage of viewing trust as a choice is that we already know some things about how people make choices and this knowledge can be applied to the study of trust decisions, as Kramer and his colleagues (1996) have done. Moreover, decisions are observable, whereas internal states are less so. Treating trust as a decision that is compatible with the expectation of ethical action from others allows us to investigate the role of beliefs about others in the trust decision. Finally, social psychologists have long known that there can be a large gap between what people indicate on rating scales that measure attitudes and beliefs and what they actually do when faced with real choices (for example, see Eagly and Chaiken 1993, ch. 4). Our interests are in what people do in situations where concerns about trust loom large.

This definition is not without some problems. Suppose in the first example you are essentially sure that the person asking for your help is a panhandler with a new twist. And suppose that you normally give money to panhandlers when they approach. Is it an act of trust when you give this person money, even if you are certain that you are not being told the truth and even if you have no expectation of ever seeing the money again? Are you not merely giving alms? Our answer would be that the situation has been constructed so that your giving money is trusting and your refusal to give is nontrusting, regardless of what you believe. The difference is in the appeal made by a panhandler on the street and the (possible) one who comes to your door with this story. The person on the street simply asks for a handout with no strings attached; the man at your door has, for whatever reason, embedded his request in a context that invites trust.

Some economic features of this definition need to be highlighted. Trusting is exploitable and potentially costly. In all cases, if the target of your trust is not trustworthy, you will suffer. If, on the other hand, the target is trustworthy, both parties are better off. You would prefer helping a person and getting your money back over not helping, and the person you help would certainly prefer to be helped. You would prefer to have Ralph finish the tree work and to pay him four hundred dollars over not having the work done, and Ralph would prefer to do the work and be paid over not doing it and not getting paid. It is a bit more subtle in your campaign for the department chair, largely because the situation we describe is asymmetric, but in running the campaigns, you both would prefer having an election in which reputations are not attacked over having campaigns in which reputations are attacked, all else being equal. In these asymmetric examples, the target of the trust has an incentive to be untrustworthy. The man at your door gets to keep your (and others') money; your friend wins the chair; and Ralph keeps your money and sleeps in.

The incentive structure of these situations is that while there are mutual gains that can be achieved through trust, there are also incentives for the other to act unethically, to choose the untrustworthy option, to fail to honor your trust. Imagine a universe of such situations—where you

Figure 3.1   A Prototypical Trust Game in Extensive Form

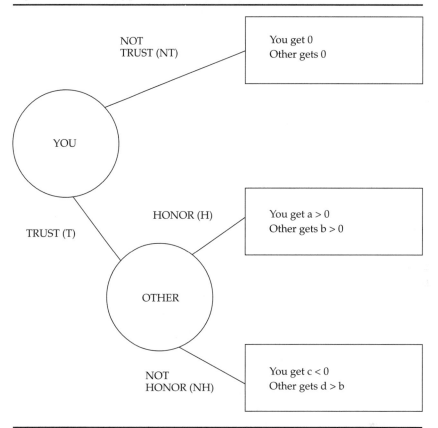

NOT
TRUST (NT)

You get 0
Other gets 0

YOU

HONOR (H)

You get a > 0
Other gets b > 0

TRUST (T)

OTHER

NOT
HONOR (NH)

You get c < 0
Other gets d > b

Source: Authors' compilation.
Note: In this representation: a, b > 0; c < 0, and d > b.

(and others) may need help on a cold night, where you (and others) may seize an advantage in an election by revealing harmful (but possibly irrelevant) information about an opponent, or where you neglect to keep your promises when it is profitable to ignore them. The prototypical structure we want to assume is that the mutual choice of trust and trustworthiness provides payoffs to both persons that are better than the payoffs for nontrust. However, the combination of trust and untrustworthiness, we assume, provides payoffs for the other that are greater than those of trustworthiness for the target, but worse than those of nontrust for the truster.

We have summarized these ideas in figures 3.1 and 3.2. There are two essential features of these arrangements: you can receive either more or

Figure 3.2   Trust Game in Normal Form

		Other	
		H	NH
You	T	a,b	c,d
	NT	0,0	0,0

Source: Authors' compilation.

less through trust than through not trusting; given that you choose to trust, the other does better by being untrustworthy. These are the elements of what has been called the Trust Game (TG) by economists (Kreps 1990; Snijders 1996). Our definition of trust adds the requirement that when the other fails to honor the trust, she violates one or more ethical rules. This requirement is not demanded by the pattern of the payoffs in the Trust Game. In the figures we have displayed this economic structure as a game in extensive (figure 3.1) and in normal form (figure 3.2).

The structure of the TG resembles a prisoners' dilemma (PD), although the two decision situations are not identical. In the TG, there is no dominating strategy for you, but there is a dominating strategy for the other. If you eliminate the dominated strategies of the other, then there is a dominating strategy for you, namely nontrusting. An important similarity between the PD and the TG derives from the following consideration: if others never honor the trust, if they always cheat, you will never trust, leading to equilibrium nontrusting (NT) outcomes. These outcomes are dominated by the trusting, honor outcome (T,H), however, much like mutual defection is dominated by mutual cooperation in the PD.

But the two types of game are dissimilar in many ways. Part of the tension in the TG is that the moves are not generally made simultaneously. The other usually knows whether or not you have trusted before making her choice, whereas you choose before knowing what she will do. This sequential property adds a potential element of reciprocation. If you trust the other, she will gain regardless of her choice because both of her payoffs following your trusting choice provide higher outcomes for her than your nontrusting choice. Part of the other's decision conflict is whether to reciprocate the benefit to you and improve your outcomes (while diminishing her own) by making the choice to honor your trust. There is also the question that we address later in the chapter: is an implicit or explicit promise to be trustworthy invoked when one is trusted?

The sequential feature of the TG also differentiates the two roles in our perceptions. We are likely to see you as facing a choice of risk versus security, or credulity versus skepticism. The other seems to be facing the choice of honor versus gain. The perceived differences between the first and second movers in the TG mirror the distinction that Keith Murnighan and Madan Pillutla (1995, 265) make in the well-known ultimatum bargaining game (UBG). They hypothesize that most of the first movers in this game see the game as "an opportunity for monetary gain," whereas the second movers, the responders, "define the situation morally." The moral connotations of a situation thus may depend on which role one occupies.

Evolution and Dynamics of Trust

At this point we want to offer some ideas about the dynamics of trusting that parallel the structure of an argument made by David Messick (1991), and others, about the nature of altruism. Clearly the trusting act can be seen as an altruistic act in that it is an act that increases the outcomes for the other while either decreasing or risking a decreased outcome for the truster. A question that has occupied many scholars from the biological as well as the social sciences is the question of how altruism can survive natural selection, which, by definition, reduces the fitness (outcomes) of those who are altruistic. This is not the place for a detailed review of this massive literature, but we can summarize several essential principles.

To make the argument clear, suppose that there are two types of individuals, altruists (As) and non-altruists (Ns), and suppose further that they differ in that the As are always altruistic (trusting and trustworthy) while the Ns are never so. Ns do not trust, nor are they trustworthy. Conducting an analysis that parallels the expected value analysis that Messick (1991) reports in the context of the prisoners' dilemma, the following generalizations can be drawn. The As in this case benefit relative to Ns when the population contains a high density of As, when a and b, the rewards for trust, are large, when d, the payoff for cheating, is low, and when c, the penalty for trusting, is small.

There is one major difference between this analysis and that reported by Messick (1991). In the earlier analysis, the As in dichotomous populations could never have a greater expected payoff than the Ns. With the case of the TG, the As can do better than the Ns. In this case a population of all As could be an evolutionarily stable state in that the Ns that invaded the population would do poorly compared with the As. The circumstances that favor As depend on values of the economic parameters and the density of As in the population.

We ask you to now imagine one embellishment of this tale. Imagine that in addition to the altruists (As) and non-altruists (Ns) there are also conditional trusters (Cs). Cs trust other trusters—As and other Cs—but not Ns. They will also not cheat when trusted. The Cs do very well because they avoid the risk of being cheated by the Ns and they get the cooperative benefits of interacting with the As and other Cs. The Cs, in this story, are similar to the reciprocal altruists described by Robert Trivers (1971) and the group-based altruists described in Messick (1991).

It is the ability of the Cs to discriminate against the Ns by refusing to trust them that gives them their advantage. Of course, this ability may be associated with some cost. Cs are more complex conceptual creatures than either Ns or As because they are capable of behaving in two ways, either trusting or not, depending on circumstances, whereas both As and Ns can do just one thing. Not only are Cs more complex psychologically and behaviorally, but they may also make mistakes in their judgments about others. The two types of mistakes they make are to trust an untrustworthy person and be betrayed, or to fail to trust a trustworthy person and forgo the gains of mutual trust. The probabilities of these errors depend on the choices made, the prevalence of trustworthiness in the population, and the ability of the Cs to discern the difference between trustworthy and untrustworthy individuals.

To suggest that the Cs have an economic advantage is not to speculate about how that ability would be manifested in a particular situation. The economic advantage may provide the *distal* "incentive" for a species to learn to discriminate against Ns, but it does not explain the precise form in which the discrimination takes place. The *proximal* cause of the behavior must also be understood.

The parallels between our argument and the arguments offered in the biological and psychological literature on the evolution of altruism are intentional. In our view, trust and other forms of prosocial behavior are closely linked. It is important to stress that arguments based on an analysis of economic or fitness advantages for some form of behavior do not imply any sort of biological determinism. The ways in which organisms and species "learn" how to use these rules may, and almost surely does, involve complex interactions between biological and cultural evolution. For a scholarly introduction to some of the psychological issues addressed in this literature, readers are referred to Donald Campbell's (1975) presidential address to the American Psychological Association, to the many responses to that address in the *American Psychologist* the following year (1976), and to more recent works that examine these issues (for example, Crawford, Smith, and Krebs 1987; Wilson 1993).

With trust, as with other forms of prosocial behavior, it is important to highlight a conflict that permeates all the literature on the evolution of altruism. As Messick (1976) pointed out decades ago, interests change as a function of the role in which you find yourself. If you are a potential recipient of an altruistic act, you have strong preferences about how others should act. You have a strong preference for others to help you to achieve your goals, to protect you from harm, to honor your rights and your freedom, and to treat you with respect. One way to induce others to treat you in these ways is to proclaim, articulate, and promote principles and rules of morality and ethics that require these actions. Such proclamations often are not very costly, and they may be quite effective. Social psychological research on influence suggests in fact that such direct appeals and exhortations may be very effective at influencing others' behavior (Cialdini 1993). This is one sense in which "cheap talk" may be quite profitable in transactions in which concerns about trust loom large, especially those involving comparative strangers.

In the role of the recipient, you have strong preferences about how others should act. However, when you are in the role of the altruist, trusting someone may be costly to you and your preferences are far less clear. David Kipnis (1996, 40) describes this difference in terms of how people feel about being trusted versus having to trust others. Most people, he asserts, like to be trusted. "To be trusted means that you are capable of managing resources that other people value. . . . It also means that you are a good person." When it comes to having to trust others, however, we may be considerably more ambivalent. "Having to trust other people is bothersome. Sometimes this bother is experienced as anxiety and sometimes as feelings of deference, fear, or anger. *But whatever the label, the feelings are negative*" (emphasis added). You may want to help another, but the costs may also be high. You may be willing to pay the costs if you could be certain that the aid would be effective, but there may be uncertainty about whether your actions are futile or, in some cases, counterproductive. To make this point clearly, examine the incentives for the two players in figures 3.1 and 3.2. The other clearly wants you to make the trusting choice because, no matter what she finally chooses to do, her payoffs are greater than those associated with the nontrusting alternative. Likewise, you have very clear preferences for what the other should do. If you trust her, you want her to be trustworthy.

You have a difficult choice because you see that the other has an incentive to cheat. She also has a difficult choice since she may get more from cheating in this episode. Life, however, consists of many episodes, and cheating in this one may come back to haunt her in a future one. The point is that both parties have very clear preferences for what they want the other party to do, even though they themselves have decision conflicts. In other words, if they could choose for each other, there would be no problem. The other would trust (for you), and you would be trustworthy (for the other). But they cannot choose for each other: they have to choose for themselves. To put this principle in a slightly different way, we generally have clearer preferences and beliefs about how others should behave than about how we ourselves should act. This distinction is consistent with the well-studied differences between how we perceive ourselves and how we perceive others (Jones and Nisbett 1971).

Our strong preferences for others' actions lead us to endorse and promote rules of ethics and morality, including exhortations to be trusting and trustworthy, that may be beneficial to us if we can induce others to follow these rules. However, we have an incentive to behave in opposition to our exhortations to others, creating a temptation to be hypocritical—to say one thing while doing another. This temptation may be dampened by our exhortations not to be hypocritical. We have a preference for others not to be hypocritical because when they act hypocritically they are usually acting against our interests and preferences.

The fact that we have clear preferences for others' actions is one reason moral and ethical systems are widely proclaimed and endorsed. Furthermore, much of the content of these systems is rule-based: "do not cheat," "keep your promises," "do not knowingly harm others," and, "do not be a hypocrite," for instance. Another important rule is: "require others to abide by the rules and punish them if they do not." These rules constitute much of our moral common sense, or our moral intuitions. Since they are widely shared, they also constitute social norms regarding acceptable behavior. We know the rules, and we know that others know them. Violations of the rules are witnessed with surprise, anger, and a sense of unfairness or injustice. We make unflattering attributions and inferences about people who fail to abide by the rules. People need not explain why they follow the rules, but they have to offer a justification when they fail to do so.

Discrimination Hypothesis

Our first hypothesis is that humans are fine-tuned to make judgments about whether people are trustworthy. In other words, we claim that humans are Cs in the abstract story we asked you to imagine about the trust game. An important question is, how do we make those judgments? To answer it, we begin by summarizing some ideas from the evolution of altruism literature. We argue that our discriminations are fast, shallow, and context-sensitive.

One crucial issue in the evolution of altruism literature is how altruistic benefits are distributed. If randomly distributed throughout the population, non-altruists would be as likely as altruists to receive them, and thus altruism would fail. What is needed is a mechanism by means of which altruists are more likely than cheaters to benefit from the acts of other altruists. Different theories describe different mechanisms to achieve this outcome. Kin selection, one of the earliest and least controversial processes, makes the allocation dependent on kin relations. In this way, to the extent that the altruistic trait is genetically coded, benefiting kin are protecting the trait so that it can be passed on to future generations. This type of altruism is selfish from the perspective of the genotype that supports the trait, thus justifying Richard Dawkins's (1976) intriguing title *The Selfish Gene*. By helping our kids (who share half our genes), we are helping the genes, even if at a cost to our persons.

Trivers (1971) goes further and explains the conditions under which even genetically unrelated individuals could exchange self-sacrificial aid and still outbreed others who decline to do so. Trivers's basic idea, that individuals help others who have helped them in the past, requires a relatively dense population in which the likelihood of multiple interactions is reasonably great. He expands his idea by positing that an individual is helped not only by another she helped in the past but also by those who know of the help. Reputation becomes an asset. Trivers is quick to note that this type of relationship is exploitable by cheaters, who mimic helpers to get the benefits while not paying the costs of helping. Thus, for the system to survive, helpers must be able to discriminate cheaters from other helpers. From the perspective of the evolution of social forms of behavior, we should expect to see the evolution of new forms of cheating and of new forms of detecting cheating.

David Wilson (1980) describes yet another mechanism that can make costly helping survive. It requires that there be a social segregation between the altruists and the cheaters, so that the altruists are more likely, in their daily lives, to interact with other altruists and not with the cheaters, who are more likely to interact with other cheaters. In this way, the benefits of help are conferred mainly on other helpers. Although there is some debate about the realism of this mechanism, there is no disputing the mathematics. The only question is whether the process actually occurs in the biological universe. Wilson claims that it does. His process does not require that individuals be able to discriminate cheaters from helpers. It only requires that some type of process segregate them. David Messick and John van de Geer (1981) provide a numerical illustration of the paradox that cheaters may do better than altruists in each of the subgroups, while altruists do better than the cheaters overall.

We have outlined three mechanisms—kin, reciprocity, and segregation—that are sufficient to implement the discrimination hypothesis. Each of these requires that the underlying proximal mechanisms be understood if the theory is to be applied to real organisms in real environments. How, for instance, does kin selection work? In some species parents must learn to recognize kin, and there are critical periods within which this learning takes place (Porter 1987). In other cases, such as that of the Belding ground squirrel, no such learning is necessary.

Female Belding ground squirrels (Spermophilus beldingi) defend territories close to the burrows where they give birth and raise their young. At some point the young males leave the territory and move to the perimeter of the colony. The females stay and colonize burrows close to the one where they were born. Thus, the sex-linked dispersal pattern and the sociology of the colony is such that females who are geographically proximal are likely to be genetically related.

This species is interesting because the females emit loud vocalizations in the presence of potential predators (Sherman 1977). When a predator—a hawk, snake, or coyote—is seen, instead of leaping for the burrow the female stands upright and emits a high-pitched alarm call that alerts neighbors to the danger (and at the same time alerts the predator to the location of the caller). Since vocalizing is riskier than diving for the burrow, the question is, why has this risky and dangerous strategy evolved? And why does it persist? Paul Sherman argues that nepotism, or kin selection, is the answer. The beneficiaries of the alarm call are generally those in closest proximity to the caller, and they are most likely to be kin of the caller. The process requires only that kin be close, not that callers "know" they are close.

This example illustrates an interesting point about the mechanisms that underlie altruistic behavior. Often the three principles are at work at the same time. With the ground squirrels, because of the dispersal patterns and the matrilineal burrow structure, females tend to help other females (males do not vocalize). Thus, there is reciprocity embodied in the network as well as nepotism. Moreover, there is a geographical segregation of altruists (females) from cheaters (males), so Wilson's model of group selection is also applicable. Nepotism, reciprocity, and group segregation all support alarm-calling in this species.

Our topic, however, is trust among humans, not alarm-calling among ground squirrels. What are the proximal processes that lead to trust among humans? We propose that these features are the same ones that support other forms of altruistic behavior, which are described in a huge empirical literature (Staub 1978). The most important of these factors are rather obvious ones. We trust (and help) people with whom we are familiar, with whom we have frequent contact, whom we believe to be similar to ourselves, and for whom we have positive regard (Staub 1978). These factors are positively correlated, naturally, in that we seek out people whom we like, and we exchange information with them, increasing our familiarity. Family members are special since we generally know them better and have stronger emotional ties with them than with others. Moreover, within families there is a genetic connection (except between husband and wife) that further rewards aid, especially aid devoted to offspring.

There is evidence that these factors may be mediated by empathic or other emotional responses in the helpers (Krebs 1975). Frequency, similarity, familiarity, and affect, in other words, may elicit trust and other forms of help because the truster has an empathic relation to the target. By an empathic relation we mean that the outcomes experienced by the target are experienced vicariously or symbolically by the truster. Our wife's sorrow is also our sorrow, and our friend's joy is partly our joy. If empathy is one of the major proximal variables that promote trust, then factors that facilitate empathy will also increase trust.

Trust is only as durable as the proximal conditions that support it. If empathy disappears, trust may also disappear. If positive affect evaporates, the behaviors that depend on the affect will also change. People monitor relationships and evaluate them both in terms of the relative value of the outcomes (Adams 1965) and in terms of procedures (Lind and Tyler 1988; Tyler, this volume). In other words, people ask whether what they get out of relationships is commensurate with what they think others are getting out of relationships, and they also ask whether the rules of the relationship are fair. Perceptions of inequities in outcomes or procedural injustice can destroy trust and its psychological foundations (Brockner and Siegel 1996). In this sense, the history of interaction within a trust relationship matters a great deal. People in such relationships function much like "intuitive auditors" (Kramer 1996), tracking their own outcomes over time and comparing them with outcomes for other people in the relationship. As a result, reciprocal trust in the relationship over time "thickens" or "thins" as a function of the cumulative history of interaction between the parties.

Trust can exist between strangers as well as between acquaintances, but the proximal features of such trust are psychologically different. First, we may trust people who come with an endorsement from acquaintances. A friend of a friend can be trusted. As Ronald Burt and Marc Knez (1996) show, the impact of gossip on judgments of another's trustworthiness can be powerful, tending to bias judgments in a confirmatory direction.

Trust can also be evoked by strangers under somewhat different circumstances. Whereas Trivers's (1971) reciprocity notion requires repeated interaction for mutual helping to work, Messick (1991) has proposed a variant of this idea, known as *group-based* altruism, that does not demand repeated contact. From a mathematical perspective, what is required is that individuals who would share aid be able to identify each other. The Cs, in the abstract story we told earlier, need only be able to tell a C and an A from an N. So suppose Cs and As have a red dot on their foreheads (assuming they have foreheads) and they use the rule, "Help anyone with a red dot on the forehead." The Cs would thrive (and, of course, the Ns would have an incentive to get a red dot). In searching for proximal causes, the question is, what cues play the role of the red dot? Messick's (1991) answer is that group membership plays this role in many situations. When group membership is made salient, a bond may be induced that facilitates trust and mutual aid. Since common group membership characterizes both parties, it induces, in effect, reciprocity.

To take a common illustration, most Americans usually do not think about their national identity while in the United States. But when two expatriates meet when they have been living abroad for a period of time, their shared "American-ness" can be palpable. People who in the United States have little or nothing in common may perceive that they are very close because of this shared group membership. People who share a group identity behave more positively toward each other than those who do not (Kramer 1991).

This type of group-based trust or altruism has some unusual properties. First, it is not extended to just anyone, only to those who are common group members. Some people, therefore, will not be trusted. Trust is a scarce resource that is not in infinite supply. If it were infinite, then we would be talking about the As in our theoretical tale, not about the Cs. The crucial thing about the Cs is that they do *not* trust everyone.

A second feature of this notion is that what constitutes the group is unspecified. The salient group boundary at one moment may be nationality, and at another moment it may be gender. The very lability of salient group identity means that whether or not group-based trust will be extended depends on the context and the details of the interaction. Canadian and American men should be more willing to trust each other following a lecture on feminism than following a lecture on Canadian-American trade disputes.

Finally, this type of trust is *depersonalized* trust, to use Marilynn Brewer's (1981) phrase. It does not depend on a history of interaction between the parties; it does not presuppose familiarity or acquaintance. It is trust that is extended to strangers in circumstances in which common identity is evoked and presumably provides relevant information about the trustworthiness of the other party. Recognition of shared identity in such contexts provides a basis for developing expectations about the other party's ethical orientation, honesty, cooperativeness, fairness, and the like. All of these dispositional inferences are useful when trying to predict the other's behavior. In this sense, depersonalized trust is presumptive trust rather than negotiated trust.

A perceived common group identity enhances not only depersonalized trust but the perception that others will be trustworthy (Messick et al. 1983). This empirical relationship between the perception of the trustworthiness of others and willingness to trust raises a vexing question about causation. Do people trust more because they believe others are trustworthy, or do people believe others are more trustworthy because they have been trusted? This is a complicated issue with evidence supporting both positions. Robyn Dawes, Jeanne MacTavish, and Hariet Shaklee (1977) report evidence that favors the "trust leads to trustworthiness" hypothesis, and Larry Messé and John Sivacek (1979) report evidence that supports both positions.

A fuller account of this relationship might stress the importance of features that evoke different views of situational appropriateness. In some contexts—for instance, in convention presentations or departmental colloquia—intellectual aggressiveness is appropriate and expected. Such behavior is inappropriate and rude at dinner parties, where courtesy and graciousness are the norms. Situations may evoke rules of appropriateness that we are to follow and that we expect others to follow as well. One approach to this type of theory has been offered in James March's (1994) eloquent account of the *logic of appropriateness*. In this account, choice does not cause expectations, nor do expectations cause choice; both choice and expectations are caused by the perception of the appropriate rules and norms of the situation, rules and norms that govern all participants. Common group membership implies that you should trust me and that I should be trustworthy. Hence, in this situation we act like Cs with regard to each other.

Shallowness Hypothesis

Here we want to introduce a second hypothesis of this essay: the *shallowness hypothesis*. This hypothesis proposes that the kind of deliberation and thought required to make a decision to trust or be trustworthy is not what psychologists call "deep" or "systematic" processing. In contrast, the hypothesis states that we decide very quickly whether to trust or to be trustworthy. You would not spend long on your doorstep thinking about whether to give the "stranded motorist" ten dollars; you would probably not spend much time deciding whether you should pursue your department's chair; and you would in all likelihood decide pretty quickly whether to pay the tree man. If you decided not to, you might spend some time working out the details of how and when you would pay him, but the decision to trust or not would probably be quickly made.

Supporting this hypothesis are several psychological principles based on the general notion that humans are imperfect information processors and decisionmakers. This notion has been systematized by the notion of *satisficing* (Simon 1957; March and Simon 1958). This concept was offered to supplant the view of human choice and decisionmaking that emphasizes rationality, thoroughness of information-seeking and analysis, coherence of preferences, and the maximization of utility or satisfaction. This alternative stresses the idea that rationality may be unreachable; that information search may be flawed, curtailed, or biased; and that preferences may not be as "well behaved" as mathematical theories suppose. Rather than maximizing satisfaction and finding the best alternative, perhaps people (and organizations) merely try to find acceptable alternatives and seek "good enough" outcomes, not "the best" outcomes.

The idea of satisficing led to the search for simple rules that could replace and approximate normatively optimal rules. These rules were called *heuristics.* To our knowledge, the earliest use of the concept of heuristics in decisionmaking and problem-solving was George Polya's (1945) advocacy of heuristic problem-solving in the solution of mathematical problems. In his influential book *How to Solve It* (1945, 112), Polya argues for the value of "heuristic reasoning," which is "not regarded as final and strict but as provisional and plausible only. . . . We may need the provisional before we attain the final. We need heuristic reasoning when we construct a strict proof as we need scaffolding when we erect a building." Polya clearly sees heuristic reasoning as an augmentation to, not a replacement for, formal mathematical reasoning. Heuristics could lead to hypotheses, hunches, and approaches, but they would have to be validated through rigorous proof. Moreover, he defines *modern heuristic* as the effort "to understand the process of solving problems, especially the *mental operations typically useful* in this process" (130, emphasis in original). Polya's definition of modern heuristic sounds almost like a definition of modern cognitive psychology.

The concept of heuristics, or heuristic reasoning, became a central component of the effort to simulate human thinking. In this domain, heuristics represent "rules of thumb" that can be useful in solving problems or in proving theorems. Allen Newell and Herbert Simon (1963, 390) put it as follows: "First, the incorporation of 'rules of thumb' in this program is highly typical of programs that have been devised for symbol identification, pattern recognition, learning, and problem-solving tasks. We call processes of this kind, which generally contribute to a result but whose results are not 'guaranteed,' *heuristic processes.*" These authors suggest two reasons why heuristic processes are employed: first, in some cases there are no ways known to perform the task that do not involve heuristic processes, and second, it is known that humans use such processes. In problem-solving programs of this sort, effective heuristics tend to be reinforced and used more frequently, while ineffective ones tend to be tried less often (Green 1963).

In the pioneering work of Daniel Kahneman and Amos Tversky (1972; Tversky and Kahneman 1971, 1973, 1974), the concept of heuristic use is contrasted with the hypothesis that humans are relatively accurate "intuitive statisticians" (Peterson and Beach 1967). On the contrary, Tversky and Kahneman argue, the processes that people use in making judgments about probabilities, frequencies, and likelihoods bear little resemblance to statistical principles. Their work demonstrates the use of heuristics like representativeness, availability, and anchoring and adjustment in judgmental contexts that highlight the difference between heuristic use and normative statistical practice. Robin Hogarth (1981), Detlof von Winterfeldt and Ward Edwards (1986), David Funder (1987), and others have claimed that the contemporary focus on the weaknesses of human cognition misrepresents reality and constitutes "a message of despair" (von Winterfeldt and Edwards 1986, 531). Jay Christensen-Szalanski and Lee Beach (1984) have argued that scientific papers that highlight cognitive inabilities are more frequently cited than papers that highlight abilities, thus providing more publicity for the weaknesses than for the strengths of human capability. We raise this issue because the sense in which we want to use the concept of a decision heuristic is the original sense in which the concept was used by Allen Newell and Herbert Simon (1963), Bert Green (1963), and others. We argue that certain social heuristics are often used as decision heuristics in circumstances in which other normative decision procedures are absent or in which their application, like theorem-proving algorithms, would be inefficient.

In contrast to the view that the use of heuristics leads to poor performance, there is good evidence in some contexts that simple heuristics can produce highly efficient and satisfactory results. We describe two well-known instances in which simple heuristics do as well or nearly as well as normative procedures. Our intent is to illustrate cases in which heuristic decision processes are impressive, not to argue that they are always so. The extent to which simple "rules of thumb" lead to performance decrements depends on the context in which they are used.

Dawes (1979) has argued that in fitting linear models to data, some types of nonoptimal linear models make predictions that are nearly as accurate as the normatively optimal model, that is, the model whose weights are selected to optimize the prediction criterion. One type of improper model that does exceedingly well is the so-called equal weight model—the one that simply weights all predictors equally. Such a model ignores information about which predictor variable is most highly correlated with the criterion and treats all predictors as if they were equally important. Dawes has shown that there is only a slight drop in predictive accuracy involved with using the simple equal weighting model in place of the optimal one. For instance, in predicting the grade point average (GPA) of graduate students at the University of Oregon and the University of Illinois, the ideal model correlated .69 with the actual GPA and the equal weight model correlated .60.

To move to a somewhat more social domain, Robert Axelrod (1984) reports on an ingenious competition in which he invited scientists to submit programmable strategies for playing the notorious prisoners' dilemma (PD) game. He conducted a round-robin tournament in which each program played with every other program. From each of these interactions, the score or total accumulated points of the two programs were recorded. A program's score for the tournament was simply the sum of its scores for all interactions. The surprising result of this tournament was that the simplest strategy submitted, Anatol Rapoport's tit-for-tat strategy, was the winner. This strategy always makes a cooperative first choice and then simply repeats the others' last choice on each subsequent trial. Tit-for-tat's success is all the more remarkable because it can never win more points than the program it is playing against. Its success is based on the fact that it encourages the other programs to be cooperative, and hence profitable for both. In a follow-up tournament held after the outcome of the first competition was publicized, tit-for-tat was again the winner, even though many programs were submitted to this second round that were explicitly designed to defeat tit-for-tat.

In this case, the simplest program of all was the best, a result that was not anticipated by the organizer of the competition. It did better than some very sophisticated programs that were designed to detect and exploit weaknesses in the other players. And it won by cooperating, which in the classical treatment of the PD game is the irrational choice. So tit-for-tat represents a case in which a simple decision heuristic, "start cooperatively, but then do unto the next other as the other did unto you on the last trial," emerged as the best of a collection of decision procedures.

In the first example, the equal weight model, it is possible to compare the success of the heuristics to uncontroversial normative models. It is also possible to specify exactly what information the heuristics is ignoring. In the case of tit-for-tat, there is less clarity about the normative solution. Indeed, no normative solution for the tournament has been offered. Many of the programs would have been normatively correct in some environments, under some assumptions, but in Axelrod's situation those assumptions were clearly not met. Despite the absence of a clear optimal solution, tit-for-tat was a genuine heuristic in that it used fewer lines of code and less information about the history of the interaction than any of the other programs.

Heuristics are rules. Some rules may be dependent on outcomes, and some may not depend on outcomes at all, like tit-for-tat, which is a simple imitative routine. Heuristics are also simple rules. We want to suggest that rule-based decisionmaking, especially when the rules are heuristics, is simpler than consequence-based decisionmaking. The individual engaged in "deep" consequentialist decisionmaking must process information about outcomes, uncertainties, and risks and combine this information with his or her preferences, risk attitudes, levels of aspiration, and willingness to tolerate uncertainty. Expected value maximization, for instance, entails the gathering of information about the available alternatives, the possible outcomes associated with the various alternatives, the likelihoods of the outcomes, and then the processing of these data in prescribed ways to select a choice.

Consequential decisionmaking, even in the simple trust context presented here, is subject to outcome-framing effects, since it is the outcomes that matter. As we have argued elsewhere (Messick and Kramer 1996), there are many ways to frame outcomes in interpersonal dilemmas. We have discussed *contextual frames* that permit you to redefine an outcome or its cause. In our first example, you could give the person on your step the money, "because ten dollars is nothing to me," thereby equating it to zero. We have also discussed temporal frames that allow you to embed the outcome in a temporal sequence (that may or may not have existence in reality). You withdraw from the race for your department's chair because "I would have come to hate the job anyway," forecasting an unverifiable outcome at some future time that justifies your decision to withdraw. If outcomes and consequences are what matters, then the ability to redefine, reframe, and reevaluate outcomes is crucial. A study by Terry Boles and David Messick (1995) attests to the power of this process. They show that, under the right circumstances, people can act as if it is better to have lost money with a wager than not to have lost money with the same wager. The power of frames has been acknowledged by March (1994, 15), who notes that this power creates an "active market for frames." When consequences matter, so do ways of framing the consequences.

When consequences matter less—Thorngate's (1980) heuristics use consequences but rely on them to a lesser degree—framing matters less; what does matter is grasping what the situation "calls for." There are always many rules that might be appropriate in a situation, and what is important from a rule-based account is the determination of the nature of the situation. March (1994, 58) proposes that, to the extent that rule-following is grounded in a logic of appropriateness, decisionmakers confront three interrelated questions. First, the question of *recognition,* which requires the decisionmakers to define what kind of a situation they confront. Second, the question of *identity,* which requires them to define what kind of a person they are in the situation. And third, the question of *rules,* which requires them to answer the question, "What does a person like me do in a situation like this?" March argues that answering such questions often entails systematic, complex reasoning. In other words, the decisionmaking process is mindful rather than mindless.

However, we would add that such questions are also answered fairly automatically in a comparatively "mindless" fashion, especially if the features of the situation that evoke them are familiar to us and seem routine (Cialdini 1993; Langer 1989). With our first illustration, if you define the situation as one of being accosted by a panhandler, then the rule evoked is your "panhandler rule." If you define the situation as a request for aid, your response is guided by your rule for helping strangers. If you see the stranger as subtly threatening you, your choice has a different texture.

How you process the situation has more to do with defining it than with considering the consequences. You may even have a default rule for ambiguity that guides you when a situation is ambiguous.

It is precisely a default heuristic of trusting, Toshio Yamagishi and Midori Yamagishi (1994) argue, that distinguishes Americans from Japanese. They point out that not trusting impedes the development of mutually rewarding relationships. Trusting strangers—what they term *general trust*—exposes the truster to risks, but it also permits exploration that may lead to highly rewarding exchanges. These authors point out that not trusting is associated with high opportunity costs in populations in which relationships vary in their value. Failing to trust is also failing to discover whether another is trustworthy and rewarding. Therefore, refusing to trust may appear rational within the context of a single interaction, but it may be globally irrational as a general rule when opportunity costs are high.

Thus, with Ralph the tree man, you may define his request as part of an economic transaction. What becomes important in this case are the rules that you consider appropriate for such transactions. If your experience is that payment for a job should be made when the job is completed, then you are unlikely to pay him up front. If your construal of the situation is that Ralph is asking your help in solving a problem he may have by waiting for your payment, your rules governing such situations are activated and you may be more willing to pay him. Again, the uncertainty is in the construal of the situation, and once that is achieved, even with the attendant uncertainty, the appropriate choice is obvious.

Rules or Consequences

There are at least three ways in which the account of a rule-based psychology of appropriateness differs from a consequentialist account. First, as we mentioned earlier, a consequentialist interpretation of the trust situation may reveal that your behavior depends on whether you believe the other to be trustworthy. However, there is no way that a consequentialist interpretation can account for the fact that your view of the other may depend on what you chose to do (Dawes 1979).

Second, outcome framing is crucial with consequentialist decisions. James Kunen (1994) provides an example in a debate about a proposed regulation that would have required equipping school buses with steel shields for the gas tanks (which are located directly under the steps and front door). It was agreed by all that the cost would come to about $1,000 per bus. Opponents of the regulation noted that the cost would be a total of $30 million, since there were 30,000 buses on the road. This seemed like a high cost. Proponents pointed out that since buses have a life expectancy of 10 years, the cost was only $100 per year per bus, or

56 cents per school day, or less than half a cent per pupil per ride. Framed this way, the cost seemed not only reasonable but trivial.

With rules, the question is whether or not a rule has been violated. This is a very different type of framing problem. We can illustrate one aspect of this type of framing by referring to the research reported by Messick and his colleagues Susanne Bloom, Janet Boldizar, and Charles Samuelson (1985). In this study, undergraduates were asked to write lists of behaviors, both their own and those of other people, that they considered either fair or unfair. We collected lists of four types of behaviors, "I-fair," "they-fair," "I-unfair," and "they-unfair." We then had a second group of undergraduates rate samples of these four types of behaviors for fairness. We discovered that the behaviors in the first person (I) received more positive (fairer) ratings than the third-person (they) items. We hypothesized that the difference was caused by the pronoun, either "I" or "they," that preceded the behavior, so we conducted a further experiment in which we switched the subjects of the expressions for half of the items and left the other half in the original form. So, for instance, some subjects rated the phrase "They steal things" while others rated the (switched) phrase "I steal things." We anticipated that the subject of the sentence would influence the rated fairness of the behaviors, but it had absolutely no effect at all. "I" acts were rated precisely like "they" acts with regard to fairness. (Frequency ratings depended markedly on the sentence subject, however, so students differentiated the sentences, just not with regard to their perceived fairness.) We took these results to mean that rule adherence or violation was evaluated more or less objectively, regardless of whether the actor was oneself or another. This is a very different pattern from that of evaluations of outcomes (Messick and Sentis 1979), in which large egocentric biases are typically found.

We concluded that rules or behaviors that are rule-relevant, like gossiping, cheating, or helping others, are relatively immune to egocentric framing. Rules, however, are verbal summaries of actions and principles. They are not the actions themselves. We hypothesized that the egocentric processes that do not influence the ratings of the verbal descriptions of behaviors influence the verbal mappings of nonverbal actions into descriptions. The biases, in other words, enter into the creation of the descriptions of reality. As one of our students told us, her roommate "steals" her food from the refrigerator while she "borrows" food from her roommate.

Karen Cates (1994) has documented that egocentric biases enter into the mapping of action into language. For her dissertation, she showed photographs depicting either positive, negative, or neutral actions to undergraduates and asked them to describe what was happening. Some of the students were told to imagine that the photograph depicted themselves, while other students were asked to imagine that the photos were of someone else. The first-person descriptions of the photos were rated as significantly more moral that the third-person descriptions. As with the study by Messick and his colleagues (1985), the ratings did not change when the pronouns were switched.

The point here is that framing disputes with rules or actions are disputes about how to describe the action, not about the evaluative valence of the outcomes. If what happened was cheating, betrayal, lying, or harming, it was ethically wrong. Rules force us to deal with the coding, classification, and categorization of behaviors, not outcomes.

The third way in which a rule-based account differs from a consequentialist account is that the latter account of why you decided not to pay Ralph might stress the risk of your money and your lack of data to forecast Ralph's reliability and honesty. But what of the account of why Ralph failed to do the work after he was paid? If the outcome is all that matters, or the feature of any situation that matters most, Ralph's behavior is predictable and sensible. He got the money and had no incentive to do the work. But this is not the way most of us would read the transaction. You would be admired for trusting Ralph (you might also be judged as naive or ingenuous), but Ralph would be condemned for having broken his word. Judgments would be made about his character and virtue. It would be the rule violation, the failure to keep his word, that triggered the emotional and moralistic responses. The way you deal with important outcomes may lead others to judge you to be foolish or clever, but the way you deal with social and ethical rules leads others to judge you as moral or immoral.

Shallow Trust

The three cases with which we began this chapter are atypical. Two of them deal with interactions with strangers, and the third deals with an unusual situation in which you and your friend have little experience. These are precisely the types of situations in which decision conflicts should be greatest. Shallow processing should occur maximally in situations that are familiar, commonplace, and frequent, with people you know and with whom you expect to have future contacts. These are scripted situations (Schank and Abelson 1977) in which behavior is habitual, well rehearsed, and automatic. These types of situations, like looking left before crossing the road, evoke fast, mindless, shallow responses that are usually appropriate. Such behavior is unremarkable because it is so banal, so undramatic. Do you count your change after a purchase? Do you check the bill at restaurants? Do you reweigh your prewrapped cheese to verify its weight or scrutinize the person who weighs your fish to make sure no thumbs are on the scale?

Sissela Bok (1978, 31) makes a strong claim for the importance of truthfulness as a sine qua non of beliefs in others' trustworthiness in her well-known principle of veracity. "Trust in some degree of veracity functions as a *foundation* of relations among human beings; when this trust shatters or wears away, institutions collapse." She goes on to note that although there are different forms of trust, the trust in the truthfulness of one's assertions has a primary status:

> [I can trust that] you will treat me fairly, that you will have my interests at heart, [and] that you will do me no harm. *But if I do not trust your word can I have genuine trust in the first three?* If there is no confidence in the truthfulness of others, is there any way to assess their fairness, their intentions to help or to harm. . . . Whatever matters to human beings, trust is the *atmosphere in which it thrives* (31, emphases added).

Individuals who recognize this point as a practical issue may decide to employ a "heuristic of veracity" across a wide range of situations, on the assumption that, on average, it is better to give people the benefit of the doubt and keep trust in others intact.

An excellent illustration of this view of trust is given by Brian Uzzi (1997). His account of a segment of the garment industry (women's better dress firms) in New York City provides a striking contrast between a purely economic, consequentialist model of producer relationships and markets and what he labels "embedded relationships": a network in which people come to know and trust each other, to make allowances for errors, and to look out for the interests of other parties in the market. As one interviewee put it, "It is hard to see for an outsider that you become friends with these people—business friends. You trust them and their work." Frequency of contact begets familiarity, trust, and trustworthiness. Uzzi points out that these same people also have dealings with others with whom they do not share this special relationship. Arms-length ties are also common, but they have a different flavor. Uzzi also notes that his interviewees discriminate like the Cs we discussed earlier. "The same individual simultaneously acted selfishly and cooperatively with different actors in their network." Trust is appropriate in one type of relationship and inappropriate in another.

Uzzi (1997) suggests that the embedded relationships he studied are characterized by three interrelated features: trust, fine-grained information transfer, and a mutual problem-solving orientation. All of these characteristics support a system in which people strive to do well and to help others to do well, who will in turn help them do well, and so on. To say that someone is "part of the family" is to use "family" in a metaphorical sense. Nevertheless, it signals the network of genetic relatedness to which kin selection refers. The phrase also implies that there are frequent interactions between the "members" and that they are aware of themselves as a group. These are precisely the conditions that support altruistic and trusting behavior, according to evolutionary theory. To see these conditions met in the garment industry is noteworthy, especially in New York, a city that has not always enjoyed a reputation for warmth and helpfulness (Latané and Darley 1970).

Another interesting example of such embedded (and emergent) trust is provided by Gary Fine and Lewis Holyfield (1996). They investigated the dynamics of collective trust development and maintenance in a most unusual organization—the Minnesota Mycological Society, an organization consisting of amateur mushroom aficionados. This organization provides an interesting setting in which to study the emergence of collective trust because of the costs of misplaced trust: eating a mushroom someone else in the organization has erroneously declared safe for consumption can lead to illness and even death. Additionally, because it is a voluntary organization, its very survival depends on the willingness to take others' motives, intentions, and competence on faith—if collective doubts about any of these issues are too great (trust in others is not sufficient), the organization will die since exit is virtually costless.

Within this interesting context, Fine and Holyfield identify three important mechanisms for the production and maintenance of collective trust: awarding trust, managing risk, and transforming trust. One way trust is created within this organization is to award trust to others even when confidence in them might be lacking. For example, there is considerable social pressure on novices to consume dishes prepared by other members at banquets—members consume these dishes because they are expected to, however anxious or cautious they may feel about doing so. The authors note that this is trust not only in the expertise of individuals but, more important, in a system of expertise. There is, as they put it rather bluntly, an *insistence* on trust. People act as if trust is in place, and if everyone does so, in a sense it is.

The insistence on and coercion of trust is organizationally adaptive, however, only if trustworthiness is in place. This brings into play the second stage: managing the risks for the group. This second and crucial element in the creation and maintenance of collective trust operates through the socialization of novices. Experts teach novices out of a sense of obligation. Fine and Holyfield characterize this kind of repayment for their own instruction in the art of identification and safe preparation of mushrooms as a form of generational justice. Novices, in turn, participate in the socialization because it helps them manage the risks of mushroom eating.

Fine and Holyfield (1996, 29) characterize the third and final stage as the *transformation of trust*: the organization is transformed from an object of trust to an arena of trusting interactions. Because the costs of misplaced trust are high, credibility is lost only once unless the mistake is reasonable. As a member acquires knowledge, they argue, trust changes:

"The basis of trust is transformed from organizational position to displayed competence. This change alters the role of the organization. At first, the organization is itself a validator, an object of trust; *later it becomes an arena in which trusting relations are enacted and organizational interaction serves as its own reward*" (29, emphasis added).

Embedded relationships of the sort described by Uzzi (1997) and Fine and Holyfield (1996) clearly allow for the emergence of "thick" forms of trust—trust characterized by dense social relations, relatively long temporal horizons, the anticipation of repeated interaction, and a positive utility for a good reputation. The trust associated with such relationships represents, in one sense, an overdetermined form of trust. We argue next that taken-for-grantedness and many of the other properties associated with shallow trust and morality can arise—perhaps somewhat surprisingly or counterintuitively—in organizations and social systems that might seem to provide only shallow relations and to support only a thin form of trust. These are the temporary groups and organizations described by Debra Meyerson, Karl Weick, and Roderick Kramer (1996). Temporary organizations have been defined as groups of diversely skilled people working together on complex tasks for limited durations. Examples of temporary groups and organizations include cockpit crews, presidential commissions, firefighting teams, theater and architectural groups, construction, auditing, and negotiating teams, juries, film crews, and election campaign organizations. The temporary group is an increasingly important form of organization, and one in which concerns about trust often are very salient.

As an organizational form, the temporary group turns traditional notions of organizing and trust upside down. These groups often work on tasks with a high degree of complexity, yet they lack the formal structures that facilitate coordination and control. They depend on an elaborate body of collective knowledge and diverse skills, yet individuals have little time to sort out who knows precisely what. They often entail high risk and high-stake outcomes, yet they seem to lack the normative structures and institutional safeguards that minimize the likelihood of things going wrong. Moreover, there is little time to engage in the usual forms of confidence-building activities that contribute to the development and maintenance of trust in more traditional, enduring forms of organization.

Temporary systems exhibit behavior that presupposes trust, yet traditional sources of trust—familiarity, shared experience, reciprocal disclosure, threats and deterrents, fulfilled promises, and demonstrations of nonexploitation of vulnerability—are not obvious in such systems. Temporary systems function as if trust were present, but their histories seem to preclude its development. In these respects, temporary groups challenge our conventional understandings regarding the necessary or sufficient conditions for the emergence of reciprocal trust.

The trust that unfolds in temporary systems can be portrayed as a unique form of collective perception and relating that is capable of managing issues of vulnerability, uncertainty, risk, and expectations. In temporary systems there is a premium on making do with whatever information, however limited, is available in advance of close monitoring so that interdependent work is initiated quickly. Swift judgments about trustworthiness cannot be avoided, since they enable people to act quickly in the face of uncertainty. People have to make consequential presumptions: no trust, no performance. It is as basic as that.

What is often distinctive about temporary systems is that they form among people who represent specialties, and the relating in a temporary system is between *roles* as much as between people. The expectation of reciprocal competent role enactment provides a basis for interdependent decisionmakers to act as if trust were present. Trust can develop swiftly because the expectations invoked most quickly tend to be general, task-based, plausible, easy to confirm, and stable.

In a temporary organization, people come together quickly and act as if trust were in place. Then, because trust behaviors are enacted without hesitation, reciprocally and collectively, they provide what Robert Cialdini (1993) aptly characterizes as social proof that a particular interpretation of reality is correct—by observing others acting in a trustworthy fashion, individuals can infer that their own trust is neither foolish nor naive.

We should note that the sort of trust found in temporary groups is not altogether different from the sort of thick trust associated with embedded relationships. For example, it is not true that there is no history in a temporary organization. The founder or leader of the group presumably has knowledge of the individual members. He or she certifies their trustworthiness, and thus trust is delegated. Delegation of this sort provides an important basis for shallow thinking in trust situations. For example, if we have great confidence in the ability of the police to keep our neighborhoods safe, we might infer that the man knocking on our door is not a criminal or suspicious character because if he were he would have been picked up by a patrol car.

In the diverse systems described by Uzzi (1997), Fine and Holyfield (1996), and Meyerson and her colleagues (1996), trust is quick, automatic, taken for granted, and shallow. Just as evil can result from mindless banality (Arendt 1963), so can goodness.

References

Adams, J. Stacey. 1965. "Inequity in Social Exchange." In *Advances in Experimental Social Psychology*, edited by Leonard Berkowitz, vol. 2. New York: Academic Press.

American Psychologist. 1976. Responses to Donald Campbell (1975), 31: 341–80.

Arendt, Hannah. 1963. *Eichmann in Jerusalem: A Report on the Banality of Evil.* New York: Viking.

Axelrod, Robert. 1984. *The Evolution of Cooperation.* New York: Basic Books.

Bok, Sissela. 1978. *Lying: Moral Choice in Public and Private Life.* New York: Vintage.

Boles, Terry L., and David M. Messick. 1995. "A Reverse Outcome Bias: The Influence of Multiple Reference Points on the Evaluation of Outcomes and Decisions." *Organizational Behavior and Human Decision Processes* 61(3): 262–75.

Brewer, Marilynn B. 1981. "Ethnocentrism and Its Role in Interpersonal Trust." In *Scientific Inquiry in the Social Sciences: A Volume in Honor of Donald T. Campbell,* edited by Marilynn B. Brewer and Barry E. Collins. San Francisco: Jossey-Bass.

Brockner, Joel, and P. Siegel. 1996. "Understanding the Interaction Between Procedural and Distributive Justice." In *Trust in Organizations,* edited by Roderick M. Kramer and Tom R. Tyler. Thousand Oaks, Calif.: Sage Publications.

Burt, Ronald S., and Marc Knez. 1996. "Kinds of Third-Party Effects on Trust." *Rationality and Society* 7(3): 255–92.

Campbell, Donald T. 1975. "On the Conflict Between Biological and Social Evolution and Between Psychology and Moral Tradition." *American Psychologist* 30: 1103–26.

Cates, Karen L. 1994. "Language and Moral Evaluation: The Role of Frequency Quantifiers, Verbs, and Other Linguistic Choices in Egocentric Morality Bias." Ph.D. diss., Northwestern University.

Christensen-Szalanski, Jay J., and Lee R. Beach. 1984. "The Citation Bias: Fad and Fashion in the Judgment and Decision Literature." *American Psychologist* 39: 75–78.

Cialdini, Robert B. 1993. *Influence: Science and Practice.* 3rd ed. New York: HarperCollins.

Crawford, Charles, Martin Smith, and Dennis Krebs. 1987. *Sociobiology and Psychology: Ideas, Issues and Applications.* Hillsdale, N.J.: Erlbaum.

Dawes, Robyn M. 1979. "The Robust Beauty of Improper Linear Models." *American Psychologist* 34: 571–82.

Dawes, Robyn M., Jeanne MacTavish, and Hariet Shaklee. 1977. "Behavior, Communication, and Assumptions About Other People's Behavior in a Commons Dilemma Situation." *Journal of Personality and Social Psychology* 35: 1–11.

Dawkins, Richard. 1976. *The Selfish Gene.* New York: Oxford University Press.

Eagly, Alice H., and Shelley Chaiken. 1993. *The Psychology of Attitudes.* Fort Worth, Tex.: Harcourt Brace Jovanovich.

Fine, Gary, and Lewis Holyfield. 1996. "Secrecy, Trust, and Dangerous Leisure: Generating Group Cohesion in Voluntary Organizations." *Social Psychology Quarterly* 59(1): 22–38.

Funder, David C. 1987. "Errors and Mistakes: Evaluating the Accuracy of Social Judgment." *Psychological Bulletin* 101: 75–91.

Green, Bert F. 1963. *Digital Computers in Research.* New York: McGraw-Hill.

Hogarth, Robin M. 1981. "Beyond Discrete Biases: Functional and Dysfunctional Aspects of Judgmental Heuristics." *Psychological Bulletin* 90: 197–217.

Hosmer, LaRue T. 1995. "Trust: The Connecting Link Between Organizational Theory and Ethics." *Academy of Management Review* 20(2): 379–400.

Jones, Edward E., and Richard E. Nisbett. 1971. "The Actor and the Observer: Divergent Perceptions of the Causes of Behavior." In *Attribution: Perceiving the*

Causes of Behavior, edited by Edward E. Jones et al. Morristown, N.J.: General Learning Press.

Kahneman, Daniel, and Amos Tversky. 1972. "Subjective Probability: A Judgment of Representativeness." *Cognitive Psychology* 3: 430–54.

Kipnis, David. 1996. "Trust and Technology." In *Trust in Organizations: Frontiers of Theory and Research,* edited by Roderick M. Kramer and Tom R. Tyler. Thousand Oaks, Calif.: Sage Publications.

Kramer, Roderick M. 1991. "Intergroup Relations and Organizational Dilemmas: The Role of Categorization Processes." In *Research in Organizational Behavior,* edited by Larry L. Cummings and Barry M. Staw, vol. 13. Greenwich, Conn.: JAI Press.

———. 1996. "Divergent Realities and Convergent Disappointments in the Hierarchic Relation: The Intuitive Auditor at Work." In *Trust in Organizations: Frontiers of Theory and Research,* edited by Roderick M. Kramer and Tom R. Tyler. Thousand Oaks, Calif.: Sage Publications.

Kramer, Roderick M., Marilynn B. Brewer, and Benjamin A. Hanna. 1996. "Collective Trust and Collective Action." In *Trust in Organizations: Frontiers of Theory and Research,* edited by Roderick M. Kramer and Tom R. Tyler. Thousand Oaks, Calif.: Sage Publications.

Krebs, Dennis L. 1975. "Empathy and Altruism." *Journal of Personality and Social Psychology* 32: 1134–46.

Kreps, David M. 1990. "Corporate Culture and Economic Theory." In *Perspectives on Positive Political Economy,* edited by John Alt and Karl Shepsle. New York: Cambridge University Press.

Kunen, James S. 1994. *Reckless Disregard: Corporate Greed, Government Indifference, and the Kentucky School Bus Crash.* New York: Simon & Schuster.

Langer, Ellen J. 1989. *Mindfulness.* Reading, Mass.: Addison-Wesley.

Latané, Bibb, and John M. Darley. 1970. *The Unresponsive Bystander: Why Doesn't He Help?* New York: Appleton-Century-Crofts.

Lind, E. Allen, and Tom R. Tyler. 1988. *The Social Psychology of Procedural Justice.* New York: Plenum.

March, James G. 1994. *A Primer on Decision Making.* New York: Free Press.

March, James G., and Herbert A. Simon. 1958. *Organizations.* New York: Wiley.

Messé, Larry A., and John M. Sivacek. 1979. "Predictions of Others' Responses in a Mixed Motive Game." *Journal of Personality and Social Psychology* 37: 602–7.

Messick, David M. 1976. "Comment." *American Psychologist* 31: 366–69.

———. 1991. "On the Evolution of Group-Based Altruism." In *Games Equilibrium Models,* edited by Reinhard Selten, vol. 1. Frankfurt: Springer Verlag.

Messick, David M., Susanne Bloom, Janet P. Boldizar, and Charles D. Samuelson. 1985. "Why We Are Fairer Than Others." *Journal of Experimental Social Psychology* 21: 480–500.

Messick, David M., and Roderick M. Kramer. 1996. "Ethical Cognition and the Framing of Organizational Dilemmas." In *Codes of Conduct: Behavioral Research into Business Ethics,* edited by David M. Messick and Ann E. Tenbrunsel. New York: Russell Sage Foundation.

Messick, David M., and Keith P. Sentis. 1979. Fairness and Preferences. *Journal of Experimental Social Psychology* 15: 418–34.

Messick, David M., and John P. van de Geer. 1981. "A Reversal Paradox." *Psychological Bulletin* 90: 582–93.

Messick, David M., Henk Wilke, Marilynn B. Brewer, Roderick M. Kramer, Patricia E. Zemke, and Layton Lui. 1983. "Individual Adaptations and Structural Change as Solutions to Social Dilemmas." *Journal of Personality and Social Psychology* 44: 294–309.

Meyerson, Debra, Karl E. Weick, and Roderick M. Kramer. 1996. "Swift Trust and Temporary Groups." In *Trust in Organizations: Frontiers of Theory and Research*, edited by Roderick M. Kramer and Tom R. Tyler. Thousand Oaks, Calif.: Sage Publications.

Murnighan, J. Keith, and Madan M. Pillutla. 1995. "Fairness Versus Self-interest." In *Negotiation as a Social Process*, edited by Roderick M. Kramer and David M. Messick. Thousand Oaks, Calif.: Sage Publications.

Newell, Allen, and Herbert A. Simon. 1963. "Computers in Psychology." In *Handbook of Mathematical Psychology*, edited by R. Duncan Luce, Robert R. Bush, and Eugene Galanter, vol. 1. New York: Wiley.

Peterson, Cameron R., and Lee R. Beach. 1967. "Man as an Intuitive Statistician." *Psychological Bulletin* 68: 29–46.

Polya, George. 1945. *How to Solve It*. Princeton, N.J.: Princeton University Press.

Porter, Richard H. 1987. "Kin Recognition: Functions and Mediating Mechanisms." In *Sociobiology and Psychology: Ideas, Issues and Applications*, edited by Charles Crawford, Martin Smith, and Dennis Krebs. Hillsdale, N.J.: Erlbaum.

Schank, Roger C., and Robert P. Abelson. 1977. *Scripts, Plans, Goals, and Understanding: An Inquiry into Human Knowledge Structures*. Hillsdale, N.J.: Erlbaum.

Sherman, Paul W. 1977. "Nepotism and the Evolution of Alarm Calls." *Science* 197: 1246–53.

Simon, Herbert A. 1957. *Models of Man*. New York: Wiley.

Snijders, Chris. 1996. *Trust and Commitments*. Amsterdam: Thesis Publishers.

Staub, Ernest. 1978. *Positive Social Behavior and Morality*. Vol. 1. Orlando, Fla.: Academic Press.

Thorngate, Warren. 1980. "Efficient Decision Heuristics." *Behavioral Science* 25: 219–25.

Trivers, Robert. 1971. "The Evolution of Reciprocal Altruism." *Quarterly Review of Biology* 46: 35–57.

Tversky, Amos, and Daniel Kahneman. 1971. "The Belief in the 'Law of Small Numbers.'" *Psychological Bulletin* 76: 105–10.

———. 1973. "Availability: A Heuristic for Judging Frequency and Probability." *Cognitive Psychology* 5: 207–32.

———. 1974. "Judgment Under Uncertainty: Heuristics and Biases." *Science* 185: 1124–35.

Uzzi, Brian. 1997. "Social Structure and Competition in Interfirm Networks: The Paradox of Embeddedness." *Administrative Science Quarterly* 42(1): 35–67.

Von Winterfeldt, Detlof, and Ward Edwards. 1986. *Decision Analysis and Behavioral Research*. Cambridge: Cambridge University Press.

Wilson, James Q. 1993. *The Moral Sense*. New York: Free Press.

Wilson, David S. 1980. *The Selection of Populations and Communities*. Menlo Park, Calif.: Benjamin Cummings.

Yamagishi, Toshio, and Midori Yamagishi. 1994. "Trust and Commitment in the United States and Japan." *Motivation and Emotion* 18(2): 129–6.

PART II

TRUST: SOCIAL BASES AND SOCIAL CONSEQUENCES

Chapter 4

Trust as a Form of Social Intelligence

TOSHIO YAMAGISHI

O NE OF THE strongest expressions of generalized distrust—that is, distrust of human nature in general—can be found in the Japanese proverb "It's best to regard everyone as a thief" (hito wo mitara dorobo to omoe). An expression of the other extreme, generalized trust, can also be found in another Japanese proverb, "You will never meet a devil as you walk through the world" (wataru seken ni oni ha nai). In nine experiments, I asked 539 students in four Japanese colleges about these proverbs in postexperimental questionnaires and found that the majority considered those who believe the former proverb to be smarter (65.7 percent versus 34.3 percent), less gullible (86.2 percent versus 13.8 percent), and more likely to be successful in life (53.9 percent versus 46.1 percent) than those who believe the latter proverb; they also indicated that belief in this proverb is more common among successful entrepreneurs (65.4 percent versus 34.6 percent). The majority of those respondents apparently believed that distrusters are smarter, less gullible, more successful, and more likely to be one of the elite than are generalized trusters. In short, they believed that distrust is a sign of social shrewdness and trust reflects credulousness and a lack of social shrewdness.

The results of experimental studies presented later in this chapter, however, provide evidence contrary to this popular belief and present a picture that high trusters are shrewder in potentially risky social interactions than distrusters. Based on these findings, I argue that distrust and lack of social intelligence constitute a vicious cycle. On the one hand, generalized distrust prevents people from engaging in further social interactions. In Russell Hardin's (1992, 517) words, "Because I have such low expectations, I am willing to test very few interactions." This unwillingness of distrusters, as "commonsense Bayesians" (Hardin 1992), to engage in social interactions deters distrusters from correcting their depressed level of trust. At the same time their unwillingness to engage in social interactions, especially risky but potentially fruitful interactions, prevents them from improving their social intelligence. Their lack of social intelligence or social shrewdness, in turn, makes them vulnerable in such risky but potentially fruitful interactions. This vulnerability has two consequences. First, their lack of social intelligence makes them more gullible when they do in fact engage in such interactions. They fail more often than they succeed in such interactions, and they learn to distrust others even more. Second, realizing their vulnerability, they avoid engaging in such interactions. It seems that either way they cannot win. By engaging in such social interactions, they learn to distrust. By not engaging in such social interactions, they lose opportunities to learn social shrewdness and improve their social intelligence or their ability to understand their own and other people's internal states and to use that understanding in social relations. Before further elaborating on this argument, let me first present relevant research findings.

Trust and Gullibility

Does trust mean gullibility? Are trustful people naive and credulous? As shown in the questionnaire results, many respondents thought that trustful people are naive and credulous, and thus gullible. Some of the psychologists working on trust also adopt this view. According to Barry Schlenker, Bob Helm, and James Tedeschi (1973, 419), for example, "interpersonal trust may be defined as a reliance upon information received from another person about uncertain environmental states and their accompanying outcomes in a risky situation." There is some experimental evidence supporting this view. For example, John Garske (1975) finds that high trusters, as measured with Julien Rotter's (1967) Interpersonal Trust Scale (ITS), have a less complex cognitive structure (that is, a less differentiated network of constructs for perceiving others) than low trusters. Based on this finding, he infers (1975, 618) that high trusters are less prudent and more gullible than low trusters; "Generalized expectancies for interpersonal trust reduce the perceived threat posed by negative others, and concomitantly lessen the necessity for discriminative vigilance in the cognitive sphere. Conversely, low trust expectancies appear to sensitize the observer to potential harmful effects." Garske (1976) bolsters this position with a finding of a negative correlation between the ITS score and intelligence and abstract thinking, as measured by a factor of Form A of Cattell's 16 PF;

that is, he finds that high trusters are less capable of abstract thinking than low trusters. Michael Gurtman and Clifford Lion (1982) have compared high and low trusters (as measured with the ITS) on the time they need to recognize adjectives displayed on a tachistoscope and find that low trusters are quicker than high trusters in recognizing adjectives descriptive of lack of trustworthiness. Based on this finding, they argue that high trusters are less vigilant at detecting signals of trustworthiness and thus are more gullible than low trusters. Peter Brann and Margaret Foddy (1988) find that compared to low trusters, high trusters tend to stay more often in a group infested by defectors and thus put themselves in a vulnerable position. These findings are consistent with the popular belief that trust is characteristic of a naive and simple personality.

We should note, however, that these results do not provide direct support for the popular belief that trust is the same as gullibility. For example, the measure of the complexity of the cognitive structure used by Garske (1975)—according to which people who evaluate a target person similarly on different personality traits have a low level of cognitive complexity—may be irrelevant to social interactions and thus may have nothing to do with gullibility. The correlation between ITS score and low intelligence and lack of abstract thinking found by Garske (1976) is significant but far from conclusive ($r = .15$). Furthermore, there is no logical or empirical basis for expecting that concrete rather than abstract thinking makes a person gullible in risky social situations. Similarly, it is an untapped empirical question whether there is a correlation between the speed with which a subject finds adjectives displayed on a tachistoscope descriptive of a lack of trustworthiness and that person's general alertness in actual social interactions. The findings that have been used as evidence supporting the popular image of high trusters as naive, credulous, and gullible individuals are thus mostly indirect at best and often irrelevant to the claim.

Whether trust means gullibility or not, of course, depends on the definition of each term. If trust is defined as "a reliance upon information received from another person about uncertain environmental states and their accompanying outcomes in a risky situation" (Schlenker, Helm, and Tedeschi 1973, 419), and gullibility as "believing another person when there [is] some clear-cut evidence that the person should not be believed" (Rotter 1980, 4), then trust is indeed the same as gullibility. That is, if we define trust as indiscriminate credulousness, it is the equivalent of naïveté and gullibility. However, indiscriminate credulousness is not the definition of trust adopted for the ITS used in the studies discussed here. Rotter (1980, 4) claims that the Interpersonal Trust Scale he developed, the most commonly used measure of trust, measures *general trust*, not indiscriminate credulousness; general trust is "believing communications in the absence of clear or strong reasons for not believing (that is, in ambiguous situations)." If we adopt this definition of general trust as a *default expectation* of the trustworthiness of others (Yamagishi 1998; Yamagishi, Kikuchi, and Kosugi 1999), general trust and gullibility are at least logically independent of each other. People who are high on general trust (high trusters) assume that other people are trustworthy until evidence is provided indicating otherwise. Gullible people are insensitive to such evidence of the untrustworthiness of interaction partners. How carefully one pays attention to such information is at least logically independent of whether one expects others to be trustworthy in the absence of relevant information. In this chapter I call those with a high level of default expectations that people are generally trustworthy "high trusters," and those who expect, without any evidence, that people are generally untrustworthy "distrusters." People who "regard everyone as a thief" are distrusters in this sense. High trusters would not regard everyone as a thief but may be watching carefully for real thiefs.

The series of empirical studies cited by Rotter (1980) provides support for his claim that trust and gullibility are independent. For example, trust as measured by his ITS has been shown to be independent of scholastic aptitude scores in several studies (Rotter 1980) and independent of assessments of gullibility by members of the same fraternity or sorority (Rotter 1967). According to J. D. Geller (1966), high trusters exhibit more trustful behavior when there is no reason to be suspicious. However, with a good reason to be suspicious, high trusters are no more trustful than low trusters. J. H. Hamsher Jr. (1968) and T. L. Wrights (1972) find that with an experience of being deceived in a game, high trusters are no more trustful of a game partner than low trusters. These and other studies cited in Rotter (1980) provide evidence that high trusters are not necessarily indiscriminately credulous or gullible.

The Vicious Cycle of Distrust and Lack of Social Intelligence

As pointed out by Rotter (1980), trust and gullibility are logically independent. On the other hand, their logical independence does not preclude the existence of causal relationships between them; one type of cognitive activities may or may not affect the other. One possible causal relationship of central interest to this chapter is in the opposite direction to the common belief that high trusters are less socially intelligent than distrusters. In fact, socially oblivious and gullible people—those who do not pay proper attention to signs of untrustworthiness—come to regard everyone as a thief because they often become victims of the "thieves."

Generalized distrust can thus be a *learned defense strategy* for gullible people who cannot protect themselves properly in risky social situations. They can avoid becoming victims in such situations by indiscriminately regarding everyone as a "thief" and choosing not to enter into these risky interactions. The best strategy for such gullible people is either social isolation or staying in established relationships with commitment partners; developing generalized distrust based on the experience of victimization ensures that they will adopt this defense strategy in the social jungle.

This defense strategy, however, is not recommended to everyone, since using it carries a cost. Generalized distrust provides protection because it leads people into social isolation or into commitment relationships with a particular partner. The cost of doing so, however, is an opportunity cost. Those who isolate themselves or limit their relations to a few commitment partners give up opportunities that may exist outside this sphere. Exploring such opportunities may be risky; for gullible people, paying the opportunity cost seems to be a better choice than setting off on such explorations and then being victimized. However, generalized distrust is not a gainful strategy for anyone who is reasonably skilled at detecting signs of untrustworthiness in risky but potentially lucrative social interactions. For socially intelligent people, developing a willingness to enter into these social interactions is a better alternative than isolating themselves. Moreover, experiences of success in such social interactions, despite some bad experiences, helps them to develop generalized trust. With generalized trust, they become more willing to enter into such interactions.

It should also be noted that distrust breeds further distrust because social isolation prevents distrusters from improving their social intelligence and skills in detecting risks in social interactions. There is a mutually reinforcing relationship between generalized distrust and gullibility or lack of social intelligence. Lack of social intelligence makes people victims, and generalized distrust thus develops even further. Generalized distrust prevents people from entering into social interactions, and thus they miss opportunities to develop the social intelligence that would make them less vulnerable.

The relationship between generalized trust and social intelligence, though mutually reinforcing in some particulars, may not be strongly so. First of all, it is unclear whether generalized trust is based on direct experience of successful social interactions. People with a certain level of social intelligence are not as likely to be exploited as less socially intelligent people and thus are not as likely to develop generalized distrust. On the other hand, they are more likely to engage in risky social interactions. They may be less likely to be exploited in each interaction than less socially intelligent people, but having more interactions, they may have more experiences of victimization in total. It is thus not as certain as in the case of distrust that experiences breed further trust. Development of generalized trust may require more conscious efforts, such as using cognitive resources (attention, memory) to develop social intelligence. This would be especially worthwhile for those who face a social environment in which opportunity costs for staying in established commitment relations are high. Those in such an environment need to learn, first, not to be discouraged by isolated incidents of victimization; they need to learn to focus on the gains of successful interactions rather than on a few negative experiences. Distrust breeds on its own, but generalized trust is available only to those who make a conscious effort to develop such a cognitive style as well as the social intelligence to detect risks in social interactions.

Trust and Education

This argument for the causal relationship between distrust and lack of social intelligence (and to some degree between trust and social intelligence) predicts a positive relationship between generalized trust and social intelligence, which I define as the ability to detect and process signs of risks in social interactions. Although social intelligence has been distinguished from other types of intelligence since the early days of intelligence research, it has not been the major focus of research in intelligence studies until recently. For example, Edward L. Thorndike argued that social intelligence—or the ability to understand self and others and to use such understandings in interacting with others—is distinct from both abstract intelligence (the ability to manipulate language or numbers) and concrete or practical intelligence (the ability to handle things physically). After the criticism of Lee Joseph Cronbach and others that social intelligence had never been defined precisely or measured properly even after fifty years, research on social intelligence stagnated for some time.

Recently, however, research on social intelligence has begun once again to attract the attention of many researchers. For example, Howard Gardner (1983) has proposed *multiple intelligences theory,* which argues that intelligence is divided into several aspects: linguistic, logical-mathematical, spatial, musical, body-kinesthetic, and personal. According to this theory, the type of intelligence valued in a particular culture as "intelligence" depends on what is necessary for adaptation within that culture. Gardner's "personal intelligence" is the ability to understand oneself and others, and thus it can be considered social intelligence in the context of this chapter. Robert L. Sternberg (1988) takes the argument even further: the intelligence needed in certain environments is neither the academic problem-solving skill that is measured by the IQ test nor the creative intelligence to handle new problems adaptively, but the intelligence involved in treating oneself and others successfully within everyday social relations. The "emotional intelligence" proposed by Daniel Goleman (1995)—the ability to control emotion, to understand other people, and to make social relations smooth—is considered social intelligence in the broader sense. Here I would draw the reader's attention to the possibility that the findings presented in this chapter—that high trusters are more sensitive than low trusters to information suggesting untrustworthiness and can judge trustworthiness more accurately—may be interpreted as an indication that high trusters are more clever and more socially intelligent than low trusters. Of course, being sensitive to information suggesting untrustworthiness, or having the ability to use such information to discern trustworthiness in untrustworthy people, is only one part of social intelligence, which, more generally, is the ability to manage social relations in order to achieve one's own goal. But this ability is at least an important part of social intelligence.

Although there is no firm basis on which to claim that formal education is positively related to the type of social intelligence discussed here, a positive relationship between level of formal education and generalized trust or distrust would provide intuitively convincing evidence against the popular belief that high trusters are naive and gullible. Figure 4.1 indicates the relationship between number of years in school and the proportion of respondents answering "most people can be trusted" to the GSS item, "Generally speaking, would you say that most people can be trusted or that you can't be too careful in dealing with people?" The figure is based on data for 1984 to 1993. It clearly indicates that the proportion of generalized distrusters (operationalized as those who believe they cannot be too careful in dealing with people) declines with formal education. Interestingly, there are two sudden drops in the trust response, one between eleven and twelve years of education, and the second between fifteen and sixteen years. The first drop indicates that high school graduates are more trustful than high school dropouts, and the second points to a similar difference between college graduates and college dropouts. A similar relationship between education and trust is also observed in responses to another GSS item, "Would you say that most of the time people try to be helpful, or that they are mostly looking out for themselves?" Although these results may simply reflect the differences in the social environments in which respondents were raised, the relationship between the relative standings of colleges and students' average level of trust, as reported in Yamagishi (1999), provides strong evidence against this interpretation.

Figure 4.2 shows the relationship between the relative standing (*hensachi*) of the college and the average level of general trust among the students of the college. The average trust score is not the average of raw scores; rather, it is the deviation from the base college after controlling for the proportion of female students. The sample included 2,790 students from 14 colleges, including two junior colleges. The correlation

Figure 4.1   Proportion of "Most People Can Be Trusted" Responses

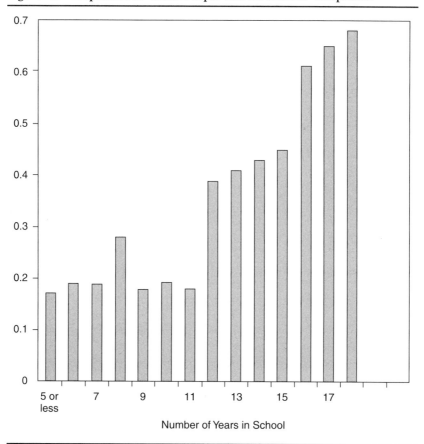

Number of Years in School

Source: Author's compilation.
Note: Responses to the GSS question, "Generally speaking, would you say that most people can be trusted or that you can't be too careful in dealing with people?"

between the relative standing of the college and the average trust score was 0.68 (p < .05). The correlation shows that the students at elite colleges are high trusters compared to students at low-ranking colleges. This finding is contrary to the popular belief that students in elite colleges are narrow-minded egoists. Furthermore, figure 4.3 shows that the relative standing of the college is negatively correlated with the students' average score on the Thief Scale, r = −.71. The correlation indicates that students at low-ranking colleges believe the proverb "It's best to regard everyone as a thief" more than do students at elite colleges.

The relationship between the relative standing of the college and the students' average trust level shown in figures 4.2 and 4.3 is consistent

**Figure 4.2   The Relationship Between the Relative Standing of Twelve
Colleges and the Average Trust Scores of Their Students**

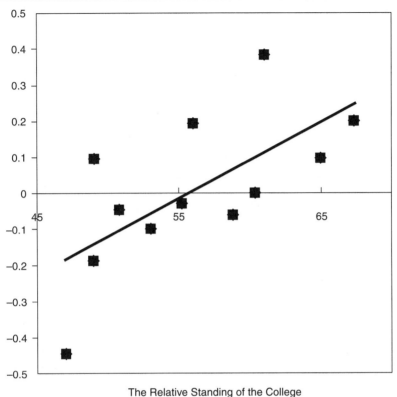

The Relative Standing of the College

Source: Author's compilation.

with the relationship between the level of education and the level of general trust shown in figure 4.1. It is possible that students at elite colleges are mostly from well-to-do families who have not experienced the miseries of life. Since they have not experienced the consequences of nasty social encounters, perhaps they naively believe in human benevolence. In contrast, students at low-ranking colleges tend to come from less affluent families. Furthermore, since they did not do as well in high school or elementary school, they may have had bad experiences at school. They may not believe in human benevolence because they have already had some miserable experiences. This seemingly convincing explanation, however, does not hold up under empirical testing, since the correlations do not exist among college freshmen. The correlation between relative standing of the college and the average trust score is 0.07

**Figure 4.3   The Relationship Between the Relative Standing of Twelve
Colleges and the Average "Thief Scale" Scores of Their Students**

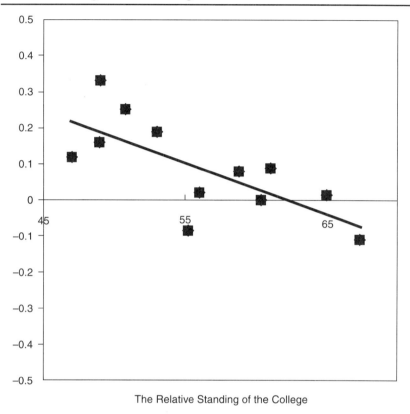

The Relative Standing of the College

Source: Author's compilation.

among freshmen. The correlation with the Thief Scale score is –.22 among freshmen. These low correlation coefficients directly contradict the alternative explanation, which would predict much stronger, not weaker, correlations among freshmen. The correlations emerge while students are at college. Higher education makes students of elite colleges high trusters.

Responses to Positive and Negative Information

The first of the series of experiments that my colleagues and I conducted on the relationship between trust and social intelligence is Kosugi and Yamagishi (1998). We investigated how high trusters and low trusters respond to information that may reveal the trustworthiness or untrustworthiness of a target person. The experiment used vignettes rather than observing actual behavior in the laboratory. Respondents were asked to imagine the situation described in a handout and to indicate what they would think in such a situation. The booklet distributed to the respondents contained fifteen scenarios. Each scenario described a situation in which a target person might betray other people's trust and behave selfishly. For example, a person who had stayed at a hotel in a foreign country for a week was charged for only one night as he checked out. He was paying cash, and there was no possibility that the hotel clerks would be able to discover his home address or his next destination. Respondents were shown scenarios such as this and asked whether the person would act in a trustworthy manner (for example, would the guest tell the hotel cashier that he had stayed for a week?) by indicating the probability of his or her behaving in such a manner. The question being examined was whether estimations of the target person's trustworthiness would be different between high trusters, who tend to trust others in general, and low trusters, who tend not to trust others. The respondents were divided into high and low trusters according to their scores on the six-item general trust scale developed by Yamagishi and Yamagishi (1994)[1] and included in the postexperimental questionnaire.

To aid in their assessments of the target person's trustworthiness, we gave respondents information about that person as well as information about the situation. In some scenarios one or two pieces of information were provided that suggested whether the target person was trustworthy. For example, in some scenarios the respondent was told that the target person had picked up trash on the street and taken it to a garbage can (positive information). In other scenarios the respondent was told that the target person had cut into a waiting line (negative information). The purpose of the experiment was to see how such information would affect the respondent's estimation of the trustworthiness of the target person, and to see whether high and low trusters responded differently to such information. Each respondent made an estimation of the target person in each of the fifteen scenarios, and these scenarios were randomly combined with five information conditions: no information about the target person; one piece of positive information; two pieces of positive information; one piece of negative information; or two pieces of negative information. The assignment of information pieces to particular scenarios in each information condition was also random.

Figure 4.4 shows two graphs of how estimation of the target person's trustworthiness changed as positive information was provided and as negative information was provided. The left margin of each graph indicates the mean probability estimation by high or low trusters that the target person would act in a trustworthy manner when no information about the target person was provided. When no information was provided about the target person, high trusters thought that the target person

**Figure 4.4   The Effect of Positive or Negative Information on High and
Low Trusters' Estimation of Trustworthiness**

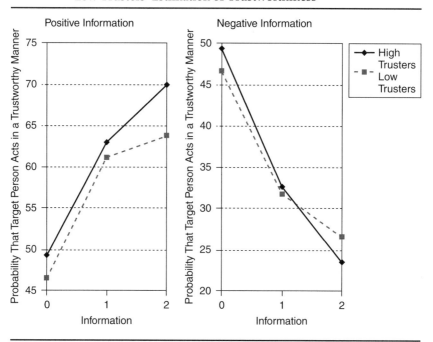

Source: Kosugi and Yamagishi (1998).

would act in a trustworthy manner to a greater extent than did low
trusters, and the difference was statistically significant. This means that
the general trust scale used to classify the respondents reflected fairly
well the degree of their general trust, that is, the extent to which they
thought that an unspecified partner would act in a trustworthy manner.

Having thus demonstrated the validity of the general trust scale, we
investigated the differences between high trusters and low trusters in
their sensitivity to information that might reveal trustworthiness or a
lack of it (positive or negative information). It is generally believed that
low trusters, who tend not to trust the benevolence of others, are more
sensitive to negative information than high trusters, who tend to trust
others, whereas high trusters are more sensitive to positive information
than low trusters. Low trusters who are always suspicious of others
would confidently deem the target person to be untrustworthy. Conversely, high trusters, with only little positive evidence, would believe
that the target person is trustworthy.

Do the experimental results support this expectation based on our
common sense? First, figure 4.4 shows that both high trusters and low

trusters were more likely to assess the target person as acting in a trust-worthy manner when positive information was provided. The differ-ence between high and low trusters in their estimation of the target person's trustworthiness especially increased when two pieces of pos-itive information were provided. As expected, high trusters rapidly raised their estimation of the target person's trustworthiness when in-formation revealing the target person's potential goodness was pro-vided, while low trusters' estimation did not rise so quickly. However, this differential sensitivity to positive information between high and low trusters was not statistically significant.

What happened when negative information was provided? Figure 4.4 shows that both high and low trusters reduced their estimation of the tar-get person's trustworthiness when negative information was provided. It further shows a difference between high and low trusters in how rapidly their estimation decreased. Contrary to the commonsense expectation de-scribed earlier, high trusters responded more quickly to negative infor-mation than did low trusters, and the differential sensitivity to negative information was statistically significant. Compared to low trusters, high trusters responded more sensitively to either positive or negative infor-mation. More generally, high trusters were more attentive or cautious and more sensitive to information revealing potential trustworthiness or the lack of it in other people than were low trusters.

This experiment was replicated using almost the same procedure as in the first experiment. There were only a few differences. For example, the maximum number of information pieces was increased from two to three. The number of scenarios was increased from fifteen to sixteen. The number of respondents (75) was smaller (there had been 257 in the first experiment). The second experiment largely replicated the findings from the first experiment, especially the most significant finding that high trusters were more sensitive than low trusters to negative information and lowered their estimation of the target person's trustworthiness more rapidly. That is, when negative information about the target per-son was provided, high trusters reduced their estimation of his or her trustworthiness more rapidly than did low trusters. As a result, high trusters' estimation fell short of the low trusters' estimation as negative pieces of information were provided. Instead of being gullible, high trusters were again shown to be more carefully attendant to information suggesting the untrustworthiness of the target person.

Predicting an Interaction Partner's Trustworthiness

Although the results of these two experiments conflict with our intuitive view of high trusters and low trusters, there is a possible alternative explanation for them. Perhaps high trusters in these experiments were more credulous than low trusters and took the words of the experimenter at face value. Furthermore, even if we are willing to accept the conclusion suggested by these results that high trusters are more sensitive than low trusters to trustworthiness-related information, a question remains: does that heightened sensitivity among high trusters lead them to make more accurate judgments in detecting untrustworthy people? To eliminate the alternative explanation and to answer this question, we conducted additional experiments.

An experiment by Masako Kikuchi, Yoriko Watanabe, and Toshio Yamagishi (1997) was designed to resolve these issues. Participants in this experiment engaged in a thirty-minute discussion in six-person groups on garbage collection issues. Then they participated in "another" experiment in which each participant played a two-person, one-shot prisoners' dilemma game with two of the other five participants. They were not informed as to who their partners were in those two games.[2] The prisoners' dilemma game was constructed in the following manner. Participants were provided by the experimenter with eight hundred yen (about eight dollars) of endowment before the experiment started. Each participant was asked to either give one hundred yen (about one dollar) to the partner or take one hundred yen from the partner. When the participant gave one hundred yen, the money was doubled by the experimenter and thus the partner received two hundred yen. So both of the two subjects received two hundred yen each when both gave one hundred yen to each other. This yielded a profit of one hundred yen for each, since each gave one hundred yen and received two hundred yen. On the other hand, when the participant took one hundred yen from the partner, the money, one hundred yen, became the participant's. The loss to the partner, however, was doubled by the experimenter, and the partner suffered a loss of two hundred yen instead of one hundred yen. Thus, if both took one hundred yen from each other, each earned one hundred yen but at the same time suffered a loss of two hundred yen, resulting in an overall loss of one hundred yen.

"Prisoners' dilemma" refers to the relationship in which cooperation yields a more desirable outcome than defection for either of the two partners and yet each defection yields a more desirable outcome than cooperation. In such a relationship, those who pursue only their own self-interest would choose defection (taking one hundred yen from the partner). If both choose defection, they have to live with the outcome of mutual defection (loss of one hundred yen), which is less desirable than the outcome of mutual cooperation.

The purpose of this experiment was to examine the participants' accuracy in judging whether other participants gave their money to the partner (cooperation) or took money from the partner (defection) in the prisoners' dilemma. For this purpose, participants had a group discussion on garbage collection issues before they participated in the prisoners' dilemma experiment. They were told that the discussion session was a part of another study and was totally independent of the experiment that followed. The real purpose of this "discussion experiment" was to give the participants an opportunity to get to know each other and learn about each other's character traits. Would they acquire in the thirty-minute discussion the cues needed to predict other participants' choices in the prisoners' dilemma experiment?

An even more important question we wanted to pursue was whether the participants' level of general trust would be at all related to the accuracy of their predictions of others' choices. In the commonsense view, high trusters are naive and credulous, and the less naive and credulous low trusters judge others' choices more correctly. On the other hand, from the previous experimental result showing that high trusters are more sensitive than low trusters to information about others' trustworthiness, we predicted that it would be high trusters who judged others' choices more correctly. The most important purpose of this experiment was to examine which of the two predictions would hold.

The experiment was conducted in the following way. Participants were paired with several other subjects: A and B or C, B and A or D or E, and so on. Each participant was informed that he or she was paired with several others, but they were not informed who their partners were. Then each participant was asked to decide whether to give or take one hundred yen from the unknown partner. It was thus impossible for the participant to base the choice between giving and taking on his or her personal liking or disliking of the partner; no one could think, for example, "I would give one hundred yen to B since B is pretty," or, "I would take from C since C is arrogant." Thus, *the decision to give or take one hundred yen was expected to reflect the participant's general character rather than his or her attitudes toward specific partners.* Those who gave one hundred yen to the partner were considered to be those who had a strong tendency to form cooperative relationships with others. Finally, it should be noted that the confidentiality of the participant's decision (whether to give or take one hundred yen) was almost completely guaranteed, not only with respect to other participants but with respect to the experimenter as well.

After having made the decision to give or take one hundred yen, subjects were informed that they had been matched with two partners. They were told which two of the other five participants they had been matched with. Then they were asked to predict whether each of the two partners had decided to give or take one hundred yen in the prisoners' dilemma experiment. To motivate the participant to take the prediction seriously, an additional bonus of one hundred yen was provided for each correct prediction.

The forty-eight participants recruited from a large subject pool at a large national university in Japan were classified into three categories—low, medium, or high truster—based on their scores on the trust scale that they had filled out at least a few weeks before the experiment. The result of this experiment indicated no statistically significant difference between the three trust levels in the cooperation rate (53 percent, 53 percent, and 48 percent among low, medium and high trusters, respectively). These three groups of participants also did not differ in their expectation of the partner's cooperation. These results are consistent with past research findings that the effect of general trust on cooperation or expectation is limited in the n-person, not the two-person, situation. General trust matters less when people interact with a particular partner in a dyadic relation since their attention is focused on that particular person.

On the other hand, high trusters were more accurate in estimating the partner's behavior (cooperation versus defection in a one-shot prisoners' dilemma game with an anonymous partner) than either low trusters or medium trusters. The result shown in figure 4.5 for the first experiment (Kikuchi et al. 1997) indicates that high trusters were more accurate in predicting other subjects' behaviors (to give or take one hundred yen) than medium trusters or low trusters. Accuracy in predicting the decision of the two partners was calculated by adding half a point when the partner acted as predicted, and zero points when the prediction failed. With this method, the participant received one point when his or her predictions for both of the two partners were correct, half a point when one prediction was correct and the other was wrong, and zero points when neither prediction was correct. Figure 4.3 shows the differences in the accuracy of prediction of other participants' choices due to differential levels of general trust as measured by the general trust scale. That is, high trusters were more accurate in predicting the behavior of other participants with whom they had had a short discussion compared with medium trusters or low trusters. The difference was statistically significant.

Furthermore, they were accurate in judging the partner's choice regardless of whether the partner actually cooperated or defected. Of the sixteen partners whom high trusters estimated to have cooperated, twelve actually cooperated (accuracy rate of 75 percent). They also estimated that sixteen partners had defected, and ten of those sixteen had actually defected (62.5 percent). Overall, high trusters' estimations were accurate twenty-two out of thirty-two times (69 percent). In contrast, low trusters were accurate only thirteen out of thirty times (43 percent), and medium trusters were accurate only twelve out of thirty-four times (35 percent). These differences in the accuracy score were statistically significant.

The same experiment was replicated by the same authors with ninety participants, and as shown in figure 4.5 (Experiment 2), it was found that

**Figure 4.5   Accuracy in Judgment of Other Participants' Choices as a
Function of Participant's Level of General Trust, from
Six Experiments**

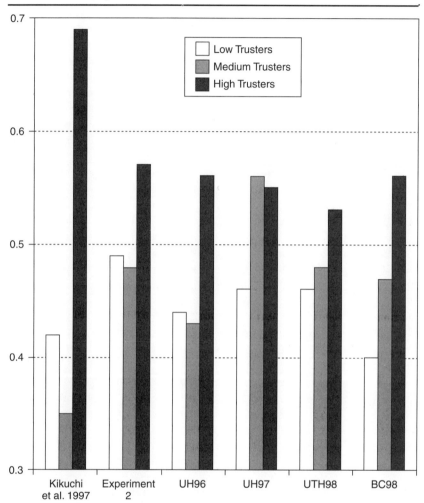

Source: Author's compilation.

high trusters were more accurate in their judgment of the other participants' choices than were medium or low trusters, although the difference, while statistically significant, was not as pronounced as in the first
experiment.

The last series of experiments presented in this chapter includes
UH96 and UH97, conducted by Yamagishi and Kosugi (1999), and additional unpublished experiments, UTH98 and BC98, conducted by

Yamagishi and his colleagues. These are basically replications of the experiment presented earlier (Kikuchi et al. 1997). The major difference between these and the previous experiment is in the participants. Participants in the first experiments were strangers, but participants in the later series of experiments were acquaintances. The participants in the later experiments consisted of two groups, each of whose members belonged to the same academic program (a small department). They had spent about a year in the same program, meeting frequently in classes.[3] Thus, their insights about other participants' personality traits should be much deeper than those of the participants in the early experiments, for whom participation in the thirty-minute group discussion was the only source of information about the other participants.[4] Otherwise, the basic design of the experiment was replicated. First, participants played a PD game with one randomly selected student from a total of thirty-three participants in UH96 and thirty participants in UH97. When they decided whether to cooperate or defect, they did not know who their partner was. They knew only that their partner was randomly selected from among all the participants. Then they answered a questionnaire that included the trust scale and other personality scales. Finally, they judged whether each of the other students from the same program had chosen to cooperate or defect. The confidentiality of their choices with respect to both the other participants and the experimenter was completely assured.

The overall cooperation rate in the first experiment, UH96, reported in Yamagishi and Kosugi (1999), was 0.47. The accuracy scores for the low, medium, and high trusters are reported in figure 4.5 (UH96). The accuracy of the judgment was calculated for each participant as the unweighted average of the proportions of correct judgments for cooperators and for defectors. For example, the accuracy-of-judgment score for a participant who judged five of seven actual cooperators as cooperators and three of eleven actual defectors as defectors is $(5/7 + 3/11)/2 = .49$. The overall accuracy of the judgment was 0.48. That is, overall, participants' judgments of their friends' behavior in the PD game were no better than random guessing. This result is consistent with the finding of Lee Ross and Samuels (1993, cited in Ross and Ward 1995) that dormitory advisers were not able to predict students' behavior in a PD game. However, the accuracy scores of high trusters were much higher than those of low trusters, and the accuracy scores of the participants were significantly correlated with their general trust score ($r = .48$). Furthermore, the accuracy score was significantly correlated with other scales that are conceptually related to general trust. First, correlation with the "honesty/fairness scale"—developed by Yamagishi and Yamagishi (1994) to measure the respondent's belief in the personal significance of being honest and fair to others—was significant ($r = .43$). Those who considered honesty and fairness personally more important were able to judge their friends' behavior in a PD game more accurately than those who cared less for being honest and fair to others. Second, the accuracy scale was correlated with the "sense of interdependence scale" developed by Nobuhito Jin (1997) to measure the belief that establishing and maintaining mutually cooperative relations is in one's own self-interest (r = .55). Those who had such a "mentality of generalized exchange" were more accurate than those who did not. Third, the proportion of their fellow students who judged each participant to have cooperated was marginally correlated to the participant's accuracy score (r = .32). That is, those who were considered by their friends to have cooperated in the experiment were more accurate in judging friends' behavior in the experiment.

The results of UH97, an almost identical replication of UH96, were consistent with those of UH96. As shown in figure 4.5 (UH97), the participant's level of trust was positively related to the accuracy of his or her judgment of the other participants' choices. The correlation coefficient between general trust and the accuracy score was statistically significant (r = .41). Figure 4.5 also reports results from two additional experiments, UTH98 and BC98. These are replications of the previous two experiments that used slightly simplified methods with forty students from another university and fourteen students from a vocational training school. As can easily be seen in figure 4.5, results from these two additional experiments are also consistent with the first two, indicating that high trusters are better than low trusters in judging what their classmates did in the anonymous, one-shot prisoners' dilemma involving real money.

In all of the six experiments reported in figure 4.5, general trust was found to have an effect on participants' accuracy in discerning defectors from cooperators among their classmates. The results of these experiments consistently indicate that high trusters are more socially intelligent than low trusters in the sense that they are more accurate in discerning defectors from cooperators.

Trust and Social Intelligence

Contrary to the common belief that trust means gullibility, the results of the series of experiments presented in this chapter consistently suggest that high trusters are more sensitive than distrusters to trust-related information, and more accurate in judging the trustworthiness of others. I have already outlined at the beginning of this chapter the rationale for this counterintuitive relationship—distrust breeds further distrust since it prevents people from exposing themselves to opportunities to develop social intelligence. Distrusters choose social isolation because they believe that "everyone is a thief." By doing so, they protect themselves from the risk of being victimized in social interactions. At the same time they pay opportunity costs.

General trust supported by social intelligence, on the other hand, allows high trusters to seek opportunities outside the security of closed social relations and to save in opportunity costs. This *relation-expanding role* of general trust, first introduced by Yamagishi and Yamagishi (1994), provides the foundation of all the experiments reported in this chapter.

Before further discussing the implications of the results of the experiments, let me briefly summarize the "emancipation theory" of trust. According to this theory, developed by Yamagishi and Yamagishi (1994), trust and commitment formation represent alternative solutions to the problem of social uncertainty. Social uncertainty is ubiquitous in human society since, in interacting with others while seeking to improve our own welfare, we expose ourselves to a risk of being exploited by others. An actor faces social uncertainty when the interaction partner has an incentive to act in a way that imposes costs on the actor; and the actor does not have sufficient information to predict whether the partner will in fact act in such a way (Yamagishi and Yamagishi 1994).

Peter Kollock (1994) provides an excellent example of social uncertainty—taken from rice and rubber markets in Southeast Asia— and observes how it promotes commitment formation between particular partners.[5] The quality of rice is immediately apparent upon simple inspection. The buyer runs little risk of being cheated on the quality of the rice he or she buys, and thus the buyer faces a low level of social uncertainty. In contrast, according to Kollock, the quality of raw rubber is hard to discern; its quality can be known only after it has been processed. Cheating on the quality is easier, and the consequence of being cheated is serious. The buyer of raw rubber thus faces a higher level of social uncertainty than does the buyer of rice. This difference in social uncertainty in the trade of rice and rubber, Kollock argues, explains the observed difference in the dominant form of trade. Rice is usually traded at an open market between relative strangers, whereas rubber is often traded between a particular producer and a broker who have formed a long-term relationship, often extending over generations. The high level of social uncertainty involved in the trading of rubber is the determining factor for the development of such committed relations between rubber producers and brokers.

Commitment formation provides the dominant means of dealing with social uncertainty in many situations. However, its effectiveness is limited to a particular social environment. This is because, while reducing the risk of being duped in interacting with unfamiliar people, commitment restrains the actors from exploring better opportunities that might exist outside the current relationship. Using terminology borrowed from economics, commitment formation reduces *transaction costs,* on the one hand, and imposes *opportunity costs,* on the other. In forming a commitment relationship with a particular partner, one obtains security (reduction in social uncertainty) in exchange for opportunities. Commitment formation is thus a gainful strategy in a situation in which outside opportunities are limited (when the general level of opportunity costs is low). On the other hand, a commitment relation becomes a losing strategy as people face more and better opportunities outside of it (when the general level of opportunity costs of staying in a commitment relationship is high). According to Yamagishi and Yamagishi (1994), general trust (or default expectations of others' trustworthiness) provides a springboard for people who are confined in the security provided by commitment relationships to leap into the outside world of opportunities. Lacking general trust and believing that "everyone is a thief," distrusters prefer to stay in the closed circuit and fail to harvest the outside opportunities. General trust "emancipates" people from the confines of the security of stable relations.

Trust in this sense—that is, trust as a positive cognitive bias in processing information about the trustworthiness of potential interaction partners—implies credulousness and thus gullibility, especially when the world outside the established relations is filled with nasty "predators." The theory of trust advanced by Yamagishi and Yamagishi (1994, 135) is in this sense a theory of the *unintended benefits of credulousness.* According to this conception, a "trusting person is the one who overestimates the benignity of other people's intentions beyond the level warranted by the prudent assessment of the available information." The experimental findings presented in this chapter, however, contradict this conception of trust. First, high trusters in Kosugi and Yamagishi's (1998) experiments more quickly reduced their judgment of the target person's trustworthiness than did distrusters when information revealing the target person's potential untrustworthiness was provided. Furthermore, high trusters in the experiment of Kikuchi and her colleagues (1997) and the six additional experiments presented in this chapter made more accurate estimations of the other participants' behaviors than did distrusters. Facing such experimental evidence against the "cognitive bias view" of general trust, I have proposed (Yamagishi 1998) the following "investment" model of trust development to explain the counterintuitive findings. General trust is not just simple credulousness but rather a by-product of a high level of social intelligence.

Having a high level of general trust (or high "default" expectations of human benevolence) helps people to leave the security of established relations and look for better outside opportunities. In a social environment full of opportunities for such "exiters," having a high level of general trust provides an advantage. And yet, leaving the secure relation and exploring better outside opportunities entails risks. In the social environment assumed, in the emancipation theory, to favor the development of general trust—an environment characterized by a high level of social uncertainty and high opportunity costs—people thus face the need to discern the trustworthiness of potential interaction partners. In such an environment, investment of the cognitive resources needed to discern the trustworthiness of others, such as attention and memory, yields a large return. Thus, it is predicted that people facing high opportunity costs and high levels of social uncertainty invest more in cognitive resources, paying more attention and more carefully processing signs of trustworthiness as they face increasing opportunities outside the closed social circle. As a result of the cognitive investment, the skills needed for discerning trustworthiness develop.

General trust, or the default expectations of the trustworthiness of others, can be a by-product of the investment in cognitive resources for improving social intelligence. Those who have invested a great many cognitive resources in developing such skills can afford to maintain high default expectations of other people's trustworthiness. By maintaining these high expectations, they can enjoy the advantage of being able to fully explore the opportunities that lie outside the established relations. At the same time they can quickly pull out of a risky relation at a faint sign of risk. Those who have not made such a cognitive investment, on the other hand, are slow to detect signs of untrustworthiness and thus are ill suited for exploring potentially fruitful but risky relations. It is prudent for them simply to assume that all people are untrustworthy ("everyone is a thief"). By making that assumption (or by keeping their level of default expectations for the trustworthiness of others low), they can avoid being victimized.

Let me finally discuss an interesting paradox in the trust-gullibility relationship. High trusters who have a high level of social intelligence are less gullible than distrusters *per social interaction*. On the other hand, they may be more gullible *in total* than distrusters since they are more willing to enter into risky social relations. The popular view of high trusters as gullible may be derived from this difference; most people who are exploited are high trusters, since they are the ones who enter into risky and yet potentially profitable relations. What people often fail to see is the other side of the coin—the benefits forgone by distrusters. Using a Chinese saying, "One has to venture into a tiger's cave to steal a baby tiger." People who have acquired a high level of social intelligence to discern trustworthiness in others are like those who have become adept at detecting the presence of adult tigers in the cave. Most of the time they can successfully seize a baby tiger and make a fortune. On the other hand, they are the only ones who are ever killed by adult tigers since those without such skills do not venture into the cave. Whether or not it is better to develop that skill and venture into tiger caves depends on how precious a baby tiger is. No one will venture into tiger caves if there is no market for baby tigers. In the same vein, neither social intelligence nor general trust will develop in a social environment in which leaving the security of a closed social circuit provides no better opportunities.

Trust and General Trust

Before closing this chapter, let me briefly discuss how general trust, defined here as default expectations of people's trustworthiness, is related to other aspects of trust. I agree with David Messick and Roderick Kramer's claim (this volume) that trust is closely related to the choice of Trust (T) in the Trust Game (see figure 3.1). There are two ways to interpret the choice of T in the Trust Game. The first is the encapsulated-interest approach advocated most strongly by Russell Hardin (this volume), according to which You in figure 3.1 has a good reason to believe that the choice of Not Honor (NH) yields less overall value to Other than that produced by the choice of Honor (H). As defined by the Trust Game, the immediate value of NH is greater than that of H to Other ($d > b$). However, the same game may be repeated as it is in the case of Trifonov and the lieutenant colonel Hardin discusses (Hardin, forthcoming). Insofar as Trifonov anticipates many games in the future, he expects that the choice of H now will yield greater overall value than the choice of NH. Using the terminology of the psychologists Harold H. Kelley and John Thibaut (1978), Other has transformed the original game depicted in figure 3.1 into an "effective" game by taking into account the implications of the present choices for future responses by You, and You somehow knows that Other has transformed the game. As Thibaut and Kelley demonstrate, there are many ways in which a given game is transformed into an effective game. For example, Other loves You, so that what Other gets from the choice of H is $a + b$ instead of b. According to this encapsulated-interest approach, trust is knowing that Other is playing a transformed game such that Other derives more value from the choice of H than of NH. In this sense, trust is reduction in social uncertainty in the Trust Game.

According to the second approach, You is playing the original Trust Game as it is and yet takes a risk in choosing T, hoping that Other will choose H rather than NH. This approach sees trust as a form of social risk-taking. There are many reasons to expect Other to choose H. It is not rational for Other to choose H unless she is playing a transformed game. But participants in experiments who play the Trust Game for money often choose H rather than NH. For example, 35 percent of the Japanese participants (Kiyonari and Yamagishi 1999) and 42 percent of the Chinese participants (Wang, Kiyonari, and Yamagishi 1999) chose H rather than NH in a cross-societal experiment of the Trust Game. Given the fact that a substantial proportion of people actually choose H for whatever reason, it is rational for You to choose T in the population where the proportion of H-choosers is greater than a certain threshold level. What is critical for the choice made by You, according to this approach, is the assessment of the probability that Other, for whom the game has been transformed, will choose H. The assessment may be based on the knowledge that You has of Other's individual character traits, including his general trustworthiness, or on the knowledge You has of the probability distribution of the trustworthy and untrustworthy people in the population. Thus, assessment of the likelihood that Other will choose H plays the central role in this approach. The assessment of the likelihood may be based on many factors, among which shallow morality, which Messick and Kramer discuss (this volume), certainly occupies a central position. General trust plays a critical role in assessing Other's likelihood of choosing H when no reputation about her is available. The findings reported in this chapter make the most sense from the second point of view.

It is important not to mix the two approaches in an analysis of trust. Trust as social risk-taking makes little sense in the first approach since trust in that approach exists in the transformation, either subjective or objective, of the game. Another game is being played in figure 3.1 by You when Other is the mother of You, an Other for whom, You knows, the choice of H brings a + b, the total value of which exceeds the value of d alone. Social uncertainty for You is reduced by this transformation, and without social uncertainty there is no social risk-taking involved when You chooses T. This is not trust, however, according to the second approach. Trust becomes irrelevant in the transformed game in which You knows that Other derives greater value from H than from NH. You knows for sure that his mother will choose H. Then the choice of T is rational for You. Whether You trusts his mother or not becomes problematic only when You does not have sufficient reason to expect that the mother has not transformed the game. Whether to choose T or NT (Not Trust) is an issue only when You is playing the Trust Game with Other, who, You knows, has not transformed it. When Other has not transformed the game, You's choice of T is a choice of risk-taking. Whether You takes the risk or not depends on his assessment of how likely it is that Other will choose H in spite of the structure of the game.

Which approach one adopts and which aspect of the Trust Game—transformation of the game or social risk-taking—one calls trust is a matter of preference. What is absolutely necessary, however, is to be clear about which approach one is taking when dealing with "trust." I have declared elsewhere (Yamagishi and Yamagishi 1994; Yamagishi 1998) that I would reserve the term "trust" only to the choice of T in the original Trust Game, giving the choice of T against a "transformer" another term, "assurance." Others may reserve the term "trust" only to the transformation of the game and give another term, "social risk-taking," to the choice of T in the original Trust Game with a "nontransformer." I would be happy with either terminology insofar as the two aspects of trust are clearly separated.

Notes

1. This trust scale and its earlier versions have been consistently successful in predicting people's behavior in a situation requiring trust (such as cooperation in social dilemma situations), demonstrating the predictive validity of this scale (Yamagishi and Cook 1993; Yamagishi 1986, 1988, 1992; Yamagishi and Sato 1986).

2. Only one of two conditions used in this experiment is presented here. The other condition is irrelevant to the discussion in this chapter and thus is not reported.

3. Each program (such as the social psychology program) consisted of up to twenty or so students per cohort. Owing to course requirements, students in the same course saw each other frequently. They also often had parties. Their bonding was much stronger than that among students in the same department in an American university.

4. Participants in this experiment did not have a discussion session before the experiment.

5. The term "commitment" is used in this chapter in a strictly behaviorist manner. That is, an actor is defined as committed to a relationship to the degree that he or she forgoes better (at the moment) alternatives. Mutual attraction and liking and a sense of loyalty to each other may emerge in such a committed relation, and when they do, they certainly strengthen the commitment. However, such psychological factors, however strongly related to commitment, are not commitment itself in this sense.

References

Brann, Peter, and Margaret Foddy. 1988. "Trust and the Consumption of a Deteriorating Common Resource." *Journal of Conflict Resolution* 31(4): 615–30.

Gardner, Howard. 1983. *Frames of Mind: The Theory of Multiple Intelligences.* New York: Basic Books.

Garske, John P. 1975. "Interpersonal Trust and Construct Complexity for Positively and Negatively Evaluated Persons." *Personality and Social Psychology Bulletin* 1(4): 616–19.

———. 1976. "Personality and Generalized Expectancies for Interpersonal Trust." *Psychological Report* 39(2): 649–50.

Geller, J. D. 1966. "Some Personal and Situational Determinants of Interpersonal Trust." Ph.D. diss., University of Connecticut.

Goleman, Daniel. 1995. *Emotional Intelligence: Why It Can Matter More Than IQ.* New York: Bantam Books.

Gurtman, Michael B., and Clifford Lion. 1982. "Interpersonal Trust and Perceptual Vigilance for Trustworthiness Descriptors." *Journal of Research in Personality* 16(1): 108–17.

Hamsher, J. H., Jr. 1968. "Validity of Personality Inventories as a Function of Disguise of Purpose." Ph.D. diss., University of Connecticut.

Hardin, Russell. 1992. "The Street-Level Epistemology of Trust." *Politics and Society* 21: 505–29.

———. Forthcoming. *Trust and Trustworthiness.* New York: Russell Sage Foundation.

Jin, Nobuhito. 1997. "Reconsidering Social Identity Theory: An Empirical Study of Within-Group Reciprocity" (in Japanese). Ph.D. diss., Hokkaido University, Sapporo, Japan.

Kelley, Harold H., and John W. Thibaut. 1978. *Interpersonal Relations.* New York: Wiley.

Kikuchi, Masako, Yoriko Watanabe, and Toshio Yamagishi. 1997. "Judgment Accuracy of Others' Trustworthiness and General Trust: An Experimental Study" (in Japanese with an English abstract). *Japanese Journal of Experimental Social Psychology* 37: 23–36.

Kiyonari, Toko, and Toshio Yamagishi. 1999. "Trusting Behavior Toward Ingroup Members in the Minimal Group Situation." *Proceedings of the Forty-seventh Annual Meeting of the Japanese Group Dynamics Association* (in Japanese): 86–87.

Kollock, Peter. 1994. "The Emergence of Exchange Structures: An Experimental Study of Uncertainty, Commitment, and Trust." *American Journal of Sociology* 100(2): 313–45.

Kosugi, Motoko, and Toshio Yamagishi. 1998. "Generalized Trust and Judgments of Trustworthiness" (in Japanese with an English abstract). *Japanese Journal of Psychology* 69: 349–57.

Ross, Lee, and Steven M. Samuels. 1993. "The Predictive Power of Personal Reputation Versus Labels and Construal in the Prisoners' Dilemma Game." Palo Alto, Calif.: Stanford University. Unpublished paper.

Ross, Lee, and Andrew Ward. 1995. "Psychological Barriers to Dispute Resolution." *Advances in Experimental Social Psychology* 27: 355–404.

Rotter, Julien B. 1967. "A New Scale for the Measurement of Interpersonal Trust." *Journal of Personality* 35(4): 651–65.

———. 1980. "Interpersonal Trust, Trustworthiness, and Gullibility." *American Psychologist* 35(1): 1–7.

Schlenker, Barry R., Bob Helm, and James T. Tedeschi. 1973. "The Effects of Personality and Situational Variables on Behavioral Trust." *Journal of Personality and Social Psychology* 39(4): 419–27.

Sternberg, Robert J. 1988. *The Triarchic Mind: A New Theory of Human Intelligence.* New York: Viking.

Wang, F., Toko Kiyonari, and Toshio Yamagishi. 1999. "Trust and Trusting Behavior in China and Japan." Paper presented at the third conference of the Asian Association of Social Psychology. Taipei, Taiwan(August 4–7, 1999).

Wrights, T. L. 1972. "Situational and Personality Parameters of Interpersonal in a Modified Prisoners' Dilemma Game." Ph.D. diss., University of Connecticut.

Yamagishi, Toshio. 1986. "The Provision of a Sanctioning System as a Public Good." *Journal of Personality and Social Psychology* 51(1): 110–16.

———. 1988. "The Provision of a Sanctioning System in the United States and Japan." *Social Psychology Quarterly* 51(3): 265–71.

———. 1992. "Group Size and the Provision of a Sanctioning System in a Social Dilemma." In *A Social Psychological Approach to Social Dilemmas,* edited by Wim B. G. Liebrand, David M. Messick, and H. A. M. Wilke. New York: Pergamon Press.

———. 1998. *The Structure of Trust: The Evolutionary Games of Mind and Society* (in Japanese). Tokyo: Tokyo University Press.

———. 1999. *From Security Society to Trust Society: Where Is the Japanese System Heading?* (in Japanese). Tokyo: Chuo Koron Shinsha.

Yamagishi, Toshio, and Karen S. Cook. 1993. "Generalized Exchange and Social Dilemmas." *Social Psychology Quarterly* 56(4): 235–48.

Yamagishi, Toshio, Masako Kikuchi, and Motoko Kosugi. 1999. "Trust, Gullibility, and Social Intelligence." *Asian Journal of Social Psychology* 2(1): 145–61.

Yamagishi, Toshio, and Motoko Kosugi. 1999. "Cheater Detection in Social Exchange" (in Japanese with an English abstract). *Cognitive Studies* 6: 179–90.

Yamagishi, Toshio, and Kaori Sato. 1986. "Motivational Bases of the Public Goods Problem." *Journal of Personality and Social Psychology* 50(1): 67–73.

Yamagishi, Toshio, and Midori Yamagishi. 1994. "Trust and Commitment in the United States and Japan." *Motivation and Emotion* 18(2): 129–66.

Chapter 5

Trust in Signs

Michael Bacharach and Diego Gambetta

I N THIS CHAPTER we embark on a reorientation of the theory of trust. The first four steps establish a new theoretical framework for determining when trust and its fulfillment are to be expected. The fifth step lies partly in the future and will implement this theoretical framework by setting out the detailed structure of the semiotics of trust, which we initiate in the last section of this essay.

In the first section we first define "trust" as a particular belief, which arises in games with a certain payoff structure. We then identify the source of the **primary problem of trust**—the problem the truster faces in answering the question "Can I trust this person to do X?"—in the truster's uncertainty about the payoffs of the trustee.[1] Departing from standard rational choice treatments, we allow that a trustee's "all-in" payoffs in a trust game may differ from his "raw" payoffs. Whether they do depends on nonobservable qualities of his. Some of these—virtues, internalized norms, certain character features—are trustworthy-making qualities in that they induce **all-in payoffs** that motivate him to resist the pull of the **raw payoffs** and instead to do X. The primary problem of trust lies in the truster's uncertainty as to whether the trustee will be governed by raw payoffs or by all-in payoffs induced by such trustworthy-making qualities.

In the second step (the second section), we first note that in virtually all games of this type that occur naturally, the truster sees or otherwise observes the trustee before deciding. She therefore can, and should, use these observations as evidence that the trustee has, or lacks, trustworthy-making qualities. We next note that, since the truster will be proceeding in this way, and given the payoff structure, there is a motive for an opportunistic trustee to "mimic"—to emit signs of trustworthy-making qualities when he lacks them. This complicates the truster's problem: she must judge whether apparent signs of trustworthiness are themselves to be trusted. Thus, the problem of trust from which we started has been transformed into a **secondary problem of trust**.

In the third step (the third section) we show how the secondary problem of trust can be recast as a particular class of signaling games. This move has two advantages. First, the theory of signaling games is a well-developed part of game theory, and the understanding of such games provided by game theory serves to illuminate the present problem. Second, signaling-game theory allows precise predictions about the conditions under which mimicry can occur and how much of it we can expect.

We then take a side step (in the fourth section) and develop signaling-game theory in a new direction. We extend it to the case in which what is signaled by a signaler is his identity. This is of crucial importance for understanding how trust decisions are made, because the secondary problem of trust is often soluble by assessing the reliability of identifying marks. This is the case every time we can determine indirectly whether a trustee has trustworthy-making qualities—by establishing whether he is the same person who has proved trustworthy in the past. The opportunists of this case are impersonators who mimic a possessor of trustworthy-making qualities by imitating that person's identifying marks.

In the fifth step we describe some salient concrete features of the complex semiotic structure of secondary problems of trust. These features, some conceptual and some empirical, must be studied and specified in order to turn our framework into a tool for the empirical analysis of real-life trust problems. Here we initiate this study and this specification. The semiotic structure involves a range of different genera of signs, a range of different kinds of costs of emitting signs, and a range of strategies for the protection of signs against the threat of mimicry.

This chapter carries a number of implications for the methodological issue of whether rational choice theory is an appropriate tool for the analysis of trust. Our analysis suggests that it is. In particular, it suggests that the subtlety and richness of the judgments made by a truster when she trusts are due only to the complexity of the game that she finds herself playing. The apparently ineffable nature of these judgments is an illusion, which we hope to dispel by describing the detail of the structure of such games. However, the particular assumptions about people's motivations that are characteristic of the currently dominant rational choice approach to trust play no role in the theory we develop here. It is, for example, not essential to our theory that trust is the product of some system of rewards and penalties that act as incentives to the trustee in repeated interactions, such as repeated prisoners' dilemmas (PDs). We treat trust as the product of underlying trustworthy-making character features—one of which can be, of course, the degree of susceptibility to rewards and punishments.

However, the presence of trustworthy-making qualities is not sufficient to induce trust. Trust has two enemies, not just one: bad character and poor information. The incidence of good character sets an upper bound on the amount of trust in a community. In this chapter we treat this incidence as given. Actual trust, however, may fall below that threshold because of the difficulties incurred communicating the presence of these qualities. We investigate only the communication deficit—what causes it and by implication how it might be narrowed. In particular, since communication is through signs, the prevalence of trust increases with the significance of signs of trustworthiness. Here we explore the determinants of the significance of such signs.

In doing so, we make use of tools that allow one to identify precise conditions under which trustworthiness is communicated and trust thereby justified. In this way we hope to foster an approach to trust research which questions the belief that trust is something mysteriously different from anything else, and aspires to the exact measurement of the conditions under which trust is rationally given.

Primary Trust

The notion of trust we investigate here is "trusting someone to do something." This notion captures a vast range of trust cases, even though it is not intended as an analysis of all varieties of trust. Its essence can be conveyed by an example. Suppose a person extends a loan to another because she expects him to do his best to repay it, when it is clear that she would do better to refuse the loan if he will make no effort to repay it, and when it is also clear that his selfish interest is to make no such effort. Then, we shall say that she trusts him to try to repay the loan. In general, we shall say that a person "trusts someone to do X" if she acts on the expectation that he will do X when both know that two conditions obtain: if he fails to do X she would have done better to have acted otherwise, and her acting in the way she does gives him a selfish reason not to do X.

We can make the notion more precise by describing the interaction as a two-player, strategic-form, noncooperative game, which we shall hereafter refer to as a **basic trust game**. This game has two players, a potential truster R ("she") and a potential trustee E ("he"). Each has two strategies: R's are labeled A and A', and E's are labeled B and B'. Figure 5.1 shows the payoffs of the truster together with the "raw" payoffs of the trustee: that is, the payoffs that would be his were he motivated by simple self-interest. The numbers 3 and −3 are purely illustrative, and x and y are any

Figure 5.1   R's Payoffs and E's Raw Payoffs

	B	B'
A	3, 1	–3, 4
A'	x, …	y, …

Source: Author's compilation.

Figure 5.2   R's Payoffs and E's Possible All-in Payoffs

	B	B'
A	3, 2	–3, –4
A'	x, …	y, …

Source: Author's compilation.

numbers that satisfy x < 3 and y > –3: thus, if the trustee chooses B, A is better than A' for the truster, and if the trustee chooses B', A' is better than A for the truster. Finally, if for whatever reason R chooses A, B' would best serve E's selfish interest. (The trustee's preferences if the truster does A' are irrelevant.)

In the loan request example, the strategies A and A' are simply the actions "lend" and "refuse"; B and B' are the conditional actions "try to repay if R lends" and "make no effort to repay if R lends." This conditionality comes from the dynamic structure of the example, in which E's action (trying or not trying) succeeds R's action (lending or refusing), which E observes. This is a very common pattern in trust situations, but not invariable, and not part of the definition of a basic trust game, which is in terms of strategies, not actions.

However, for all the truster knows, there is no need for the trustee's payoffs–that is, his all-things-considered, or "all-in," payoffs—to be identical with his raw payoffs. Perhaps the borrower's upbringing has instilled in him a horror of not repaying debts, so that his payoffs are as in figure 5.2. If we simplify by supposing that this is the only other possible case, the primary problem of trust consists, in effect, in identifying which of the two payoff structures really governs E's actions.

The remainder of the definition of basic trust games concerns what the players know. We assume, first of all, that there is mutual knowledge between R and E that R can do either A or A', and that E can do either B or B'.[2] Second, there is mutual knowledge of R's payoffs, but in general only E knows E's payoffs: a basic trust game is thus a "game of asymmetric information" concerning E's payoffs. However, we assume that there *is* mutual knowledge of E's raw payoffs. What only E knows, however, is whether his all-in payoffs coincide with, or differ from, his raw payoffs.[3]

Basic trust games are paradigms of primary problems of trust and by no means exhaust the range of such problems. They simplify in several ways, some of which we record later in the chapter. Here we draw attention to two. For there to be a problem for R whether to trust E, it is not necessary that the forces pushing E toward B' be E's raw payoffs (selfish interests); the same problem arises for R if she is concerned that E may be guided by unselfish, even noble or spiritual, reasons for choosing B'. For example, R has a trust problem if she thinks it possible that E has no intention of repaying her because he plans to give all his future unspent earnings to cancer relief. We have chosen to characterize the bad-case payoff structure, which would lead E to do B', as selfish only for the sake of concreteness and simplicity.

Basic trust games abstract from "multiple peril." In a basic trust game there is only one way (B') in which trust can be disappointed, and there is a single bad-case payoff structure, which puts R in peril of B', that of figure 5.2. Often, however, there may be several such perils, each favored by a different "raw" type. A traveler in an unknown city with a plane to catch, seeing a waiting cab, may wonder, "Can I trust that driver?" She may be concerned about more than one scenario. He might be driven by greed and take a roundabout route (B') for the sake of money, or he might be libidinous and molest her (B"). Such cases, and yet more elaborate ones, can be handled by exactly the same methods we develop for basic trust games, at the cost only of some increase in complexity.[4]

We shall say that, in a basic trust game, the truster R **trusts** the trustee E if *R expects E to choose B.* We assume that all-in payoffs govern choice; hence, if R trusts E, R will do A. We therefore call A the **trusting act** and B the **trusted-in act**. The trustee E will be said to be **trustworthy** if the following obtains: *if E believes R trusts him, E chooses B.* Since all-in preference guides choice, for E to be trustworthy his all-in payoffs must diverge from his raw payoffs.

If R thinks E is trustworthy, it now follows—almost—that R will trust E and do A. What follows, more precisely, is that there is an equilibrium in which this is so. There is a consistent state of affairs in which R trusts E and so does A, and E thinks R trusts him and so does B. This is an equilibrium, because E's doing B fulfills R's expectation, and R's doing A fulfills E's expectation.[5]

Trust-Warranting Properties

There are many possible properties, and even kinds of property, that can make a trustee trustworthy. Some of these take the form of the reasons the trustee has to choose B. One such reason is his very belief that the truster is trusting him (Dasgupta 1988; Gambetta 1988; Hausman 1997; Hirschman 1984; Pettit 1995).[6] Another class of reasons are generated by values held by the trustee that make him put a high value on an (A, B) outcome in itself and override the raw preference he has for B' given that the truster will do A. These include general moral principles supporting altruistic behavior, and context-specific norms such as those that govern teamwork. Other properties making for trustworthiness are individual character traits and evolved or cultural dispositions. These properties may make E trustworthy either through some unreflective mechanism of habit or internalized norm or by making E see the force of reasons to be trustworthy. Another important consideration that may lead E to do B is his susceptibility to possible rewards and punishments, a subject we take up later in this section.

From a game-theoretic standpoint, all these properties have the effect of transforming the trustee's raw payoffs. They replace them with "all-in" payoffs, or evaluations, on which the trustees place a higher value on B than on B' (given that he thinks R expects him to do B). The particular case of altruism has often been modeled thus, as a value that transforms a person's first-order, raw payoffs into higher-order, all-in payoffs (Kitcher 1993; Nagel 1978).

We call any property (or combination of properties) of a trustee in a basic trust game that suffices for him to be trustworthy in it a **trust-warranting** property for that game.[7] We assume that in a basic trust game both parties know perfectly well which properties of trustees are trust-warranting in the game, and indeed, that this is mutual knowledge.

By contrast, R may know much or little about whether E has trust-warranting properties. Every degree of informedness is conceptually compatible with R's asking herself the primary question. However, across an extremely broad range of empirical cases, the way in which R acquires whatever information she has about the matter is much the same. In the rest of this chapter we focus on this information process.

Before turning to it, we must address one important point. We have said that, in a basic trust game, there are always properties of E that R must know E has if trusting E is to be warranted, and that these are "payoff-transforming" properties of E. At first blush, this claim seems to be false in an important subclass of basic trust games. In this subclass trust is usually thought to be warranted in virtue of features of the situation that R knows about other than such properties of E. It is the subclass in which the encounter whose payoffs are given in figure 5.1 has a sequel in which R will have opportunities to punish a B' choice, or reward a B choice, if she has trusted. The trustee will therefore be concerned that R will punish him if he does B', or that the reputation he earns with R will adversely affect his dealings in the sequel with her or others who hear of it. Both in classical economics (Hume, Smith) and in much contemporary rational choice writing on trust and reputation, this forward payoff structure is said to provide E with strong enough reasons, in the form of incentives, to be trustworthy.

It may seem that this solution to the primary trust problem eliminates the need for R to be concerned about E's trust-warranting properties. However, what matters is not these raw future payoffs alone, but the way in which E's knowledge of them transforms the raw payoffs to B and B'. Into this transformation enter dispositions of E to be swayed by these possible sequels, including his time preference and his imagination (Selten 1978). Given E's dispositions (for example, given his insensitivity to the fact of being trusted), a known system of sufficiently great punishments and rewards will usually incline E toward B'. But it does not follow from this that for a given system of known punishments and rewards his dispositions become irrelevant. On the contrary, for any plausible such system there are usually values of dispositional variables that make E untrustworthy, as well as values of them that make him trustworthy. The way such variables can tip the balance is just the same in the case of raw payoffs spread over time as it is in the case of raw payoffs in a one-shot encounter.

It was exactly for reasons of this kind that American mafiosi, according to the Mafia boss Vincent Teresa, decided not to have dealings with black people. There was no punishment severe enough for the prospect of it to keep them under control. Once that was clear, the sign "black" was enough to banish trust. Blackness, in the Mafia world, had become a sign of the absence of a nonobservable trust-warranting property, namely, of not responding to the prospect of punishment.

Secondary Trust

Krypta and Manifesta

The truster seldom knows the trustee's trust-relevant properties directly from observation. True, one may say, "I could see at once that he was an honest fellow." But it is in signs that one *sees* it. One observes, for instance, physiognomic features—the set of the eyes, a firm chin—and behavioral features—a steady look, relaxed shoulders—and treats them as evidence of an internal disposition. Trust-warranting properties—honesty, benevolence, love of children, low time preference, sect membership—may come variably close to being observable. But, except in limiting cases,[8] they are unobservable, and signs mediate the knowledge of them.

Let us call unobservable properties of a person **krypta**. Those krypta of a person that are his trust-warranting properties in a basic trust game we call his **t-krypta** in that game.[9]

The truster in a basic trust game may have sources of knowledge of the trustee's inner properties, and in particular his t-krypta, other than direct observation. Nothing in the notion of a basic trust game excludes background knowledge or knowledge gotten from others; similarly, nothing excludes direct observation of features of the trustee that *are* directly observable. These various sources may combine to allow the truster to know, or at least form considered beliefs about, the trustee's t-krypta. A truster may observe the tweed jacket and shooting stick of a woman in a departure lounge and infer that she is to be trusted to look after the truster's bag while he posts a last-minute letter. Or a truster, recognizing the trustee, by her face or signature, as someone who has always repaid loans in the past, may infer that she has now, as then, those properties of character and liquidity that make her creditworthy. Or finally, a truster, having heard of the trust-warranting properties of a person of a certain description, may try to match that description with the person in front of her: "Is this the person picked out by the signs of identification I heard of?" Sometimes signs from different sources give contrasting evidence: the credit card details look fine, the signature looks fine, but—as one of the authors of this chapter knows from experience—if the man speaks with an Italian accent, R may still be reluctant to accept credit card payment. Sign reading is a fundamental part of deciding whether to trust. Correspondingly, the deliberate use of signs, or signaling, is a fundamental part of making oneself appear trustworthy.

By a person's **manifesta** we mean any observable features of him. "Features" of a person include parts or aspects of his body, pieces of his behavior, and his appurtenances. Whether a feature of one of these kinds is observable depends on the situation. In face-to-face encounters one's face is a manifestum. At the immigration desk the passport one carries is a manifestum. In the street the jacket a woman wears is a manifestum. Depending on the medium of interaction, a feature can be a manifestum or remain hidden. The telephone reveals the voice but not the face; the Internet reveals neither the voice nor the face but still reveals an electronic address, a language, and a style of writing.

Manifesta may be evidence relevant to, or signs of, krypta, and in particular of t-krypta. An open look is a sign of honesty. A business suit is a sign of respectability. An accent is a sign of one's social and ethnic origins. A signature is a sign of personal identity. A skullcap is a sign of piety. A declaration is a sign of good intentions. A hesitation is a sign of dishonesty. Excessive protestation is a sign of insincerity. Such manifesta can be read by R, allowing her to make inferences about E's krypta and hence his trustworthiness. They may reveal that E is motivated or otherwise disposed to do B if he thinks R trusts him to, or that he is not so disposed.

Inferences from prima facie manifesta are sometimes sound; the observable features (the tweeds, the signature, the name, the accent, the club membership) may in some cases be good enough signs. Sometimes, however, it is not certain that signs of trust-warranting properties are to be trusted. Herein lies what we call the "secondary problem of trust."

A manifestum may be a sign of a krypton without being a reliable sign of it.[10] (Sometimes indeed a manifestum offered as a sign of a krypton may even reduce the probability that it is rational to assign to the krypton.) The significance of manifesta is captured by the phrase "He seemed so trustworthy," uttered after trust has been misplaced. Most signs are less than fully reliable, but we do not have in mind this commonplace. In the case of signs of t-krypta, there are special forces at work that threaten reliability.

Opportunists

We now define a type of interactant in a basic trust game, the **opportunist**, who is not only untrustworthy but also manipulative. An opportunist has these properties: he is rawly motivated: if an opportunist E knew he was trusted to do B, he would do B', for the sake of the extra raw payoff; he is manipulative: if he could obtain trust at low enough cost, he would do so, then betray it. The first is just the property of being guided by raw payoffs. The second property goes beyond the first: the opportunist is not just lacking in trust-warranting properties (love of babies, strength of will, devoutness, responsiveness to being trusted, diagnostic skill), but is proactively deceptive.

An opportunist is a type of interactant in a basic trust game, not necessarily a type of person. A person might be trustworthy in one encounter but an opportunist in another. This is because some trust-warranting properties may vary over time in a given person—people change. Some trust-warranting properties are stable, others not. "I trusted him, but he must have changed since I knew him years ago." He had become an opportunist. Finally, some trust-warranting properties are local rather than global. Someone may be solidly trustworthy as a father and yet an opportunist with his colleagues or the Inland Revenue. Love of children may be a krypton that sustains trustworthiness only in specific relationships. Honesty, by contrast, is a property that warrants trust in a wide range of encounters.

Now suppose there is a manifestum, m, that people take to be evidence of a krypton, k. Then, deliberately displaying m is a possible strategy for convincing someone that you have k. In the language of signaling theory, displaying m is a way of signaling that you have k. Both k's and non-k's may have a motive for signaling that they have k.[11] Rich people sometimes wear expensive clothes to show that they are rich; poor people sometimes wear expensive clothes to seem to be rich. Benevolent uncles smile to show they are benevolently disposed; wicked uncles smile to seem to be benevolently disposed. The deceptive instances of the strategy we call "mimicking."[12] More precisely, a **mimic** of k through m is a person who does not have k and deliberately displays m in order to be taken by another to have k.[13]

Mimic-Beset Trust Games

The possible presence in the world of opportunists means that a truster must beware of mimicry in interpreting manifesta of the trustee. Suppose that k is some t-krypton and m is a manifestum that is usually taken to be a sign of k. Then the truster should argue as follows: "An opportunist would wish to make me trust him to do B, then betray me by doing B'. He would know that to get me to trust him it would help to get me to believe he has k. There may be opportunists around. Therefore, this m-bearer may not have k but may instead be an opportunist mimicking k through m. The m I observe, though it may be produced by a k-possessing and therefore trustworthy trustee, cannot be taken at face value." Apparent guarantors of trust might be the manipulations of a wolf disguised as an old lady.

We shall call an encounter a **mimic-beset trust game** if it is a basic trust game with these features: (1) there is some positive probability that the trustee is an opportunist; and (2) the truster observes a manifestum or manifesta of the trustee. More precisely, before the truster and trustee have to choose their actions, there is an observational episode in which the trustee may, if he wishes, display a certain manifestum, and the truster observes it if he does. We suppose that the vast majority of basic trust games, and indeed of small-number problems of trust more generally, include some observation by trusters of manifesta of their trustees. Recall that any piece of observable behavior, including a message, counts as a manifestum; whence it follows, for example, that every trust-involving interaction initiated by a trustee contains an episode of the kind described.

Imagine that the truster is approached by a stranger who tells her a hard-luck story and asks her for money. The truster values a world in which she gives money and the story is true and values negatively a world in which she gives money and the story is false. As the stranger speaks, he has the opportunity to look the truster in the face, or else he may look down at the ground. The t-krypton is honesty, the manifestum is the action of looking the truster in the face. If we like, we can complicate this story to make it more realistic without changing the essential structure of the trust game. For example, it may be that there are two displayable manifesta, looking in the face and offering an address, or indeed many. Similarly, the t-krypta may be many and various. It is clear that very many basic trust games are mimic-beset trust games.

Secondary Trust

If a truster is playing a mimic-beset trust game, she should give her trust only with caution. She should exercise care in this example not only if the stranger looks down, but also if he looks her in the face. The assumptions of mimic-beset trust games imply that whenever there is a question "Can I trust this person to do B?" a truster must first, and need only, answer another question: "Is the manifestum m of the trust-warranting cryptic property k that I observe a reliable sign of k?" Or, in brief, "Can I trust this sign of k?" The conditions under which manifesta of t-krypta may be trusted or distrusted constitute a special topic in trust—the "problem of secondary trust."

If we are right that typically problems of trust are mimic-beset trust games, then the problem of secondary trust is the key to answering the two questions that normative trust theory should be concerned with: "When is it rational to trust someone to do something?" and, "How can I, who am trustworthy, convince the truster that I am?" The first question is asked by the truster, the second by the trustee who has trust-warranting properties. A theoretical understanding of the secondary problem of trust directly answers the truster's question. It also indirectly answers the trustworthy trustee's question: he should, if he wishes to be trusted and if he thinks the truster rational, display those manifesta that can be trusted as signs.

There is, moreover, one secondary problem of trust that pervades all interactions between any two people that are spread over time. Present behavior can have no effect on future payoffs, and so future payoffs can provide no present incentives, unless a fundamental condition is present in the future encounters. This is the condition that the truster knows that her interactant is . . . who he is! This condition is necessary whatever the specific nature of the successive interactions (whether they are simple repetitions of a fixed basic trust game, opportunities for reciprocation, opportunities for punishment, or whatever). For, as we show later in the chapter, identity itself is a krypton.

Secondary Trust and Signaling

In the first section we suggested that secondary trust almost always accompanies, and is often the key to solving, problems of primary trust. In this section we do two things: first, we show how the theory of signaling that developed in economics, biology, and game theory (Spence 1974;

Zahavi 1975), when combined with the notion of a mimic-beset trust game, provides a clear analytical framework for understanding secondary trust. Mimic-beset trust games can be recast as a class of signaling games. Rational trust can therefore be explained, up to a point, as the beliefs that a receiver has in an equilibrium of a signaling game. Second, we expand signaling theory to treat "signaling via identity," a mode of signaling that is of key importance when the basic trust game is repeated over time and reputation is invoked in solving problems of trust. Signaling via identity has until now received little attention (but see Bacharach 1997; Tadelis 1996).

Signaling Theory

A signal is an action by a player (the "signaler") whose purpose is to raise the probability that another player (the "receiver") assigns to a certain state of affairs or "event." This event could be anything. As it happens, in many cases studied in the literature the event is that the signaler is of a certain "type"; for example, in a famous early study (Spence 1974) the event is that the signaler is a worker of high rather than low productivity. In these cases what is being signaled is what we have called a krypton of the signaler.

Within signaling theory most attention has been paid to a class of games in which there are three kinds of agents: k's, non-k's (both of whom can send some signal from a specified list), and receivers. There is something the receiver can do that benefits a signaler whether or not he is k, but it benefits the receiver only if the signaler is k, and otherwise hurts her. The benefits to k and non-k signalers need not be equal. Thus, k's and receivers share an interest in the truth, but the interests of non-k's and receivers are opposed: non-k's would like to deceive receivers into thinking they have k, in order to receive the benefit, while receivers have an interest in not being deceived. The interests of k's and non-k's are also usually opposed because the activity of the latter damages the credibility of the signals of the former.

The main result in signaling theory is that in a game of this kind,[14] there is an equilibrium in which at least some truth is transmitted, provided that the possible signals include one, s, that is cheap enough to emit, relative to the benefit, for signalers who have k, but too costly to emit, relative to the benefit, for at least some of those who do not.

If the cost relationships are such that all and only k's can afford to emit s, the equilibrium in which they do so is called "separating" or "sorting." In such an equilibrium, signals are quite unambiguous, and the receiver is perfectly informed. No poisoner seeks to demonstrate his honesty by drinking from the poisoned chalice.

But the cost conditions may also give rise to dirtier equilibria, so-called semi-sorting ones. In a semi-sorting equilibrium (SSE), a signal s is emitted by all k's but not only k's; a certain proportion of non-k's emit it too. Here, although observing s is evidence for the receiver in favor of k, it is not conclusive evidence; it makes it more likely that the signaler has k but does not imply that he does. A determined mimic can even try to make an audience believe that he is an operatic singer, by lip-synching. The higher the proportion of non-k's who use this signal, the less conclusive is the evidence.

The conditions on the parameters of a signaling game necessary for it to have a sorting equilibrium or a semi-sorting equilibrium are well known. It has a sorting equilibrium, in which a k always emits s and a non-k never emits s, if two conditions hold: the benefit to a k of being treated as a k exceeds the cost for him of emitting s; and the benefit to a non-k of being treated as a k is less than the cost for him of emitting s. In brief, a k can afford to emit s, and a non-k cannot. We call these the Can and the Cannot conditions. (They are called the "incentive compatibility condition" and the "nonpooling condition" in game theory.) And the signaling game has an SSE, in which all k's emit s and a certain proportion p of non-k's, less than one, also do so, if these two conditions hold: the Can condition; and the benefit to a non-k of being treated as a k is exactly equal to the cost for him of emitting s: that is, a non-k can just afford to. We call the latter the Can Just condition. We can also calculate p in terms of the cost and benefit parameters.

There is evidence that many—perhaps most—cases of krypton signaling in animal life are not sorting but only semi-sorting equilibria (Guilford and Dawkins 1991). The same appears to be true of human life. For example, verbal reports of inner states such as beliefs and intentions may be regarded as a very large family of krypton signals. Telling lies is commonplace; all such reports are suspect when the signaler has a motive to deceive. Yet whenever a hearer doubts a verbal claim, it remains likely that the speaker's making it is on balance evidence for the krypton (raising, not lowering, the probability the hearer assigns to the krypton), since otherwise the speaker acted counterproductively. If so, then the utterance is a semi-sorting signal of the krypton. If a man wearing a UPS uniform rings your doorbell, the chances are that he is a UPS delivery man.

The relevance of signaling theory to the problem of trust lies in a simple connection: mimic-beset trust games are instances of signaling games. In a mimic-beset trust game there is a trustee who may or may not have k and who can, if he so decides, display a manifestum m to a truster. Both k trustees and non-k trustees are interested in getting the truster to believe that they have k.[15] To complete the demonstration of the correspondence between the two kinds of game, it remains only to note that the *display of* m may be regarded as a *signal* s (and displaying m as emitting the signal s).

Our definition of a mimic-beset trust game is silent about whether the opportunist will in fact mimic. For a basic trust game to be mimic-beset, as we have defined this term, it is enough that the trustee has an opportunity to display a manifestum and that he may be an opportunist, and so prepared to mimic, if it suits him. We can now use the correspondence with signaling games to give precise conditions in which mimicry will occur, assuming that the truster and trustee are "subjects of game theory." More than this, we can say how much mimicry will occur, when any does—that is, what proportion of opportunists who have a chance to mimic does so. The nub of the matter is this: *opportunistic trustees in a mimic-beset trust game mimic at least sometimes if the associated signaling game has a semi-sorting equilibrium.*[16] We may conclude that opportunists sometimes mimic if and only if the Can condition is satisfied for a k and the Can Just condition is satisfied for a non-k. And we can determine the proportion of opportunists who do.

Signaling theory is thus a powerful tool: it delivers specific answers to the questions of when, and how much, false signaling will occur. However, crucial for the experience of the solutions it offers are strong assumptions about the players' background knowledge: they know the sizes of the benefits, and of the cost of emitting s, for both k's and non-k's; and a receiver knows the base-rate probabilities that a signaler is k and non-k. When she peers through the peephole and sees a stranger in a UPS uniform, as she wonders whether to confer the benefit of opening the door she has in mind the general incidence of criminality, the ease or difficulty of acquiring a disguise, and the value to a criminal of what he would get from securing entry.

One of us recently filled the truster role in a mimic-beset trust game with an SSE. Bacharach was approached by an apparently (m) desperate young man in a public park. He turned out to be an opportunistic non-k mimicking k through m. Bacharach gave him money despite his uncomfortable awareness that there was a chance of this, and because that chance seemed to be outweighed by the chance that the young man was genuine and by the awfulness of his plight if he was. The former chance depends, in the theory, on the base-rate incidence of opportunism, on the size of the donation, and on the difficulty of "putting on" the m that Bacharach observed, which was a detailed and convincing performance. He and the young man both played their parts just right in an SSE of a mimic-beset trust game.[17]

Signaling theory provides a framework for analyzing, in a wide if somewhat idealized class of cases, rational krypton signaling of both informative and deliberately misleading kinds. It thus serves as a basis for an analytical account of the secondary problem of trust. But it provides only a framework. The explanations it gives remain abstract and incomplete. They are cast in terms of a benefit (from being thought k) and costs (of emitting each possible signal) that are given no structure in the theory and themselves receive no explanation. In the remainder of the chapter we begin to fill the gap that is left.

Identity Signaling

Signaling via Individual Identity

In this section we analyze an extremely widespread strategy for using manifesta to give evidence of a special kind of krypton, identity. This strategy gives rise to a special problem of secondary trust—trust in signs of identity. When it is used, the truster employs, instead of the three-layered inferential structure

$$m \rightarrow k \rightarrow t,$$

the four-layered structure

$$g \rightarrow i \rightarrow k \rightarrow t,$$

where t denotes trustworthiness, k denotes k-ness, i denotes identity, m denotes presence or absence of a manifestum of k, and g denotes presence or absence of a kind of manifestum that is a sign of identity, called a "signature." The threat of mimicry of k through m is replaced by the threat of mimicry of i through g.

Signaling via identity (which for the sake of concision we call "identity signaling") arises in dynamic contexts. In particular, it does so when a basic trust game is played repeatedly. Unless players are locked in a room and monitor each other constantly, there is the possibility that partners may change. Whenever this is so, the repeated basic trust game is a basic trust game with random rematching. In such a game, the trustee may wish to signal his identity so as reassure R that he is the same person R encountered before.

Identity signaling pays, when it does, by enabling the signaler to exploit a reputation. The latter is not always straightforward. This is because the fact that someone is the bearer of a certain reputation is frequently a krypton of that person! For example, Armani has a reputation for selling well-designed clothes, but to exploit this reputation a seller must convince customers that he is Armani. Islamic Jihad has a reputation for carrying out its threats against hostages, but to exploit this reputation a group of kidnappers must convince governments that they belong to Jihad. The IRA has devised a special secret code—known to the British police—that they use when they issue warnings about bombs they have placed. Not only does the code make the information credible because it reidentifies a group that has acquired a reputation for planting bombs, but so long as it remains secret, it also makes the telephoned information credible because it creates an obstacle for would-be IRA impersonators who would like either to play nasty pranks or to plant a real bomb to discredit the IRA.

Identity signaling is a strategy for signaling a krypton that works by giving evidence of another krypton, that of being the reputation-bearer. It can be an efficient means of krypton signaling, partly because identity signals can be very cheap, and partly because it capitalizes on certain preexisting beliefs of the receiver. The signaler does not need to send a signal to induce these beliefs. They are of two kinds: the signaler's reputation with the receiver, and the "trait laws" believed by the receiver. We first consider trait laws.

Commonsense belief systems contain trait laws. These laws of constancy are of two kinds: individual trait laws, of the form "once a k always a c," and categorial trait laws, of the form "one X a k, all X's k's." A categorial trait law is a schema in which both k and X are variables. It is not of the form "all Swedes are fair-haired" (a specific reputation of Swedes), but rather, "all people of a given nationality have the same hair color," or, "hair color is a national characteristic." Similarly, an individual law is not of the form "Alderman Brown is a stuffy so-and-so," but rather, "someone's degree of stuffiness is the sort of thing that doesn't change." There is no need for a trait law to be as rigid as this: k may be not a sure property but a merely probabilistic or tendential one, as in, "within each nationality, the *probabilities of various hair colors* are the same for all persons," or, "a given individual's tendency to cheat is constant over time." In this chapter we deal only with sure k's, but this is for simplicity, not because the logic of our argument requires it.

A reputation is formed in someone's mind by, as it were, experiencing a krypton. An **experience krypton**—a generalization of the economic notion of an "experience good" (Nelson 1970)—is a krypton that is revealed by interacting in a certain way with its possessor. That a merchant sells a good wine is revealed by buying wine from him; a woman's honesty is revealed by trusting her to repay a loan; an organization's readiness to execute hostages if its demands are not met is revealed by not meeting those demands. The outcome of the interaction reveals to one interactant whether the other has the krypton.

We can put this in terms of a basic trust game: a t-krypton k is an experience t-krypton if the truster discovers whether the trustee has k by trusting her. The interpretation is that the outcome of the trusting act and the trustee's act reveals to the truster whether the trustee has k: more precisely, the outcome of (A, B) reveals that he has k, while the outcome of (A, B') reveals that he does not.[18]

This discovery gives birth to a reputation for k-ness or non-k-ness, and so for either trustworthiness or untrustworthiness. If the trustee remains anonymous, however, reputation will be stillborn. For a reputation to issue an advantage, for its value to be realized, its owner must reveal himself to those who believe in it. That is, he must engage in signaling behavior in which he signals his identity by displaying an appropriate manifestum.

Manifesta used to signal identity are usually of a kind we call "signatures." A **signature** is a manifestum that is drawn from some fixed family, called a stock. Stocks are all alike in some respect: one stock is the set of all possible English proper names, another the set of all possible fingerprints, another the set of all possible uniforms, another the set of all possible embroidered emblems.

Suppose that a trust game with rematching is enriched as follows. Before a trustee plays for the first time, she acquires a signature from a certain stock, by a "heteronymous" mechanism, that is, a mechanism that ensures that the signature differs from all other allocated signatures, thus avoiding the possibility of "mistaken identity." Genetic variety does this for fingerprints and faces (and other features that keep being discovered, such as odors); the size of the set of common names almost does it for the standard mechanism of name allocation (help yourself). On any occasion on which this trustee plays a game, she is able to display her signature if she wishes.

Here is how the identity signaling mechanism works to allow a trustee who has k to show that he has. Suppose that on some occasion this trustee chooses to display his signature. His truster on this occasion, R, if she trusts him, soon finds out whether he is k (since k is an experience krypton). Thereafter, whenever E encounters R again, E is in a position to provide evidence that he is E simply by displaying his signature. Provided that R remembers it, she can infer (from heteronymity) that he is the previously encountered trustee who turned out to have k, and she can conclude (from the individual trait law "once a k always a c") that he still has k.

The simplest example of such a repeated trust game with random rematching and identity signaling is a sequence of face-to-face encounters with random rematching and facial display. It has been suggested that human facial recognition evolved because this capacity allowed interactants in collective action problems to keep track of interactants who had proved cooperative (Barkow, Cosmides, and Tooby 1992). If so, then what took place was identity signaling in which the signature stock was the set of possible human faces.

Face-to-face interactions are (still!) the kind that first spring to mind. They have the properties—key advantages, as we explain elsewhere—of being costless to display and almost impossible to reproduce. It is perhaps because it is easy to forget how lucky we are to be able to count on facial recognition in so many of our dealings that we may overlook that individual identity is a krypton, and that even when people repeatedly interact the problem of signaling who you are is often far from trivial. In particular, the further that interaction departs from ideal face-to-face conditions, the less safe are signalers of personal identity from the corruption of their signals by the mimicking activities of impersonators.

Identity signaling often provides a highly efficient way of signaling a krypton, for example, a t-krypton that implies trustworthiness. One reason is that it is easy to contrive stocks with heteronymous allocation mechanisms and signatures that are very cheap to display, both of which tend to characterize stocks of symbolic signatures. The ultimate source of the efficiency of identity signaling, however, is the presence in the receiver population—in our case, the population of trusters—of pre-existing beliefs in trait laws. The identity signaling strategy capitalizes efficiently on these beliefs.

Indeed, we can regard the identity signaling mechanism as a prime example of applying the following very general maxim for signalers: seek background beliefs that link the krypton with another more efficiently signaled one. Reputation works as a means of signaling krypta when, but only when, both halves of this recipe are present. The general maxim has wide application in the world. As the schemas at the beginning of this section show, a truster's inferences contain two sorts of links: from manifesta to krypta, and from krypta to krypta. Optimizing a signaling strategy may often involve inducing the receiver to follow a quite roundabout route, going through several krypton-krypton links leading from a signalable krypton to the one that counts; many krypton-signaling mechanisms (for example, Spence's) are indirect in this way.[19] However, it must be remembered that we have been idealizing away from uncertainty by considering only rigid trait laws; when beliefs connecting krypta are only partial or probabilistic, increasing the roundaboutness of the mechanism decreases its power.

Categorial Identity Signaling

So far we have focused on the individual case. Consider now a class or category of people X all of whom are k's. X's may be able to mark themselves with a group signature g (that is, a signature that is displayed by all X's but by no non-X's). Suppose they do. Suppose further that a truster R discovers as a result of an interaction with some individual X—for instance, x—that x has k. Thereafter, if R has an encounter with any X—for instance, x'—and the latter displays g, R can conclude (by heteronymity) that x' is an X, and therefore (by the categorial trait law "one X a k, all X's k's") that x' has k.

Categories have both advantages and disadvantages over individuals as units of identity for purposes of signaling trustworthiness. Because categories can be large, a reputation for k-ness can be built, and travel, much more rapidly. It may be that, with respect to certain kinds of krypton, people are more inclined to believe in categorial than individual trait laws (people may indeed believe unduly in national characters and ethnic traits), partly because the former provide simplified, more cognitively tractable views of the world (Tajfel 1959). Categories are more powerful in various ways; for example, social groups may be able to secure observance of trait laws through social influence on their members, while individuals may lack analogous means of keeping themselves in line over time.[20]

On the other hand, if the identity signaling mechanism for showing that you have k is to work, a signature must be fixed over occasions of interaction. For an individual this just means coordinating her display behavior over time. Earlier we merely assumed that she could do this effortlessly. This is often indeed the case, but not always: to display her personal identification number (PIN), for instance, or the distinctive clothes she wore, the would-be self-identifier must recall it. But this is often not hard. By contrast, a category of people can get identity signals to work only by coordinating across members to adopt matching signatures. So the most likely categories to use categorial identity signaling are not just sets of people who share any old k, but sets that already have enough cohesion as a group to facilitate this coordination. Consider an example reported by Robert Frank (1994, 207): many New York couples advertise for a governess in Salt Lake City, having learned that people brought up in the Mormon tradition are trustworthy to a degree exceeding that of the average New Yorker. Mormons have the right kind of cohesion and can coordinate their signatures; people who love children have no such cohesion and therefore cannot coordinate their signatures. Hence, if k is the property of being diligent in looking after a child left in your care, the krypton "Mormon," which is a sign of k, can be signaled via identity, while the krypton "children-loving," which is also a sign of k, cannot be.

The Management of Manifesta

In the previous two sections we argued that signaling theory provides a general analytical framework for understanding the phenomenon of secondary trust. Signaling theory, however, is abstract and incomplete. It does not arm our imagination with the tentacles it needs to grasp the infinite variety of signs that can be emitted by trustees and processed by trusters in mimic-beset trust games. Its abstractness makes it difficult even to see many of the trust problems we regularly face as what they are, signaling games that involve trust in signs.

In particular, signaling theory lacks a concrete semiotic structure. Yet this is indispensable for introducing order into the variety of signs of trustworthiness, and for accounting for the varied strategies of "sign management" that people use. There is scope, above all in humans, for creating new signs, for discovering latent ones, and for protecting signs against mimics. Protective measures are in turn threatened by stratagems to get around them, giving rise to a relentless semiotic warfare in which technology plays a major part. We see bank notes, forgeries, watermarks, forged watermarks; we see smiles, false smiles, scrutiny, and dark glasses. In the last section we made a beginning in the task of delineating the concrete structure of signs and their management by describing one important general strategy for signaling krypta, identity signaling. In this section we pursue this enterprise. First we briefly discuss the routes by which a manifestum may come to signify a particular krypton. We then give a taxonomy of manifesta and discuss the relative advantages for the signaler of manifesta of the different taxa. Third, we go on to describe some techniques of "sign management," including the "protection" and "multiplication" of signs. Then we recount a pair of real incidents that posed primary problems of trust: we show that the theory we have developed provides an analytical reconstruction of the truster's intuitions on that day. By the same token, the truster's intuitions illustrate the richness and subtlety of the reasoning that sustains our everyday decisions as trusters about whether to trust, and our everyday moves as trustees in managing signs.

"Model Comes Before Mimic"

The literature on mimicry, which has developed in biology, includes some applications of signaling theory but is mainly concerned with the variety of forms and functions of animal signaling (Hauser 1996). Almost nothing has been written about the human case.

In biology, the standard dynamics begins with the emergence in a first phase of a mutant of some k-possessing type of organism. This mutant bears a manifestum m, which gives it a selective advantage over other k-possessors because a certain type of receiver learns to associate k with m. For example, k is toxicity, m is a bright marking, and receivers are predators. In a second phase a mutant of non-k (say, nontoxic) organisms emerges that also bears m. It too is selectively advantaged, in this case over non-k's without m. As this variety ("mimics") multiplies, its advantage, as well as that of m-bearing k's ("models"), diminishes, in both cases because the correlation of m with k becomes weaker as mimics multiply.[21]

We have seen that, in any SSE of a signaling game in which the signal is a display of a manifestum m, each non-k that displays m is a mimic of k through m. But SSEs fail to capture other aspects of the notion of mimicry. In particular, the signaling-game model describes no real-time process through which m comes to signify k. Indeed, for all that this model says, the significance of m can spring into existence at the same moment as the deceitful use of the same m. But almost always, in animal and human affairs, "model comes before mimic." The standard way in which an m comes to be evidence of a krypton k for receivers at time t is the growth of an associative belief: before time t there has been a history of experiencing krypta associated with independent evidence of k-ness.[22] Signaling theory does not deny this explanation of the evidential force of s; it only fails to model it. This is because it is an equilibrium theory with no dynamics. All it says about the evidential force of a manifestum in an SSE is that in such a state the probabilities with which k's and non-k's use s are known to the receiver; it says nothing about how the receiver comes to know them. In one interpretation she works them out a priori from various data, including those on benefits and costs; on this interpretation, the equilibrium, complete with the significance and rate of deceptive use of the signal, springs into existence. But, equally, there is nothing to stop us from interpreting the SSE as the outcome of a learning process like the one sketched here.

Kinds of Manifesta

The main result of signaling theory implies that a manifestum m is secure against mimicry if and only if it is cheap enough for a k to display and too expensive for an opportunist to display. We have called these two conditions the Can and Cannot conditions. The study of the reliability of different kinds of signs of krypta in general, and of t-krypta in particular, can usefully be organized in terms of these conditions.

Cues   One favorable case is that m is a "cue" of k. A "cue of k" is a manifestum whose display is costless for k-possessors.[23] An example is an honest look, or, in identity signaling, one's handwriting or voice.[24] Since in a signaling game the benefit from being thought k is positive for a k, any cue of k satisfies the Can condition. There is no guarantee that cues satisfy the Cannot condition: if assuming an honest look were easy enough, the Cannot condition would fail and honesty would be mimickable through an honest look. However, cues usually have at least some positive cost for non-k's. If so, signaling theory implies that sometimes k's can rely on the cue of k to convince: namely, when mimics have little to gain. Often, though not always, the cue is "there anyway" and the k need take no action to manifest it: these are "automatic cues." When cues are automatic, a k can take it easy. Indeed, he need hardly be aware of the cue's effect to benefit from it, as we shall see.[25]

Evolution has equipped us with many cues. These may be categorial, such as signs of gender, or individual, such as signs of age. Cues of this kind are often costly, sometimes impossible, to mimic. Some, like the face, could have evolved, together with a remarkable ability to discriminate the faces of other humans, because they are advantageous in that they sustain cooperation by making identity signaling cheap and safe from mimics. By contrast, other biological cues of identity, some of which are still being discovered, may have evolved for reasons unrelated to co-operation or may be just random individual differences that become observable with the right technology; insofar as they are heteronymous, these manifesta can be employed for reidentification. British banks may soon introduce new devices at their cash dispensers, "palm readers" or "finger readers," that trade on the fact that in no two individuals is the shape of the hand, or even a single finger, the same. They will replace PINs, which are kept safe from imitation by mimics only by secrecy.

An interesting class of cues emerges as a by-product of the life each individual lives. As we grow older, our diet, occupation, and lifestyle shape our limbs, looks, and quirks. Cues of this kind also apply to cate-gories of people, who share a language, a pronunciation, and practices of many sorts.

Symbolic Manifesta   An unfavorable case is that m is symbolic, in the sense that it consists in a configuration of characters, however these may be physically realized. It is exemplified by names, logos, and oaths. What makes this case unfavorable is that among the physical realizations there are usually some that are very cheap for anyone, non-k's included, to pro-duce. The efficient production cost of a verbal claim or a false signature is virtually zero. Symbolic manifesta are attractive because the signaler ef-fortlessly meets the Can condition, but since they violate the Cannot con-dition their evidential value is under threat. The expansion of the scope for ultra-cheap transmission of symbol-strings is indeed a major cause of the growth of mimicry in our time. However, the Cannot condition is not necessarily violated, even if the costs of producing the manifestum are zero, for the costs of producing m may not be, as we shall see, the only costs of displaying it.

Symbols are characteristic of actual identity signaling. Symbolic sig-natures, individual or categorial, abound. Like other symbolic mani-festa, they are vulnerable to the mimic if the production element in cost dominates. We do indeed find much mimicry of identities through sym-bolic signatures, both of a personal kind (impersonation) and of a catego-rial kind (posing). However, it may sometimes be that mimicking the trustee E, or a category of trustworthy X's (and hence indirectly k) through some g, is more costly than mimicking k directly through some m. For even though the Cannot condition fails to be satisfied on the pro-duction side, there are often ways specific to identity signals in which E, or X's, can raise the cost of mimicry to would-be mimics.

Fakeable Manifesta   A second important unfavorable case is that m can be faked. Faking is not the same thing as mimicry: what is mimicked is a krypton, what is faked is a certain kind of object. Mimicry uses all sorts of techniques, from lying to plastic surgery, from makeup to the imitation of bodily movements. Fakery is one technique among others. If I mimic a rich man by wearing an expensive suit, I do not fake or forge the suit. If I mimic a devout person by wearing a skullcap, I do not fake the skullcap. If, however, I mimic a rich man by wearing what looks like but is not an expensive suit, then I employ fakery to execute mimicry. If I write your name on a check so that it is taken for yours, I forge something to execute mimicry. And if, to convince customers that my roadside restaurant has a good kitchen, I place cardboard mock-ups of dump trucks in the parking area, I fake trucks as part of a strategy to mimic an establishment where one eats well.

The objects that are faked or forged in these examples are not true manifesta but "quasi-manifesta." By definition manifesta are observables: if m is a manifestum, a truster can tell by looking (smelling, hearing) whether a trustee is displaying an m. But if a thing can be faked, then ipso facto trusters cannot tell whether what is displayed is that thing. A fakeable object o (or type of object o) is one that can be simulated by another, o'. For faking to be successful, it must be possible for an observer to mistake o' for o.

The following definition of fakery will do for our purposes. First, generalize the notion of manifesta to "exhibits." An exhibit is a displayable feature of a person (for example, a part of his body, a behavior, an object attached to him) of which one aspect is observable (that is, is a manifestum), and the other is not: call this the "latent component." Consider any exhibit (m, n) (where m denotes the manifestum and n the latent component). To fake (m, n) is to display an exhibit (m, n') where n' differs from n, with the object of convincing an interactant that it is (m, n). To do this successfully, n' must be observationally indistinguishable from n. An opportunist, to convince a truster that he is to be trusted, may display a fake testimonial or a fake smile. The latent component of the testimonial is its authorship, and the latent aspect of the smile is the emotion that it expresses or fails to express.

An important class of cases in which false signaling by faking occurs is that in which displaying a real m satisfies the Cannot condition. For example, m is a certificate that can be obtained only if you can prove to the issuing office that you are k. In this class of cases, it may be that the best hope of falsely signaling k is by faking m. For it may be that, although displaying m is prohibitively costly for a non-k (the signal display-m satisfies the Cannot condition), displaying a fake m is not, because k's have no particular advantage in producing the manifest component of m.[26]

Sign Management

So far we have described the characteristics that, by helping or hindering the satisfaction of the Can and Cannot conditions, militate for or against the effectiveness of *given* signals. The question naturally arises: how can we expect signalers, and in particular trustworthy and opportunist trustees, to optimize over alternative signals and over variables, which may affect the costs to them and others of using given signals? We call the ensemble of such optimizing activities "sign management." In this section we discuss two important principles of sign management, protection and the multiplication of signs.

Humans are often faced with situations in which the Cannot condition fails, and indeed fails badly, so that even quite high rates of mimicry still leave mimics with a profit. Trusters and trustworthy trustees have developed many strategies to combat these situations. One such strategy is protection.

To "protect" a manifestum m of a t-kryptum k is to implement the Cannot condition by deterring would-be mimics from either producing or displaying. But to be successful, the strategy must do this without endangering the Can condition: the cost of, say, punishing mimics must be affordable by trustworthy trustees (k's). There may be alternative manifesta that would convince trusters without any protection, but these may be so expensive to produce or display as to violate the Can condition. What is important is that the sum of the costs of production, display, and protection be too high for mimics but affordable for k's. As it happens, a common strategy is cheap manifesta combined with strong protection.

Protection strategies are of several kinds: they may be directed at detecting mimics in the act of faking or fraudulently displaying manifesta, or they may demonstrate at a later stage that a mimicry has taken place. The mimic is then punished. Such strategies may be put in place by trustworthy trustees, trusters, or some coalition. Thanks to efficient legal systems, firms can practice effective identity signaling of quality by incurring the trivial cost of displaying a name or a logo. Even if there are manifesta that support tolerable equilibria when unprotected, through their production and display costs alone these are frequently more costly in toto than such symbolic signatures when protected.

It may be that groups successful in category signaling tend to have members who are not cryptic but relatively transparent to each other. Mormons are no doubt better than non-Mormons both at recognizing Mormons and at recognizing non-Mormons. In particular, we may expect successful category signalers to have good negative as well as positive recognitional capacities, for this allows them to detect mimics and so to operate protection strategies. For this reason, signaling via identity of X-membership tends to be more feasible the more familiar to each other are members of the category X. (In the individual case this reaches an extreme degree: a person is very expert at telling who is, and who is not, himself!)

A type of sign management activity as important as protection is the choice of which signals to use. This may involve searching for or designing new signals. The "model" is often in a position to raise the cost of mimicking her through her manifestum, by modifying it to make this more expensive, or by choosing or sometimes inventing a new type of manifestum. For example, fakeable manifesta may be rendered harder to forge by introducing some costly device in their production, such as digital watermarks that can identify photographs transmitted on the Internet. Several episodes in the history of fashion are of the latter type: when a garment becomes more affordable, it stops being a reliable sign of opulence, and those who intend to signal their opulence by the way they dress must switch to costlier ones. If the trustworthy trustee can pursue such a strategy at a low enough cost to herself, she can banish the threat of mimicry. Generally, a failure of the Cannot condition to obtain through mimicry costs in one category can be made good by raising those in another.

A feature of a krypton that militates against mimicry is multiplicity of its manifesta. Say that good eating-places are frequented by many patrons who are mostly local people. When I see that a place is crowded, I may think, "Ah! that looks like a good place for lunch." But when I enter, I may notice that all the patrons are tourists. This leads me to conclude that this cannot really be a good restaurant. The problem for the mimic is not just that the technical difficulty of the simulation accelerates with the dimension of the manifestum, but that it is very easy to forget one and give the game away. A good mimic must be thorough and display all the characteristic signs of a k. How multiple the manifesta of a krypton are depends on the "bandwidth" of the signaling stage of the game. It is often thought to be easier to mislead someone about yourself when nothing is exchanged but strings of ASCII symbols, as in Internet communication, than in face-to-face encounters. When a customer opens a bank account in New York, he is given a PIN and asked to specify three further identifiers: his mother's maiden name, the name of his elementary school, and a password of his choice. The base-rate incidence of mimicry in New York is probably higher than in Oxford, where only two identifiers are requested.

An ethnic group with a long history is usually very robust because the constellation of manifesta that identify it is extensive. Art Spiegelman reports that, during the German occupation of Poland, his father used to travel to town by tram. It had two cars: "One was only Germans and officials. The second, it was only the Poles. He always went straight to the official car." There a simple salute "Heil Hitler" was enough not to call attention, whereas "in the Polish car they could smell if a Polish Jew came in." It was harder for a Polish Jew to mimic the nuanced multiple signs of a Polish Gentile than the fewer superficial manifesta of a pro-Nazi (Spiegelman 1991, 142).

Two Incidents

One of us was recently stopped by a young man at the door of the college library. He said to Gambetta: "I am a student, and I've forgotten the code to get into the library. Could you please let me in?" His nonverbal manifesta matched his claim. He looked like a plausible Oxford undergraduate; he also had what to Gambetta seemed an honest look. Still, the library is full of precious books (raw benefit), while his verbal claim was costless; his scruffy looks are socially approved among today's students and thus cheap not only to produce but also to display (low cost of mimicry). Before making a decision, Gambetta looked at him with suspicion (closely observed his manifesta) and probed him with questions designed to establish the krypton in question—to establish whether he really was what he claimed to be. Hardly a minute later, Gambetta ran into a group of about ten people chatting in the cold at the entrance to a college seminar room. One of the group said: "There's going to be a seminar in the Wharton Room, but we're locked out. Could you let us in please?" That room is full of precious paintings and furniture (raw benefit), but Gambetta did not think twice before letting the whole group into the room.

Why was he more suspicious of one person than of many? Had we not been writing about the problem we would hardly have noticed the curious difference between the two incidents in terms of the truster's reaction. In the first, Gambetta sought further evidence of the claim before believing in the student's trustworthiness, and in the second he did not. Even the second incident might have been an instantiation of an SSE: the group of people might have been a mimicking team planning to rob the room clean once Gambetta let them in and then left. Yet he took the claim to be honest and believed that the members of the group had the krypton in question—that they were genuine seminar participants stuck in the cold. We tend to perceive our reactions of this kind as guided by intuition, and as therefore not governed by complex computations. But this is only because we are so good at this activity; it comes naturally to us, even though it entails reading a rich web of signs and rapidly computing sometimes complex cost-benefit balances.[27] The key manifesta Gambetta observed were that the trustee was a group and that the group members looked like graduate students and academics. Unreflectingly, Gambetta must have formed a rough idea of the cost relative to the benefit of assembling a whole group of people, and of supplying them all with the right looks for the staging of an elaborate act of concerted mimicry. Given these estimates, the conclusion that it was too expensive followed easily. Had the group asked to be let into the room where the college's silver is kept (very high raw benefit), Gambetta's conclusion would have been different.

Reflecting on the behavior of the trustees in these examples from the point of view of the trusters shows the potential of signaling theory for predicting fine details of people's sign management strategies. Neither the student nor the group of academics intentionally chose in the morning to wear their looks as manifesta for displaying to Gambetta later that day. Had they been untrustworthy opportunists they would have prepared for such encounters, and done so, but the trustworthy trustees did not expect to run into the difficulties they did and made no preparations. By simply keeping to their normal style, and so conforming to the conventions of their categories, they convinced the truster. A substantial part of the look of an academic or a student is a set of automatic cues: pale complexion, drooping shoulders, an absent air. Such cues give the true k-possessor two distinct advantages over her would-be mimics. Because they are cues, the Can condition is necessarily met. Because they are automatic, the k-possessor does not have to be on her toes, planning, her strategic faculties activated. (One needs to worry about cues only when they are counterindications.) Cues need to be natural to be automatic. Just as the student unreflectingly wears his pale complexion, so too she unreflectingly dons her tracksuit top or her Doc Martens. Automatic cues are information manna that supports all human intercourse—whose success depends on the correct identification of krypta—and, in particular, does much to engender trust only when it is warranted.[28]

The fact that in displaying such non-natural automatic cues as Doc Martens no conscious intentionality is involved is consistent with our tendency to tailor our appearance in a way that deals with incidents of these kinds. If the same signaling situation arises day after day, what is at first a conscious intention tends to become habitual and internalized. But it remains an intention, for all that, on this simple test: were one to be made aware of the issue by, for example, losing a suitcase containing all one's clothes, one would choose to re-outfit oneself with similar manifesta—for example, with new clothes in the same style—with the explicit intention of signaling one's t-krypta. In short, the intention does not have to be "occurrent" but only "triggerable." So conforming to the dress codes and outward practices of one's group can be explained as a broadly intentional act, with the purpose of signaling membership of that group.

This example illustrates that the secondary problem of trust, "trust in signs," is present in many daily encounters. It also illustrates that a krypton is often indicated by several manifesta that, in our truster role, we need to disentangle before we can roughly compute their cost and decide on their reliability. As trusters, we do not usually need to bother about the Can condition; typically, we already know from experience that k-possessors can afford to display m.[29] But we do need to judge whether the Cannot condition is satisfied: given the raw benefit, could a mimic afford this manifestum? This is often a complex task, since in analyzing the affordability of signs we face a very wide array of sources of sign cost. But we are often good at it owing to the richness of our background knowledge. It matters for the Cannot condition that the absence of a norm against down-dressing reduces the total cost of a scruffy look, but we come to the problem knowing what the norms are and easily marshaling this knowledge. Sometimes the analysis of costs of signs is less obvious. The longer it takes to acquire a certain look or accent, the more expensive it is for a mimic to assume it: to look like an academic costs nothing extra to academics, and something to nonacademics; by contrast, to look like a student costs little to both students and nonstudents of the right age group. The analysis can produce surprises. Although one person is generally less menacing than a group, this is not so when the menace is of mimicry: the number of people involved increases the cost of mimicking because this demands coordination and consistency. Confidence artists do better as loners.

Conclusion

Several scholars have expressed skepticism about the specificity of problems of trust. One upshot of our reorientation of the theory of trust is just such a skeptical conclusion: the problem of trust is not, in its essentials, sui generis. This conclusion, however, is not nihilistic; we do not suggest that the problem of trust thereby evaporates. Rather, we reformulate it, within a more general yet robustly analytical framework. Trust is a complex phenomenon, but one whose main elements are met in other domains of decisionmaking. We have emphasized here those elements that have to do with how to read signals of hidden qualities when these signals may be meant to mislead. We have pointed out that this "secondary problem of trust" is almost always present, and we have stressed its analogy with the problem of how to read quality signals elsewhere. The problem of the truster with respect to trustworthiness is the problem of the employer with respect to productivity, of the dog with respect to the belligerence of the hissing cat, and of the predator with respect to the toxicity of the striped worm.

We have said comparatively little about the hidden qualities, the t-krypta themselves. We have noted that the hidden qualities that are relevant for trustworthiness vary greatly with what the trustee is being trusted to do, and with cultural and other determinants of preferences. It is certainly possible, and we do not wish to deny, that there are high-level human dispositions that render people trustworthy in general, or at least over a very wide range of basic trust games. They may, for example, include a positive responsiveness to the very fact of being trusted. To this extent the full analysis of trust may involve attitudes that are indeed peculiar to games of trust. We are agnostic about the existence of dispositions of this kind—attitudes primed specifically in trust cases. We are also neutral as to whether such dispositions, if they exist, are themselves explicable by methods of rational choice theory.

The fundamental problem for the truster, however, is independent of the existence or nature of such dispositions. That problem is the decoding of signs, including deliberate signals. The key quality that, in the circumstances, determines trustworthiness may be as unmysterious as the size of a bank balance or membership in a profession. Even where deep t-krypta are at work, it is often not the deep t-krypton itself that determines trustworthiness but a mundane quality known to be correlated with it, such as an identity. The question for the truster is whether the trustee has qualities that she believes, in virtue of experience or common sense or on some other basis, to make for trustworthiness, not the sometimes deeper question of why these properties do so. Yet answering this shallower question is a complex business, because in games of trust there is a motive for the unscrupulous to mimic trustworthiness by displaying its signs.

The ceaseless semiotic warfare between mimics, on the one hand, and their trustworthy models and potential dupes, on the other, rather than being the proper target of a single essay, defines an entire field of research that, for the case of humans, has barely been opened. Its overall outcome, at any one time, yields the amount of trust society enjoys. Insofar as people can observe, and read, reliable signs of trustworthiness, we can conclude that mimics have backed away or been fought off. But even in these happy circumstances models and dupes should not rest on their laurels. Mimics are always in the offing.

Appendix

Glossary

All-in payoffs are those that motivate an agent once self-interest and all other considerations are taken into account.

A *basic trust game* is a two-player—a potential truster and a potential trustee—strategic-form, noncooperative game. Each player has two strategies: in the loan example, the strategies of the truster are simply the actions "lend" and "refuse," and those of the trustee are to "repay" and "not repay" if the loan is made. There is mutual knowledge of the truster's payoffs, but only the trustee knows his all-in payoffs: a basic trust game is thus a "game of asymmetric information" concerning the trustee's all-in payoffs. However, there is mutual knowledge of the trustee's *raw* payoffs. What only the trustee knows is whether his all-in payoffs coincide with, or differ from, his raw payoffs.

Krypta are unobservable properties of a person. Those krypta of a person that are his trust-warranting properties in a basic trust game are his t-krypta in that game.

Manifesta are any observable features of a person. "Features" include parts or aspects of his body, his behaviors, and his appurtenances.

A *mimic* is an opportunist who deceives by displaying a manifestum that is a sign of a krypton he does not possess.

A *mimic-beset trust game* is a basic trust game in which there is some positive probability that the trustee is an opportunist and the truster observes a manifestum or manifesta of the trustee.

An *opportunist* in a basic trust game is an interactant who has two properties: he is motivated by raw payoffs, and if he could obtain trust at low enough cost, he would do so, then betray it. An opportunist is not just lacking in trust-warranting properties but proactively deceptive.

The *primary problem of trust* consists in identifying which of the two payoff structures really governs a trustee's actions.

Raw payoffs are those that motivate an agent who pursues only his self-interest in the narrowest sense.

The *secondary problem of trust* concerns the conditions in which manifesta of t-krypta may be trusted or distrusted. To answer the question "Can I trust this person to do X?" a truster must first, and need only, answer another question: "Is the manifestum of the trust-warranting krypton k that I observe a reliable sign of k?" In brief: "Can I trust this sign of k?"

A *signature* is a manifestum used to signal identity, which is drawn from some fixed stock of manifesta, which are all alike in some respect: one stock is the set of all possible English proper names, another set of all possible fingerprints, another the set of all possible uniforms, another the set of all possible embroidered emblems.

A *trusted-in act* in a basic trust game is the trustee's response expected by a truster when the truster believes a trustee is trustworthy in that game.

A *trusting act* in a basic game is the act chosen by the truster when the truster expects the trustee to be trustworthy in that game.

A person *trusts* someone "to do X" if she acts on the expectation that he will do X, for example, to "repay" a loan when there is mutual knowledge between them that two conditions obtain: if he fails to do X she would have done better to have acted otherwise, and her acting in the way she does gives him a selfish reason not to do X.

Figure 5.3   E's Raw Payoffs in Multiple Peril Game

	B	B′	B″			B	B′	B″
A	1	4	0		A	1	0	4
A′	—	—	—		A′	—	—	—
	Greedy Type					Libidinous Type		

Source: Author's compilation.

A *trust-warranting property* is any property (or combination of properties) of a trustee in a basic trust game that suffices for him to be trustworthy in that game.

A *trustee* is trustworthy in a basic trust game only if, believing the truster trusts him, he chooses X.

Several colleagues have sent us comments on an earlier version of this essay, some of which have led to changes and improvements. Not all the points that deserved attention, however, receive it here, mostly because of lack of space. We are particularly grateful to Tyler Cowen, Jon Elster, Russell Hardin, Susan Hurley, David Laitin, and Gerry Mackie.

Notes

1. We use bold characters throughout the text to mark the terms we define in the appendix.

2. By this we mean that each knows that the other knows it, each knows this, and so on, up to some finite degree.

3. In the language of games of incomplete information (Fudenberg and Tirole 1991; Ordeshook 1986), there is more than one "type" of E, of which one is characterized by the raw payoffs and one or more others by other payoffs; in general only E knows E's type. In this respect, but not in all, basic trust games resemble "principal-agent" problems with adverse selection and R as principal.

4. Corresponding to perils B′ and B″ are types of trustee whose raw payoffs are shown in figure 5.3.

5. There are cases, often regarded as canonical cases of trusting, that are not covered by this notion. It is often thought that in prisoners' dilemma (PD) games and games of the family of Rousseau's Stag Hunt mutual trust can

produce cooperative outcomes. Because such trust is symmetric, with each player both a truster and a trustee, our asymmetric notion cannot be directly applied. There is, however, in PD games and kindred symmetric games a close bilateral analogue of our unilateral notion, and there is a bilateral trusting equilibrium that goes with it. If we interpret the standard PD matrix as showing raw payoffs, then both have the same raw payoffs, and both are uncertain about the relation between the raw and all-in payoffs of the other. The present notion extends easily. To illustrate, consider the following simple expression of the idea that mutual trust can yield (C, C) in the PD. Say that a player "trusts" the other if she expects him to do k, and that a player is "trustworthy" if the following is true of her: if she trusts the other player, this makes her prefer to do k herself, despite the fact that she rawly prefers to defect. Then there is an equilibrium in which both are trustworthy, both trust, and both do k.

6. This reason for preferring B to B′ takes us outside the standard framework of game theory, because part of it consists of a belief that E has about R's expectations. In standard game theory, R's act-choice (here A) typically affects E's preference over B and B′, but R's reason for this act-choice does not: the primitive objects of preference are acts given others' acts, not acts given others' reasons for acting. Despite the nonstandard character of such preferences, however, there is no difficulty in describing an equilibrium in which E has them. The equilibrium described at the end of the first section, in which R trusts a trustworthy E, is an example. By definition, a trustworthy E chooses B if he thinks R trusts him. E's preference for B when he thinks R trusts him might be produced either by E's derived belief that R will choose A or, nonstandardly, by E's belief that R trusts him. And the argument that the described situation is an equilibrium is independent of which of these beliefs produced it.

7. We have assumed here that if the trustee has a trust-warranting property k, then (given the belief that she is trusted) she *definitely will* do B. But this oversimplifies. Mormons are valued as trustworthy baby-sitters, but there may be some bad Mormons. Here, then, k only makes doing B probable. The whole analysis can easily be generalized to this case, which is perhaps the only one we can expect ever to find in reality.

8. A limiting case is "perceiving as." For example, a smile may be seen as a friendly smile: the disposition is in the content of the perception and not inferred (see, for example, McDowell 1994).

9. We have assumed that there is no plasticity about what R can observe: some features she observes costlessly and automatically, in the base interaction; others she cannot observe but can only infer from the observables and background knowledge. Other features are not like that: get closer to a crocodile on a polo shirt and you can see whether it is a Lacoste one or not. If getting closer is costly and chosen, then this choice variable should be modeled as part of the description of the game that is played. In the basic trust game and the variants of it that we consider in this chapter, we abstract from scrutiny by R of this kind, for the sake of simplicity and without affecting our essential argument.

10. Thus, in our (stylized) treatment, a t-krypton k is sure evidence of trustworthiness, but manifesta are in general unsure evidence of k.

11. We often speak of k's and non-k's rather than of people who have and do not have k. A krypton has been defined as a property, so one should perhaps speak of an agent's "having" k rather than of agents who "are" k, or "of" k's. But sometimes the latter is smoother, and it does no harm, since corresponding to every property there is a type—the possessors of the property.

12. The "mimicry" defined here is *deceptive* mimicry; there are also varieties of nondeceptive mimicry. I may mimic to amuse. I may also mimic a type of person (X) who is known to have k, by copying some manifestum m of X-ness, to convey that I am k, when I am k; although this behavior is deceptive, it is so only incidentally, and there is no reason in general why X's should lose by it; indeed, they may benefit from it if they too display m in order to convey that they are k, by the reinforcement of the association between m and k. This is a form of "Mullerian" mimicry (Pasteur 1982).

13. Mimicry may also be negative—"camouflage." There are often manifesta of a trustee that are likely to be interpreted by the truster, rightly or wrongly, as indicating not-k, and so untrustworthiness. Both an honest k who expects to be unjustly perceived if he displays such a manifestum m and an opportunist non-k who is afraid of being detected if he does, have a reason to camouflage, that is, to take steps *not* to show m. For our purposes here, we consider deceptive camouflaging as a special case of mimicking, since the strategy of camouflaging non-k-ness by suppressing m is just that of mimicking k through displaying the notional manifestum "no m."

14. Other scenarios besides this one are treated in signaling theory, but we shall not consider them.

15. So far we have suggested, about the trustworthy trustee's preferences, only that, in the circumstances in which the truster expects B and so chooses A, the trustee prefers (A, B) to (A, B'). Given that he is trusted, he prefers to fulfill rather than to let down trust. But nothing has been said about his preference for being trusted or not trusted in the first place. Both cases are possible. Let us say that in a basic trust game the trustee is "willingly trustworthy" in the first case, that is, he is trustworthy and prefers to be trusted. Suppose someone is trustworthy because doing B, though onerous, is felt to be an obligation. Then he is also willingly trustworthy if he wishes, all in all, to take on such onerous obligations. If a krypton k makes someone trustworthy but not willingly trustworthy, the mimic-beset trust game is an only slightly different signaling problem, and its signal-theoretic solutions are essentially the same.

16. We here take it for granted that if there is a semi-sorting equilibrium, players conform to it. Some of the games in question also have "pooling" equilibria (in which k's and non-k's behave in the same way); these generally appear implausible, even though, notoriously, principles for excluding them involve unsettled questions about rational belief revision in multistage games. To establish the statement in the text we need only show: (1) in an SSE of the signaling game a non-k signaler sometimes

emits s (that is, displays m); (2) this emitting of s is a case of mimicking k via m. The first condition comes directly from the definition of an SSE. To see the second condition, recall that for E to mimic k via m is for E to display m in order to raise the probability that R attaches to E's being k. In an SSE, using s always raises the probability that the receiver attaches to your having k. Say that in the equilibrium a non-k uses s with probability p. By definition of an SSE, $0 < p < 1$. Let the population fraction of k's be f. If the receiver observes the non-k's s, she assigns the probability $Pr(c; s)$ to his being k, where $Pr(c; s) = f/[f + p(1 - f)]$, by Bayes's theorem, since $Pr(s; c) = 1$. This ranges between f (when $p = 1$) and 1 (when $p = 0$). On the other hand, if the receiver observes no s, she assigns the probability $Pr(c; not-s) = 0$. Hence, using s raises the probability that the receiver attaches to k from 0 to some positive number, as long as $f > 0$ (there are some k's in the population).

17. There is more than one plausible way of modeling the situation. If the size of a donation in a begging game is conventionally given at D, and the truster's preferences are like Bacharach's, we have a mimic-beset trust game as defined here, and it has an SSE in which the truster is just prepared to pay D to a mendicant displaying m if a non-k's payoff from D is just equal to the cost of mimicry (he can just afford to mimic) and the proportion of non-k's who mimic is equal to KZ, where K is the odds that an arbitrary beggar is k and Z is the ratio of the utility the truster gets from paying D to a k and the regret she suffers from paying D to a non-k. Such an equilibrium might arise over time through adjustments in D or in the level of the performance.

18. Evidently act-outcomes often reveal t-krypta less definitively than this. The hustler may feed the truster a few Bs, though lacking the t-krypton; an honest man by contrast may occasionally succumb to the lure of B', though possessing it. Our definition of "experience krypton" defines only an ideal case, which may be relatively rare.

19. In Spence's model, the property k (high productivity) is correlated with another (academic prowess). The k's strategy for demonstrating the former is to signal the latter, which he credibly achieves by displaying a manifestum (a certificate) that he can afford to get and a low-prowess job applicant cannot. He leaves it to the employer to draw the inference from prowess to productivity.

20. There are two ways in which the presence of non-k members can undermine categorial identity signaling: it undermines social belief in the trait law; and these members are able to mimic k-ness by using the group signature—for as long as the cost of the latter is the same for all group members, the Cannot condition fails if the Can condition is met. An important example of this mechanism occurs when group membership (i-ness) is taken as evidence *against* k, so that i members who are k have an honest motive to camouflage i-ness by suppressing a manifestum m that acts as an involuntary signature of i-membership. For example, it is difficult for k members of an ethnic minority that is reputed to be non-k to signal successfully that they are k by merely camouflaging their ethnicity, because it is just as easy for opportunistic non-k members to camouflage it. On the

other hand, such camouflage may be an important method of escaping from the trap of their group identification (their i-ness) in cases where this acts only as an initial filter. Those who are not excluded summarily by their i-ness may have an opportunity to signal their k-ness by some further signal that they can afford and their non-k fellow i's cannot.

21. Since in general there is some fitness cost in displaying m, in general an equilibrium is eventually reached in which, for mimics, the fitness benefit from the now imperfect correlation just covers fitness cost (the Can Just condition is met), while for models it still more than covers the fitness cost (the Can condition is met). This equilibrium is an SSE of an appropriately specified game. Notice that for this process to take place it must be that the cost of mimicry is not too high: it must be lower than the fitness benefit of being taken for a k when there are not yet any mimics. But the cost of mimicry must be higher than the cost of displaying m for a model.

22. This describes how a well-founded associative belief, between an m and a certain k, forms in the mind of a *rational* truster. In this chapter we do not consider the variously *biased* or *erroneous* associative beliefs of which there are plenty in the real world: from the ancient Greek belief that beauty means goodness (*kalos k'agathos*) to the many extravagant folk injunctions still around today about whom one should trust (people who use words sparingly, people who look you straight in the eyes) or not trust (redheads, people with thin lips, women, people from the city, people from the country).

23. It is the marginal cost of display that is zero, not necessarily the historic cost of developing the capacity to display it.

24. This sense of "cue" resembles Hauser's (1996). Although k's who display a manifestum m may do so as a signal of k, they may also display m for some other reason, and indeed in some cases without any purpose. Rich people often wear expensive clothes with no thought of conveying anything about their wealth, but merely to make a bella figura; as an unintended by-product, they give evidence of their wealth. In such cases m is a cue of k, even though it is costly to produce, because it is not a costly input *into the activity of inducing a belief in k-ness.*

25. It may be that m is a cue of k but is also costless to display for *some* non-k's. In this case the truster ought to be concerned about taking m at face value (that is, as indicating k and so trustworthiness) even if she is sure there are no opportunists (say because it is common knowledge that the penalty for opportunist behavior is certain death). For she may think that non-opportunistic egoism is possible. Suppose, for instance, that all k's have wide-set eyes and most non-k's have narrow-set eyes, but some non-k's (say 10 percent) have wide-set eyes. Say the population is 50 percent k and 50 percent non-k. Then, if R sees that E has wide-set eyes, she should deduce that there is a one-in-eleven chance of E's being non-k. According to the payoffs, it may or may not be wise to trust E.

26. In real cases of Spence's scenario, the signaling strategy for demonstrating high productivity (demonstrating academic prowess) contains a third step,

in which fakery can play a part. An employer, for instance, observes not the quality of your performance at college but a certificate or transcript. The piece of paper you show has two elements, the second element of which, the provenance of the piece of paper, nonmanifest, and could be such that the certificate is no evidence of prowess. It is no evidence of prowess if you have counterfeited it, that is, if its provenance is not the transcript office of the university.

27. Intuitive judgments can involve complex computations. A substantial literature in cognitive psychology describes processes for framing impressions of people from their behaviors; much of this literature emphasizes that these processes are often "automatic" and without conscious awareness. Yet in some of it (see, for example, Kunda and Thagard 1996) the automatic, unaccessed processes have considerable complexity.

28. When cues are symbolic signs, like the styles of dress in the example, they usually give less security, other things being equal, because they are cheaper for the mimic to reproduce.

29. For example, we know that students can afford to look like students, for what it is to "look like a student" is to look the way that, in our experience, they usually do. This reason for not having to make calculations about the Can condition is due to the process of associative learning described earlier.

References

Bacharach, Michael. 1997. "Showing What You Are by Showing Who You Are." Working paper. New York: Russell Sage Foundation.

Barkow, Jerome H., Leda Cosmides, and John Tooby. 1992. *The Adapted Mind: Evolutionary Psychology and the Generation of Culture.* Oxford: Oxford University Press.

Dasgupta, Partha. 1988. "Trust as a Commodity." In *Trust: Making and Breaking Cooperative Relations,* edited by Diego Gambetta. Oxford: Blackwell.

Frank, Robert. 1994. *Microeconomics and Behavior.* 2d ed. New York: McGraw-Hill.

Fudenberg, Drew, and Jean Tirole. 1991. *Game Theory.* Cambridge, Mass.: MIT Press.

Gambetta, Diego. 1988. "Can We Trust Trust?" In *Trust: Making and Breaking Cooperative Relations,* edited by Diego Gambetta. Oxford: Blackwell.

Guilford, Tim, and Marian Dawkins. 1991. "Receiver Psychology and the Evolution of Animal Signals." *Animal Behaviour* 42: 1–14.

Hauser, Marc D. 1996. *The Evolution of Communication.* Cambridge, Mass.: MIT Press.

Hausman, Daniel. 1997. "Trust in Game Theory." Discussion paper. London: London School of Economics.

Hirschman, Aerbert O. 1984. "Against Parsimony: Three Easy Ways of Complicating Some Categories of Economic Discourse." *American Economic Review Proceedings* 74(2): 88–96.

Kitcher, Philip. 1993. "The Evolution of Human Altruism." *Journal of Philosophy* 90(10): 497–516.

Kunda, Ziva, and Paul Thagard. 1996. "Forming Impressions from Stereotypes, Traits, and Behaviors: A Parallel Constraint-Satisfaction Theory." *Psychological Review* 103(2): 284–308.

McDowell, John Henry. 1994. *Mind and World.* Cambridge, Mass.: Harvard University Press.

Nagel, Thomas. 1978. *The Possibility of Altruism.* Princeton, N.J.: Princeton University Press

Nelson, Phillip. 1970. "Information and Consumer Behavior." *Journal of Political Economy* 78(2): 311–29.

Ordeshook, Peter C. 1986. *Game Theory and Political Theory: An Introduction.* Cambridge: Cambridge University Press.

Pasteur, Georges. 1982. "A Classificatory Review of Mimicry Systems." *Annual Review of Ecological Systems* 13: 169–99.

Pettit, Philip. 1995. "The Cunning of Trust." *Philosophy and Public Affairs* 24(3): 202–25.

Selten, Reinhard. 1978. "The Chain Store Paradox." *Theory and Decision* 9: 127–58.

Spence, Michael A. 1974. *Market Signaling: Informational Transfer in Hiring and Related Screening Processes.* Cambridge, Mass.: Harvard University Press.

Spiegelman, Art. 1991. *Maus: A Survivor's Tale.* New York: Pantheon.

Tadelis, Steven. 1996. "What's in a Name? Reputation as a Tradeable Asset." Working paper. Cambridge, Mass.: Harvard University, Department of Economics.

Tajfel, Henri. 1959. "The Anchoring Effects of Value in a Scale of Judgments." *British Journal of Psychology* 50: 294–304.

Zahavi, Amotz. 1975. "Mate Selection: A Selection for a Handicap." *Journal of Theoretical Biology* 53: 205–14.

Chapter 6

Reputations, Trust, and the Principal Agent Problem

JEAN ENSMINGER

I S TRUST purely strategic? Or does trust begin precisely where the ability to make rational calculations leaves off? There is much disagreement in the trust literature over even this fundamental distinction despite a recent explosion of interest in the concept of trust among social scientists. Why should this concept be of interest to economists? It has been suggested that trust can substitute for monitoring in agency situations, and even more broadly it has been argued that a failure of trust significantly reduces the gains of economic cooperation (Putnam 1992). In this chapter I consider a case of extreme trusting behavior with high economic risks and benefits. The pastoral-nomadic Orma of East Africa employ hired herders in their cattle camps and in some cases actually adopt these young men as their fictive sons. Although the innovation of kinship makes this case look superficially like the "social trust" associated with group identity discussed by Tom Tyler (this volume), I argue in this chapter that appearances can be misleading. I interpret this case as one of calculated self-interest (see Hardin, this volume) in the context of principal-agent theory, wage efficiency, reputation, and the insights of the anthropological literature on reciprocity.

The Orma of northeastern Kenya were until recent times largely subsistence, nomadic-cattle pastoralists herding in a rather lush environment bordering the coast of Kenya near the Somali border. They are still primarily cattle-dependent, though they have added whatever diversification they can find. They are now two-thirds sedentary and very much tied to the commercial cash economy; they regularly sell their livestock to purchase their daily food and other needs. (For further details on the Orma economy, see Ensminger 1992.) These considerable trans-formations in their economic adaptation, particularly their sedentariza-tion in large villages that have been long overgrazed, have necessitated great changes in their herding relationships. Although the Orma al-ways made use of remote cattle camps to keep the dry stock in the most ideal grazing and watering conditions, their use of these camps far from the watchful eye of the herd owner is even more extensive today. This has put great strain on the family labor supply for wealthy households with large herds and is all the more exacerbated by the fact that these very same wealthy families tend to educate their sons, who are then un-available for this work. Increasingly the Orma have turned to poor rela-tions and nonrelations to herd for pay in the cattle camps. The resources at stake are tremendously valuable, and the herding conditions, riddled with the risks of wild animals and bandits toting AK-47s, are difficult. One of the Orma strategies for dealing with these very high agency costs is to develop close personal ties, sometimes even culminating in adoption, with faithful hired herders.

This extreme form of accommodation to high agency costs involves the substitution of trust for monitoring. But is this trust purely strategic, or does it require consideration of a non-utilitarian perspective—perhaps, in this case especially, a perspective that incorporates social identity and what Tyler (this volume) refers to as social trust? If trust is purely strategic, why does it work for the Orma as a substitute for su-pervision? And how do these contracting parties get on this escalator of increasing trust and cooperation that appears to land them ultimately in the place where all employers would love to be—with employees who are totally loyal to the firm and no longer require supervision?

Moving Beyond Agency Theory to Incorporate Trust

Specialization and division of labor are both increasing among the Orma. Poor households derive a significant portion of their income from sources other than the sale of their herds. Rich households, on the other hand, are increasingly taking advantage of larger economies of scale in livestock production. We might be inclined to predict a movement to-ward purely contractual wage labor to create these larger economies of scale, but we find instead that more informal methods of increasing the labor force persist.

Agency theory (Alston 1981; Alston and Higgs 1982; Fama 1980; Fama and Jensen 1983a, 1983b) teaches us that agency costs arise as the division of labor intensifies in a hierarchical situation. Whenever an individual (identified in the literature as a "principal") engages another individ-ual (identified as an "agent") to whom some decisionmaking authority is granted, a potential agency problem exists (Jensen and Meckling 1976, 308). Agency costs stem from the fact that the interests of principals (herd owners in this case) and their agents (hired herders) may diverge, and consequently the principal incurs transaction costs in monitoring the behavior of the agent. Michael Jensen and William Meckling (1976, 308) put it this way:

> If both parties to the relationship are utility maximizers there is good reason to believe that the agent will not always act in the best interests of the principal. The *principal* can limit divergences from his interest by establishing appropriate incentives for the agent and by incurring monitoring costs designed to limit the aberrant activities of the agent.

One focus of agency theory has been to explain the choice of contract given the nature of the supervision required. Thus, in their study of agrarian contracting in the southern United States, Lee Alston, Samar Data, and Jeffrey Nugent (1984) argue that fixed-rent and sharecrop contracts reduce the need for direct supervision of labor, and it is therefore not surprising that such contracts are preferred over wage contracts by farmers with fewer supervisors (Alston and Higgs 1982, 351). Similarly, we can understand much about the way in which Orma herd owners structure their relations with hired herders as an adaptation to huge monitoring costs.

Agency theory goes a long way toward explaining labor relations and contracting among the Orma. But the actual adoption of herders carries these relationships into a domain not well specified by the economic theory of contracts. As Robert Pollak (1985) notes, characteristically different qualities are associated with family and hired labor. One would assume that for the Orma the advantages of family labor are great, for precisely the reasons noted by Pollak—transaction costs are reduced. But the way in which kin relations reduce transaction costs is not well understood either.

Turning a more or less explicitly contractual relationship into a kinship relationship moves the exchange in the direction of what anthropologists refer to as "generalized reciprocity" (Sahlins 1972), and by its very nature this movement implies less precision in the specification of the contract, less monitoring, and greater tolerance for long-term debit flows in the relationship.

Marshall Sahlins (1972) distinguishes three qualitatively different forms of reciprocity that fall along a continuum, he argues, from generalized to balanced to negative. Generalized is the form of reciprocity most commonly found among close kin and characterizes the nature of the relationship we usually expect between parents and their children. Here the flow may be unidirectional without any explicit expectation of balance, or at least not over any short time frame. These relations are notable for the fact that careful accounts of aid are not kept and the relationship can sustain a very long—perhaps permanent—period of one-way flow. As one moves toward balanced reciprocity, which is characteristically found among friends, one may freely give aid but with the expectation that the aid will be reciprocated equivalently and in a timely fashion. In other words, people are keeping score, often closely. A balanced reciprocity relationship that can tolerate longer repayment schedules and longer periods of one-way flow is characteristic of closer relationships that lie toward the generalized end of the continuum. At the opposite end of the spectrum we have true negative reciprocity, which is characteristic of theft and dealings with enemies or total strangers. Here the goal is to get something for nothing and to reciprocate as little as possible.

What is notable about the adoption of Orma hired herders is the way in which the original contractual relationship moves from balanced (if not somewhat negative) reciprocity to something closer to fully generalized reciprocity between the two parties. Clearly one aspect of this transition is a reduction in the account-keeping of who is indebted to whom, much as one sometimes finds within nuclear and extended families. At the very least, even if the relationship continues to balance out in terms of effort and reward, long-term deficits in either direction may be run up without serious concern to either party.

Although this unusual solution to the agency problem is consistent with principal agent theory, the developing literature on trust has better explored this particular aspect of exchange in "committed" relationships and brings new insights to bear on this category of cases. The special characteristics of this relationship also point to the relevance of anthropological literature on reciprocity.

The Subject of Trust

There is a growing interest among sociologists, political scientists, economists, and scholars who study organizational behavior in the subject of trust. Much of the interest in trust is associated with its impact on cooperation. It has been argued that a certain amount of trust may be necessary in order to reach optimal levels of cooperation. In societies where people have low levels of trust, opportunities for exchange may be forgone. Thus, it has been proposed that there are detrimental economic consequences to a national decline in trusting behavior (Putnam 1992).

The Orma practice of adopting hired herders as fictive kinsmen clearly changes the nature of the relationship considerably and specifically embodies a higher degree of trust. But what, then, is this magic elixir called trust that makes agency problems go away? In the purely rational self-interest accounts of James Coleman (1990) and Russell Hardin (this volume; 1993, 505), "you trust someone if you have adequate reason to believe it will be in that person's interest to be trustworthy in the relevant way at the relevant time." In other words, you trust when you have sufficient knowledge of the other party's incentive structure and competence to be confident that he or she will fulfill the behavior that you expect of them.

But to Toshio Yamagishi and Midori Yamagishi (1994, 136), this is merely one form of trust, what they refer to as "knowledge-based trust." This is trust based on information that we have about a partner, including their competence and reputation. But Yamagishi and Yamagishi identify a second form of trust that they label "general trust." This is a cognitive bias based on a belief in the goodwill and benign intent of the partner. "A trusting person is the one who overestimates the benignity of the partner's intentions beyond the level warranted by the prudent assessment of the available information."

One way of thinking about the difference between Coleman's and Hardin's use of the term and Yamagishi and Yamagishi's is to see it as the difference between risk and uncertainty. In the rational account we trust because we can assign probabilities to the expected gains from cooperation with another. As Hardin (1993, 516) notes, "My estimation of the risk is my degree of trust in you." And further: "The degree of trust I have for you is just the expected probability of the dependency working out well." And finally, in game-theoretic metaphor (515): "One should open with a cooperative move in the hope of engaging the other also to be cooperative. This is not merely a moral injunction. It is a rational claim of self-interest. One should open with cooperation when the expected long-run benefits of iterated cooperation outweigh the short-term risk of loss."

In contrast, Yamagishi and Yamagishi focus on uncertainty. They note that trust involves an overestimate that is neither "warranted" nor "prudent" based on available information. I take this to mean that appropriate probability assessments are not possible (thus differentiating their sense of trust from the Coleman-Hardin sense of it as risk); indeed, Yamagishi and Yamagishi refer to this case as trust under "social uncertainty." Put more succinctly, Yamagishi and Yamagishi cite Lewis and Weigert (1985): "Knowledge alone can never cause us to trust" (970), for "trust begins where simple prediction ends" (976).

In a similar vein, one might be easily tempted to assume that the fact of turning a contractual hired herder relationship into a kinship relationship looks a great deal like an effort to create a common identity, much as Tyler (this volume) argues that "social trust" is the foundation of a nonstrategic form of trust. But the very strategic nature of such a move demonstrates what is really going on.

In the following case I attempt to demonstrate that even the extreme form of trusting behavior that we find among the Orma can be characterized as "encapsulated self-interest" according to Hardin's (this volume) usage. As Hardin (1993, 526) notes:

> A full account of rational trust must be grounded in reasons for expecting another to fulfill a trust and in reasons for holding general beliefs about trustworthiness. These are addressed, respectively, by the incentive account of trustworthiness that justifies and explains trust and by the common-sense Bayesian account of learned trust. The commonsense Bayesian is little more than an inductivist who generalizes from the past to the future.

Obviously the truster's and trustee's reputations loom large in the analysis. But as Hardin (1993, 515) also correctly notes, the "general social conditions" affect the statistical probability that trusting behavior will be repaid by trustworthiness. In this context the "general social conditions" have a direct impact through the mechanism of reputation, the evaluation of which is tied to norms of appropriate conduct.

The Case Study

Orma Herding Relationships

Among the Orma, herding relationships exist on a continuum from related individuals who are neighbors and share herding duties to individuals of absolutely no relationship who herd for a household on more or less contractual terms. In the past household imbalances between stock and labor were resolved primarily by coresidence in nomadic camps and common herding and sharing of subsistence production. Under such conditions supervision was direct and pervasive. As sedentarization increased and a larger number of stock had to be kept in cattle camps, such informal relations became more formalized and individualized. Young men from poor families began working away from home and exclusively for their wealthy patrons.

Almost all East African pastoralists make extensive use of cattle camps. These camps afford ideal conditions for herd mobility in order to maximize access to grazing and water resources. Because the cattle camps are unencumbered by households, including the elderly and infirm, and are left in the care of agile young men who often travel with nothing more than a spear, milking gourd, and hide for sleeping, their mobility is uninhibited. The stock are also far out of the control of the head of the household, who often is the owner of the majority of the herd, thus creating an agency problem. Cattle camps among the Orma (as among most East African pastoralists) easily roam one hundred miles from the residential village, sometimes moving daily. They typically hold 60 to 100 percent of a household's livestock, which is likely to be the entire source of income and wealth of the family. Supervision is difficult, and there is an inevitable conflict of interest between the absentee herd owner (the principal) and the on-site, day-to-day decision-maker, the herder (or agent). Indeed, this problem is a favorite subject of discussion among Orma elders, who spend endless hours developing monitoring and incentive strategies to overcome it. It is accurate to say that a high level of suspicion and distrust of hired herders is the norm, though one does tend to encounter the attitude that while other people's hired herders are not to be trusted, one's own are exceptions.

The Agency Problem Among Orma Herders

Cattle herding under the conditions that pertain in East Africa is a risky venture. Losses of 70 percent were recorded for both the 1974 and 1984 droughts, but good husbandry reduced these significantly for some exceptional herd managers (Ensminger 1992).[1] Although careful husbandry can lessen the dangers of all of these risks, managing a herd is hard work indeed. As has been pointed out to me on numerous occasions by herd owners, it is not easy to lift a five-hundred-pound steer out of the mud. Such a task is backbreaking work that takes the effort of at least four men with poles to support the underbelly of the animal as it is righted—often over and over again. Herd owners use this example to dramatize the difference between the care a herd owner would provide for his own animals and that commonly provided by hired herders. They maintain that in the absence of the herd owner, or at least his son, a hired laborer would not make the effort to lift stock that are stuck in the mud, as happened to large numbers of weakened stock in both 1975 and 1985, following the first rains after a severe drought.

The costs to a herd owner of not finding good workers for the cattle camp are legendary. In the following account an elder describes the problems associated with long-distance management.

> The ones doing the best work in the cattle camp are in their parents' camp and not herding for pay. Those are their cattle. The employees—there are so many things they don't do. First, they don't want to herd. There are young boys who are supposed to help them and they leave all the work to the young boys. The hired herders just pass the time and demand to be paid. They may leave a child to herd 7 or 8 days and give them no rest for even a day. There are so many like this these days. Second, they don't check the cattle when they arrive at the end of the day—they don't look for lost cattle. Third, they may leave the cattle camp and go visit a nearby village and say they are looking for a lost cow, but come back and say they couldn't find it. If cattle are lost they must be found immediately or they will never be found. So the owner loses his cow. Nowadays, people have noticed. If someone has lost a cow the boy won't get paid. This is the an-

swer. Others decide to pay the salary even if the herder has lost a cow, but then they fire the boy. Others tell the boy to find the cow and if he does, then he will be paid. Then sometimes the boy goes and never comes back. These are the problems. Not everyone is like this. Some who herd for pay do a very good job. The owners trust them.

Strategies for Overcoming the Agency Problem

Given the great risks involved, one would expect pastoralists to be extremely reluctant to engage hired laborers. Indeed, Louise Sperling (1984) finds that the Samburu avoid this practice for precisely this reason. Over the long term the Samburu relieve labor shortages by practicing polygyny (thus producing their own labor force), and over the short term by borrowing the children of close relatives for years at a time or by herding cooperatively with other members of their settlement. The Orma also engage in all of these practices.

Among the Orma there were in fact large increases in household size between 1980 and 1987 for rich households (from 10.9 to 15.5). These increases occurred not only because fertility and polygyny rates were higher but also because fewer sons split off and more joint families stayed together upon the death of the father.

But many Orma households still find themselves in need of additional labor, in part because the Orma are more sedentary than most East African pastoralists; by 1987 fully 63 percent of households were permanently settled in the Galole area. Sedentarization requires a greater dependence on the use of cattle camps: grazing conditions are far inferior in settled villages than in nomadic villages, and much more stock (often even milking stock) must be kept in the cattle camps, often for far longer periods of the year. Also, the relatively severe labor shortage in the wealthiest Orma households may have arisen because of greater inequality in the distribution of wealth among the Orma than among most other East African pastoralists. Among the wealthy Orma, a high portion of young men are at school, employed with a cash income, married early and settled down in a permanent village, or kept out of the cattle camps by their mothers, who now often prefer to have their sons near them rather than in the distant camps.

The result is that wealthy sedentary households employed on average 1.2 hired laborers in 1979, and 1.1 per household in 1987, about 80 percent of whom herded in the stock camps. Of the hired herders in 1979, 46 percent were relatives. (Sisters' sons and daughters' sons together made up almost half of this group.) Significantly, however, 54 percent of hired herders had no relationship whatsoever to the household. It should be noted that the Orma still place an exceedingly high premium on having at least one close relative of the family in the cattle camp. This person should preferably be a son, but at the very least a sister's, daughter's, or brother's son, who can act as a supervisor over the others. One elder described the need for relatives in the cattle camp this way:

> We cannot only depend on hired labor. Even if you have no son old enough to be in the cattle camp, your own son, no matter how young he is, must be there. He sends information even if he cannot order around the others. Every household must have one son in the cattle camp. If people don't have children they must get someone to whom they are related—a brother's son or sister's son. But these ones must be supervised. You need counter-checking.

The Orma concur with Sperling's report (1984) of the Samburu attitude that one can better trust a close relative as a herder than a nonrelative. But why exactly are close relatives more trustworthy than nonrelatives? When I asked the Orma what type of person they could most readily trust as hired herders, there was a quick and definite answer—sisters' sons. These are considered absolutely the most reliable people to hire as herders. When pressed to explain why such relatives are particularly trustworthy, the Orma began by explaining that it has something to do with "control." One somehow has more "control" over a sister's son than, for example, a brother's son, who is not a bad candidate as a hired herder but clearly inferior to a sister's son. Before long my informants said that the "control" is linked to the fact that sisters' sons receive important gifts from mothers' brothers, and this is why the nature of the bond makes them especially trustworthy.[2] They have more to lose by failing to live up to expectations. Indeed, approximately one-quarter of the hired herders in my sample of herders who are relatives are sisters' sons. It was clear from my discussions with the Orma on this topic that property relations are tightly bound up with "control" and "trust." Another explanation offered for preferring this relationship was that one can "punish" a sister's son and needn't worry about repercussions, as might occur across clans, for example. In short, one trusts those whom one can control, and one controls those who have the greatest interest in doing what you wish them to do.

Clearly, the first preference is to have a son in the cattle camp, and failing that, another relative who has clear financial incentives to produce good results. When no relatives are available, the herd owner or his sons living in the sedentary village increase their supervision of the cattle camps by visiting them more frequently. Trusted relatives herding in nearby cattle camps are also regularly grilled for information on the health and condition of the cattle and the performance of the hired herders.

Herd owners also employ financial incentives to increase the work performance of their hired herders. The usual herder contract among the Orma stipulates that the herder will receive food, clothing, and one female head of stock per year. These conditions are negotiated at the outset but make up only the minimal wage contract. Employers make use of all sorts of incentives to sweeten the arrangement if the herder is perceived to be doing a good job. For example, in any given year they commonly make frequent gifts of clothing above and beyond the norm, they may be generous in their gifts to the youth's parents, they may allow the herder to pick the particular head of stock he will receive as annual payment, and they may give a second animal per year in the form of Muslim alms (*zakat*).

For those herders who perform up to standard, the rewards in the form of additional payments may well exceed the equivalent of three times the standard herding contract of one cow per year. In addition, the herder receives many benefits from the patron that are harder to quantify. He may have privileged access to information, concerning both politics and livestock trading, he may be extended credit, and he may enjoy other privileges associated with the status afforded elites in the society, such as better dress, better nutrition, and access to better health care. Also, his poor relations, especially his mother and father, have someone to whom they can turn in times of need.

In the following account, an elder who is a long-term employer of hired laborers describes how one knows who the good laborers are, and having found them, how one steers and rewards their behavior with incentives:

> If [a hired herder] is bad he is just bad-natured. The good ones are good-natured. The bad ones cannot be made good. Such people you pay and get rid of. If he has not completed 12 months he gets no pay and is fired.
>
> [The ones you want] are respectful and don't get angry with you. To reward him you give him clothes. You allow him to select his own cows for his salary. (This makes him very happy because he knows the best cattle.) Sometimes people even employ married laborers. With these ones you can take care of the family. Even our own children can go to the cattle camp after they marry. The employer must look well after the family while the boy is in the cattle camp or he will refuse to go. The family must be given enough milk and food.
>
> Now the ones who herd well get a salary of 1 cow as well as 1 cow for *zakat*. Instead of giving *zakat* to someone else, the herd owner gives it to the boys in the cattle camp. I myself paid the bridewealth of two boys who herded well for me in the cattle camp. Ali Mohamed [pseudonym] worked 5 years and married Galole Shure's [pseudonym] daughter. After he married he stayed with me another 6 years. I don't even remember how much I have paid to him. I even gave bridewealth from my own daughters to that man. I have never met the parents of that boy; he is a Wardei [descendant of an Orma who was captured by the Somali during the wars of the 1860s], but he did good work. All the boys doing well in the cattle camp get similar treatment from people. It is not only me. All the other people have ways of helping them. Those who don't work well don't get this treatment.

The practice of awarding above-market wages is similar to what Carl Shapiro and Joseph Stiglitz (1984) label an "efficiency wage." They argue that such wages provide a means of reducing shirking by increasing the costs to workers of being caught. In other words, if workers are being paid above market value, the loss to them of losing the job is greater, thus decreasing the likelihood that they would wish to risk losing the employment by being caught shirking. This, I would argue, is the mechanism by which they get on the escalator of increasing trust.

The ultimate gesture on the part of a herd owner is to pay the man's bridewealth after many years of loyal service or to marry the hired herder to one of his own daughters. After the marriage the owner will extend his care to the wife and children of the herder. At this point the herd owner may formally adopt the hired herder as his own son. The Orma talk fondly of such relationships in paternalistic terms, and most wealthy households can point to at least two or three such individuals for whom they have paid bridewealth in the previous decade. After the hired herder marries he often establishes an independent household if he has accumulated sufficient cattle to do so. This represents the end of the formal hired herder relationship, but if the hired herder resides nearby, the herd owner may still call upon him in times of emergency.

If after marriage the hired herder does not have the resources to become independent, he may stay on with the herd owner. Although his salary ceases, the herd owner takes on responsibility for the maintenance of the hired herder's household. This is the point at which the Orma recognize the relationship as an adoption. After marriage the hired herder is generally not stationed in the cattle camp, as is the norm for married sons; his base becomes the permanent sedentary village or the nomadic village. However, like the herd owners' own sons, he takes on the role of supervisor and may make frequent trips to the cattle camp to supervise the herd boys there. He also does extensive traveling to scout grazing and water conditions, collect medicines from the district headquarters, and market stock. What develops in effect is a hierarchical labor structure with increasing specialization.

Although these adopted sons are generally talked about as "just like my own sons," there are in fact differences. The herd owner may take corporate responsibility for any wrongs committed by the adopted son, just as he would for his own sons, but the adopted son does not inherit. However, adopted sons are generally of an older generation than a man's own sons (they arguably have received their inheritance while the herd owner is alive), and they are often given the role of executor of the estate upon the death of the father—that is, they take charge of dividing the stock among the sons, often according to the elder's wishes or accepted norms.

The enduring nature of these fictive kin relations is illustrated by one family that has managed to maintain such relationships across generations. The former hired herder still lives next to the man for whom he herded, even though he is now a man in his fifties of modest independent means with three wives of his own. This former herder not only had his bridewealth paid for him but was also sent to Mecca on the Hajj. His sons now herd for the wealthy elder, as their father did before them.

The Power of Reputation

Both herd owners and hired herders have ample opportunity to choose short-term gain over long-term cooperation. At any given moment either party may be in significant arrears in the relationship. Given that the bulk of the contract wage is paid only once a year, the herd owner has ample opportunity to default on the relationship before each annual payment. One old man is notorious for refusing to pay hired herders even after they have finished their twelve-month contract. Elders are routinely called in to adjudicate the disputes. Even worse, the herd owner may fail to fulfill the "just" expectations of a long-term hired herder by not paying his bridewealth at the appropriate time, as happened in a much celebrated case in 1998. Similarly, hired herders face constant temptations to shirk on arduous work, not to mention the potential for outright theft of livestock. In another case in 1998 a new hired herder received his annual payment early (after only two months of work) as a signal of generosity from the herd owner. But the herder rapidly revealed himself to be completely unworthy, and the herd owner had to let him go well before he had worked off the twelve months of salary that he had already been paid. In spite of the moral hazard demonstrated in these cases, reputation is usually a significant deterrent against short-term gain for both owner and employee.

Should it be perceived that an owner has treated a herder unjustly—as, for example, the old man who always tries not to pay—or that the herder's loyal performance warrants the payment of his bridewealth but the owner has not so volunteered, the owner will have tremendous difficulty attracting quality herdsmen in the future. As one elder put it, "The herd boys know who the 'bad' old men are." When asked why a man would pursue such a strategy, one elder replied, "It is stupid! He only gets bad herd boys who are after food and not getting on well with their family."

One wealthy elderly man, whom many Orma considered disagreeable, was known to be antisocial and remained nomadic in part because of his inability to get along with people. During the 1985 drought the herders who worked for him sold some of his cattle and ran off with the money, leaving Orma territory completely. Ordinarily repercussions would have followed—the families of the young men would have felt compelled to repay the stolen stock in order to maintain the good name of the family. Normal practice would have dictated that they take corporate responsibility. In this case, there was no such sentiment. Public opinion sided with the herd boys; they were judged (even by the elders) to have been justified because they had been so poorly treated by the old man.

Although sample sizes do not permit quantitative confirmation, the elders are convinced that other "scrooges" such as this elder also fared extremely poorly during the drought. The elders believe that such men's cattle died in larger numbers owing to neglect, and that many were in effect "stolen." Not coincidentally, three elders who fared far better in the drought are highly respected, considered good managers, and have reputations for treating their hired herders exceptionally well. As one elder put it:

> The drought was what gave the boys the chance to cheat. The cattle left this area. People here had to be taking care of their families here [in the permanent village]. Usually we frequently visit the cattle camp—that helps a lot. People can check and see if a cow is missing. There is less supervision during a drought.

Because the cattle were so far removed from their owners, many herd boys had the opportunity to "settle the score," so to speak, with the "bad" old men. The prospects of employment outside of the district also enabled the young men to violate accepted behavior with impunity as long as they had no intention of returning to Tana River District.

Such behavior did not characterize the vast majority of hired herders, for whom the hope of future rewards, although not specifically negotiated, provided a clear incentive to perform well in herding activities in the absence of direct supervision. Over the long haul it is obvious whether the milk yields of the cattle indicate that they have been well cared for in the cattle camps, and whether morbidity and mortality of the stock are within the bounds expected, given existing conditions.

Conclusions

One of the most striking aspects of Orma labor relations is their informality and imprecision. One might well ask why herd owners who pay some workers according to a fixed contract don't do the same with those they pay two and three times as much. Instead, they choose to compensate these individuals through far vaguer forms based largely on gifts and enforced by reputational effects. This strategy works, I would argue, not entirely because it allows compensation to be tailored ex post facto to actual job performance, much as a bonus might be, but rather, because it reduces monitoring costs. (Gary Miller, in this volume, discusses the same characteristic of delayed reward in corporate America.)

Herding productivity is extremely difficult to measure given the vast array of uncontrolled variables that may confound measurement of the efforts of the hired herder—drought, disease, wild animals, and enraged farmers, for example. If I tell you up front that I will be tripling your wage, I probably want to be quite specific about what I expect in return performance. But this is exactly what the Orma herd owner cannot specify. On the other hand, if I reward work based on a consensus of what is deemed reasonable after the fact, given the applicable circumstances, we both risk the sanction of reputational effects but are not bound by a contract that might have been inappropriate given the unforeseen circumstances. Alternatively, I may extend a bonus up front in the hope of enticing you into even more superior performance (much like an efficiency wage) or signaling that I wish to promote you to the next level of effort and reward, but again, I expect a performance that can only be defined ex post facto, given the highly unpredictable circumstances.

This ex post facto evaluation works only in combination with trust on the part of each party during the period when each is a net creditor to the other. Thus, trust is used through the many iterations of the relationship as each party complies with the consensus norm concerning fair effort and compensation. Should either party default at either time, they pay the price of lost capital or reputation. In either case the loss is greater at higher levels of the iteration. In other words, much as Shapiro and Stiglitz (1984) suggest, the cost of shirking increases for the hired herder at higher wage levels, for he may begin back down at the bottom when he seeks reemployment elsewhere. Similarly, the capital loss and reputation loss to the herd owner for defaulting in the final stages of the relationship—at the point where a hired herder should reasonably expect bridewealth, for example—are extremely high, as we saw in the case described earlier. In that instance a group of hired herders, having observed many instances of the herd owner's "cheapness," stole many animals from him simultaneously during a drought. Because public consensus sided with the herd boys, it was the herd owner's reputation that suffered most, and he had great difficulty finding good workers thereafter.

Although the Orma clearly prefer relations that give them "control" over laborers, as is the case with sons and other close relatives who are economically dependent on them, they substitute "trust" when they have to. Under these circumstances the herd owner does everything possible to construct the choice environment in such a way as to maximize the probability that trust will be rewarded with trustworthiness. In much the same way that Hardin (1993) suggests, each party trusts in small steps, testing the waters and measuring the response of the other as well as possible, and in this stepwise progression the level of trust and risk escalates over time. Gradually the herd owner reduces his supervision and the herder tolerates longer periods between remuneration. Both parties depend in this endeavor on the norms of "fair play" to enforce their expectations through reputation.

The longer one spends building a reputation, the less likely one is to risk it by taking one quick gain. Reputation builds to greater and greater levels as one consistently forgoes greater opportunities for rewards from cheating. As a consequence, each increase in reputation also creates greater opportunity costs for shirking, as the future value of one's reputation grows. The relationship is self-reinforcing in this sense.

The actual adoption of a hired herder clearly moves the nature of the relationship from a contractual one to a more trusting one. But contrary to superficial appearances, this is not so much about the creation of trust due to a new common identity with the adoptee (see Tyler, this volume) as it is about calculated self-interest (see Hardin, this volume). From the context of agency theory, the most interesting quality of this transformation in the relationship is that we associate the move in the direction of generalized reciprocity with looser account-keeping and less direct monitoring of the daily performance of agent and principal. I believe this is what the elder discussed earlier is trying to capture when he remarks about one such relationship with a herder, "I don't even remember how much I have paid to him."

This suspension of account-keeping is in fact the essence of trust. Trust has replaced the need to monitor daily performance, thus gradually relieving both parties of a great accounting burden. In its final stages this form of trust appears to be the antithesis of strategic calculation. But as we examine the process by which it evolves, we see that in fact it is quite carefully calculated. This usage contrasts with the perspective of Williamson (1993), who wishes to reserve the term for non-calculative behavior. Trust occurs neither randomly nor prematurely. It occurs in direct measure to a decreased risk of the probability of cheating on the parts of both the principal and the agent, and this assessment is based on their incentives for long-term cooperation, their reputations, and the general social context of norm enforcement. This is a story about trusting in order to diminish accounting for very calculated reasons.

The case study on which this chapter is based stems from approximately four years of anthropological fieldwork with the Orma of Tana River District in Kenya (July 1978 to February 1981, April through December 1987, and parts of the summers of 1994, 1996, 1998, and 1999). The author wishes to thank the following foundations and institutions for generous grant support during these field trips: the National Science Foundation, the John D. and Catherine T. MacArthur Foundation, the Rockefeller Foundation, the National Institutes of Health, the Ford Foundation, Fulbright-Hays, the Beijer Institute, and Washington University.

The author also wishes to acknowledge the stimulating intellectual affiliation afforded by the Institute for Development Studies, University of Nairobi, and research clearance granted by the Office of the President, Government of Kenya.

Notes

1. Common dangers that befall Orma herds but can be mitigated by careful husbandry are: weight loss or death due to drought conditions or failure to move stock to the best grazing; weakening of calves due to overmilking; failure to assist cows giving birth; failure to vaccinate stock against endemic diseases; attack by wild animals (especially lions and wild dogs); loss of stock in thick bush; attacks on stock by farmers if cattle are allowed to encroach upon farms; exposure to disease if herders take stock into tsetse fly-infested areas; death following the first rains after a drought when the stock are in a weakened condition and easily get stuck in the mud; and— increasingly common in recent years—cattle rustling by armed bandits.

2. This "control" does not stem from the "power of the curse," which influences these relations in some other East African societies.

References

Alston, Lee. 1981. "Tenure Choice in Southern Agriculture, 1930–1960." *Explorations in Economic History* 18: 211–32.

Alston, Lee, Samar Data, and Jeffrey Nugent. 1984. "Tenancy Choice in a Competitive Framework with Transactions Costs." *Journal of Political Economy* 92(6): 1121–33.

Alston, Lee, and Robert Higgs. 1982. "Contractual Mix in Southern Agriculture Since the Civil War: Facts, Hypotheses, and Tests." *Journal of Economic History* 42(2): 327–53.

Coleman, James. 1990. *Foundations of Social Theory.* Cambridge, Mass.: Harvard University Press.

Ensminger, Jean. 1992. *Making a Market: The Institutional Transformation of an African Society.* New York: Cambridge University Press.

Fama, Eugene. 1980. "Agency Problems and the Theory of the Firm." *Journal of Political Economy* 88(2): 288–307.

Fama, Eugene, and Michael Jensen. 1983a. "Agency Problems and Residual Claims." *Journal of Law and Economics* 26: 327–49.

———. 1983b. "Separation of Ownership and Control." *Journal of Law and Economics* 26: 301–26.

Hardin, Russell. 1993. "The Street-Level Epistemology of Trust." *Politics and Society* 21(4): 505–29.

Jensen, Michael, and William Meckling. 1976. "Theory of the Firm: Managerial Behavior, Agency Costs, and Ownership Structure." *Journal of Financial Economics* 3: 305–60.

Lewis, J. D., and A. Weigert. 1985. "Theory of the Firm: Managerial Behavior, Agency Costs, and Ownership Structure." *Social Forces* 63: 967–85.

Pollak, Robert. 1985. "A Transaction Cost Approach to Families and Households." *Journal of Economic Literature* 23(2): 581–608.

Putnam, Robert. 1992. *Making Democracy Work: Civic Traditions in Modern Italy.* Princeton, N.J.: Princeton University Press.

Sahlins, Marshall. 1972. *Stone Age Economics.* New York: Aldine de Gruyter.

Shapiro, Carl, and Joseph Stiglitz. 1984. "Equilibrium Unemployment as a Worker Discipline Device." *American Economic Review* 74(3): 433–44.

Sperling, Louise. 1984. "The Recruitment of Labor Among Samburu Herders." Working Paper 414. Nairobi, Kenya: University of Nairobi, Institute for Development Studies.

Williamson, Oliver. 1993. "Calculativeness, Trust, and Economic Organization." *Journal of Law & Economics* 36(1): 453–86.

Yamagishi, Toshio, and Midori Yamagishi. 1994. "Trust and Commitment in the United States and Japan." *Motivation and Emotion* 18(2): 129–66.

Chapter 7

Clubs and Congregations: The Benefits of Joining an Association

Dietlind Stolle

T HE SOCIAL capital school has proposed that one of the important mechanisms for generating good democratic outcomes is participation in networks of voluntary associations (Putnam 1993, 1995a, 1995b). In his study of Italy, Robert Putnam regards the density of membership in associations as one indicator of regional social capital, showing powerfully the effects of different levels of membership density on several societal outcomes and on the effectiveness of government performance (Putnam 1993; see also Case and Katz 1991; Fukuyama 1995; Granovetter 1985; Hagan, Merkens, and Boehnke 1995; Jencks and Peterson 1991; Knack and Keefer 1997).

Networks of civic engagement, norms of reciprocity, and trust constitute the heart of social capital. To Putnam (1993, 89ff), these three elements of social capital belong together, although he stresses and builds his argument on the assumption that membership in social networks such as soccer clubs, singing groups, and bowling leagues facilitates democratic mobilization and socialization effects.[1] "Internally associations instill in their members habits of cooperation, solidarity, and public-spiritedness. . . . Participation in civic organizations inculcates skills of cooperation as well as a sense of shared responsibility for collective endeavors."[2] It is plausible and almost self-evident that groups of voluntary associations produce certain goods that are available to the group itself. However, it has not been satisfactorily proven *whether* and *how* voluntary associations create trust and other payoffs that benefit the wider society outside of the group, although such an assumption underlies contemporary theories of social capital. In other words, we do not truly know whether voluntary associations fulfill this function, and if so, how.[3]

In his studies of the United States, for example, Putnam assumes that declining membership in associations is the cause for all kinds of social evils, such as reduced levels of trust and cooperative attitudes in the U.S. population (Putnam 1995a). In his work on Italy, Putnam uses the indicator of regional associational membership as one important predictor of the region's institutional performance (Putnam 1993, 89ff).[4] Both works essentially assume the validity of a micro theory of social capital that posits a causal link between association membership and other civic attitudes and behavior that benefit the wider society. However, is it correct to use the density of membership in any type of association in a given region as an indicator of that region's level of trust and norms of reciprocity? To what extent can associations serve as the causes and creators of trust and cooperative values? Are all associations alike in their ability to develop trust and other social capital traits among their members? What are the specific mechanisms in associations that are responsible for the potential learning of trust and cooperative attitudes? To answer these questions, we need to examine how the different components of social capital, such as association membership, trust, and cooperative attitudes, relate to each other sequentially.

Problems arise in obtaining answers. First, even though at the macro level the relationship between associational membership, other indicators of civic behavior, and governmental performance is evident and strong in Putnam's study of Italian regions, there is no micro theory of social capital that explicitly states which aspects of social interactions matter for the creation of generalized trust and norms of reciprocity. Such a micro theory needs to define the theoretical causal connection between the structural and cultural components of social capital.

The second related problem is the lack of empirical research about the causal relationship between these aspects of social capital. So far, very few data sets combine cultural indicators of generalized trust and cooperation with structural measures of individual associations or interactions, the content of their work, and the degree of social contact.[5] National and cross-national surveys that include questions on generalized attitudes, such as the American National Election Studies, the General Social Surveys, or the World Value Studies, do not give detailed information about the respondent's involvement in different types of associations. As a result, group-level characteristics as causes of social capital production cannot be directly identified; we do not know whether trust and cooperative attitudes increase linearly with the length of time spent in any type of association or other social interaction, or whether it is a function of a particular type of involvement or a special type of group. Answers to these two questions would not only enhance our understanding of the sources of generalized trust but are critical to the construction of a micro theory of social capital.

This chapter addresses two related research questions. First, even though we find association members to be more civic and trusting, to what extent can these effects be attributed to the group experience per se, as opposed to self-selection? Second, to what extent can we distinguish between the effects of group membership that pertain strictly to the group itself and those that influence the wider society? To investigate the link between individuals' civicness and trust, their group attitudes, and their involvement in associations, I have constructed and administered a questionnaire to identify the traits of individuals and the associations to which they belong. The questionnaire includes items on several social capital indicators as well as information about group activities and the nature of involvement and interaction within the group. I personally gathered data for nearly one thousand association members of various local groups nested in several associational types in Germany, Sweden, and the United States.

The Centrality of Generalized Trust for Social Capital Research

Research about the causal relationship between cultural and structural components of social capital brings together insights from the school of political and social participation and the school of civic attitudes and behavior. Most empirical studies on the effect of voluntary associations have shown that, relative to nonmembers, members of associations exhibit more democratic and civic attitudes as well as more active forms of political participation. Gabriel Almond and Sidney Verba (1963) and many other authors have found that members of associations are more politically active, more informed about politics, more sanguine about their ability to affect political life, and more supportive of democratic norms (see, for example, Billiet and Cambré 1999; Hanks and Eckland 1978; Olsen 1972; Verba and Nie 1972). Others have noticed that the number and type of associations to which people belong, and the extent of their engagement within these associations, are related to political activity and involvement (Rogers, Barb, and Bultena 1975). In later research, Verba and his colleagues have found that members of voluntary associations learn self-respect, group identity, and public skills (see, for example, Dekker, Koopmans, and van den Broek 1997; Moyser and Parry 1997; Verba, Schlozman, and Brady 1995; Yogev and Shapira 1990).

To these findings, the social capital school adds the insight that membership in associations should also facilitate the learning of cooperative attitudes and behavior. In particular, membership in voluntary associations should increase face-to-face interactions between people and create a setting for the development of trust. This ingroup trust can be used to achieve group purposes. Further, the social capital school claims that through mechanisms not yet clearly understood the development of interpersonal trust and cooperative experiences between members tends to be generalized to the society as a whole (see also Boix and Posner 1996; Knight, this volume). In this way the operation of voluntary groups and associations contributes to the building of a society in which cooperation between all people for all sorts of purposes—not just within the groups themselves—is facilitated.[6]

Generalized attitudes of trust extend beyond the boundaries of face-to-face interaction and incorporate people not personally known. They are indicated by an abstract preparedness to trust others and to engage in actions with others (see Yamagishi and Yamagishi 1994; Yamagishi, this volume). These attitudes of trust are generalized when they go beyond specific personal settings in which the partner to be cooperated with is already known; they even go beyond the boundaries of kinship, friendship, and acquaintance. In this sense the scope of generalized trust should be distinguished from trust in personal relationships. This more immediate form of trust may be called private or personalized trust; it results from cooperation and repeated interactions with one's immediate circle, whether that be a family, community, or voluntary association. The scope of generalized trust also needs to be distinguished from identity-based forms of trust that include only people one knows personally as well as those who fit into a certain social identity that one holds (see Brewer 1981; Kramer, Brewer, and Hanna 1996; Messick 1991; Messick and Kramer, this volume). Even though identity-based trust is "depersonalized" in this conception of trust, total strangers cannot be trusted. Total strangers cannot be categorized easily into a known social identity.

The important question is how the trust that we obviously build for people we know well can be extended and used for the development of *generalized* trust, or trust for people we do not know well. In Russell Hardin's (1993) words (see also Hardin, this volume), how do we develop a general level of expectation of trustworthiness? How do we make the leap of faith to people we do not know? How do we generalize and feel comfortable with those about whom we do not have much information? How is generalized trust institutionalized? In short, we need a mechanism that explains the development of generalized trust.

Several mechanisms have been suggested and discussed. Hardin (1993), for example, argues that general expectations about others' trustworthiness are strongly influenced by an individual's previous experiences (see also Hardin, this volume). It has also been suggested that participation in school, family, work, and community is likely to have "strong internal effects" on the building of civic virtues (Mutz and Mondak 1998; Newton 1997). In addition, the role of government and public policies has been brought into the debate about the development of generalized trust (Levi 1998; Sides 1999; Stolle 2000).

In this chapter I examine the capacity of voluntary associations to facilitate generalized trust, since social capital theorists assume the existence of this capacity. With voluntary associations as with other potential sources for generalized trust, the task is to specify the mechanisms and aspects of the interactions that are either beneficial or inhibiting for generalized trust.

Arguments about the importance of voluntary associations in fostering trust and civic attitudes have been criticized for focusing too narrowly on certain types of secondary associations as the main source of social capital. For example, Deborah Minkoff (1997) emphasizes the importance of checkbook associations, whereas Michael Foley and Bob Edwards (1996) point out the significance of social movements for the creation of social capital. Other critics note that more informal contacts and gatherings, such as with friends or in cliques, can be equally productive. Alternative forms of social interaction can strengthen civil society and hence democracy. However, neither the social capital school nor its critics have sufficiently tested the actual potential of various social interactions for the development of trust and civicness. The goal of this chapter is to fill some of these gaps in social capital and trust research. I have selected the most prominent mechanism of social interaction, namely, membership in voluntary associations, and examined its facilitative and mobilizational potential for various civic values and attitudes, such as generalized trust.

Hypotheses and Research Design

The first and most problematic issue concerning these research questions is the possibility that people self-select into association groups depending on their original trust or general civicness level. This is a classic problem of endogeneity. People who trust more or who are more civic might be more easily drawn to membership in associations, whereas people who are less civic or less trusting might not join in the first place. This concern is depicted in figure 7.1.

In other words, it could be that although we seek to observe the rounded arrow, our results are driven by the relationships depicted by the black arrowhead. Social capital theory has not sufficiently dealt with this problem (but see Brehm and Rahn 1997). Ideally one would track association members over time in order to filter out the separate influence of group membership per se on civicness, controlling for the self-selection effects. However, we do not have the longitudinal data available, primarily because collecting such data would entail enormous

Figure 7.1   Association Data Set, by Country

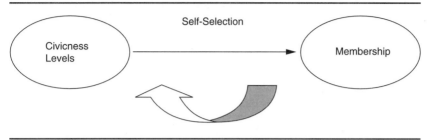

Source: Author's compilation.

costs. The more efficient strategy then is to sample members from different kinds of groups. With my self-collected data set with association members in several groups, nested in various associational types in three countries, we can test whether civic attitudes and behaviors are really a product of membership effects.

In addressing this problem, it is critical to determine whether the membership itself has a separate effect on the development of civic attitudes and behavior, disregarding whether self-selection is at work. The question is whether the group socialization period within an association *adds* to the building of the individual's trust, civic engagement, and cooperation that can be used *outside* of the group life.

To determine added membership effects with my data set, which includes association members from several groups, I compare members of associations who joined for only short periods with members who have participated for a long time. This comparison tests whether the additional membership effects exist, namely, whether the length of time spent in an association causes civic outcomes. I use a categorical variable in this analysis to measure different periods of membership for each respondent. The variable makes seven distinctions, which range from very short periods of membership (a few months) to major parts of the respondent's adult life. Assuming that the association members in the sample are somewhat similar in terms of their attitudes and behavior, this variable—length of membership—reveals the learning effects in associations.[7]

The second issue that this chapter clarifies relates to the differences between associations. Even though we might find that associations are virtuous, they need not be equally virtuous. Are all associations alike in their capacity to develop trust and other social capital traits among their members? We can take advantage of the presence of ten associational types in my data set to examine their distinct capacities to develop trust and civic attitudes and behavior. To understand better which types of associations are connected to civic outcomes and trust, another comparison is undertaken, namely, between members of different associational types, which are distinguished by several dummy variables.

These variables—length of membership and associational types—are the main independent variables for the analysis that follows. I test their ability to explain an array of several indicators of trust and civic values and behavior that relate to the group and to the society at large. The selection of the dependent variables by distinguishing between group-related and society-related indicators of civicness is my third contribution to the social capital debate. If the major claim of the social capital school about the significance of secondary voluntary associations for democracy is correct, then we ought to see that membership has an added effect on society-related indicators of civicness, and especially on generalized trust in a variety of social and apolitical groups. In short, the main purpose of this chapter is to test whether and in which associations membership effects actually exist. In addition, the analysis reveals how far these effects reach into the wider society.

The Data

My data set includes responses to a questionnaire with several items on various types of social trust, societal engagement, community involvement, group activity, and associational membership. The questionnaires were distributed to members of associations in Germany, Sweden, and the United States in 1996, 1997, and 1998. I usually went to an association meeting, observed interactions, and (either during a break or at the end of the meeting) asked all members to fill in the questionnaire. The questionnaire usually took twenty to forty minutes to complete. The respondents were nearly all of the members who attended a particular meeting, training session, rehearsal, or competition.[8]

To control for regional differences and their impact on social capital, I selected association members who reside in the capital cities of the two European countries, in Berlin and Stockholm; the greater Philadelphia area was chosen as an equivalent city in the United States. This choice of cities allowed me to test my hypotheses in a range of metropolitan areas in advanced industrialized democracies. All in all, I selected forty-nine local groups, comprising ten different types of association. Table 7.1 summarizes the associations studied in each country and the number of respondents per associational type.

The associational types were selected in order to test several propositions of the social capital theory and its critiques. For example, bowling leagues and church choirs, as well as groups from similar types of association sectors, were chosen mainly because social capital theory focuses on these apolitical associations as the typical sources of social capital generation. Other types of associations chosen exhibit more public-oriented purposes. Two assumptions can be made about associations that seek to provide public goods rather than to develop a private interest: there may be a higher self-selection bias with members of such organizations, and

Table 7.1   Association Data Set, by Country

Associational Type	Number of Associations/Respondents		
	Sweden	Germany	United States
Boule leagues	9/116	—	—
Bowling leagues	2/39	7/70	3/108
Church choirs	7/148	4/125	7/133
Pet groups	1/19	—	—
Parents' groups	3/34	—	—
Sports groups	—	2/47	—
Self-help groups	—	1/19	—
Political groups	—	—	2/32
Neighborhood organizations	—	—	1/9
Total	22/356	14/261	13/282

Source: Author's compilation.

civic attitudes and behavior in such organizations may develop in a different pattern. For example, for Sweden I chose parents' groups (*Farsor och Morsor*)—whose members go on so-called night walks for the purpose of trying to stay in contact with adolescents in their neighborhoods—a type of association prevalent there, and for the United States I selected a neighborhood group and political organizations, such as the League of Women Voters and campaign volunteers. The choice of such organizations beyond solely apolitical groups allows for the testing of hypotheses about associations directed to different purposes.[9]

Dependent Variables

Measuring Aspects of Social Capital

This chapter constitutes a test of an array of different types of civic attitudes, such as generalized trust, and behaviors and their potential roots in associations. I make two types of distinctions. One is between public and private forms of social capital (see also Stolle and Rochon 1998). Private social capital captures those attitudes and behaviors that mainly benefit the members of the voluntary association and group life itself. Such forms of social capital might be exclusive and not accessible to people outside of a particular group. Therefore, the use of private forms of social capital for situations outside of each group, that is, for situations of cooperation with people less known, is not as obvious. The use of private social capital for democracy is more limited. However, private social capital may still function as an asset to those who regularly interact with each other. Public social capital, on the other hand, includes attitudes and behavior that go beyond the group life itself. For example, it includes generalized values, which tend to influence behaviors in settings outside of group life and wherever the individual enters potential cooperation games. The assumption of the social capital school is that the attitudes, values, and behaviors learned in associations can be used elsewhere. If this proposition is true, we should find that members who have experienced group life for longer periods of time are also, for example, more trusting, in a generalized sense, toward all people, not just toward their fellow members. The question is whether group membership has an effect on both private and public forms of social capital.

The second distinction is between attitudes and values as well as behaviors. Do attitudes and values that have been shaped and socialized over long periods of time change through the experience of membership in associations? Is the experience of membership too short-lived to have an impact on the change of attitudes and values (Newton 1997)? Can associational membership cause changes in behavior?

I selected nine different attitudinal and behavioral indicators of private and public forms of social capital. They all have in common that they tap a certain sense of engagement, a readiness to cooperate, to give the benefit of the doubt, to commit, to get involved, and to trust. The choice of so many dependent variables is supposed to depict a wide array of aspects of social capital, even though generalized trust should be seen as the heart of social capital. In the following, the measurements along these two dimensions of private and public forms of social capital are discussed in turn. The exact question wording, scaling techniques, and reliability measures can be found in the appendix.

Private Social Capital: Group-Related Behavioral and Attitudinal Change
Here I introduce three measures for group-related *behavioral* indicators as they describe aspects of private social capital:

1. *Activity levels for the group:* This variable is constructed from individual scores on a two-item scale, both of which depict the respondent's engagement with projects and tasks within the group. Generally members of Swedish groups are twice as engaged as those in German or U.S. groups.

2. *Level of socializing outside of the group activities:* This variable is based on one questionnaire item that captures the respondent's socializing pattern with members of the associational group outside of group

life, for example, after the rehearsal or after the practice. Members of bowling leagues in all three countries, for example, are particularly social beyond the regular group life.

3. *Conversational breadth:* This variable is constructed from individual scores on several questions about the respondent's conversation topics within the group. The questions range from conversations about private issues or about professional, societal, political, and neighborhood questions to topics related to the hobby or group tasks. Generally members of U.S. associations exhibit a slightly higher conversational breadth.

I use two measures for group-related *attitudinal* indicators as aspects of private social capital:

4. *Ingroup trust:* This variable measures the trust that association members have for their fellow members. High ingroup trust is partially a function of group size. Larger groups, especially large choirs, do not exhibit as much ingroup trust (correlation is $r = -.42$ for the whole sample, significant at $p < .0001$). Smaller groups, such as the self-help group, all show high ingroup trust. Generally U.S. groups exhibit more ingroup trust than Swedish or German groups.

5. *Commitment level:* This item depicts the individual's commitment to his or her particular association.

All three behavioral indicators and the two attitudinal indicators are classified as private forms of social capital, because they are directed solely at the members of the group. It is not obvious how activity levels of the group, socializing with members after the meetings, and conversational breadth directly affect attitudes and behavior outside of group life.[10] Potentially, and according to theories of social capital, we would also expect a connection between ingroup trust and types of trust that are related to the outside world, such as generalized trust. But we have no evidence of this relationship.[11] It is my hypothesis that membership as measured in length of time spent in one of the selected groups has a positive impact on these types of behaviors and attitudes.

Public Social Capital: Society-Related Behavioral and Attitudinal Change
I test one of the aspects of public social capital, society-related behavioral change, using two measures:

6. *Civic engagement outside the group life:* Civic engagement in communities constitutes one type of behavior that is useful for the larger society. This variable, a four-item scale, captures the respondent's activities at the neighborhood or community level, outside of the

actual group life. Of course, members of neighborhood organizations are most active in neighborhood and community projects. Generally members of U.S. groups are much more involved locally than members of Swedish or German groups.

7. *Vote in local elections:* This straightforward indicator measures whether the respondent has voted during the last local election. Since members in voluntary associations are generally more engaged and more politically active, there is not much variation in responses. Most members in the sample voted. However, not all members in U.S. associations vote, and they are least active in U.S. bowling leagues and neighborhood organizations.

I use two society-related attitudinal indicators as aspects of public social capital:

8. *Generalized trust:* Generalized trust is the most important aspect of public social capital. I used a six-item scale, all of the items tapping a presumption of the trustworthiness of either people in general or highly abstract groups of people such as fellow citizens, strangers, and foreigners. Generally members of Swedish associations are significantly more trusting than members of U.S. or German groups.

9. *Approach toward new neighbors:* This variable tries to tap the respondent's attitudes toward strangers. The item asks the respondent to imagine a scenario in which a new family moves into the neighborhood and to choose the kind of contact the respondent would establish. The answers suggest four different responses: doing nothing, waiting for an initiative from the neighbor family, starting a conversation, or inviting the family over. The link here is that associational membership over time and the social contacts established in groups could eventually spill over into a more open and inclusive approach in other settings.

In short, all of these attitudinal and behavioral indicators of public social capital tap the potential of activity and engagement, as well as openness, acceptance of otherness, and trust, for use in various situations, especially in contact with persons unknown. The social capital school assumes that such attitudes can be the product of regular and face-to-face interactions with other people and cooperation experiences within a group.

Control Variables

The regression models for each of these indicators include the main independent variables—namely, the distinctions between associational types and between different periods of participation—as well as other types of control variables that are related to civic and trusting attitudes and behavior. These control variables are mainly personal resource variables, such as age, education, income, gender, and length of residence in the municipality. One additional control variable is of special importance. It captures the respondent's additional memberships beyond the association I visited. It could certainly be that the respondent is a member of several other associations that also exert influences on his or her behavior and attitudes. I have no information on how long respondents have been members of other associations, nor do I know more about the specific circumstances of that additional involvement. However, at least we can control for multiple memberships and identify whether they are related to the social capital indicator in question. In the following discussion, I examine in turn each set of private versus public social capital indicators.[12]

Results

Group-Related Behavioral Change

The first set of dependent variables captures behavior within the group: activity levels, levels of socializing outside of group life, and conversational breadth.

As predicted, all three indicators show very strong added membership effects, demonstrated by the coefficients for the length-of-membership variable. The longer the period of time respondents have been members of any of the selected associations, the more active they are, the more they socialize with each other outside of group life, and the more they converse about various issues. These results hold for all three countries, with the exception of conversational breadth in Sweden. The logic is that the members become more familiar with each other, more attached (see discussion in the next section), and more committed to the association and to their fellow members. This obviously breeds an openness to talk more widely, to socialize more after hours, and even to take on more tasks.[13]

There is also something in the nature of the associational type that allows members to be more active, more conversational, and more likely to socialize. For example, members of U.S. neighborhood groups are significantly more active and less conversational than members of bowling leagues. (See the coefficients for group dummies in tables 7.2, 7.3, and 7.4.) In addition, socializing patterns outside of group life are significantly related to a group measure of fun orientation. This variable indicates whether most association members view getting seriously involved with the given hobby or other interest or socializing as the main goal of each associational meeting (table 7.3). The higher group value of socializing is,

(Text continues on p. 217.)

Table 7.2 Group-Related Behavioral Change: Activity Levels (OLS Regression Results)

Independent Variables	Standardized Coefficients (t-Value)		
	United States	Germany	Sweden
Personal resources			
Age	−.10	.05	−.18***
	(−1.6)	(.6)	(−3.0)
Education	−.06	.16**	.19****
	(−.10)	(2.2)	(3.3)
Income	−.06	.02	.01
	(.9)	(.3)	(.3)
Gender	.22****	−.10	−.02
	(3.2)	(−1.3)	(−.3)
Length of residence in municipality	.07	.05	.02
	(1.1)	(.8)	(.3)
Group-related variables			
Length of membership	.30****	.27****	.36****
	(4.2)	(3.8)	(5.6)
Number of additional memberships	.15**	.10	.14**
	(2.3)	(1.5)	(2.4)
Members of political groups	−.11*	—	—
	(−1.5)		
Members of church choirs	.00	−.08	−.11
	(.4)	(−1.1)	(−1.2)
Members of neighborhood groups	.24****	—	—
	(3.9)		
Members of self-help groups	—	.07	—
		(.9)	
Members of parents' groups	—	—	−.00
			(−.3)
Members of pet groups	—	—	−.06
			(−.9)
Members of boule leagues	—	—	−.18*
			(−2.0)
Constant (unstandardized)	.39	−.64	.51
	(1.3)	(−1.7)	(1.4)
Number of cases	238	246	327
Adjusted R^2	.17	.11	.24

Source: Author's compilation.
Notes: United States: Bowling leagues were excluded. Germany: Bowling and sports groups were excluded. Sweden: Bowling leagues were excluded.
*p < .10; **p < .05; ***p < .01; ****p < .001 (two-tailed test)

Table 7.3   Group-Related Behavioral Change: Level of Socializing Outside of Group Life (OLS Regression Results)

Independent Variables	Standardized Coefficients (t-Value)		
	United States	Germany	Sweden
Personal resources			
Age	−.09	−.01	.02
	(−1.2)	(−.2)	(.3)
Education	−.08	−.04	.01
	(−1.2)	(−.6)	(.2)
Income	−.01	−.07	.05
	(.2)	(−1.0)	(.8)
Gender	.09	−.08	.05
	(1.3)		(.8)
Length of residence in municipality	−.13*	.01	−.03
	(−2.0)	(.2)	−(.5)
Group-related variables			
Length of membership	.32****	.35****	.26****
	(4.5)	(5.1)	(3.7)
Number of additional memberships	.08	.00	1.0
	(1.2)	(.0)	(1.6)
Members of political groups	.03	—	—
	(−.4)		
Members of church choirs	.11	−.03	−.01
	(−1.2)	(−.35)	(−.8)
Members of self-help groups	—	−.21***	—
		(−3.1)	
Members of parents' groups	—	—	−.16**
			(−2.5)
Members of pet groups	—	—	−.16**
			(−2.3)
Other controls			
Fun orientation within group	.01	.25***	.21***
	(.13)	(2.6)	(2.7)
Constant (understandardized)	1.3**	.83**	.21
	(2.3)	(2.2)	(.5)
Number of cases	270	246	242
Adjusted R^2	.09	.20	.13

Source: Author's compilation.
Notes: United States: Bowling and neighborhood groups were excluded. Germany: Bowling and sports groups were excluded. Sweden: Bowling and boule leagues were excluded.
*p < .10; **p < .05; ***p < .01; ****p < .001 (two-tailed test)

Table 7.4   Group-Related Behavioral Change: Conversational Breadth (OLS Regression Results)

Independent Variables	Standardized Coefficients (t-Value)		
	United States	Germany	Sweden
Personal resources			
Age	−.15**	−.20**	−.22***
	(−2.3)	(2.4)	(3.6)
Education	.06	.07	.06
	(.8)	(.9)	(.9)
Income	.04	−.02	.04
	(.6)	(−.25)	(.6)
Gender	.11	−.08	.23****
	(1.6)	(−1.1)	(3.8)
Length of residence in municipality	−.05	−.01	.06
	(−.7)	(−.01)	(1.0)
Group-related variables			
Length of membership	.16**	.30****	−.05
	(2.2)	(4.1)	(.7)
Number of additional memberships	.16**	.14**	.14**
	(2.4)	(2.2)	(2.4)
Members of political groups	−.01	—	—
	(−.2)		
Members of church choirs	−.05	−.15**	−.05
	(−.6)	(−2.2)	(−.7)
Members of neighborhood groups	−.12*	—	—
	(−2.0)		
Members of self-help groups	—	−.04	—
		(−.5)	
Members of parents' groups	—	—	.15**
			(2.4)
Members of pet groups	—	—	−.11*
			(1.8)
Constant (unstandardized)	.35***	.37****	.45****
	(3.0)	(3.3)	(4.4)
Number of cases	270	247	272
Adjusted R²	.07	.10	.13

Source: Author's compilation.
Notes: United States: Bowling leagues were excluded. Germany: Bowling and sports groups were excluded. Sweden: Bowling and boule leagues were excluded.
*p < .10; **p < .05; ***p < .01; ****p < .001 (two-tailed test)

Figure 7.2   Activity Levels in Several Associational Types

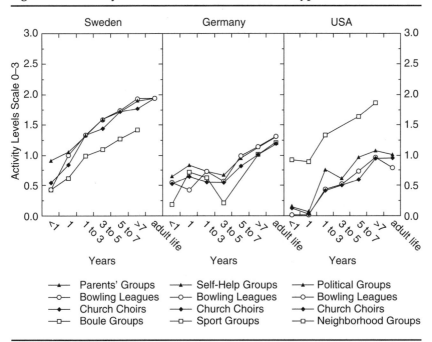

Source: Author's compilation.

of course, significantly related to individual socializing patterns outside
of group life. Furthermore, in Germany members of self-help groups socialize significantly less than members of sports groups and bowling
leagues. This is also true for members of Swedish parents' and pet groups.
It is not entirely clear whether these results can be attributed to added
membership effects or self-selection. To get a better picture, activity
levels are plotted along the variable length of membership in figure 7.2.

The figure shows adjusted means of activity levels (adjusted for age,
education, income, and gender), which were plotted along the increasing
time of membership. The lines indicate that activity levels rise steeply
with longer membership periods in all three countries, but they start at a
slightly higher level of activity in Sweden when members have just joined.
In addition, we do not see significant differences between associational
types, as already indicated by the regression analysis for activity levels
(table 7.2). Figure 7.2 suggests two points. First, length of membership is
the dominant variable driving the results. Second, we do not see strong
self-selection effects with regard to associational type, that is, members
do not self-select into special types of associations on the basis of their
activity levels (with the exception of U.S. neighborhood groups).

For all three indicators, activity level, socializing, and conversational breadth, personal resource variables, such as education, age, income, gender, and the length of residence in the municipality, are controlled. Some of these resource variables work differently in the three cultural contexts. For example, in the United States female association members are significantly more active and engaged than male members; this is not the case in the European cities. In Sweden we find a strong gender influence on the level of conversational breadth. Women share significantly more topics in their associations than do men, even more so than in Germany and the United States. In all three countries it is the younger people in associations who share several conversational topics widely, an interesting generational effect that should not go unnoticed. Another similarity in all three national settings is that personal resource variables do not strongly affect private social capital (behavioral aspects).

The number of additional memberships per respondent outside of the association I visited also indicates some influence. Whereas members with several memberships do not seem to socialize more outside of their group life, generally they are more active and converse on a wider array of issues. It is not certain whether this is an indication of self-selection, in which case the number of additional group memberships stands for the special characteristics of a "joiner nature,"[14] which might affect group-related behaviors. An alternative interpretation would be that the given behavioral change is caused by an increasing number of individual memberships.

These results are perhaps not surprising—we expect group life to influence certain behaviors of the members that have to do with the group itself. It is less certain that attitudes would change as well.

Group-Related Attitudinal Change

The second set of variables includes attitudes that relate to the group and its members, namely, ingroup trust and commitment to the group. Attitudes are not influenced so easily during one's lifetime. They are formed and developed over long periods of time and through daily contact with institutions, the family, schools, friends, and so on. The results are therefore not as clear-cut with respect to attitudinal changes as with behavioral indicators.

Ingroup trust, measured at the individual level, is not strongly influenced by the actual group experience but more intensively by personal resources. Only in the United States do longtime association members trust their fellow members more than people who joined the group not too long ago, as shown in table 7.5. There is no such influence in the European cases. Older members in the United States trust their fellow members more than do younger members.

Table 7.5 Group-Related Attitudinal Change: Individual Ingroup Trust (OLS Regression Results)

Independent Variables	Standardized Coefficients (t-Value)		
	United States[a]	Germany	Sweden
Personal resources			
Age	.19***	.10	−.08
	(2.8)	(1.1)	(−1.3)
Education	−.10	.09	.09
	(−1.5)	(1.2)	(1.3)
Income	.05	−.09	.00
	(.8)	(−1.3)	(.07)
Gender	−.06	−.16**	−.12*
	(−.8)	(−2.1)	(1.7)
Length of residence in municipality	−.03	−.04	−.08
	(−.4)	(.5)	(−1.2)
Group-related variables			
Length of membership	.13*	.03	.07
	(1.9)	(.4)	(1.0)
Number of additional memberships	.04	.08	.11*
	(.6)	(1.3)	(1.7)
Members of political groups	.04	—	—
	(.6)		
Members of church choirs	.11*	—	−.08
	(1.7)		(−1.0)
Members of self-help groups	—	.12*	—
		(1.8)	
Members of bowling groups	—	.14*	—
		(1.7)	
Members of parents' groups	—	—	.02
			(.4)
Other controls			
Betrayed by a known person	−.10	.9	.13**
	(−1.6)	(1.4)	(2.1)
Constant (unstandardized)	6.5****	.91***	1.1****
	(8.7)	(2.9)	(5.1)
Number of cases	267	246	272
Adjusted R²	.10	.07	.04

Source: Author's compilation.
Notes: United States: Bowling leagues and neighborhood groups were excluded. Germany: Sports groups and church choirs were excluded. Sweden: Bowling leagues and pet groups were excluded.
[a] Note that the measure for ingroup trust in the U.S. sample is a 1–10-point scale and therefore different from the ingroup trust measure in the European cases. See also the appendix.
*p < .10; **p < .05; ***p < .01; ****; < .001 (two-tailed test)

Figure 7.3   Ingroup Trust in American Associations

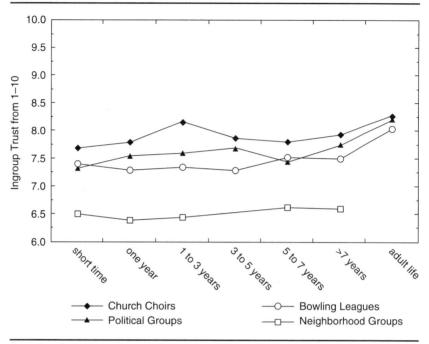

Source: Author's compilation.

However, in each associational group members seem to create a certain trust level that does not change very much with increased time of membership. For example, members of U.S. church choirs seem more trusting in comparison to members of neighborhood organizations and bowling leagues. But the difference between members who have participated in a church choir for a long time and those who just joined is not as stark (see figure 7.3). In sum, ingroup trust is a group-specific phenomenon that is influenced by some personal resources. The added membership effects are generally low.

Individual commitment levels are measured only in the U.S. sample. This variable is interesting because it is determined by other group-related attitudes and behavior. Members who trust their fellow members more and who are more active in their groups are also more committed to the associational life of their group (see table 7.6). Even controlling for these effects I find that more time spent in a given group influences commitment levels positively.

As figure 7.4 also demonstrates, commitment levels are fairly similar when people enter an association; they rise rapidly in the first months

**Table 7.6   Group-Related Attitudinal Change: Commitment
to Associational Life in the United States
(OLS Regression Results)**

Independent Variables	Standardized Coefficient (t-Value)
Personal resources	
Age	−.11*
	(−1.8)
Education	−.08
	(−1.4)
Income	.00
	(.0)
Gender	.06
	(1.0)
Length of residence in municipality	.01
	(.2)
Group-related variables	
Length of membership	.23****
	(3.7)
Number of additional memberships	0.4
	(.7)
Members of political groups	.05
	(.8)
Members of church choirs	.27****
	(4.0)
Members of neighborhood groups	.04
	(.7)
Other controls	
Individual ingroup trust	.28****
	(5.1)
Individual activity level	.15**
	(2.5)
Constant (unstandardized)	1.7****
	(5.2)
Number of cases	268
Adjusted R^2	.31

Source: Author's compilation.
Note: Bowling leagues were excluded.
*p < .10; **p < .05; ***p < .01; ****p < .001 (two-tailed test)

Figure 7.4   Commitment Levels in American Associations

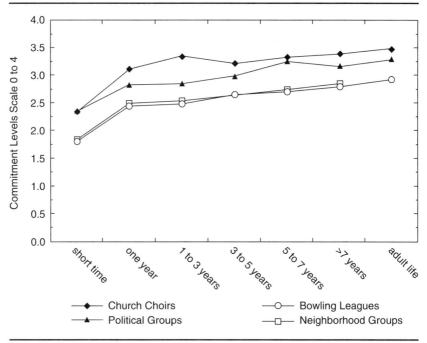

Source: Author's compilation.

of membership, and from there they continue to rise over longer membership periods. Still, commitment levels are highest in U.S. church choirs, a result of the additional dimension that members share religious values. Participation in a U.S. church choir thus means more than the weekly meeting of a hobby group.

We must be careful, however, with the interpretation of these results. Ingroup trust, and particularly commitment levels, could also explain length of membership.

In sum, attitudes that focus on the group or group members are not as clearly connected to the membership experience over time as the behavioral patterns discussed earlier. More predominantly, ingroup trust is influenced by personal resources and to a degree by the type of association. Commitment levels are clearly related to the time spent in the association generally, but the levels vary according to the type of association. Even though we find effects from the length of group membership on attitudes toward the group, we have to keep in mind that these attitudes, such as ingroup trust and commitment, do not directly benefit the larger society outside of the particular group. They cannot easily be utilized in another context.

Society-Related Behavioral Change

The results are different with the third set of variables, which includes measures of civic engagement in the respondent's community and voting in local elections. The question with regard to civic engagement is whether members become more engaged in their communities once they have joined an association for longer periods of time. The proposition is that association membership mobilizes members to get involved in their neighborhoods and communities. The answer is not obvious: in the United States and even more so in Germany, they do; in Sweden, on the other hand, they do not. Table 7.7 indicates that in Sweden those who have participated in associations for long periods of time are even significantly less active and engaged in their communities.

This is certainly a puzzling finding that needs more explanation. Generally civic engagement levels are lower in the European cases, and particularly in Sweden. (Perhaps the type of involvement is different in Sweden.) The regression results in table 7.7 and figure 7.5 indicate that members of Swedish church choirs and parents' groups are significantly more active than members of pet groups and boule leagues, for example. So it is very much the type of group the respondent has joined that is related to his or her civic engagement in the community. However, an interesting logic seems to emerge. People who want to fix things in their communities and who want to be active join certain associations. However, the longer members participate in their associations, the less likely they are to invest their energies outside of them, with the exception of Swedish parents' groups. As a result, the members' engagement levels in their communities drop.

In the United States to a certain degree, and particularly in Germany, members become more engaged the longer they participate in an association (see figure 7.5). In the Philadelphia area, younger people, women, and those who have lived in their community for longer are more likely to be active in their neighborhoods. Members of political groups and those in neighborhood organizations are significantly more active than members of bowling leagues. In Germany it is not the type of association that affects civic engagement as much as the length of membership.

Besides additional memberships, two other control variables were included in this model, namely, political efficacy and a measure of how often the respondent reads local news. In all three countries members with higher levels of political efficacy, those with more memberships, and those who read the local newspapers are more engaged in local affairs. The coefficients for these three variables are relatively large, leading me to conclude that, with the exception of Germany, civic engagement in communities is mainly determined by factors other than the experience

Table 7.7   Society-Related Behavioral Changes: Civic Engagement Outside of Group Life (OLS Regression Results)

Independent Variables	Standardized Coefficients (t-Value)		
	United States	Germany	Sweden
Personal resources			
Age	−.14**	−.12	.17***
	(−2.3)	(−1.3)	(2.6)
Education	.05	.04	.03
	(.8)	(.5)	(.5)
Income	.09*	−.11	.00
	(1.7)	(−1.4)	(.1)
Gender	.12**	.02	.04
	(2.1)	(.25)	(.7)
Length of residence in municipality	.11**	−.05	−.01
	(2.1)	−(.6)	(−.2)
Group-related variables			
Length of membership	.11*	.19**	−.22****
	(1.7)	(2.3)	(−3.6)
Number of additional memberships	.15***	.12*	.19****
	(2.7)	(1.7)	(3.3)
Members of political groups	.15**	—	—
	(2.4)		
Members of church choirs	.08	−.00	.18***
	(1.1)	(−.1)	(2.6)
Members of neighborhood groups	.15***	—	—
	(3.0)	—	—
Members of sports groups	—	−.05	—
	—	(−.6)	—
Members of parents' groups	—	—	.24****
	—	—	(4.2)
Members of bowling leagues	—	—	.07
	—	—	(1.1)
Other controls			
Political efficacy	.21****	.13*	.11*
	(3.8)	(1.9)	(1.8)
Follow municipal or local newspaper	.31****	.32****	.25****
	(5.7)	(4.3)	(4.2)
Constant (unstandardized)	−.13	.07	−.21*
	(.8)	(−.4)	(−1.7)
Number of cases	268	181	275
Adjusted R^2	.37	.13	.26

Source: Author's compilation.
Notes: United States: Bowling leagues were excluded. Germany: Bowling leagues and self-help groups were excluded. Sweden: Pet and boule groups were excluded.
*p < .10; **p < .05; ***p < .01; ****p < .001 (two-tailed test)

Figure 7.5   Civic Community Engagement in Three Countries

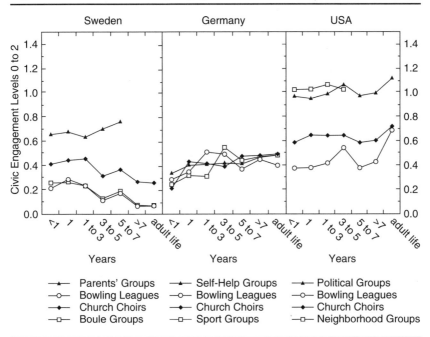

Source: Author's compilation.

of associational membership in a social group. The number of additional memberships (outside of the groups I visited) plays an important role in the U.S. sample, and again, we cannot be sure whether this indicates something about a "joiner nature" or about the effects of multiple memberships on civic engagement in the community. For civic engagement, we need to understand better the actual mobilizational sources that lead people to join certain associations in which members are more active in their communities—such as neighborhood groups, political groups, and parents' groups—in the first place. The country differences between the European and U.S. cases are also worth further investigation. In sum, it is not predominantly the course of the membership and the added experience of the group that influence civic engagement levels—again with the exception of Germany (and members of U.S. bowling leagues).

This result is also confirmed by examining voting habits, as shown in table 7.8. The possibility that voting is influenced by patron-client relationships in the three cities under consideration—Stockholm, Berlin, and Philadelphia—can be excluded because this is not how local elections are organized in these three metropolitan settings. Therefore, voting in local

Table 7.8   Society-Related Behavioral Change: Voting in Local Elections (Logit Analysis)

Independent Variables	Coefficient (Wald Statistic)		
	United States	Germany	Sweden
Personal resources			
Age	.02*	.06	.02
	(4.1)	(1.4)	(.7)
Education	.05	.32*	−.00
	(1.0)	(3.8)	(.0)
Income	.13	−.33	.13
	(1.6)	(1.1)	(.3)
Gender	−.21	1.9	−.05
	(.3)	(2.6)	(.0)
Length of residence in municipality	−.47**	−.31	−.08
	(5.4)	(.4)	(.5)
Group-related variables			
Length of membership	.03	1.0***	−.11
	(.1)	(6.7)	(.3)
Number of additional memberships	.08	.19	.55**
	(.8)	(.18)	(4.6)
Members of political groups	3.03**	—	—
	(4.2)		
Members of church choirs	1.0	−2.9**	1.33**
	(1.0)	(4.8)	(4.6)
Members of bowling leagues	.59	—	1.62
	(.33)	—	(1.6)
Other controls			
Political efficacy	.15	−1.08	.20
	(.41)	(1.6)	(.3)
Follow municipal or local newspaper	.98****	.28	1.23**
	(13.6)	(.1)	(5.3)
Constant	−3.8**	−3.6	−1.7
	(6.1)	(1.9)	(1.2)
Cox and Snell R^2	.20	.15	.16
χ^2 (df)	58.901 (12)	27.33 (10)	32.696(11)
−2-log likelihood ratio	225.985	36.991	95.173
Percent predicted correctly	80	95	90
Number of cases	263	168	190

Source: Author's compilation.
Notes: United States: Neighborhood groups were excluded. Germany: Bowling and sports groups were excluded. Sweden: Pet, boule, and parents' groups were excluded.
*p < .10; **p < .05; ***p < .01; ****p < .001

elections is an act that contributes to the public good in the respondent's region.[15] Except in Germany again, group life has no influence per se. Surely members of political groups vote more (in the United States) than do members of bowling leagues and neighborhood groups. Members of Swedish church choirs, who are also more active in their communities, vote more than do members of boule, pet, and parents' groups. In addition, reading the local newspaper has positive effects on voting in local elections in Sweden and the United States. But in these countries the additional time in a group does not contribute to the increased chance that a member votes locally.

In short, only in Germany, and to a lesser extent in the United States, do we see that the length of time spent in a voluntary association has additional mobilizing effects on an individual's social and political behavior outside of group life, especially in the community where he or she lives. Membership in certain groups, such as political groups, neighborhood organizations, parents' groups, and church choirs in Sweden (not church choirs in the other two countries), are related to more civic engagement. However, the results on societal behavioral indicators suggest that these group differences are more a matter of self-selection than an actual effect of experiences within the group. In some German groups and a few U.S. groups, however, we see that civic engagement increases with the time an individual spends in the association.

Society-Related Attitudinal Change

The most important aspects of public social capital are attitudes that depict the readiness to cooperate and openness to strangers. Generalized trust measures those aspects well. In a village, town, region, or nation in which most citizens trust each other, they will also want to cooperate with each other. They are ready to engage in projects, activities, and problem-solving because they are not afraid to approach each other. In addition, generalized trust is an attitudinal resource for individual civic action, life satisfaction, and egalitarianism values (for aggregate results, see Inglehart 1997; Uslaner 2000).

The following analysis identifies whether generalized trust and openness toward strangers change with the time spent in certain types of voluntary associations. The test is particularly important, not only for the social capital school, but also for theories about the sources of generalized trust that are central to this volume.

The empirical test did not withstand the strong claims of the social capital school. Generalized trust is not significantly influenced by added membership effects. In none of the national subsamples was the length of membership variable significant, as the results in table 7.9 show. Personal resources and experiences seem to determine generalized trust. Older

Table 7.9   Society-Related Attitudinal Change: Generalized Trust (OLS Regression Results)

Independent Variables	Standardized Coefficients (t-Value)		
	United States	Germany	Sweden
Personal resources			
Age	.15**	−.01	−.15**
	(2.2)	(−.06)	(−2.4)
Education	−.03	.03	.15***
	(−.5)	(.4)	(2.6)
Income	.14**	.02	.19***
	(2.2)	(.2)	(3.0)
Gender	−.11	.05	.03
	(1.6)	(.6)	(.4)
Length of residence in municipality	−.09	−.09	.07
	(1.4)	(−1.3)	(1.0)
Group-related variables			
Length of membership	.10	−.05	.04
	(1.4)	(−.6)	(.6)
Number of additional memberships	.11*	.05	.08
	(1.8)	(.7)	(1.4)
Members of political groups	.08	—	—
	(1.1)		
Members of church choirs	.21***	.16**	.15**
	(2.8)	(2.2)	(2.2)
Members of neighborhood groups	.04	—	—
	(.7)		
Members of self-help groups	—	.04	—
		(.5)	
Members of parents' groups	—	—	.14**
			(2.4)
Members of pet groups	—	—	.12**
			(2.0)
Other controls			
Parents in past	.09	.21***	.15***
	(1.5)	(3.2)	(2.8)
Betrayed by someone known	.01	−.14**	−.03
	(.2)	(2.1)	(−.5)
Constant (unstandardized)	1.03****	1.2****	1.37****
	(6.2)	(6.5)	(9.5)
Number of cases	257	218	286
Adjusted R²	.13	.10	.15

Source: Author's compilation.
Notes: United States: Bowling leagues were excluded. Germany: Bowling and sports groups were excluded. Sweden: Boule and bowling leagues were excluded.
*p < .10; **p < .05; ***p < .01; ****p < .001 (two-tailed test)

people are more trusting in the United States, whereas in Europe we can say the opposite. This result shows that in a cross-national perspective trust is not necessarily linked to the older generation. Income has positive effects on trust in Sweden and in the United States—one can afford to trust more when there is not so much at stake. The number of additional memberships outside of the group I visited is weakly related to generalized trust in the United States, but not in Germany and Sweden. The implication of this finding is discussed in the concluding section.

Two additional control variables were included in models of generalized trust—personal experiences with parents and experiences with people in the immediate environment. (See the appendix for the exact question wording.) The first indicator measures parental socialization influences during the respondent's childhood; it turns out to be a significant predictor of generalized trust in the European cases. In a distrusting, cautious environment—one in which, for example, children are warned to be careful around strangers—generalized trust probably cannot fully develop. The bivariate correlation is r = .27 for the whole sample (significant at the p < .001 level). The second indicator, which measures the experience of being betrayed by someone known to the respondent, also appears to be an influence on generalized trust in Germany, but not in the other two countries.

Controlling for these resources and experiences, I still find group differences. In all three countries members of church choirs are significantly more trusting than members of bowling, boule, and sports groups. In Sweden this is also true for members of pet groups. The comparison between members of church choirs and members of bowling leagues is depicted in figure 7.6.

For this part of the analysis I have selected only members of those associational groups that are the same in all three countries, namely, bowling leagues and church choirs. I show adjusted means of generalized trust for all the different-length categories of participation. There are several observations to be made with this figure. Generally members of church choirs are significantly more trusting compared to members of bowling leagues, with the exception of German bowling leagues. This is true even when they first join these groups, a result that points to the high likelihood of self-selection effects. Members with higher trust levels self-select into certain groups, such as church choirs. However, and more important, in most of these cases we do not find an added effect of membership, with the exception of U.S. bowling leagues.

All of this evidence taken together suggests that we are dealing here with self-selection effects. People who decide to join an association probably do so in the context of higher trust. Furthermore, people who become members of certain types of associations, such as church choirs, do that also in the context of higher trust levels compared to people who,

Figure 7.6   Church Choirs and Bowling Leagues in Three Countries

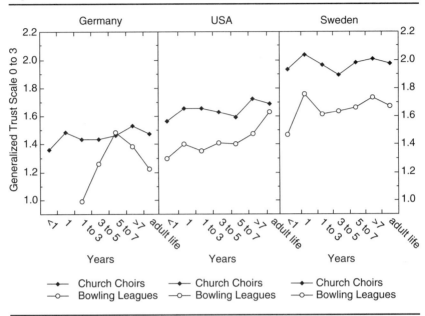

Source: Author's compilation.

for example, join bowling leagues. Does this result imply self-selection? We cannot be entirely sure, but the fact that the entry levels of trust are fairly distinct for different associational types in all three countries seems to indicate that differences predated the entry into membership. Ironically, and in seeming justification of the argument about "bowling alone," membership in U.S. bowling leagues represents an exception in that longer membership affects generalized trust (see figure 7.6).

The results are similar when examining openness toward strangers (tested only in the U.S. sample). Such openness is strongly influenced by general attitudes, such as generalized trust, and by personal resources, such as gender and age (see table 7.10). Women and younger people think that they would be generally more open and inviting toward newly arrived neighbors. Those with more association memberships generally, as well as members of bowling leagues and neighborhood groups, are significantly more open than members of political groups. However, being a member of a certain group for a longer time does not make an individual more open toward newly arrived neighbors (see coefficient for length-of-membership variable).

Figure 7.7 confirms that the length of membership is not very influential in supporting respondents' openness toward newcomer families in

Table 7.10   Society-Related Attitudinal Change: Openness Toward Strangers in the United States (OLS Regression Results)

Independent Variables	Standardized Coefficients (t-Value)
Personal resources	
Age	−.14**
	(−2.0)
Education	.02
	(.4)
Income	−.03
	(−.4)
Gender	.16**
	(2.3)
Length of residence in municipality	.02
	(.3)
Group-related variables	
Length of membership	.07
Number of additional memberships	.16**
	(2.4)
Members of church choirs	.18
	(1.6)
Members of neighborhood groups	.15**
	(2.2)
Members of bowling groups	.19*
	(1.7)
Other controls	
Generalized trust	.23****
	(3.5)
Number of cases	253
Adjusted R^2	.09

Source: Author's compilation.
Note: Political groups were excluded.
*p < .10; **p < .05; ***p < .01; ****p < .001 (two-tailed test)

their neighborhood. There seems to be a boost in the early joining phase, but it is not an attitude that lasts over the course of the membership.

Conclusion

Evidence for the social capital theory of the effects of associational membership is hard to generate. However, the key to understanding the mobilizing and civic potential of voluntary associations is to examine the

Figure 7.7   Openness Toward Strangers

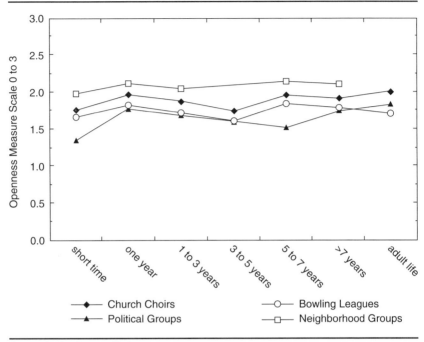

Source: Author's compilation.

added membership effects that result from the socialization experience of the group. One way to do that is to sample members from various associations and to merge information on these specific groups with data about individual members. I have done this with my self-collected data set. Even then, with associational membership being such a special, short-lived effect in an individual's lifetime, it is very hard to filter out any relationships whose significance is due to a particular membership experience.

However, this study included important tests of the social capital theory, and the new insights contribute to constructing a micro theory of social capital and to theories of generalized trust. Besides the social associations that the social capital school considers important, the study looked at political, self-help, and community groups. This purposeful selection of associational types allows the generalization of the results to a wide range of formal associations. Because the samples originated in metropolitan areas in a variety of advanced industrialized democracies, we should expect to find similar results in metropolitan areas of other Western countries. However, in rural or developing areas where associations play a more pivotal role in everyday life, the findings may be different. Let me recapitulate the results and discuss their implications.

First, membership in voluntary associations does have many different functions and mobilizational effects that serve as learning schools for civic skills (Verba, Schlozman, and Brady 1995). The analysis has demonstrated that members do indeed learn certain skills, attitudes, and behavior; most of them, however, can be utilized only in the group context. The added influence of group life is strongest on group-related behavioral indicators, such as group tasks and responsibilities, the level of socializing with group members outside of group life, and conversational breadth. In addition, membership over longer periods positively affects commitment levels and ingroup trust, at least within U.S. groups. I characterize these attitudes and behaviors as private social capital because they are not universal and cannot be generalized to other settings. We do not know, for example, whether the ability to take on tasks and responsibilities for the group also translates into a readiness to get involved in other cooperative situations. Similarly, we do not know whether the ability to develop commitment and ingroup trust can be utilized in a different context.

Second, the follow-up question was to understand whether members who join groups for longer periods learn more generalized and universal skills, attitudes, and behavior. The findings with regard to indicators of public social capital are less convincing. Out of the two behavioral and two attitudinal indicators, only those of civic engagement in communities and voting were related to membership over time in Germany, and there was a weak group effect on civic engagement in the United States. Otherwise in Sweden and the United States, none of the public social capital indicators were an outcome of added membership effects. This is a disturbing finding for social capital theory: associations' side effects and payoffs relate mainly to the group itself, not to the wider society. The importance of those types of associations in the data set used here, however, has been said to bring about generalized and universal attitudes and behavior. This connection could not be confirmed empirically.

The main reason then for the finding that voluntary associations do indeed accommodate more trusting, more open, and more civicly engaged people has to be self-selection. As further analysis indicated, people who trust more self-select into certain types of associations. (See further evidence for self-selection in Stolle 2000.) This is an enormously important finding for social capital theory. The results verify our common understanding as developed by social capital theory about the connection between membership in voluntary associations and trust, civic engagement, and openness to strangers, but they do not verify strongly that these types of interactions are *causes* for these generalized attitudes and behavior.

There is one caveat to be made in relation to this finding. Might it be possible that it is not the membership in a specific group that contributes to the building of civic attitudes and behavior, and particularly to generalized trust, but the multitude of associational memberships that gives rise to such influences? I included the measure of additional memberships in the analysis as a control variable. The limitation is that the data set provides neither the length of participation in other groups nor more information about the additional groups. Therefore, self-selection effects resulting from a "joiner nature" and added effects from multiple memberships cannot be clearly distinguished. However, the results revealed that additional memberships matter significantly for some of the societal indicators, but only weakly for generalized trust in the United States and Sweden. Yet the effect is not consistent enough and not strong enough to explain the causal relation between membership and social capital. In addition, even if the multitude of associational memberships was important, we ought to find an influence at the micro level—that is, an influence with just one membership—because multiple memberships most likely work as an accumulation of a single experience.

Third, some associations are more virtuous than others. For example, members of church choirs are more trusting in a generalized sense. In Sweden members of church choirs are more civicly active and vote more than members of other groups. Membership in church choirs is also linked to high private social capital, since we find high commitment levels and high ingroup trust in U.S. church choirs, for example. Members of U.S. neighborhood organizations are particularly active in their groups, but also, beyond that, they engage in civic projects in their communities more than members of other associations. My analysis so far has indicated that most of these effects that reach into the wider society seem to be driven by self-selection. Members of church choirs join such groups at a higher level of generalized trust and with more openness to strangers than individuals who join bowling leagues.

Fourth, it is an advantage to have a cross-national sample available to test several social capital hypotheses. The advantage is clearly that a test reveals which hypotheses hold cross-nationally. In the analysis presented here, the relationship between civic indicators and length of membership could be confirmed in all three countries with behavioral group-related measures. The length of membership is positively related to activity levels and socializing patterns in all three cases. The relationship between length of membership and indicators of public social capital as well as other attitudinal variables, on the other hand, varied according to the cultural context of the respondents. There are also strong country differences in trust levels, civic engagement, and attitudes toward strangers that cannot be explained by the influence of membership alone (an issue not discussed in this chapter). These insights demonstrate that the different cultural and institutional structures in the three countries independently affect the relationship between membership and civicness. The difficulty is to explain why these indicators work so differently in these settings and to identify all the aspects of civil society that are connected to these phenomena.

Several questions remain before we can draw any conclusions about the role of voluntary associations in learning generalized attitudes such as trust. Even though my data set constitutes a good alternative to following members of associations over the course of years, we still need to better understand the extent to which we can distinguish between self-selection and added membership effects. Integrating the length-of-membership variable into the analysis was a worthwhile effort, but we need to compare its effects more efficiently to those of self-selection. I suggest the following avenues for research and analysis in order to advance our insights into social capital theory. First, it would be worth collecting panel data on association members of a wide array of groups. This would allow us to better distinguish self-selection effects from effects of sustained joining over time. At the same time we would be able to test a wider range of hypotheses related to social capital theory because we could include several types of groups and group structures. Second, we need to know more about those factors in civil society and national institutions that directly affect the structure of group life. For example, we need to know more about why Swedish groups are more active than groups in other countries.

Finally, and most important in the context of this volume, the short-lived experiences of group life do not satisfactorily explain the development of generalized trust. Moreover, in this analysis negative experiences with others who are important to us are less important to our generalized expectation of others' trustworthiness than Hardin's insights would lead us to expect. At the same time parental socialization matters for generalized trust. However, compared to these effects and the group influences analyzed here, country variations in generalized trust are strongest (see Stolle 2000). Theories of the sources of generalized trust should embrace these results. Empirically, two areas are the most promising for developing further insights into generalized trust development. On the one hand, we need to further explore other forms of social interaction, for example, the contacts at the workplace and in the community that are connected to trust creation. On the other hand, we need to systematically analyze family socialization practices[16] and the effects of governments and national institutions on trust development in a cross-national perspective. Generalized trust and civic values may be mainly determined by such factors.

Appendix: Operationalizations of Concepts

Private Social Capital: Group-Related Behavioral Change

1. *Activity levels for the group:* This variable is constructed from individual scores on a two-item scale.

    - Item 1: "Have you within the last year planned or prepared a project for the association, maybe together with your fellow associational members?"
    - Item 2: "Have you had in the past, or do you have at the moment, a responsibility task within the association?"

    Dichotomous answer possibilities. Cronbach's alpha of two-item scale = .60.

2. *Level of socializing outside of the group activities:* This variable is measured by only one item:

    - Item: "Do you also meet some of the other associational members outside the organized associational life?"

    Answer possibilities in four categories.

3. *Conversational breadth:* This index sums the individual answers for seven questions about various conversational topics to an individual average. The higher the index, the more wide-ranging the topics of conversation the respondents have with other association members in their groups.

    - Question: "In case you have conversations, what do you talk about? Please choose all the suitable alternatives."

    Answer possibilities include the following conversational topics: private lives, professional lives, societal questions, politics, life in the immediate living environment and local questions, common hobby, and other interests and hobbies.

Private Social Capital: Group-Related Attitudinal Change

4. *Ingroup trust:* This variable is constructed by a question on a four-point scale.

    - Item: "Would you say that in general you can trust the members of your association more than other people?"

    Answer possibilities include trusting their fellow members "a lot more than other people," "a little more than other people," "as much as other people," or "less than other people." Within the U.S. sample, an additional ingroup trust variable was included: a measure of trust toward other group members on a scale of 1 to 10.

5. *Commitment level:* One survey item asks about the individual's commitment to his or her particular association.

- Item: "Personally, how committed do you feel to this choir?"

The answer possibilities range from "not at all" to "very strongly" and can be given in five categories. Indicator is available only in the U.S. sample.

Public Social Capital: Society-Related Behavioral Change

6. *Civic engagement outside of group life:* This variable is a four-item summated rating scale. The common dimension of the four items was confirmed by factor analysis (see factor loadings in parentheses). The extraction method was unweighted least squares.

- Item 1: "Have you participated in a community/neighborhood project?" (.847)
- Item 2: "Have you initialized a community/neighborhood project?" (.598)
- Item 3: "Have you financially supported a community/neighborhood project?" (.705)
- Item 4: "Name the community project you had in mind when you answered the last questions." (.742)

The first three items allow three different answers that range from "strong involvement" to "no involvement." The last item allows a dichotomous answer. Cronbach's alpha of four-item scale: .81.

7. *Vote in local elections:* This variable measures whether the respondent voted during the last local election.

- Item: "Did you vote in the last state election in Pennsylvania (or other state)?"

Answer possibilities are dichotomous.

Public Social Capital: Society-Related Attitudinal Change

8. *Generalized trust:* The generalized trust scale consists of six questionnaire items. The common dimension of the six items was confirmed by factor analysis.

- Item 1: "How much do you trust another fellow citizen?" (.711)
- Item 2: "How much do you trust a stranger?" (.701)

- Item 3: "How much do you trust a foreigner?" (.643)

- Item 4: (statement for agreement or disagreement) "In our society we have to be concerned about constantly being cheated." (.576)

- Item 5: "Would you think that one can trust other people, or should one be careful with others?" (.539)

- Item 6: (statement for agreement or disagreement) "Whatever a lot of people say, most do not stand up for others." (.498)

The extraction method was unweighted least squares. Items 1, 2, and 3 were part of a larger battery of questions about trust toward other groups of the population; answer possibilities could be given in four categories according to strength of trust. Items 4 and 6 were scaled in five categories, according to agreement level. Item 5 was scaled in two categories. The addition of these six items to a summated rating scale produced a scalability coefficient Cronbach's alpha = .76.

9. *Openness toward strangers:* This variable is somewhat unusual and has not typically been asked in other surveys. It tries to tap the respondent's attitudes toward strangers.

- Item: "Assume that a family from another area is moving into your neighborhood, not too far from your own house/apartment. Which of the following would you consider doing? Choose only one."

The answer possibilities ranged from "inviting the person/family over to my house" to "starting a conversation," "waiting until the person/family initiates the social contact," or "doing nothing at all."

Other Variables

Number of Additional Memberships   This variable adds the memberships indicated in a list of twenty-five types of associations. It ranges from zero (no additional membership) to a maximum of ten additional associational memberships.

Length of Membership   This variable measures the length of time the individual has spent in the group that I visited.

- Item: "Since when have you been a member of this particular association?"

In most questionnaires this question could be answered in seven categories: "less than a year," "for a year," "more than one year and less than three years," "between three and five years," "between five and seven years," "more than seven years," and "my whole adult life."

Fun Orientation (group measure)   This variable measures the extent to which associational members see their meetings as a possibility to socialize as opposed to a serious practice of hobbies or interests.

- Item: "When you come together with the other associational members, at training, at competitions or at other times, do you usually talk a lot, or do you pursue the activity without much conversation?"

Answers were distinguished in five categories and averaged per group.

Parental Socialization   This variable taps parental socialization influences in the respondent's childhood.

- Item: "When you were small, did your parents teach you to be careful in contact with strangers? For example, did they tell you to avoid contact with people you did not know? Please choose just one alternative."

The answer choices included "they told me to be very careful," "they told me to be a little careful," and "they did not tell me to be careful in contact with others/strangers."

Betrayed by Someone Known   This variable attempts to measure whether the respondent has been betrayed by someone to whom he or she is close. It results from a battery of subquestions on the following item:

- Item: "Have you been cheated in your life by someone?"
- Subquestion: "Have you been cheated in your life someone you knew?"

Possible answers: yes or no.

The completion of this project as supported by a grant provided by The Aspen Institute Nonprofit Sector Research Fund. The fieldwork for this project was made possible by research grants from the Princeton University Center of International Studies, the Center of European Studies, the Council of Regional Studies, and the MacArthur Foundation, as well as by a grant from the New Jersey chapter of the Swedish Women's Organization. I also thank Jonathan Krieckhaus, Marc Hooghe, Larry Bartels, Sheri Berman, Nancy Bermeo, Christian Welzel, Melissa Marshall, Job van der Meer, Jan Teorell, and two anonymous reviewers for helpful comments on earlier drafts of this chapter.

Notes

1. These types of groups stand for a whole range of socializing groups and are used here as examples to illustrate the larger point about which groups matter.

2. Putnam (1993, 89ff) also cites the external effects of voluntary associations as intermediaries between citizens and governments. Regionally, the higher the density or number of such groups, the more effectively community members can overcome collective action problems and collaborate for mutual benefit. The crosscutting and overlapping involvements initialized in voluntary associations in a community strengthen the local network of interaction, which in turn facilitates the solution of local or communal issues. See also Tocqueville (1835/1966) as a proponent of both the internal and external effects of voluntary associations.

3. See a constructive discussion of the missing mechanism between the experiences of interaction and generalized expectations of cooperation in Knight (this volume). See also Hardin's discussion (this volume) of the spillover from local group participation and ingroup trust to generalized trust.

4. Another reason for this choice of associational membership as the most important social capital indicator has been, of course, that measurements of membership in associations as opposed to other types of social interactions or attitudinal data have been readily available.

5. However, see the group-level studies that investigate membership influences on political and social views and behavior other than trust by Eastis (1998) and Erickson and Nosanchuck (1990).

6. For some empirical evidence on the correlation between associational membership and generalized attitudes and behavior, see Almond and Verba (1963), Brehm and Rahn (1997), Hooghe and Derks (1997), Seligson (1999), and Stolle and Rochon (1998, 1999). The theoretical relationship between membership in voluntary associations and democratic payoffs in the wider society has been discussed in Gundelach and Torpe (1997), Foley and Edwards (1996), Boix and Posner (1996), and Jordana (1999).

7. However, there might be the possibility of an additional endogeneity problem. In a model, explaining ingroup trust, for example, a coefficient for length of membership that is significantly different from zero might not indicate only added membership effects. It could certainly be that members who do not develop strong ingroup trust in their fellow association members drop out of the association at some point, so that all of those left have developed strong ingroup trust. As I discuss later in the chapter, it is possible that parts of my results are driven by this phenomenon.

8. In each association there were usually one or a maximum of two people who refused to fill in the questionnaire. The overall response rate in relation to present association members is approximately 95 percent. Therefore, the possibility of bias through self-selection of respondents can be discounted.

9. Other than the purposeful choice of specific associational types, the forty-nine different local groups were chosen on a random basis. I usually called central agencies of the associational type in the cities for names, addresses, and telephone numbers of specific groups. I then made a selection according to criteria such as availability, size, and convenience. In the case of bowling leagues, I chose teams that were present during the

training times on a given day in a huge bowling hall in Berlin and in a suburb near Philadelphia.

10. It certainly could be the case that socializing and conversing in a group contribute to the formation of generalized values such as trust. However, research has shown that there is not much evidence that membership in more conversational and more social groups over time contributes to the development of generalized trust (see Stolle 2000).

11. In fact, I found that ingroup trust and generalized trust are inversely related (see Stolle 1998).

12. Because the personal resource variables and the group variables work differently in different countries, the samples are separated into country samples. As a consequence, the sample size shrinks.

13. There is a possibility, however, that those who talk more and who take on more tasks are also the ones who stay in an association for long periods, whereas all the others drop out. However, if this were the case, we would need to have a general dropout rate of at least 60 percent in Sweden and about 80 percent in the United States and Germany for such a high increase in group-related civic behavior to occur. These numbers were calculated under the conservative assumption that members who drop out are not at all engaged or active. The dropout rate N_d/N can be calculated as follows:

$$\frac{N_d}{N} = 1 - \left[\frac{\text{(activity average for recent joiners)}}{\text{(activity average for long-term joiners)}} \right]$$

14. This expression refers to the possibility that an individual may enter into multiple associational memberships because of personal characteristics and resources.

15. See a discussion about voting in local elections as an act of patron-client relationships in Putnam (1993).

16. See an interesting explanation for changing trust levels caused by family socialization in Bennich-Björkman (1998).

References

Almond, Gabriel A., and Sidney Verba. 1963. *The Civic Culture.* Princeton, N.J.: Princeton University Press.

Bennich-Björkman, Li. 1998. "Strong Individuals, Weak Society? Child Rearing and the Decline of Social Capital After World War II." Paper presented at the Social Capital and Political Science Workshop at the European Consortium of Political Research Joint Sessions, Warwick, U.K. (March 1998).

Billiet, Jaak, and Bart Cambré. 1999. "Social Capital, Active Membership in Voluntary Associations, and Some Aspects of Political Participation: An Empirical Case Study." In *Social Capital and European Democracy*, edited by Jan W. van Deth, Marco Maraffi, Kenneth Newton, and Paul F. Whitley. New York: Routledge.

Boix, Carles, and Daniel Posner. 1996. "Making Social Capital Work: A Review of Putnam's *Making Democracy Work.*" Working paper 96-4. Cambridge, Mass.: Harvard University, Center for International Affairs.

Brehm, John, and Wendy Rahn. 1997. "Individual-Level Evidence for the Causes and Consequences of Social Capital." *American Journal of Political Science* 41(3): 999–1023.

Brewer, Marilynn B. 1981. "Ethnocentrism and Its Role in Interpersonal Trust." In *Scientific Inquiry and the Social Sciences,* edited by Marilynn B. Brewer and Barry E. Collins. San Francisco: Jossey-Bass.

Case, Anne C., and Lawrence Katz. 1991. "The Company You Keep: The Effects of Family and Neighborhood on Disadvantaged Youth." Working paper 3705. Cambridge, Mass.: National Bureau of Economic Research.

Dekker, Paul, Ruud Koopmans, and Andries van den Broek. 1997. "Voluntary Associations, Social Movements, and Individual Political Behavior in Western Europe." In *Private Groups and Public Life: Social Participation, Voluntary Associations, and Political Involvement in Representative Democracies,* edited by Jan van Deth. London and New York: Routledge.

Eastis, Carla M. 1998. "Organizational Diversity and the Production of Social Capital: One of These Groups Is Not Like the Other." In *Beyond Tocqueville: Civil Society and Social Capital in Comparative Perspective,* edited by Bob Edwards and Michael W. Foley (a thematic issue of *American Behavioral Scientist*) 42: 66–77.

Erickson, Bonnie, and Terrance A. Nosanchuck. 1990. "How an Apolitical Association Politicizes." *Canadian Review of Sociology and Anthropology* 27(2): 206–19.

Foley, Michael W., and Bob Edwards. 1996. "The Paradox of Civil Society." *Journal of Democracy* 7(3): 38–53.

Fukuyama, Francis. 1995. *Trust: The Social Virtues and Creation of Prosperity.* London: Hamish Hamilton.

Granovetter, Mark. 1985. "Economic Action and Social Structure: The Problem of Embeddedness." *American Journal of Sociology* 91(3): 481–510.

Gundelach, Peter, and Lars Torpe. 1997. "Social Capital and the Democratic Role of Voluntary Associations." Paper presented at the Workshop on Social Capital and Politico-Economic Performance, European Consortium of Political Research Joint Sessions, Bern, Switzerland (February 27–March 4, 1997).

Hagan, John, Hans Merkens, and Klaus Boehnke. 1995. "Delinquency and Disdain: Social Capital and the Control of Right-Wing Extremism Among East and West Berlin Youth." *American Journal of Sociology* 100(4): 1028–53.

Hanks, Michael, and Bruce K. Eckland. 1978. "Adult Voluntary Associations and Adolescent Socialization." *Sociological Quarterly* 19(3): 481–90.

Hardin, Russell. 1993. "The Street-Level Epistemology of Trust." *Politics and Society* 21(4):505–29.

Hooghe, Marc, and Anton Derks. 1997. "Voluntary Associations and the Creation of Social Capital: The Involvement Effect of Participation." Paper presented at the Workshop on Social Capital and Politico-Economic Performance at the European Consortium of Political Research Joint Sessions, Bern, Switzerland (February 27–March 4, 1997).

Inglehart, Ronald. 1997. *Modernization and Postmodernization: Cultural, Economic, and Political Change in Forty-three Societies.* Princeton, N.J.: Princeton University Press.

Jencks, Christopher, and Paul Peterson. 1991. *The Urban Underclass.* Washington, D.C.: Brookings Institution.

Jordana, Jacint. 1999. "Collective Action Theory and the Analysis of Social Capital." In *Social Capital and European Democracy,* edited by Jan W. van Deth, Marco Marraffi, Kenneth Newton, and Paul F. Whiteley. London: Routledge.

Knack, Stephen, and Philip Keefer. 1997. "Does Social Capital Have an Economic Payoff? A Cross-Country Investigation." *Quarterly Journal of Economics* 112(4): 1251–88.

Kramer, Roderick M., Marilynn B. Brewer, and B. A. Hanna. 1996. "Collective Trust and Collective Action: The Decision to Trust as a Social Decision." In *Trust in Organizations: Frontiers of Theory and Research,* edited by Roderick M. Kramer and Tom R. Tyler. Thousand Oaks, Calif.: Sage Publications.

Levi, Margaret. 1996. "Social and Unsocial Capital: A Review Essay of Robert Putnam's *Making Democracy Work.*" *Politics and Society* 2(1): 45–55.

———. 1998. "A State of Trust." In *Trust and Governance,* edited by Valerie Braithwaite and Margaret Levi. New York: Russell Sage Foundation.

Messick, David M. 1991. "On the Evolution of Group-Based Altruism." In *Games Equilibrium Models,* edited by Reinhard Selten, vol. 1. Frankfurt: Springer Verlag.

Minkoff, Deborah. 1997. "National Social Movements and Civil Society." In *Social Capital, Civil Society, and Contemporary Democracy,* edited by Bob Edwards and Michael W. Foley. (A thematic issue of *American Behavioral Scientist*) 40: 606–20.

Moyser, George, and Geraint Parry. 1997. "Voluntary Associations and Democratic Participation in Britain." In *Private Groups and Public Life: Social Participation, Voluntary Association, and Political Involvement in Representative Democracies,* edited by Jan W. van Deth. London and New York: Routledge.

Mutz, Diana, and Jeffrey Mondak. 1998. "Democracy at Work: Contributions of the Workplace Toward a Public Sphere." Paper presented at the annual meeting of the Midwest Political Science Association Meeting, Chicago (April 23–25, 1998).

Newton, Kenneth. 1997. "Social Capital and Democracy." In *Social Capital, Civil Society, and Contemporary Democracy,* edited by Bob Edwards and Michael W. Foley. (A thematic issue of *American Behavioral Scientist*) 40: 575–86.

Olsen, Marvin E. 1972. "Social Participation and Voting Turnout." *American Sociological Review* 37(3): 317–33.

Putnam, Robert D. 1993. *Making Democracy Work: Civic Traditions in Modern Italy.* Princeton, N.J.: Princeton University Press.

———. 1995a. "Bowling Alone: Democracy in America at the End of the Twentieth Century." Nobel Symposium. Uppsala, Sweden.

———. 1995b. "Tuning In, Tuning Out: The Strange Disappearance of Social Capital in America." *PS: Political Science and Politics* 28(4): 664–83.

Rogers, David L., Ken H. Barb, and Gordon L. Bultena. 1975. "Voluntary Associations Membership and Political Participation: An Exploration of the Mobilization Hypothesis." *Sociological Quarterly* 16(3): 305–18.

Seligson, Amber L. 1999. "Civic Association and Democratic Participation in Central America: A Test of the Putnam Thesis." *Comparative Political Studies* 32(3): 342–62.

Sides, John. 1999. "It Takes Two: The Reciprocal Relationship Between Social Capital and Democracy." Paper presented at the annual meeting of the American Political Science Association, Atlanta.

Stolle, Dietlind. 1998. "Bowling Alone, Bowling Together: Group Characteristics, Membership, and Social Capital." *Political Psychology* 19(3): 497–526.

———. 2000. "Communities of Trust: Public Action and Social Capital in Comparative Perspective." Ph.D. diss., Princeton University.

Stolle, Dietlind, and Thomas R. Rochon. 1998. "Are All Associations Alike?" In *Beyond Tocqueville: Civil Society and Social Capital in Comparative Perspective,* edited by Bob Edwards and Michael W. Foley. (A thematic issue of *American Behavioral Scientist*) 42: 47–65.

———. 1999. "The Myth of American Exceptionalism: A Three-Nation Comparison of Associational Membership and Social Capital." In *Social Capital and European Democracy,* edited by Jan W. van Deth, Marco Marraffi, Kenneth Newton, and Paul F. Whiteley. London: Routledge.

Tocqueville, Alexis de. 1966. *Democracy in America.* Garden City, N.Y.: Doubleday. (Originally published in 1835)

Uslaner, Eric M. 2000. "The Moral Value of Trust." Unpublished manuscript.

Verba, Sidney, and Norman Nie. 1972. *Participation in America: Political Democracy and Social Equality.* New York: Harper & Row.

Verba, Sidney, Kay Lehman Schlozman, and Henry E. Brady. 1995. *Voice and Equality: Civic Volunteerism in American Politics.* Cambridge, Mass.: Harvard University Press.

Yamagishi, Toshio, and Midori Yamagishi. 1994. "Trust and Commitment in the United States and Japan." *Motivation and Emotion* 18(2): 129–66.

Yogev, Abraham, and Rina Shapira. 1990. "Citizenship Socialization in National Voluntary Youth Organizations." In *Political Socialization, Citizenship Education, and Democracy,* edited by Orit Ichilov. New York: Teachers College Press.

Chapter 8

Patterns of Social Trust in Western Europe and Their Genesis

GERRY MACKIE

MACHIAVELLI (c. 1519/1970, 160–64) thought that it was impossible for a corrupt people either to create or to maintain a free government (except in the rare happenstance that a good prince leads them to good customs). Constitutional features suited for an uncorrupted people are not suited to a corrupted people; political institutions should be designed to vary by political culture, to use today's terminology. Among its other virtues, republican Rome enjoyed a high level of social trust; the Senate, for example, so trusted the goodness of the plebs that it entertained an edict that individuals voluntarily return one-tenth of an unknown quantity of war booty that had fallen into their hands, and the plebs, rather than simply ignoring such an edict, contested its enactment, according to Machiavelli (c. 1519/1970, 243). However, several of the institutions that were good for uncorrupted republican Rome were bad for corrupted imperial Rome. In his own day, Machiavelli continued, Italy was corrupt above all other lands; France and Spain were corrupt as well, but each was united by a king constrained by the rule of law. In German lands, by contrast, it was as in ancient Rome: citizens were trusted to contribute voluntarily their share of taxes and they did so, such was their goodness and respect for religion; this was because they were isolated from Romance customs and because they maintained social equality within their states. Machiavelli's Tuscany too was free of lords and gentry, and thus a candidate for republican rule. A principality was best in a climate of inequality and low trust, and a republic was best in a climate of equality and high trust.

On first reading, Machiavelli's attention to the differences in corruption between populations seems to be quaintly archaic, and his cross-cultural comparisons comically provincial, and thus, his notion that the same institution might have different consequences in different cultures is obscured. Robert Putnam (1993) resurrected the notion, however, in his study of the introduction in 1970 of the same imposed institutions of regional government throughout Italy and their subsequent course of development. He finds that the performance of the regional governments varies sharply according to the degree of civic community in the region; further, that higher civic involvement in the 1900s foretold both higher civic involvement and economic development in the 1970s by region; and finally, that such variations in civic involvement seem to be stable back to at least the early Middle Ages. The same institutions had different effects in different cultural settings. It is also interesting that Machiavelli's Tuscany (together with neighboring Emilia-Romagna) was near the top of Putnam's civic community index. Civic community involves social trust—the capacity for collective action, according to Putnam.

Social trust came within the ambit of modern political science with Gabriel Almond and Sidney Verba's *Civic Culture* (1963, 261–99), a comparison of political attitudes and democracy in five countries. Interpersonal trust eases the formation of secondary associations, which in turn support the stability of democratic rule. Ronald Inglehart (1990, 44), in survey research on the advanced industrial countries, offers a civic culture hypothesis with a model that relates stable democracy secondarily to differentiated social structure and primarily to a political culture of civicness, as indexed by interpersonal trust and two other components; economic development contributes positively to social structure and political culture, but not directly to democratic stability. Edward Muller and Mitchell Seligson (1994) have challenged Inglehart, arguing that his civic culture attitudes have no effect on the change in democracy from 1980 to 1990, and further that interpersonal trust is a consequence, not a cause, of democratic rule. Inglehart (1997, 174) has responded that his model is relevant to the stability of democracy, not to short-term change in the level of democracy, and that new models of democratic stability using data from the forty-three-country World Values Survey (WVS) yield an even more prominent place for interpersonal trust. For example, data from the forty-three countries worldwide show a correlation of $r = .72$ ($p = .0000$) between stable democracy and interpersonal trust (Inglehart 1997, 174).

I do think that something like civic culture and its associated social trust contributed to the original European transition to political and economic modernity. That does not mean that I subscribe to a cultural determinism such that some peoples are destined to enjoy democratic peace and prosperity and other peoples are not. My purpose is to seek the micro foundations of civic culture, because, if we can precisely identify and understand the geneses of social trust, then we can recommend traditional and novel institutions that advance social trust, civic action, and democracy. I do not confidently identify those micro foundations in this programmatic essay, but as an example of what I intend I refer the reader to my analysis of Chinese foot-binding and African female genital-cutting. Different explanations of those practices result in different reform strategies. A patriarchal-oppression theory would recommend feminist revolution in Sudanic Africa; a functionalist theory would propose alternative puberty rituals and new roles for the inflicting midwives; a legalist theory would advocate punishable prohibition and propaganda; a modernizationist theory would point to economic development; and so on. All such recommendations have failed. My convention explanation of the practices recommends associations of parents who pledge not to engage in the practice, and this reform strategy has robustly succeeded (Mackie 1996, 2000). Understanding culture does not mean surrendering to it; on the contrary, understanding how culture works helps us to escape its cage.

The next section examines *Eurobarometer* survey data on trust attitudes in twelve different countries in Western Europe. Differences in trustingness and perceived trustworthiness are stable over time and between countries. There seems to be a gradient of social trust across Europe—the high pole in the northwest and the low pole in the southeast. Other cross-cultural studies find a related cluster of differences between the northwest and the southeast. The following section offers a hypothesis to account for the trust gradient—there is a coincident gradient in traditional family structure. In the traditional northwest new couples establish their own household, women marry late, and youth work as servants in outside households; in the traditional southeast new couples move into the groom's father's household, women marry early, and work outside the household is shameful. I propose that these features of family life are a special type of Schelling convention that happens to regulate access to reproduction, and that because they are universal and persistent Schelling conventions they are likely to be independent of and prior to other explanatory factors. The Mediterranean honor complex in the southeast is also such a marriage-strategy convention appropriate to the Mediterranean climate, but the cultivation of a trustworthy disposition is the marriage strategy more appropriate to the climate and partly related family patterns of the northwest. One problem with the hypothesis is that southeast family patterns are not the neat opposite of the northwestern pattern. However, the more pronounced variability in family pattern and in other factors on the Italian peninsula makes it an ideal setting for further elaborating and testing the hypothesis.

Patterns of Trust in Western Europe

Eurobarometer Data

Comparable data on trust among the publics of the European Community (EC) are available from *Eurobarometer* surveys undertaken in 1980, 1986, 1990, 1993, and 1996. Surveyors state: "I would like to ask you a question about how much trust you have in people from various countries. Please tell me whether you have a lot of trust, some trust, not very much trust, or no trust at all." The mean for respondents from a given country is calculated by applying the coefficients 4, 3, 2, 1, respectively to the answer codes, "no reply" excluded, and 2.50 is the nominal mean.[1] Respondents are asked to rate their own country, the remaining EC countries, and varying collections of countries outside the EC. For 1980 the data include respondents' rating of their own country for Belgium, Denmark, Germany, Greece, France, Ireland, Italy, Luxembourg, the Netherlands, and Great Britain, a total of ten countries; for 1986, 1990, and 1993, add Spain and Portugal for a total of twelve (EC-12); and for 1996, add Sweden, Finland, and Austria, for a total of fifteen countries (EC-15).[2] Thus, for 1996, as an example, we can construct a fifteen-by-fifteen matrix that displays the country mean of respondents' ratings, illustrated in table 8.1. A column lists the ratings of nationalities by those in the country labeled at the top of the column; for example, the column headed "Belgium" includes trust ratings of the fifteen different EC countries (including of their own country) by respondents in Belgium. A row lists the ratings of one nationality by respondents in each of the EC-15 countries; for example, the row labeled "Belgians" includes trust ratings of the Belgians by each of the EC-15 countries (again including Belgians rating Belgians).

It turns out that people always rate people of their own country (a rating I label "own-trust") as much more trustworthy than the average judgment of trustworthiness of that people by the respondents from all of the remaining countries. (The mean of all own-trust ratings is 3.29; the mean of all ratings by other nationalities is 2.70.) Indeed, with a few marginal exceptions among the lowest-trust countries (Italy and Greece), people rate their own people as more trustworthy than any of the remaining nationalities. Whatever the source of this positive own-country bias, it distorts rankings that are otherwise quite consistent, and so, unless otherwise indicated, own-trust is excluded from all the measures I report. Returning to table 8.1, the right-hand side marginal is an unweighted average of the trust ratings of one nationality by each of the other nationalities, a Europe-wide rating of the relative *trustworthiness* of that nationality. The bottom marginal is an unweighted average of the trust ratings bestowed by one nationality on each of the other nationalities, a measure of the relative *trustingness* of each nationality. There is

Table 8.1 Trust Among EC-15 Nationalities

1996—All	Belgium	Denmark	Germany	Greece	Spain	France	Ireland	Italy	Luxembourg	Netherlands
Belgians	3.10	2.97	2.76	2.36	2.69	2.96	2.85	2.65	2.74	3.00
Danes	2.97	3.60	2.94	2.30	2.76	2.93	2.92	2.78	2.97	3.36
Germans	2.62	2.96	3.51	2.04	2.65	2.83	2.70	2.79	2.85	2.88
Greeks	2.47	2.51	2.47	3.35	2.35	2.48	2.61	2.38	2.47	2.48
Spanish	2.59	2.68	2.59	2.57	3.42	2.74	2.73	2.65	2.76	2.81
French	2.74	2.68	2.90	2.43	2.29	3.24	2.83	2.72	2.89	2.49
Irish	2.67	2.99	2.42	2.47	2.53	2.67	3.49	2.50	2.58	2.85
Italians	2.40	2.50	2.39	2.45	2.54	2.52	2.80	2.87	2.63	2.33
Luxembourgers	3.18	3.13	3.03	2.40	2.72	3.02	2.94	2.74	3.52	3.28
Dutch	2.78	3.31	2.86	2.24	2.83	2.86	2.93	2.85	2.99	3.38
Portuguese	2.60	2.69	2.44	2.52	2.63	2.68	2.77	2.42	2.69	2.85
British	2.71	3.12	2.32	2.12	2.07	2.39	2.67	2.65	2.39	2.91
Swedes	3.00	3.42	3.02	2.52	2.85	2.99	2.92	2.89	2.98	3.34
Finns	2.92	3.19	2.87	2.42	2.71	2.90	2.91	2.79	2.94	3.25
Austrians	2.84	3.22	3.04	2.33	2.66	2.69	2.91	2.65	2.95	2.91
Swiss	2.92	3.25	3.14	2.52	2.90	2.92	2.98	2.91	3.04	3.15
Norwegians	2.91	3.51	2.95	2.40	2.80	2.97	2.92	2.78	2.90	3.31
Mean	2.79	3.04	2.80	2.44	2.67	2.81	2.88	2.71	2.84	2.98
Mean-own	2.77	3.01	2.76	2.38	2.62	2.78	2.84	2.70	2.80	2.95

(Table continues on p. 250.)

Table 8.1 *Continued*

1996—All	Portugal	Great Britain	Sweden	Finland	Austria	Mean	Mean-Own	Own-Trust	Excess Own-Trust
Belgians	2.24	2.84	3.22	3.07	2.93	2.83	2.81	3.10	1.10
Danes	2.27	3.07	3.57	3.31	2.94	2.98	2.94	3.60	1.23
Germans	2.20	2.25	3.12	2.90	3.09	2.76	2.71	3.51	1.30
Greeks	2.01	2.43	2.87	2.67	2.50	2.54	2.48	3.35	1.35
Spanish	2.29	2.57	2.84	2.59	2.57	2.69	2.64	3.42	1.29
French	2.53	2.24	3.03	2.91	2.61	2.70	2.66	3.24	1.22
Irish	2.19	2.72	3.24	2.94	2.53	2.72	2.66	3.49	1.31
Italians	2.32	2.48	2.79	2.49	2.42	2.53	2.23	2.87	1.29
Luxembourgers	2.38	2.85	3.30	3.07	3.05	2.97	2.94	3.52	1.20
Dutch	2.30	3.08	3.33	3.14	2.95	2.92	2.89	3.38	1.17
Portuguese	3.23	2.79	2.95	2.66	2.48	2.69	2.66	3.23	1.22
British	2.32	3.32	3.43	3.18	2.58	2.68	2.63	3.32	1.26
Swedes	2.25	3.03	3.59	3.36	3.04	3.01	2.97	3.59	1.21
Finns	2.19	2.98	3.49	3.70	2.93	2.95	2.89	3.70	1.28
Austrians	2.14	2.88	3.52	3.30	3.57	2.91	2.86	3.57	1.25
Swiss	2.48	3.00	3.49	3.38	3.23	3.02			
Norwegians	2.24	3.06	3.65	3.49	2.99	2.99			
Mean	2.33	2.80	3.26	3.07	2.85	2.82			
Mean-own	2.27	2.77	3.24	3.05	2.84	2.79			

Source: Author's compilation.

no need to weight the averages, because there is no reason why the accuracy of trust judgments by people in small countries should differ from those by people in large countries. By this arrangement of the data, we have attained three variables of interest: trustworthiness, trustingness, and own-trust.

Cross-country survey comparisons are fraught with problems and hazards. Such issues cannot be rehearsed in this limited space, but at a minimum, let us assess whether the trust judgments extracted from the *Eurobarometer* surveys are stable across time and across countries. Are the trust judgments stable across time? Begin with trustworthiness. Bivariate correlations of average *trustworthiness* judgments across survey years 1980, 1986, 1990, 1993, and 1996 are strong and significant, ranging from .87 to .99 as measured by Pearson's r (each at a significance of .000), and ranging from .55 to .88 as measured by Kendall's tau (each at a significance of .01 or better).[3] Bivariate correlations of average *trustingness* across the survey years range from .42 (p = .179) to .88 (p = .001) as measured by Pearson's r, and range from .47 (p = .06) to .87 (all the remaining correlations significant at .03 or better) as measured by Kendall's tau. Finally, correlations of *own-trust* range from .57 to .89 (.01 > p > .001 for six correlations, .05 > p > .01 for three correlations, and p = .07 for one) as measured by Pearson's r, and, excluding 1980 (correlations are positive but not significant except for 1986), range from .38 (p = .09) to .59 (the remaining correlations significant at p = .03 or better). The three variables are stable across time, extraordinarily so as such things go.

Are trust judgments stable across countries? Here, rather than comparing the marginals, we are comparing the matrix entries by column. We compare, first, the fifteen-by-fifteen trust judgments (as always, excluding own-trust—the diagonal is vacant) expressed in the 1996 survey, and second, the average of the twelve-by-twelve trust judgments expressed in all the surveys from 1980 to 1996. Generally, rankings are strongly and significantly correlated between countries, with the exception of rankings by respondents in Greece. For the 1996 data, thirteen of the fourteen Kendall correlation coefficients of rankings by respondents from Greece with rankings by respondents of the other countries are negative (and two of those coefficients report as conventionally significant). In the 1996 sample rankings by respondents in Portugal appear to be unrelated to rankings by respondents in other countries. Excluding Portugal and Greece, the median number of positive and significant (.05 or less) correlations between one country's rankings and another's is 10 (out of a possible 12), and these significant correlations range from .42 to .92. (Pearson's correlation coefficients are similar, and generally stronger and more significant.) For the average of trust judgments from 1980 to 1996 for twelve countries, the Kendall coefficients for correlations between rankings by respondents from Greece and rankings by other countries are mildly positive but not significant. For the average of all years, Portugal's rankings correlate positively with those of other countries (six at a significance of .05 or better, and three at a significance between .05 and .10); the 1996 Portugal sample is a lone anomaly— Portugal 1996 differs more from other years' samples than any similar comparison in the database, suggesting either some extraordinary event or corrupt data. For all years, and excluding Greece, the median number of positive and significant (.05 or less) correlations between one country's rankings and another's is 8 (out of a possible 10), and these significant correlations range from .49 to .86. (Again Pearson's correlation coefficients are similar, and generally stronger and more significant.) With the exception of Greece, and the anomalous 1996 Portugal sample, trust judgments are stable across countries.

Since trust judgments are stable across time and stable across countries, it is likely that the surveys are capturing some social reality rather than reporting some artifact of methodology. The judgments are stable, but there is also evidence of a few long-term changes. Germany and Italy showed much lower levels of trust in the 1950s than they did in the 1980s and 1990s, presumably related to their defeat in World War II, or perhaps past low trust contributed to their earlier lack of democracy (Inglehart 1990, 438; Inglehart 1997, 359). The German increase leveled off in the 1980s, and the Italian increase leveled off in the 1990s.

What do the trust rankings tell us? The EC-12 sorts into three groups with respect to trustworthiness. First, Luxembourg, the Netherlands, Denmark, and Belgium are highest in trustworthiness—label them "the North Sea" for short. Second, France, Germany, Great Britain, and Ireland, are intermediate—label them "Intermediate" for short. Third, Spain, Portugal, Greece, and Italy are lowest—label them "the Mediterranean" for short.[4] The sort is similar for trustingness, except for the oddity that the highly trustworthy and highly own-trusting Luxembourgers are very low in their trusting of other nationalities. For a closer look, examine figure 8.1, which shows the trustworthiness of the twelve nationalities (arranged from "least trustworthy" to "most trustworthy" on a 1980 to 1996 average) by year of sample. Figure 8.2 shows the trustingness of the twelve nationalities (arranged from "least trusting" to "most trusting" on a 1980 to 1996 average) by year of sample. Figure 8.3 shows the ups and downs of own-trust from year to year.

Three observations are manifest in the charts. First, *Italy is considered not only the least trustworthy but the least trustworthy by far;* this assessment is shared by the Italian respondents themselves, who rank lowest in own-trust among the twelve nationalities (see figure 8.3). Also, Italians are among the least trusting. Second, trustworthiness rankings are noticeably lower in the 1996 sample than in the samples for the other years, but own-

Figure 8.1   Trustworthiness (EC-12 Average)

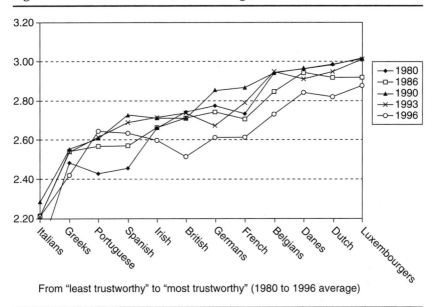

From "least trustworthy" to "most trustworthy" (1980 to 1996 average)

Source: Author's compilation.

Figure 8.2   Trustingness (EC-12 Average)

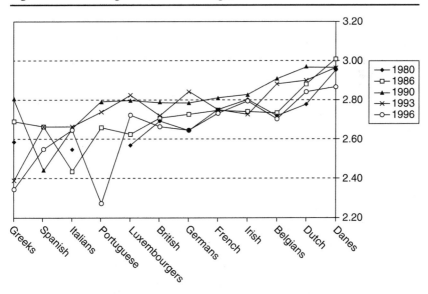

Source: Author's compilation.

Figure 8.3   Own-Trust (EC-12 Average)

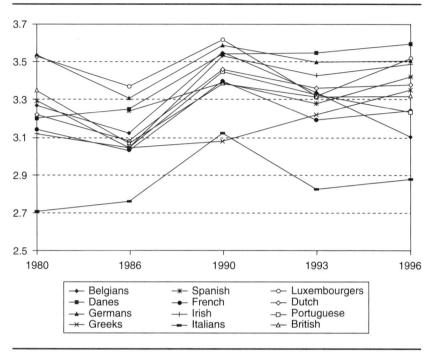

─◆─ Belgians	─✳─ Spanish	─○─ Luxembourgers
─■─ Danes	─●─ French	─◇─ Dutch
─▲─ Germans	─+─ Irish	─□─ Portuguese
─✕─ Greeks	─▬─ Italians	─△─ British

Source: Author's compilation.

trust increases to near high levels in 1996—*from 1993 to 1996 respondents in the EC-12 came to trust other nationalities less but trust their own nationality more.* Is this related to controversies over unification? I don't know.

Third, *trustworthiness, trustingness, and own-trust are correlated.* I have already mentioned that a positive own-country bias seems to be exhibited in the own-trust ratings. Is this bias arbitrary from country to country, so that assessments of the trustworthiness of people in one's own country do not resemble the assessments of them offered by one's European neighbors? Remarkably, own-trust ratings resemble the trustworthiness ratings of the outsiders in each case: for 1996 the Pearson correlation coefficient between own-trust and trustworthiness is .74 (p = .002), and for all years it is .80 (p = .002). Next, trustingness and trustworthiness could each be stable but not necessarily related to one another. Are the most trustworthy also the most trusting?[25] Yes: the Pearson correlation coefficient between trustworthiness and trustingness for 1996 is .62 (p = .01), and for all years it is .75 (p = .005).[6] Noise is obvious in the data. The survey question captures both personal and political dimensions of trust. "Do you trust the Germans?" could mean, "Do you trust German people?" or, "Do you trust Germany?" Own-trust from year to year goes up and down in the same direction for nearly every country; there must be an exogenous factor—economic confidence?—driving that fluctuation in level but not ranking. Similar moods affect trustworthiness and trustingness, although to a lesser degree, and with some divergence, for example, between own-trust on the one hand (up) and trustworthiness and trustingness on the other (down) in 1996 (charts not shown).

The data on social trust among the EC-12 indicates a social trust gradient across Europe, with highest trust at a northwest pole and lowest trust at a southeast pole. The 1996 survey includes complete data on Sweden, Finland, and Austria, and also trust by people from EC-15 member countries—Switzerland, Norway, Hungary, Poland, the Czech Republic, Slovakia, Turkey, and Russia. Trust is highest for the Swiss, Swedes, and Norwegians, and lowest for the eastern Europeans and then the Turks, replicating the gradient. The data on high trust for Switzerland, Sweden, Norway, and Austria also suggest that the northwest pole may be associated with Germanic (including Scandinavian) speakers, corresponding to Machiavelli's observations five centuries ago.

Similar Studies

Geert Hofstede (1980, 1991) was able to administer a job-related attitudes survey to the employees of local subsidiaries of IBM in more than fifty countries across the world in 1968 and 1972. With factor analysis he found the answers sorting into three dimensions, but from theoretical concerns he distinguished two strands in one of the dimensions to yield a four-dimensional model of differences in culture: social inequality, individualism, masculinity and femininity, and uncertainty avoidance. I want to pay attention to his inequality (his label is "power-distance") index and to his individualism index, which are correlated (more inequality is associated with less individualism, −.67, p = .001) and also happen to be the two that load on the same factor. Each is correlated with national wealth and with distance from the equator: the more inequality, the closer to the equator and the less wealth; the more individualism, the more wealth and the further from the equator. The inequality index purports to indicate "the extent to which the less powerful members of institutions and organizations within a country expect and accept that power is distributed unequally" (Hofstede 1991, 28). Worldwide, countries where a Romance language is spoken ranked medium to high on the inequality index (more unequal), and countries where a Germanic language is spoken ranked low (more equal). Hofstede (1991, 32–33) speculates that the difference is rooted in family experiences:

> In the large power-distance situation children are expected to be obedient towards their parents. Sometimes there is even an order of authority

among the children themselves, younger children being expected to yield to older children. Independent behavior on the part of the child is not encouraged. *Respect* for parents and other elders is seen as a basic virtue; children see others showing such respect, and soon acquire it themselves. . . . In the small power-distance situation children are more or less treated as equals as soon as they are able to act. . . . The goal of parental education is to let children take control of their own affairs as soon as they can. Active experimentation by the child is encouraged; a child is allowed to contradict its parents, it learns to say "no" very early. Relationships with others are not dependent on the other's status; formal respect and deference are seldom shown. . . . There is an ideal of personal independence in the family.

As for the next index, individualism "pertains to societies in which the ties between individuals are loose; everyone is expected to look after himself or herself and his or her immediate family. Collectivism . . . pertains to societies in which people from birth onwards are integrated into strong, cohesive ingroups, which throughout people's lifetime continue to protect them in exchange for unquestioning loyalty." Europeans, Germanic or Romance, rank high (individualist) on the individualism index, and the English-speaking countries rank highest worldwide. Again, the range of the index is surmised to be rooted in family experiences: individualism in the nuclear family and collectivism in the extended family (Hofstede 1991, 50). More exactly, however, says Hofstede (1980, 229; 1991, 66), individualism is related to universalism, and collectivism to particularism, which resolves the apparent anomaly that high individualism is associated in another study with high interpersonal trust.[7] Looking at both power distance and individualism in Europe alone, they are negatively correlated, as they are worldwide, and three clusters are apparent: strongly individualist and egalitarian Great Britain, individualist and egalitarian Germanic and Scandinavian countries, and individualist and moderately inegalitarian Romance countries plus Belgium. Hofstede's inequality index is significantly correlated with my *Eurobarometer*-derived trustingness variable (Pearson's $r = -0.60$, $p = .05$), as is his individualism index ($+0.60$, $p = .05$).

The 1990 to 1993 World Values Survey in forty-three societies contained the question, "Generally speaking, would you say that most people can be trusted or that you can't be too careful in dealing with people?" and two possible answer codes, "Most people can't be trusted," and, "Can't be too careful." I compared the independent WVS trust data from the relevant European countries to the trust data I derived from the *Eurobarometer* survey. WVS-trust correlates in expected directions with my 1990, 1996, and average trustworthiness, trustingness, and own-trust variables. For WVS-trust and my average trustingness, $r = .69$ ($p = .03$). I do not know why WVS-trust is not more strongly related to my trustingness and trustworthiness—perhaps because the WVS data are nominal and the *Eurobarometer* data are ordinal-interval. Inglehart (1997, 352, 358–61) also reports data from the survey project on income inequality and on associational memberships for the forty-three societies. Both WVS-trust and my average trustingness are strongly and significantly correlated with more associational memberships, and both WVS-trust and my 1996 trustingness are strongly and significantly correlated with more income equality, recalling Machiavelli's observations on corruption, inequality, and republicanism. Also, Hofstede's inequality index is correlated with WVS-trust ($r = -0.61$, $p = .02$), as is his individualism index ($+0.53$, $p = .06$). It is remarkable that a factor extracted from Hofstede's survey, limited to apparently inconsequential on-the-job attitudes, relates to independent measures of trust taken twenty years later.

Emmanuel Todd relates worldwide macro-level variations in family structures to variations in ideology (1985) and variations in cultural development (1987). Todd's work is admirably parsimonious, but too bold for my intellectual tastes. Nevertheless, I find his broader hypotheses suggestive, and his narrower discussion of family structure and development in Europe useful. Todd asserts that generally economic development is preceded by the demographic development of a fall in the rates of mortality and fertility, a trend that in turn is preceded by the cultural development of a rise in the rate of literacy. Further, worldwide, literacy is positively correlated with mean age at marriage, more so with mean age at marriage of women (.83). (Even male literacy is more strongly associated with later female age of marriage than with later male age of marriage, .79 compared to .65.) Looking at Europe, there are correlations between age at marriage of women over twenty-seven years around 1840, literacy rates of over 70 percent around 1850, and national product exceeding $10,000 in 1979—but no relation between these variables and industrialization in 1860 as indexed by rail track per capita. Early cultural development (late age of female marriage and higher literacy) and higher current national wealth are found in Norway, Sweden, Finland, Denmark, the Netherlands, Belgium, Luxembourg, Germany, and Switzerland— almost the same set of countries that rank highest in the *Eurobarometer* trust measures.[8]

There are two different exceptions here, each interesting. First, notice the absence of Great Britain from both the list of countries experiencing early cultural development and the list of current higher-trust countries. Older historiography emphasizes the industrial revolution, its beginning in Great Britain, and the apparent diffusion of industrialization and associated modernization through Europe and beyond; however, Todd's data (and much recent historiography) suggest that the industrial revolution is not an independent prime mover but rather a dependent component within a longer and larger process of change. (Its onset in Great Britain was perhaps related to the combination of coal and iron resources and fortuitous location for world commerce and conquest.) What is remarkable is that despite its lead in the industrial revolution, Great Britain ranks behind the countries of early cultural development and current high trust in national product per capita in 1979 (and by 1993 ranks *below* Italy in per capita gross domestic product).[9] This suggests that there are important relationships between early cultural development, later economic development, and social trust, and, if Todd's data are correct, that the absence of Great Britain from the present list of countries of higher trust may not be due to measurement error. If such a pattern of relationships is posited, however, then Germany becomes the exception—high in cultural and economic developments but medium on both trustworthiness and trustingness. The countries of intermediate trust—France, Germany, Great Britain, and Ireland—are geographically intermediate, but with the exception of Ireland in the twentieth century, they are also the largest of our countries in territory and population.

Explaining Western European Patterns of Social Trust

Candidate Explanations

What explains the social trust gradient across Europe? The behavioral consequences of Protestant belief as contrasted to those of Catholic religious belief? The colder climate in the northwest and warmer climate in the southeast? Differences in customs or values between Germanic and Romance culture areas? The advance in economic development in the northwest due merely to its fortuitous location at the center of the new Atlantic-oriented world system? Different tendencies in family structure between the two regions? Idiosyncratic features not captured by our methodologies? These are among the major issues in comparative politics and historical sociology. Late female age of marriage, nuclear families, declining mortality and fertility, literacy, interpersonal trust, associational membership, population density, urbanization, industrialization, occupational specialization, wealth, subjective welfare, stable democracy, and other salient variables are all associated in a widely recognized modernization complex. Properly sorting out the intricate and sometimes reciprocal causal relationships between these processes is an unending challenge. I offer one plausible yet incomplete hypothesis, gladly conceding that nothing can be settled by the data and analysis in this meager essay.

The Marriage-Strategy Hypothesis

Tacitus (quoted in Goldthorpe 1987, 10) observed that German customs of family life differed considerably from those of the Romans, including primacy of the nuclear family, lack of clans or lineages, probably monogamy, and possibly late marriage: "The young men were slow to mate . . . the girls too, are not hurried into marriage." I propose that persistent differences in family structure—more precisely, different marriage-strategy equilibria ultimately account for the social trust gradient across Europe. The social trust gradient from the northwest to the southeast in Europe corresponds to the broad categorization of traditional European family structures by the Cambridge family historians John Hajnal (for example, Hajnal 1983) and especially Peter Laslett (1983). Laslett discerns four broad types of family household in traditional Europe, distinguished by thirty-three tendencies of difference. The first type corresponds to the northwest, the second is intermediate, the third ("Mediterranean") corresponds to the southeast, and the fourth, which I shall not discuss, is eastern Europe (beyond the EC-12). The first set of tendencies has to do with household formation. The tendency in the northwest is for neolocal residence: the newly married couple sets up residence on its own. The tendency in the southeast is for the newly married couple to stay in the father's household; new households fission off from the joint household for reasons unrelated to marriage. Household formation seems to structure many of the remaining variables, according to Laslett. (This conjecture is not borne out, however, on closer examination of southeastern marriage patterns, as we shall see.) Neolocal residence implies a large proportion of nuclear households, generally limited to parents and unmarried children. Patrilocal (groom's father's) residence implies a large proportion of joint households, including grandparents, adult brothers, and grandchildren.

A second important set of tendencies distinguishing the northwest European marriage pattern is late age at marriage, especially late age at first marriage of women. This implies a narrow age gap between spouses and a late age at first birth of children. This is supposed to follow structurally from neolocal residence, because the couple has to work and save to afford marriage. The southeast, in contrast, tends to experience early age of female marriage, implying a large age gap between spouses and early maternity. Also in northwest Europe, the proportion of permanently celibate individuals marrying was comparatively higher. The third important tendency is dubbed "addition to household of life-cycle servants"; in other words, in the northwest youth left home to work as temporary servants in outside households, especially households at the stage of having young children to care for. This seems to follow structurally from neolocal residence: the couple with young children needs help (recall, these are the days of peasant subsistence), and the servant youth need to earn money in order to establish their own households ("save for their nest egg"). Life-cycle service is "very common" in the northwest and "not uncommon" in the Mediterranean. But in parts of southern Italy and Greece it is "shameful" to work for non-kin (Banfield 1958; Barbagli and Kertzer 1990, 381; Campbell 1964, 285).

The northwest European pattern of late age at first marriage of women is "quite remarkable and unlike anything elsewhere in the world" (Levine 1989, 92; see also Seccombe 1992, 56). The pattern may have originated in the marriage practices of the Germanic tribes, the political economy of the manorial system of the high Middle Ages, developing Christian marriage rules, or in other factors, and various combinations thereof, but it seems to have emerged decidedly after the Black Death (Levine 1989, Seccombe 1990). Whereas it was once believed that the nuclear family is a consequence of industrialization, the received view now is that the northwest European nuclear family was rather one of the factors contributing to early industrialization (Goode 1963; Laslett 1983; Todd 1987; cf. Seccombe 1992). Indeed, adapting Seccombe, since several societies achieved technological capacities as good as or better than those of northwestern Europe, only to stagnate or regress, the unique marriage pattern must be suspected as a necessary factor in the initial transition to modernity.[10]

The marriage pattern contributed to that transition in a number of ways. Late marriage reduces fertility and thus reduces mortality crises and increases average longevity; the reduced number of children also increases parental investment per child. Neolocal late marriage requires, and the associated longevity justifies, greater investments in physical and human capital by the marrying parties—especially, in comparison, by females who accumulate both for ten or more years between puberty and first marriage. With marriage partners more equal in age, the average duration of marriage increases, and women (and their children) are less likely to be widowed and paupered in their later childbearing years. Life-cycle service permits men and women to accumulate capital for marriage, redistributes youth from less productive to more productive holdings, and introduces youth to a variety of settings and skills (adapting from Seccombe 1992, 239–41). The frustrating delay in marriage also cultivates habits of self-control and future orientation in the population.

Some contrasts between Germanic and Romance marriage patterns go back for many centuries. Why the regional homology and the millennial persistence? To tackle the question, we have to understand the concept of a Schelling convention.

Conventions Regulating Access to Reproduction

Game theory is the study of interdependent choice. The most necessary and deeply interdependent choices a human makes have to do with reproduction. Moreover, many crucial aspects of courtship, marriage, and child-rearing are a matter of coordination. This gives rise to what I call conventions regulating access to reproduction. Elsewhere this concept allows me to explain two perplexing practices. Female genital mutilation in Africa persists despite modernization, public education, and legal prohibition. Female foot-binding in China lasted for one thousand years but ended in a single generation. I show that each practice is a self-enforcing convention (in Schelling's sense), regulating access to reproduction, and maintained by interdependent expectations on the marriage market (Mackie 1996).

Schelling said that the coordination game lies behind the stability of institutions and traditions yet can also explain rapid change.[11] How can the same mechanism explain both stability and change? Look at a sample coordination game, as in game B of figure 8.4. (Generally, for the games in figure 8.4, there are two players, each player has two strategies, the lower-left payoff in any box is that of player Row-Chooser, and the upper-right payoff in any box is that of player Column-Chooser. Assume that the players cannot talk to each other, and that they play pure strategies, not a probabilistic mixture of strategies.) If Row-Chooser chooses row 1 and Column-Chooser chooses column 1, then they coordinate on R1C1 and carry home a payoff of two each; the same is true if they coordinate on R2C2. If coordination fails—say they choose R1C2, or R2C1—then each gets nothing. The usual illustration of this is whether to drive on the left side of the road or the right. It does not matter which side I drive on so long as everyone else does the same.

Consider now game A in figure 8.4. Here only R1C1 is an equilibrium choice. Game A does not represent a coordination problem; for that, there must be at least two proper coordination equilibria, according to Lewis (1969). Game B of figure 8.4 does represent a coordination problem. So does game C. In game C, R1C1 is better for each player than R2C2, and R2C2 is better for each player than the miscoordination at R1C2 or R2C1. If people are stuck at inferior equilibrium R2C2, they may lack a concerted way to move to superior equilibrium R1C1. Game D also represents a coordination problem, but now with a bargaining aspect. Here Column-Chooser does best at R1C1, while Row-Chooser does best at R2C2, and each likes either of these coordination equilibria better than miscoordination at R1C2 or R2C1; this game has all the ingredients of power and tragedy. *Any* game with two or more proper coordination equilibria represents a coordination problem.

Singling out a coordination equilibrium is a matter of concordant mutual expectations. If there are two of us and we can talk, then we can each promise to choose either right or left, and the promise is self-enforcing. If there are hundreds of us, express agreement is difficult. Many conventions suggesting a single choice of equilibrium in a coordination problem are not expressly agreed to; rather, they are tacit. Schelling urges that there is no logical solution to the tacit coordination problem; rather,

Figure 8.4   Game Matrices

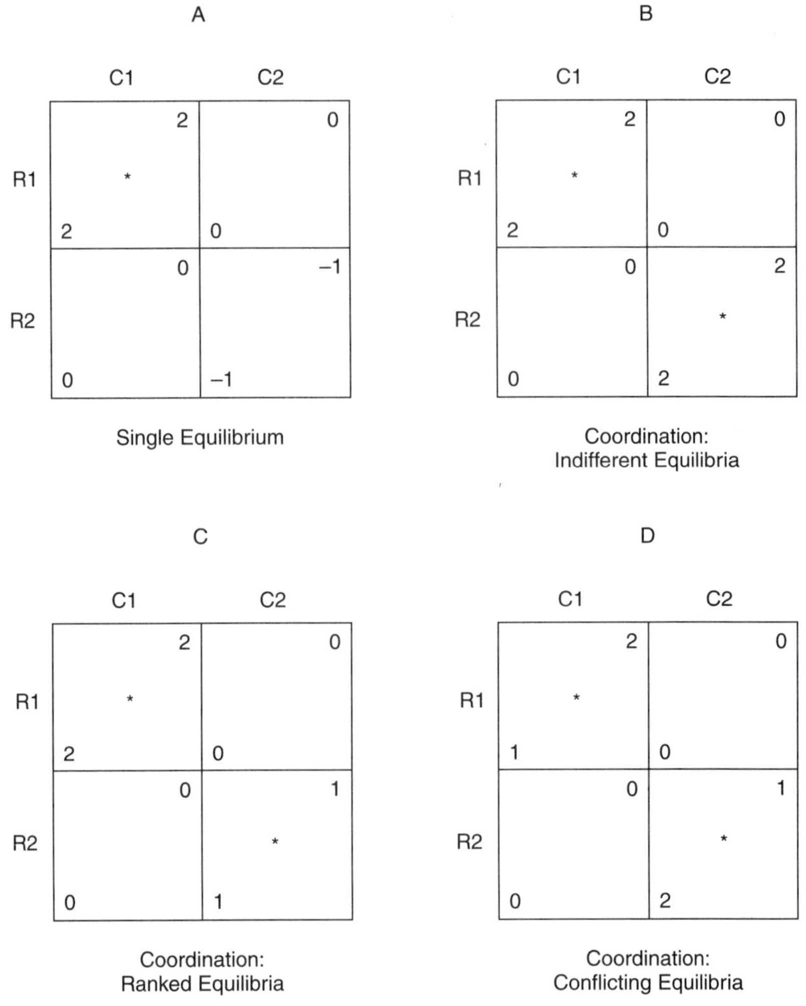

A

	C1	C2
R1	2 *	0
	2	0
R2	0	−1
	0	−1

Single Equilibrium

B

	C1	C2
R1	2 *	0
	2	0
R2	0	2
	0	2 *

Coordination:
Indifferent Equilibria

C

	C1	C2
R1	2 *	0
	2	0
R2	0	1
	0	1 *

Coordination:
Ranked Equilibria

D

	C1	C2
R1	2 *	0
	1	0
R2	0	1
	0	2 *

Coordination:
Conflicting Equilibria

Source: Author's compilation.
* = Equilibria choices

solutions are suggested by their psychological salience. The salient choice is not uniquely *good*, just noticeably *unique*. It all depends on what the players believe about each other. In novel play of game C, absent credible communication, superior R1C1 stands out as the salient choice for most people. But in a recurring game, precedent is strongly salient. If we played the same game 1C yesterday at R1C1, then R1C1 is the salient choice today. If the choice yesterday was inferior R2C2, R2C2 is weakly salient today, and if R2C2 was the result in our last ten games, it is strongly salient in our next. Coordination by precedent is convention.

At 5:00 A.M., Sunday, September 22, 1967, Sweden switched from driving on the left to driving on the right (Hardin 1988; Ullman-Margalit 1977). Sweden, or at least its authorities, saw driving on the left as more like the game in 1C than the one in 1B. The rest of Continental Europe drove on the right, so as international traffic increased, visitors to Sweden caused accidents by driving in the wrong lane, as did nonchalant Swedes abroad. So Swedes would be better off driving on the right, moving from R2C2 to R1C1 in something like game 4C. Even if the millions of Swedes were each convinced that driving on the right would be better, they could never spontaneously, by some invisible hand, get to the better coordination equilibrium. Convention is self-enforcing: any one person driving to the right to demonstrate its advantages would end up dead. In left-driving Pakistan a local religious party decreed that the pious had to drive on the right. The decree was rescinded in two weeks following a number of serious accidents (Bedi 1994).

Some features of family life are conventions of this type, and other features are not. A feature is a convention to the extent that a choice is interdependent between the parties and it is in the parties' interests to make a coordinated choice. Discussions of family structure often emphasize inheritance practices—whether land is impartible or partible, for example. Whether inheritance is impartible or partible is not a convention, or is only weakly conventional, because the property that one family transmits to its children does not depend, or only weakly depends, on what another family transmits to its children; a weak dependence might occur, say, if a certain type of land parcel was complementary in the local agricultural market. Whether the Addams family bequeaths its total one hundred acres to one child and compensatory nonland shares to the remaining three children or bequeaths twenty-five acres to each of the four children matters little to the Barney family.[12] However, marriage-formation practices are deeply interdependent between families, and marriage is defined as the fact that two parties make the same choice—each other—for the purposes of reproduction. If the local convention is that a daughter on the marriage market is equipped with a dowry of a certain content and value, then it matters immensely to the families with sons on the local marriage market that the Addams family has failed to properly dower Letitia.

Marriage Strategy as an Independent Variable

Conventions regulating access to reproduction are nearly universal in local marriage markets and stubbornly persistent there because of the strong interdependence of marriage choice. Consider, say, the cooking practices of a household. What one house cooks does not depend on what another house cooks (except for the soft constraints of input prices and local knowledge). To deviate from the local norm of cooking might mark one's family as creative, or maybe odd, but it is not fatal. Consider now age of marriage. If the local convention is for males to marry at thirty-five and females at fifteen, then individuals seeking to marry away from those means face a smaller pool of eligible mates from whom to choose. The smaller the mate selection pool, the lower the quality of match, down to absence of acceptable match and consequent reproductive death. For individuals who wish to marry and reproduce, there are strong incentives to comply with any convention regulating access to marriage. The convention persists in the ongoing marriage market, which is sufficient, but in addition, parents, nearly all of whom will have complied with it, transmit the expectations to their offspring. Those who do not wish to marry and reproduce, or who defy the conventions, tend not to have offspring to carry on their peculiar traditions. An anthropologist (Goody 1983, 209–10) presumably unfamiliar with the particulars of the Schelling convention observes:

> Once established as a trend a particular age of marriage may be difficult to vary; a late or early age may have to continue as a norm in situations very different from that in which it had its functional origins, not as a survival but because people are locked into a particular system. In my own experience the very high differential age of marriage found among the Konkomba of northern Ghana (late for men, early for women) has proved very resistant to modification, despite the wishes of many young men and women, and the pressures from outsiders; *the brides are simply not there to enable a sudden change to take place.* When variations in an already established "norm" do occur, they may arise from a number of factors which are specific to an individual case; it has been suggested that, at Colyton, Devon, in the later seventeenth century such changes were due to a desire to adjust the number of children to a favorable or disastrous sequence of events, so that the age of marriage reacted to local changes in the economy or demography. [references omitted, emphasis added]

Demographers sometimes portray age at marriage as an equilibrating device. Say that in a frontier society the number of males exceeds the number of females; then, assuming no polyandry, females are equitably distributed by increasing the difference between male and female marriage age, males marrying older and females marrying younger or both. Individuals acting individually cannot depart from the age convention, but the value of the convention might change nonintentionally in response to changes affecting all or most members of the intramarrying group.

Neolocality and patrilocality are each alternative Schelling conventions—brides and grooms from different families in the same market must each expect one type of residence or another. Consider a local marriage market, and the larger set of overlapping marriage markets within a cultural region, that is at a neolocal equilibrium. If a boy or girl wishes to find a partner who expects patrilocal residence, he or she faces a much smaller marriage pool, perhaps an empty pool, and thus an inferior match or reproductive death. There is further entrenchment at a neolocal equilibrium, since a boy who proposes departing to patrilocality would have to convince his parents to take into the residence a bride and subsequent grandchildren, and it is unlikely that the inherited neolocal housing structure would be large enough for that, not to mention the parents' expectations; a girl's family might reduce her dowry since it is going to the groom's family rather than to the new couple. Similarly, at a patrilocal equilibrium, a boy or a girl seeking a partner who expects neolocal residence faces a smaller or empty marriage pool. The equilibrium is further entrenched in that the boy is unlikely to obtain from his parents resources for independent residence, and the girl's family is not likely to provide the additional resources for residence conventionally provided by the boy's family. Of course, there are those who defy the conventions, but their deviation may result in less successful biological reproduction, and more surely will result in failed cultural reproduction of the deviant trait as children and grandchildren are relentlessly attracted back to mean values on conventions.

The tradition of life-cycle service is also a convention. For teenagers and younger adults to work annual stints with other families means that other families must need and want work from outsiders and are willing to accept residence of non-kin; under a no-service equilibrium, a youth seeking outside work would find no family needing or wanting to hire him. Life-cycle service is associated with neolocality, and its absence is associated with patrilocality: the small nuclear family household needs outside help when its children are small, but the large extended family household does not. Also, later age of marriage, especially for females, is associated with neolocality, and early female age of marriage with patrilocality. Under neolocality, boys and girls must accumulate sufficient capital to establish their independent household, both by their own work and by waiting for the parents' bequests at retirement and death, which delays marriage. Under patrilocality the male needs his father's permission to marry and the younger female goes directly from her parents' supervision to her husband's family's supervision. However, in noticing the associations among these somewhat independent conventions—neolocal with late marriage and service, and patrilocal with early marriage and no service—we must not commit the error of expecting that we will observe optimal institutions. Just because it would be better for all concerned if neolocals married late and had available service does not mean that such conventions will be what we observe, because, such as in the case that Goody observed, the relevant parties can be stuck at a welfare-inferior equilibrium that no one of them can escape alone. That is an advantage of the convention approach: it can help us explain what is anomalous for structural-functionalism, for example, the many ills that follow from neolocality, early marriage, and no service in traditional southern Italy, or the consequential occurrence of patrilocality and late marriage in north-central Italy.[13]

I noted earlier that a great many variables are interrelated in a modernization syndrome. Here I want to propose that conventions regulating access to reproduction—specifically neolocality, early female age of marriage, and life-cycle service—are together a strong candidate for being one of the necessary and primal factors in the original transition to modernity. Observed early in the historical record, these conventions are locally almost universal and stubbornly persistent, thus suggesting considerable independence and causal priority.[14] Observing such universality and persistence, Wally Seccombe (1992, 24) asks: "Why do the great majority of families in a society share so many features in common? What ensures their similarity with one another and induces new family branches to replicate the form of their predecessors?" His answer neatly summarizes the standard sociological repertoire for explaining such structural homology: the dominant mode of production (the local political economy?), an independent cultural kinship ideal inspiring widespread emulation and conformity, desire for family reputation for compliance with local norms, and norm compliance variously enforced by legal codes, community surveillance, and the heads of households. However, contrary to economic determinism, a study of variation in postmarital residence, female age at marriage, and prevalence of household servants among regions of Italy finds a "persistence over time of regionally distinctive nuptiality patterns, even as economic systems changed"; "cultural norms" are somewhat independent of "political economy" (quoting Barbagli and Kertzer 1990 on Rettaroli 1990). Moreover, I am dubious in principle of the norm-compliance account and believe that the convention account is more promising, especially in deriving a delimited conformity from the desire for reproduction rather than having to assume conformity as an all-purpose but arbitrarily invoked primitive.

Pierre Bourdieu (1976, 117–18), in his essay on marriage strategies as strategies of cultural reproduction, acutely observes that ethnology "has borrowed not only concepts, tools, and problems but also an entire theory of practices from the legalistic tradition . . . [a tradition] that speaks the language of the *rule* rather than that of the *strategy*." The legalistic approach imagines that individual action is motivated by reference to a local unwritten law, called a norm, that is associated with some unwritten sanction. Norms persist because they are habitually transmitted from parent to child. Bourdieu's innovation was to reject legalism in favor of his habitus, "a whole system of predispositions inculcated by the material circumstances of life and by family upbringing." Habitus is an advance on legalism but retains the bibliophilic imagery of culture as a book of rules (explicit for the legalists, implicit for Bourdieu) handed down from parent to child, of people as "cultural dopes." A rational-choice approach to culture (which may be defined as the distribution of beliefs within an intramarrying group) portrays it as constraints on individual action arising from local interdependencies of action—as in conventions regulating access to reproduction. A local cultural practice of neolocality, for example, is not the result of parents teaching their children to be neolocal but rather persists as a convention that is very costly for individuals on the marriage market to ignore. (Consider how unlikely it would be for one to satisfy a desire for patrilocal marriage in Ohio.) The convention is so strong that actors may even fail to realize that there are alternatives to it. One observes that children speak the same language as their parents and in the absence of variation in the observed population erroneously assumes that the cause is parental training. Notice, however, that children of immigrants to the community, because of the power of convention, speak in the language and accent of their peers, not their parents (Harris 1998; Mackie 1999).

Francis Fukuyama (1995) argues that there is an important relationship between family structure, trust, and national prosperity, but a surprising one. Fukuyama dubs the surprise "the paradox of family values" (61–127): in an informal but instructive cross-national comparison, he finds that the stronger and larger the family, the lower is both social trust and national prosperity. Fukuyama reports this association but does not adequately explain it. He ascribes culture, including ethics and family structure, to "inherited ethical habit" (34), which is "totally arational in its substance and in the way it is transmitted" (33). He rejects "rational choice" explanations of culture and imagines that the only alternative explanation of culture is that people "adopt such attitudes without thinking much about them and pass them on to their children, so to speak, with their toilet training" (38). Fukuyama's toilet-training theory of culture, following Weber, explains northwest European family structure and high trust as a consequence of the adoption and bibliophilic transmission of Protestant religious beliefs. But why, with so much eagerness and sacrifice, did the northwest Europeans flock to the Protestant sects? I argue that their religious beliefs were rather a consequence of the prior culture emergent from their family structure.

The toilet-training theory says that "because culture is a matter of ethical habit, it changes very slowly" (40). Some cultural regularities change slowly, but some change almost instantly. Foot-binding, for example, was nearly universal for one thousand years but ended entirely in less than a generation (Mackie 1996). Some cultural regularities change slowly, some change quickly, and the toilet-training theory, although of venerable sociological heritage, explains neither (Harris 1998; Mackie 1999). Incidentally, Fukuyama confuses rational choice theory, which assumes only actors who have consistent purposes, with vulgar economics, which assumes that humans are egoists who seek the heaping up of material goods. Vulgar economics is, of course, useless for explaining human purposes that violate its assumptions. Fukuyama also unwittingly shares the behavioral assumptions of vulgar economics: he thinks that individuals are naturally selfish and are moral only if society habituates them to be so (35).[15] I argue for a rational choice approach: a concrete account of cultural reproduction, explained by distinct mechanisms subject to constraints, as opposed to the typical socialization story where arbitrary habits are passed on by rote indoctrination. A more accurate understanding of the mechanisms of culture also allows for more effective policies to promote welfare-enhancing cultural change.

Trust or Honor?

Assume that humans strongly desire to raise successfully their biological children. The various forms and aspects of marriage serve this end. Because of the desire for children, each party prefers marriage to non-marriage, and thus marriage is a deeply interdependent choice and a co-ordination equilibrium. Females are certain of maternity, but males are not certain of paternity. (Who was it who quipped that maternity is a fact, but paternity is an opinion?) In the standard case the female requires assurances of resource support for the bearing and rearing of children, and the male requires assurances of paternity confidence. Families advertise their male offspring as capable of providing both generous and sustained support, and their female offspring as both fertile and faithful. Under conditions of resource equality, humans compete in conveying the many signs of trustworthiness to possible marriage partners. Under conditions of resource inequality, conventions of honor (as male vigilance and as female modesty) emerge as signs of higher desirability. Trust and honor each serve the purpose of guaranteeing the risky marriage transaction, but each is an effective strategy only against its own type—trust with trust and honor with honor.

The honor conventions of male prowess and female modesty, sometimes described as the Mediterranean cultural pattern, can be derived from past conditions, not of resource shortage, but rather of resource un-predictability. Fernand Braudel (1966, 231, 235, 238, 244) emphasizes the unity of the Mediterranean climate:

> a climate, which has imposed its uniformity on both landscape and ways of life . . . identical or near-identical worlds . . . on the borders of coun-tries as far apart and in general terms as different as Greece, Spain, Italy, North Africa . . . undeniable homogeneity, both from north to south and from east to west. . . . The disadvantage of this climate for human life lies in the annual distribution of rainfall. It rains a good deal . . . but the rains fall in autumn, winter, spring. . . . The "glorious skies" of the summer semester have their costly drawbacks. Everywhere drought leads to the disappearance or reduction of running waters and natural irrigation. . . . A few changes in temperature and a shortage of rainfall were enough to endanger human life.

There is far more potential variance in male reproductive success than in female reproductive success. Resource unpredictability results in more mortality among males as compared to females and results in more re-source inequality among families; male death and family stratification conspire to produce a shortage of marriageable males (Braudel's [1966, 415] Mediterranean: "We may assume that as a rule women were in the majority"). The shortage of males intensifies positional competition among families offering daughters on the marriage market, and the families of women compete to marry upward (hypergyny), provide dowries, and assure paternity confidence; at an extreme of resource inequality, polygyny, formal or informal (sequential monogamy, mis-tresses) emerges. Bobbi Low (1990) uses Murdock's standard cross-cultural sample to explore the relationships between variance in male resource control as proxied by nonsororal polygyny, on the one hand, and environmental variables, on the other hand. Among other things, she finds that as the seasonality of rainfall increases, so does polygyny; also, polygyny increases with pathogen stress. ("In the towns of the Sicilian cereal latifundia, where only men cultivated the land, adult male death rates exceeded adult female death rates probably because males were more exposed through their work to a torrid climate and to malaria" [Benigno 1989, 178].)

Thus, under greater resource inequality, families advertise the honor of the line, the purity of their females, and their commitment to the values of chastity and fidelity, the so-called modesty code. Local conventions of modesty emerge, among them claustration, veiling, foot-binding, and in-fibulation. Female modesty in these circumstances is a positional good (valued not for attaining a standard but for its rank—not "excellent" but "best") and thus is driven to maximum affordable values on the conven-tions: "One wrong word about his sister and he'll kill you," "The errant daughter shall die," and so on. It is a matter of family honor that its sons not only fulfill the reproductive obligations of marriage but attempt multiple low-cost liaisons—a mixed reproductive strategy.[16] The contrast between the northwestern marriage strategy of trust and the southeastern strategy of honor is developed in the next section.

The contrast between the northwestern and southeastern family patterns is also arguably related to differences in climate, disease mortality, and their interaction. It is not that the north is colder and the south hotter, except as that may affect disease mortality.[17] Rather, it is that the northwestern climate is less extremely variable than the Mediterranean in the ways that matter to agricultural production, and it is also more predictable.[18] More predictable resources lead to less inequality between families and greater expected longevity in the northwest. To understand regional differences in disease mortality we must consult William McNeill's *Plagues and Peoples* (1977, 57): by the beginning of the Christian era, "four divergent civilized disease pools had come into existence, each sustaining infections that could be lethal if let loose among populations lacking any prior exposure or accumulated immunity." As the scope of conquest and trade expanded, the Roman disease pool of the West was connected to the Chinese disease pool of the East, with calamitous population collapse for both empires at the extremes of the new confluence. The Roman Mediterranean populations contracted from the third century on and collapsed after the Justinian plague in the late fifth century. The Germanic barbarians invaded the Western Roman Empire, or more precisely, wandered in to take over vacant land. This occupation made a bad situation worse, because as Roman and Germanic "masses began to commingle, living as close neighbors and intermarrying, disparate ethnic groups were exposed to the ravages of alien diseases for which they lacked effective antibody defense" (Seccombe 1992, 57). Whether owing to the macro parasitism of imperial domination of the peasantry in the south, as McNeill believes, or the differential micro parasitism of disease, population growth was greater after the Justinian collapse in the Germanic north than in the Romance south. Later the Black Plague of 1346 to 1350 and its many weaker successors hit all of Europe hard, but it hit the Mediterranean the hardest. (The possible explanations are detailed by McNeill 1977, 146–54.) I would add that perhaps small households in the north and large households in the south contributed to the differential mortality. In the 150 years after the first plague, the population center of Europe shifted from northern Italy to the low countries, as did the centers of commerce and conquest (The shift is made vivid in the population maps constructed by Kees Terlouw 1997.), Thus, again, now with respect to disease, expected life span was more predictable in the northwest. Less inequality of resources and more longevity support neolocality and late marriage.[19]

Trust as a Marriage-Strategic Disposition

There are five major tasks in the life cycle (Seccombe 1992, 25). First, to achieve a livelihood. Second, to acquire household space. Third, to get married. Fourth, to bear and raise children. Fifth, to provide for aging parents. The second, third, and fourth tasks typically involve conventions that regulate access to reproduction. Assume that residence, age of marriage, and service are such conventions. Consider first the northwest European case of neolocal residence and late age of marriage. The husband and wife are of comparable maturity. The wife has attained comparable human capital, perhaps a distinctive skill. She has also probably spent some time away from her family, but even if not, a twenty-six-year-old is certainly more independent than a sixteen-year-old. Each spouse hails from a small nuclear family, which has some reputation but comparatively little power to enforce the honor of its sons and the modesty of its more independent daughters. Consider next the stylized southeast European case of patrilocal residence and early age of marriage. (The stylization is useful but misleading, as I explain in the next section.) The husband is mature, but the wife is much younger; the man tends to have more power, the woman tends to be less responsible. The wife has attained simple domestic skills, but no other distinctive human capital. She has spent no time away from her family and has less of a sense of independence. Each spouse hails from a large patrilocal family for whom reputation is everything and which has the power to enforce the honor of its sons and the modesty of its daughters. In the northwest, marriage is a contract negotiated by two independent individuals (with parental agreement); in the southeast, marriage is a contract negotiated between two families (with the children's agreement).

Assume that men and women want to have their own biological children. If that is the goal, the problem for the woman is resource support for bearing and raising her children, and the problem for the man is assurance that the children are his own. These are major problems. Although it is probably obvious to most readers of this chapter that reckless promiscuity and penury is not the way to go in a marriage, these background assumptions are learned practices that do not seem so obvious to those of our fellow citizens populating the daytime television talk shows. Under the southeastern marriage system, the modesty of the immature and dependent young bride is guaranteed by the jealous honor of her family and by vigilant supervision before and after marriage. The resource reliability of the groom is guaranteed by the honor of his family, under whose supervision the couple will reside; even if the son turns out to be useless, his family will make good the keep of the children, if only for the sake of its reputation. The primary negotiators of the marriage are the two families, who each insist on marrying as well as possible into a family of honor.

(Of course, the couple's wishes cannot be denied, but notice how zealously the honor family supervises the introduction of prospects.) Transgressions are deterred by the prospect of destruction of the family's honor—for an individual member to damage his family's honor is to damage his own central interests. The northwestern marriage market is quite different. The mature and independent female and the male are certainly concerned about their reputations. However, these reputations do not follow from direct physical supervision by their respective families, but rather from dispositions inculcated by parents and cultivated by individuals. The reliability of the female's marriage pledge is guaranteed by neither the thorough physical supervision of her family, which is impossible because of its smaller size and her much longer wait until marriage, nor the broader incentives of the larger patrilocal family to safeguard its honor, but rather by her trustworthiness. The male's potential resources are indicated not only by inheritable family resources but by his ability to earn and save in work beyond the parental family; the reliability of his marriage pledge is best guaranteed not so much by the honor of his family as by his own signs of trustworthiness. If parents desire children and grandchildren (and that is one of my assumptions), then it is in the parents' interest under this system to teach their children to be trustworthy. Anyway, individuals who do not exhibit the signs of trustworthiness do less well on the marriage market, and under subsistence conditions those who were in fact untrustworthy tended to be less successful in raising children to adulthood.

Notice the powerful consequences of a convention of life-cycle service, a temporary stage of work outside the family before starting one's own family (perhaps the equivalent today is college). First, children must be trained to make favorable decisions even when not under family supervision. Second, children attain an outside perspective on affairs and, if lucky, several new skills. Third, familiarity and cooperation with distant kin or non-kin are shown to be possible. Fourth, we get something like the strength of weak ties. (For the idea that new information or new opportunities are more likely to be learned from distant acquaintances than from close relations, see Granovetter 1973.) Neolocal households à la Montegrano in southern Italy are almost isolated cliques. In contrast, identically small neolocal households in the northwest, linked through life-cycle service involving annual and sequential household residence of equal-status outsiders, inhabit a more complete network of ties. To be fit for the intimate apprenticeship necessary to acquire sufficient capital for marriage, the youth must be prominently trustworthy.

The first and fifth major tasks of the life cycle are to obtain a livelihood and to care for aging parents. Under patrilocal residence, there comes a time for the old man to retire, and ideally there is a stable transfer of household authority to one of the sons. Nevertheless, under the supervisory constraints of commonly expected common residence, the aged grandparents need not fear neglect because they are daily present with lingering authority even if resented. And a marrying son, although he needs parental permission to marry, need not worry about attaining his own means of production, since marriage does not mean leaving the household. Matters are quite different under neolocal residence and its variants. In order to marry, son and daughter must accumulate and receive from parents sufficient means of production to establish their own household. Generally, this is impossible without large transfers from the couple's parents. A resource dilemma arises between the parents and the children. The children need the parents' capital to establish their own households, but once the parents transfer the capital, they lose certainty of care in their old age. The neolocal parents' only security is the trustworthiness of their children to honor the pledge of care. Therefore, it is in parents' interest to raise trustworthy children. In the patrilocal household, it is in the father's interest to inculcate the norm "obey your father." In the neolocal household, it is in the father's interest to inculcate the norm "fulfill your promises."

Thus, it may be no mere accident that the high-trust countries in northwestern Europe traditionally exhibited one marriage pattern and the low-trust countries in the southeast exhibited another. It may be that the marriage patterns generated variations in social trust as a by-product. Further, recall that Hofstede's index of inequality and his index of individualism were negatively correlated with one another, and each also proved to be correlated with the measures of trustingness derived from *Eurobarometer* and the World Values Survey. At one pole we have southern latitude, more inequality, obedience to parents, local collectivism, extended families, fewer associational relationships, and lower trustingness; at the other pole we have northern latitude, more equality, independence from parents, individualism, nuclear families, more associational memberships, and higher trustingness.[20] According to Todd, a later female age of marriage is associated with higher literacy worldwide. The logic of the relationship is obvious: if women have time to learn before they marry, they transmit that learning to children, and at the national level earlier literacy is associated with later wealth. In the case of the original northwest European transition to modernity, I have identified an additional linkage from later age of marriage to economic development: the unavoidable marriage strategy of cultivating trustworthy dispositions resulting in persons who are independent and individualized yet at the same time, because of their trustworthiness, capable of forming and re-forming in civic, political, and economic associations beyond the immediate family.

Discussion

Problems with the Marriage-Strategy Hypothesis

Laslett (1983) proposed that neolocal residence structurally induces late age of female marriage and life-cycle service. These three traits are associated in northwestern Europe and, as I have argued, additively generate trust. However, southeastern Europe is not the neat opposite of northwestern Europe. Students of the Italian family (Barbagli 1991; Benigno 1989; Macry 1997) have identified three broad traditions of family formation.[21] The first, characterized by neolocal residence and late age of marriage, is found in the cities of northern and central Italy (and in Sardinia). The second, characterized by patrilocal residence, late age of marriage, and life-cycle service, is found in the countryside of northern and central Italy, where agriculture was typified by annual sharecropping or family farms. The third, characterized by neolocal residence and early age of marriage, is found in southern Italy, where agriculture was typified by agrotowns of farmworkers employed by large estates or by tiny peasant plots (greater resource inequality). Life-cycle service is absent in southern Italy (Arru 1990; Da Molin 1990). On the Iberian peninsula, in a similar pattern, patrilocality and early marriage are found in the north, patrilocality and late marriage are found in the center, and neolocality and early marriage are found in the south (Benigno 1989, 175). Empirically, neolocal residence does *not* structurally induce late age of female marriage or life-cycle service. This may count against Laslett's structural interpretation of the relations between the variables, but it is not inconsistent with the convention account.

Trust is higher in northern Italy, lower in central Italy, and lower still in southern Italy. Consider Putnam's (1993, 97 and throughout) celebrated study of civic culture in Italy: low trust and low political and economic development are found in the southern region, and high trust and high political and economic development are found in the north-central region. The lower-trust south is characterized by neolocal residence and small nuclear families, and the higher-trust north-central area by patrilocal residence and large joint families. Clearly, then, postmarital residence alone has nothing to do with trust! The large joint families of the higher-trust north-central area and their late-marrying daughters are associated with a particular style of sharecropping in the past. Land was owned by an urban elite who annually contracted with a family head for the exclusive labor of family members, and the landlords, who paid a fixed percentage of the crop, demanded larger work crews (Kertzer 1989). Whether the joint family emerged in response to landowners' demands or landowners' demands emerged in response to the joint family, I do not know.

The large patrilocal family, being well suited to guarding the chastity and fidelity of its women, is capable of living in rural isolation. What about the small neolocal family in the more fiercely honorable south? "Throughout most of southern Italy, the division of land into individual farmsteads was rare or nonexistent" (Da Molin 1990, 504). It is curious that such families are found in dense villages admirably suited for jealous surveillance of all by all, particularly of the honor of the women. Moreover (and notice the negative superlatives):

> In southern society, to go into service was considered to be humiliating and a disgrace; in some cases it was almost better to starve. To leave one's home to work as a servant in another home was considered to be absolutely unforgivable. The southern male, and in particular the head of the household, protected the honor of his women, be they wife, daughter, sister, or mother. An "honored" daughter (a daughter with a good reputation) only left her family and home after marriage. It was absolutely inconceivable that a girl should leave home to enter service for a period and co-reside with another family; if she did so before marriage, she could never return to live in the family home. (521)

The traditional southern pattern of neolocal residence, early age of marriage, and no life-cycle service is the worst of all possible family worlds but, owing to its conventional nature, impossible for any one family to escape from. One must establish one's own household with few resources at an early age. Hiring outside help when the children are small is impossible; thus, the wife has no time to invest in new human capital. The transmission of human capital from teenager to toddler so common under life-cycle service does not occur. Poverty follows. Parental death, unemployment, sickness, or senility are calamitous to the precarious nuclear unit. Laslett (1988) takes note of the "nuclear-hardship" of the neolocal family, its vulnerability to misfortune, its dependence on the broader community, and corresponding institutions of poor relief in England and elsewhere. The neolocal family is also found in southern Italy, but without the corresponding community institutions. Banfield (1958, 105) studied a neolocal low-trust village in southern Italy. The thematic apperception test stories that Banfield invoked from the distrustful Montegrani were 90 percent about calamity and misfortune (similar tests in northern Italy and in Kansas yielded threefold and sixfold fewer proportion of calamity stories, respectively), and no wonder: "No matter how hard parents struggle, the family may suddenly be destroyed and reduced to beggary." Banfield (1958, 139–52) offers two explanations for the amoral familism and suspicion of Montegrano. First, trust is higher in northern Italy, and there one finds the extended family. The greater poverty and insecurity of the neolocal household makes for distrust. One finds the nuclear family in northwest Europe, however, and higher trust there than in northern Italy. Second, Banfield hypothesizes that the northern and southern Italy family patterns vary by traditions of land tenure leading to renters in the north and hired hands in the south. The traditions of land tenure themselves, however, might have evolved in adaptation to a prior local family pattern.

Conclusion

Under my convention approach, postmarital residence, age of marriage, and forms of service can be both somewhat independent of one another and stable in value. The distinguishing cause of first transition to modernity may have been neolocality, late age of marriage, and life-cycle service. Late female age of marriage may also encourage female literacy and thus general literacy and an explosion of human capital. Late female age of marriage tends to supplant honor with trust (compare Cook and Hardin, forthcoming). Late-marrying patrilocal families that sharecrop together on a contract basis may extend trust beyond the nuclear family. Life-cycle service may underwrite trust and cooperation beyond the radius of family. Advancing economic development increases trust, according to the survey data, regardless of prior family structure, and economic development tends to induce neolocality, later age of marriage, and work outside the household. Trust is subject to equifinality. (The same effect might follow from any one of several different causes.) This does not mean that anything goes, just that the theorist might have to specify more than one genesis for more than one variety of trust.

It may be that neolocal residence, late female age of marriage, and life-cycle service additively generate trust. Thus, we find highest trust in northwestern Europe, which had all three traits; lower trust in the north of the Mediterranean peninsulas, which had late female age of marriage and some life-cycle service; and lowest trust in the south of the peninsulas, which had neolocal residence alone.

I have been bold in stating my marriage-strategy hypothesis for the sake of effective presentation, but I am humbly aware of the sketchiness of the theory, of the loose ends and inconsistencies, of the inappropriately monocausal overemphasis on trust and family, of the neglect of political history, and of the paucity and ambiguity of supporting data. The hypothesis requires both more detailed modeling and more comparative-historical testing and refinement. A proper theory would detail relationships between background demographic variables, biogeography, political economy, and the several conventions regulating access to reproduction. A worldwide comparison is out of the question, and a Western European comparison is not only beyond the comprehension of any single researcher but afflicted with uncontrolled variables and incomparable data sources. Italy, however, is an ideal laboratory for testing an elaborated hypothesis, because of fewer uncontrolled variables and more comparable data, but above all because of the abundance of distinguishable cases and the very wide range on all the variables of interest—production, reproduction, nature, and trust.

This chapter is part of a larger project called "Climates of Trust." I especially thank Diego Gambetta and Russell Hardin, and also Mark Hansen and the other participants in the workshop that occasioned this volume, and an audience at the Trust and Information Seminar at Oxford University. I am also thankful for comments and suggestions from others. I am responsible for the contents.

Notes

1. Means are taken directly from the 1990, 1993, and 1996 *Eurobarometer* publications; I use rawer response data from 1980 and 1986 *Eurobarometer* publications to calculate means equivalent to those reported in later years.

2. Whenever in this chapter I report a 1980 to 1996 mean, it is constructed for the EC-12 of 1986, 1990, and 1993, treating Spain and Portugal as missing values in 1980, and excluding Sweden, Finland, and Austria from the EC-15 in 1996.

3. Pearson's r is a measure of the linear association between two series of interval-level data that ranges from -1 for perfectly negative correlation to $+1$ for perfectly positive correlation; Kendall's tau is a measure of the similarity between two ordinal rankings and ranges from -1 to $+1$ if, as here, the data matrix is square.

4. Do the measures vary because of different meanings for the equivalents of "trust" in the various languages? The survey evidence suggests that this is unlikely. First, trustworthiness rankings are highly similar across countries, regardless of the language of the survey question. Second, own-trust rankings are highly similar to trustworthiness rankings, again regardless of language. Language does not determine reality. With respect to Russell Hardin's (this volume) observations on cross-language differences in the term "trust," it may well be that there is neither a word for nor the reality of trust in a small closed society. There would be, however, a need for trust in the urban societies of Europe. The need for trust is the same reality from one modern European setting to another, even if labeled trust in the United Kingdom and confiance in France, and even if the level of trust varies from one country to the next. Trust and confiance denote the same problem, even if the more nuanced meanings of each term vary.

5. The projection heuristic of John Orbell and Robyn Dawes (1991) is capable of explaining social trust or its absence as the by-product of imperfectly informed agents projecting their own trustworthiness or lack thereof onto unknown others. See Mackie (1997) for a full discussion.

6. Hardin (this volume) argues that trustworthiness begets trust. My provisional view is that trustworthiness is conceptually prior to trustingness, but that trustworthiness and trustingness are causally reciprocal (see Mackie 1997).

7. The same apparent anomaly was rediscovered and resolved in the same fashion thirty years later by Toshio Yamagishi and Midori Yamagishi (1994) in their studies of comparative responses of Japanese and Americans in social-dilemma decisionmaking experiments. "Individualist" Americans trust more than "collectivist" Japanese in these experiments, suggesting that the proper contrast is between universalistic Americans and particularistic Japanese in the placement of trust. See Mackie (1997) for further discussion.

8. According to Todd, mid-nineteenth-century Scotland enjoyed late female age of marriage and high literacy, but England did not. If these variables are related to social trust, then social trust as measured by the survey question may now generally be higher in Scotland than in England.

9. Measured in terms of either exchange rates or purchasing power standards (Statistical Office of the European Communities 1994). Thus, it is not a complete surprise that students in York in Great Britain free-ride in prisoners' dilemma decision experiments significantly more than those in Turin in northwestern Italy—from 12 to 16 percent more, depending on the experimental condition (Burlando and Hey 1997). *Eurobarometer* data for 1976, 1980, and 1986 on Italians' trust of other Italians by region show the northwest as the most trusted region. Interestingly, the northwest Italians cooperate more when the game is repeated among the same subjects, but the British do not.

10. Patricia Crone (1989, 148, 152–54), in her excellent summary of "The Oddity of Europe" in history, remarks that "medieval Europe was backward in comparison with medieval China or the Islamic world, but it was not visibly different in kind. Of course it had its peculiar features, but so did other civilizations, and it is only in retrospect that medieval Europe can be seen to have contained an unusual potential." She cites the northwest European marriage pattern as one of its distinguishing peculiarities.

11. This account of conventions as solutions to coordination problems, as developed by Schelling (1960) and Lewis (1969), is adapted from Mackie (1996).

12. Hume had a concept of conventions and cited inheritance practices as an instance of convention. Schelling interprets choice of equilibrium in repeated coordination games as a matter of convention harking back to Hume's concept. In an unpublished paper I attempted to follow up on Hume and explain inheritance practices as conventions in Schelling's sense. I concluded that inheritance practices were not conventions, and that conventions were more likely to be found associated with more interdependent marriage practices. This led to the discoveries in Mackie (1996).

13. The relations between these conventions, and their interdependence and independence, requires further work. There appears to be no tension between

patrilocality and either early or late marriage, for example, but considerable tension between neolocality and early marriage.

14. Conventions regulating access to reproduction can depend on more fundamental demographic variables. For example, if life expectancy is brief, then neolocality does not pressure late age of marriage, because children inherit at an early age.

15. I think that humans are naturally moral. Fukuyama (1995, 370) rather incoherently affirms this view as well.

16. These ideas are borrowed from the brilliant work of Dickemann 1979.

17. Hot temperatures are unmistakably associated with an increase in aggressive behaviors. In the United States there are highly significant correlations between the warmth of a city and violent crime arrest rates. Controlling for heat, and for race, there is also a weaker but puzzling correlation between southern culture and violent crime. Heat and culture are hotly debated as substitute hypotheses. However, they may be complementary, with independent effects from heat and from a lingering southern U.S. culture of honor rooted in reproductive conventions (for suggestive evidence, see Fischer 1989). For an entry into the heat literature, consult Anderson and Anderson (1996).

18. Low (1990), a biologist of reproduction strategies, offers a useful formal distinction between extreme variation and unpredictability.

19. These speculations have to do with understanding the origins of the European transition to modernity and do not imply any geographical determinism with respect to current transitions to democracy.

20. Compare Cook and Hardin (forthcoming), who say that small communities with strong oversight of individuals tend to organize cooperativeness with general norms and the sanction of shunning, while more urban communities organize cooperativeness through many relatively specific networks, hence through trust as encapsulated interest. Our conceptions are parallel but differ in important details.

21. The southern family pattern has changed radically with modernization but nevertheless exhibits distinctive traits, as detailed in Jurado-Guerrero and Naldini (1997).

References

Almond, Gabriel, and Sidney Verba. 1963. *The Civic Culture.* Princeton, N.J.: Princeton University Press.

Anderson, Craig A., and Kathryn B. Anderson. 1996. "Violent Crime Rate Studies in Philosophical Context: A Destructive Testing Approach to Heat and Southern Culture of Violence Effects." *Journal of Personality and Social Psychology* 70(4): 740–56.

Arru, Angiolina. 1990. "The Distinguishing Features of Domestic Service in Italy." *Journal of Family History* 15(4): 547–66.

Banfield, Edward C. 1958. *The Moral Basis of a Backward Society.* Glencoe, Ill.: Free Press.

Barbagli, Marzio. 1991. "Three Household Formation Systems in Eighteenth- and Nineteenth-Century Italy." In *The Family in Italy from Antiquity to Present,* edited by David I. Kertzer and Richard P. Saller. New Haven, Conn.: Yale University Press.

Barbagli, Marzio, and David Kertzer. 1990. "An Introduction to the Study of Italian Family Life." *Journal of Family History* 15(4): 369–83.

Bedi, Rahul. 1994. "Pakistan: Religious Right Puts Bhutto in a Spot." InterPress Service, May 27, 1994.

Benigno, Francesco. 1989. "The Southern Italian Family in the Early Modern Period: A Discussion of Co-residential Patterns." *Continuity and Change* 4: 165–94.

Bourdieu, Pierre. 1976. "Marriage Strategies as Strategies of Social Reproduction." In *Family and Society: Selections from the Annales,* edited by Robert Forster and Orest Ranum. Baltimore: Johns Hopkins University Press.

Braudel, Fernand. 1966. *The Mediterranean, and the Mediterranean World in the Age of Philip II.* Vol. 1. Berkeley: University of California Press.

Burlando, Roberto, and John D. Hey. 1997. "Do Anglo-Saxons Free-Ride More?" *Journal of Public Economics* 64(1): 41–60.

Campbell, J. K. 1964. *Honour, Family, and Patronage.* Oxford: Clarendon Press.

Cook, Karen S., and Russell Hardin. Forthcoming. "Networks, Norms, and Trustworthiness." In *Norms,* edited by Karl-Dieter Opp and Michael Hechter. New York: Russell Sage Foundation.

Crone, Patricia. 1989. *Pre-industrial Societies.* Oxford: Blackwell.

Da Molin, Giovanna. 1990. "Family Forms and Domestic Service in Southern Italy from the Seventeenth to the Nineteenth Centuries." *Journal of Family History* 15(4): 503–28.

Dickemann, Mildred. 1979. "The Ecology of Mating Systems in Hypergynous Dowry Societies." *Social Science Information* 18: 163–95.

Fischer, David Hackett. 1989. *Albion's Seed: Four British Folkways in America.* Oxford: Oxford University Press.

Fukuyama, Francis. 1995. *Trust.* New York: Free Press.

Goldthorpe, J. E. 1987. *Family Life in Western Societies.* Cambridge: Cambridge University Press.

Goode, William J. 1963. *World Revolution and Family Patterns.* New York: Free Press.

Goody, Jack. 1983. *The Development of the Family and Marriage in Europe.* Cambridge: Cambridge University Press.

Granovetter, Mark. 1973. "The Strength of Weak Ties." *American Journal of Sociology* 78(6): 1360–80.

Hajnal, John. 1983. "Two Kinds of Pre-industrial Household Formation System." In *Family Forms in Historic Europe,* edited by Richard Wall. Cambridge: Cambridge University Press.

Hardin, Russell. 1988. *Morality Within the Limits of Reason.* Chicago: University of Chicago Press.

Harris, Judith Rich. 1998. *The Nurture Assumption.* London: Bloomsbury.

Hofstede, Geert. 1980. *Culture's Consequences: International Differences in Work-Related Values.* Beverly Hills, Calif.: Sage Publications.

———. 1991. *Cultures and Organizations.* London: HarperCollins.

Inglehart, Ronald. 1990. *Culture Shift in Advanced Industrial Societies.* Princeton, N.J.: Princeton University Press.

———. 1997. *Modernization and Postmodernization: Cultural, Economic, and Political Change in Forty-three Societies.* Princeton, N.J.: Princeton University Press.

Jurado-Guerrero, Teresa, and Manuel Naldini. 1997. "Is the South So Different? Italian and Spanish Families in Comparative Perspective." *Journal of Mediterranean Studies* 30: 42–66.

Kertzer, David I. 1989. "The Joint Family Household Revisited: Demographic Constraints and Household Complexity in the European Past." *Journal of Family History* 14(1): 1–15.

Laslett, Peter. 1983. "Family and Household as Work Group and Kin Group: Areas of Traditional Europe Compared." In *Family Forms in Historic Europe,* edited by Richard Wall. Cambridge: Cambridge University Press.

———. 1988. "Family, Kinship, and Collectivity as Systems of Support in Pre-industrial Europe: A Consideration of the 'Nuclear-Hardship' Hypothesis." *Continuity and Change* 3(2): 153–75.

Levine, David. 1989. "Recombinant Family Formation Strategies." *Journal of Historical Sociology* 2(2): 89–115.

Lewis, David. 1969. *Convention: A Philosophical Study.* Cambridge, Mass.: Harvard University Press.

Low, Bobbi S. 1990. "Human Response to Environmental Extremeness and Uncertainty: A Cross-cultural Perspective." In *Risk and Uncertainty in Tribal and Peasant Economies,* edited by Elizabeth Cashdan. Boulder, Colo.: Westview Press.

Machiavelli, Niccolò. 1970. *The Discourses.* Harmondsworth, Eng.: Penguin. (Originally published c. 1519)

Mackie, Gerry. 1996. "Ending Foot-binding and Infibulation: A Convention Account." *American Sociological Review* 61(6): 999–1017.

———. 1997. "Trust as Bond, Trust as Exit." Unpublished paper.

———. 1999. "Family and Character." Unpublished paper.

———. 2000. "Female Genital Cutting: The Beginning of the End." In *Female Circumcision: Multidisciplinary Perspectives,* edited by Bettina Shell-Duncan and Ylva Hernlund. Boulder, Colo.: Lynne Reinner.

Macry, Paolo. 1997. "Rethinking a Stereotype: Territorial Differences and Family Models in the Modernization of Italy." *Journal of Modern Italian Studies* 2(2): 188–214.

McNeill, William H. 1977. *Plagues and Peoples.* New York: Anchor Books.

Muller, Edward N., and Mitchell A. Seligson. 1994. "Civic Culture and Democracy: The Question of Causal Relationships." *American Political Science Review* 88(3): 635–52.

Orbell, John, and Robyn Dawes. 1991. "A 'Cognitive Miser' Theory of Cooperator's Advantage." *American Political Science Review* 85(2): 515–28.

Putnam, Robert D. 1993. *Making Democracy Work.* Princeton, N.J. : Princeton University Press.

Rettaroli, Rosella. 1990. "Age at Marriage in Nineteenth-Century Italy." *Journal of Family History* 15(4): 409–25.

Schelling, Thomas C. 1960. *The Strategy of Conflict*. Cambridge, Mass.: Harvard University Press.

Seccombe, Wally. 1990. "The Western European Marriage Pattern in Historical Perspective: A Response to David Levine." *Journal of Historical Sociology* 3(1): 50–74.

———. 1992. *A Millennium of Family Change*. London: Verso.

Statistical Office of the European Communities. 1994. *Eurostat: Rapid Reports, Economy and Finance*. 1994. Vol. 4. Luxembourg: Office for Official Publications of the European Communities.

Terlouw, Kees. 1997. "A General Perspective on the Regional Development of Europe from 1300 to 1850." *Journal of Historical Geography* 22(2): 129–46.

Todd, Emmanuel. 1985. *The Explanation of Ideology: Family Structures and Social Systems*. Oxford: Blackwell.

———. 1987. *The Causes of Progress: Culture, Authority, and Change*. Oxford: Blackwell.

Ullman-Margalit, Edna. 1977. *The Emergence of Norms*. Oxford: Clarendon Press.

Yamagishi, Toshio, and Midori Yamagishi. 1994. "Trust and Commitment in the United States and Japan." *Motivation and Emotion* 18(2): 129–66.

PART III

TRUST: NETWORK, ORGANIZATIONAL, AND INSTITUTIONAL BASES

Chapter 9

Why Do People Rely on Others? Social Identity and the Social Aspects of Trust

TOM R. TYLER

T HE CONCEPT of trust has emerged as a central issue in recent discussions of the organizational dynamics of groups ranging from ork organizations to political and social systems (Braithwaite and Levi 1998; Tyler and Kramer 1996). In this discussion I focus on one issue concerning the role of trust in such group dynamics—the importance of trust in the authority relations of groups, organizations, and societies. My particular concern is with the influence of trust on the willingness of the people within groups, organizations, or societies to defer to group authorities, follow organizational rules, and, when encouraged to do so by their leaders, act in ways that help their group.

It is typically suggested that being able to trust others is crucial to being willing to take the risks associated with productive social exchange. In other words, trust is a form of social capital. It facilitates relations between people and groups. The argument presented here extends this suggestion to authority relations, suggesting that, if people trust authorities, group functioning is facilitated because the people within an organization are more willing to act in ways that aid the organization, for example, by accepting rules and decisions made by group authorities (Tyler and Blader 2000; Tyler and Huo 2000). If so, then groups can function more effectively when their members trust group authorities. This argument suggests that groups, as well as the individuals within them, have an interest in creating and maintaining the social conditions under which trust can occur.

Let me begin by suggesting that there is empirical evidence to support the argument that trust in authorities has value for groups. In a previous paper (Tyler and Degoey 1996) I tested empirically the argument that trust in organizational authorities has desirable social consequences for those organizations. I did so by examining the influence of trust on the willingness to defer to group authorities in several types of groups.

In that analysis I defined trust as an attribution that people make about the motives of a group authority. If people trust a group authority, it means that they judge that authority to be concerned about their needs, to have their best interests at heart, to care about their views, to consider those views when making decisions, and to try to be fair to them. In other words, trust reflects the assessment that the motives of an authority are benevolent and caring—that the authority is motivated to act in ways that take into account the welfare of the people within the group.

My analyses indicate that trust in the motives of group authorities, as expected, encourages both voluntary deference to their decisions and feelings of obligation to obey social rules. In each case the findings of several different studies converge on the finding that trustworthiness facilitates voluntary deference to rules and authorities (see also Tyler and Blader 2000; and Tyler and Huo, 2000).

In the case of voluntary deference to the decisions of organizational authorities, the issue addressed is whether the members of organizations defer to group authorities because they favor the decisions made by those authorities or because they trust the motives of the decision-makers. In analyses addressing this question, I consistently find that trust in the motives of the authority has an influence on deference to decisions and feelings of obligation to obey rules that is distinct from the influence of the favorability of the decisions made by that authority. In fact, the influence of motive inferences is typically stronger than is the influence of the favorability of decisions.

It is particularly important that the trustworthiness effects outlined are distinct from the influence of judgments about the favorability of the decisions made by group authorities, or of members' ability to control the outcomes of those decisions when dealing with authorities. In other words, it is important to show that trust does not simply reflect the experience of receiving favorable or desired outcomes from an authority. These instrumental factors do influence behavior, but none of the outcome indices have been found to be as influential as inferences about the trustworthiness of the motives of an authority. Further, inferences about trustworthiness are distinct from judgments about outcome favorability.

That trust in the motives of an authority encourages voluntary deference to the decisions of authorities and heightens feelings of obligation to obey social rules is important because organizations benefit when their members voluntarily defer to social rules. Authorities find it difficult to manage groups, organizations, or societies using strategies based on their control over resources that can be used as incentives or their threats of harm or sanctioning of group members.

Typically authorities have, at best, a limited ability to influence the favorability of the outcomes for group members or to alter the risk of detection and punishment for rule-breaking (Tyler 1997a). Hence, authorities value, and benefit from, the willingness of group members to cooperate voluntarily by deferring to authorities and rules.

Trust is important because it is a key antecedent of the willingness to cooperate voluntarily. It therefore encourages behaviors that facilitate productive social interaction. Because of its important social implications, we need to explore the psychology of motive attributions to understand why trust encourages voluntary deference—that is, to better understand the nature of trust in group authorities.

Trust as Predictability

One orientation toward trust suggests that trust is an expectation or estimate of the future behavior of others. For example, Oliver Williamson (1993) describes trust as "calculativeness" regarding the probable future actions of others, while Morris Zelditch and Henry Walker (1984) refer to trust in terms of "validity," a judgment about the probable future behavior of others. Social dilemma researchers describe trust as an expectation about the future reciprocity of others (Dawes 1980). All of these conceptions of trust link it to estimates of the future behavior of others—typically whether others will reciprocate any cooperative behaviors that a person might undertake. If people believe that others will reciprocate their own cooperative behaviors, then they are more willing to engage in cooperative exchanges with those others. Each of these models links the willingness to cooperate to the expected gains and losses of such cooperative behavior, outcomes that depend on what others do in response to cooperation.

The conception of trust as predictability is rooted in a particular conception of what people want from other people. That model is described by the social exchange model. It suggests that people want resources from others and engage in organized life in order to exchange resources. Further, within interactions, people are motivated by the desire to maximize their gain of resources and minimize their losses. Hence, people focus on the probable behavior of others so that they can behave strategically, maximizing their attainment of desired resources and minimizing personal costs. To do so, they need to have an estimate of what others will do in response to their own behavior.

Although there is widespread support for the importance of expectations about the behavior of others in shaping cooperative behavior, there are also signs that this explanation is not a complete model of the psychology of trust. For example, Peter Brann and Margaret Foddy (1988) examine the cooperative behavior of people within a social dilemma setting. They find that those high in trust in others, as measured by Julian Rotter's (1966) Interpersonal Trust Scale—which measures general trust in others with whom one has had no personal experience—feel a moral obligation to cooperate and do so irrespective of what others in their group are doing or are expected to do. If others are overusing resources, and are expected to do so in the future, the "rational" behavior is to overuse resources oneself. However, those high in trust in others continue to underutilize resources, irrespective of their judgments about the behavior of others. They do so because they feel an obligation to the group. Such feelings of obligation reflect a social orientation toward the group that is distinct from calculations about anticipated personal gain or loss owing to the actions of others (Tyler and Dawes 1993). There is something involved in such behavior other than a simple response to the expected behavior of others with whom one is dealing.

Similarly, Robyn Dawes, Alphons van de Kragt, and John Orbell (1990, 199) review the literature on free-rider problems and find that identification with the group to which one belongs decreases one's propensity to engage in noncooperative behavior that removes resources from a common pool of resources. Interestingly, this effect is found "in the absence of any expectation of future reciprocity, current rewards or punishments, or even reputational consequences." Again, people feel an obligation to the group that develops out of identification with the group and group values. That identification shapes their behavior, leading to cooperation that is distinct from that based on expectations about the behavior of others.

Deference and Social Trust

I would argue for a broader conception of the psychology of deference that includes attention to social orientations and, in particular, to the social aspects of trust. I refer to trust that is social in character as *social trust*. My goal is to explore social aspects of trust in the context of authority relations.

What makes trust social from my perspective is that it develops from the social bonds or social identification within a group, organization, or society. Social connections of these types lead people to trust that others will be motivated to act toward them in ways that are benevolent and caring. If, for example, an authority is the authority for my own group, I believe that that authority cares about my welfare and will do what is right for me and for others in my group. I do not need to have a clear expectation about what that person will do, and I may not be in a position to form such an expectation, but I do believe that, whatever the authority does, it will be something that facilitates my well-being.

My suggestion is that deference becomes more social and less strongly linked to expectations about what others will do when people are involved in ongoing social relationships of the type that exist within groups. Why does deference become more social in the context of ongoing relationships? Because an important aspect of people's interaction with others involves the creation of social identity. The work of social identity theorists and researchers has made it increasingly clear that people use others as a source of self-relevant information (Tajfel 1978; Tajfel and Turner 1986; Turner et al. 1987). In other words, people both define themselves through their association with groups and organizations and use their membership in groups to judge their social status, and through it their self-worth (Smith and Tyler 1997; Tyler, Degoey, and Smith 1996). In the context of groups with which people have social connections, people's trust judgments become more strongly linked to identity concerns, and less strongly linked to resource exchange.

A core aspect of the social identity approach to the relationship between people and groups is the suggestion that identity concerns are distinct from concerns over resource exchange. Within social identity research this distinctiveness is demonstrated in studies using the minimal group paradigm (Hogg and Abrams 1988). Within that paradigm people are divided into groups on an arbitrary basis that has no relationship to the exchange of resources—for example, according to their preference for various forms of art. Once so divided, people exhibit ingroup favoritism and outgroup derogation. These actions are motivated by concerns with identity enhancement. Hence, the findings of mere categorization research suggest that identity concerns are a second important motive that influences the thoughts, feelings, and actions of group members, even when resources are not being exchanged. The present analysis extends this argument from intergroup relations to the study of authority dynamics within groups—that is, to intragroup dynamics.

Although psychological theories have traditionally focused on the relationship of group members to group authorities as an issue of resource exchange (consider vertical dyad linkage theory, for example, see Chemers 1983, 1987; Dansereau, Graen, and Haga 1975; Vecchio and Gobdel 1984), I would suggest that this relationship is also about the definition and validation of social identity—the issue addressed by social identity theory. Such identity concerns are distinct from issues of resource exchange and may emerge as more important under some circumstances.

When people deal with others, especially authorities, their experience with those others communicates information that is used to infer the motives or intentions of those authorities. These motives and intentions communicate information about a person's social status. Hence, respectful treatment by authorities communicates to people that they are valued members of groups, while disrespect conveys lack of status.

One key aspect of high-quality treatment is that it leads to the inference that the motives of social authorities are benevolent, caring, and, hence, worthy of trust. When authorities treat a person with dignity and respect, they are saying that they, as authorities, affirm that person's position and are concerned about his or her well-being. In other words, people evaluate their position within groups by considering their treatment by authorities, using it to infer the probable motives of group authorities.

Identity issues influence group viability because people respond to the group through a social identity that is shaped by this information. Those who feel respected and valued by the group respond by following group rules and acting on behalf of the group, that is, by deferring to authorities (Smith and Tyler 1997). Hence, people who receive treatment that communicates high status respond to such information by deferring to group authorities and group rules (Smith and Tyler 1997; Tyler, Degoey, and Smith 1996).

Such information about social identity is communicated by several aspects of the quality of the treatment received from authorities. First, it is typically linked to people's assessments of the fairness of decision-making procedures—the procedural justice effect (see Lind and Tyler 1988; Tyler and Lind 1992). One important reason that organizations develop and maintain institutions that enact "the rule of law" is that people who regard the decisionmaking procedures of their organization as fair identify more strongly with their organization and are more willing to defer to its rules.

Second, the quality of the treatment received from others is linked to evaluations of several aspects of procedures that are strongly associated with judgments of their fairness. I have collectively labeled assessments of these aspects of procedures "relational judgments" (Tyler and Lind 1992). Two of these judgments involve evaluations of the quality of interpersonal treatment. The first is an assessment of the degree to which one is treated with politeness and dignity, treatment that affirms one's favorable status within the community. The second is an evaluation of the neutrality of the actions of authorities—their honesty, lack of bias, evenhandedness, and use of objective and factual criteria in decisionmaking. This assessment also communicates that one has favorable status by showing that group decisions are reasonably made, and do not favor others. I will refer to these two judgements as reflecting "quality of treatment."

These two judgments about the actions of authorities, as well as other aspects of their behavior, influence the third relational judgment: the assessment of the motives of authorities, or "social trust." People are strongly influenced by whether they judge the actions of the authorities

Figure 9.1   The Influence of Relational Judgments

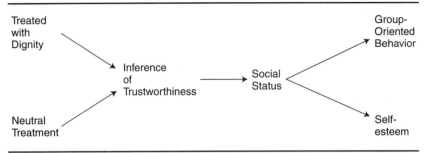

Source: Author's compilation.

to be the result of a motivation to be benevolent and caring. Together these three relational judgments communicate to individuals information about their standing within the group, as understood by the authorities who represent the group. This argument is shown in figure 9.1.

The importance of motive inferences about authorities that are based on their behavior toward group members can be illustrated by considering two seemingly paradoxical research findings. First is the finding that biased or unfair actions by authorities sometimes have little or no negative effect on their evaluations by citizens (Tyler 1990). This occurs when citizens infer that the motives of the authority are benevolent even if their overt actions are sexist, racist, or in other ways biased.

Conversely, authorities can create formal frameworks designed to treat people fairly, such as formal grievance procedures, but those frameworks can fail to have positive consequences if people do not infer that they are benevolently motivated. For example, companies benefit from having employee grievance procedures only if employees infer that management is actually interested in considering the opinions expressed in such procedures. If employees do not feel that managers are truly interested in the views they articulate, the company does not gain by having formal procedures that allow the expression of opinions.

In both cases, it is the inference that people make about the motivation for actions they have experienced when dealing with group authorities that shapes their responses to those authorities and to the organization they represent. Hence, the key issue is the degree to which people infer that authorities are concerned, caring, and hence trustworthy. This trustworthiness is social in character in the sense that people are not focused only on whether they can predict what the authorities will do. Because they lack information or expertise, they may be unable to make an inference about the authorities' probable future behavior. Instead, they trust that whatever that behavior is, it will be behavior that takes their welfare into account.

Evidence for Social Trust

What type of evidence would support the argument that authority relations are, at least in part, motivated by social motivations and identity concerns? In this discussion I describe several types of evidence that support this argument. All develop from studies about experiences with social authorities.

The first evidence in favor of a "social" element to trust develops from findings about when people care about the quality of their treatment by authorities (that is, dignity, neutrality). According to a social conception of trust, people should care about how they are treated by authorities when that treatment has an influence on their identity. So, for example, if a person draws his or her identity from membership in a group, then the way the individual is treated by an authority from that group has an impact on his or her identity. Under that circumstance, the individual should care about how he or she is being treated.

When talking about the influence of the quality of the treatment people receive, past studies have meant the degree to which people react to their experiences by evaluating whether they have received procedural justice and/or treatment consistent with relational criteria of justice. As noted, these criteria are neutrality, treatment with dignity and respect, and, most important, treatment leading people to infer that the motives of the authorities with whom they are dealing are trustworthy.

Although procedural justice and relational criteria can be distinguished conceptually, when we look at the results of studies in which people are evaluating their experiences, the two judgments are found to be highly intercorrelated. Judgments of the degree to which treatment is fair in "relational" terms typically explain around 70 to 80 percent of the variance in procedural justice judgments. Because the two ideas are so highly related, in this discussion I combine them and compare the importance placed on procedural or relational judgments ("quality of treatment") to the importance of instrumental issues, such as outcome favorability or control over the outcome.

As predicted by an identity-based model, people care more about the quality of their treatment by authorities when they have a personal relationship with those authorities or share their values. Further, people care more about how they are treated by authorities when those authorities are members of their own group. Finally, they care more about the quality of their treatment by authorities when they identify more strongly with the group the authority represents.

In each case people care more about the quality of their treatment by authorities, including having more concern about their trustworthiness, when the authorities' behavior toward them is more relevant to their social identity. In these situations in which quality of treatment matters, people have social bonds or identity connections with the authority, or the group that authority represents, and use treatment by the authority to define themselves and assess their self-worth.

There is also direct evidence that the quality of the treatment that people receive from authorities influences their sense of self in terms of their self-esteem. An individual's inference that an authority with whom she is dealing is not benevolent and caring toward her has a negative impact on her self-esteem.

Finally, there is evidence that the impact of the quality of the treatment that people receive from social authorities is mediated by changes in people's assessment of their social status. Two aspects of status are important. The first is pride, an assessment of the status of the group(s) to which a person belongs. The second is respect, an assessment of a person's status within the group. Both status judgments are affected by inferences about the trustworthiness of social authorities. Those who feel that they cannot trust the authorities feel that the group those authorities represent has lower status, and that they have lower status within the groups those authorities represent.

These findings suggest that, as hypothesized (see figure 9.1), lack of trust in the motives of societal authorities damages inferences about the status of the group and damages a person's belief that his own status in the group is high. We consider each of these arguments in more detail.

Personal Relationships and the Importance of Trust

One finding that supports an identity perspective is that people are more concerned about the trustworthiness of authorities when they have an ongoing personal relationship with them. Since people draw more of their sense of self and social identity from a group if they have a personal connection to the group or to group authorities, this is consistent with an identity perspective.

Elsewhere (Tyler and Degoey 1996) we have illustrated the importance of social connections by demonstrating that inferences about the trustworthiness of a managerial authority more strongly influence the willingness to voluntarily accept the decisions of that authority when the authority is a friend or when the employee expects to have a long-term social relationship with the authority. In each case in which a social connection exists, trust shapes the willingness to accept decisions.

This finding suggests that trust-based deference is tied to the social connection between the individual who is voluntarily deferring and the authority to whom he or she is deferring. The existence of a social connection is important because people are more strongly influenced by the status-relevant information communicated to them by people with whom they share social connections. In other words, people feel that their treatment by those who are more strongly connected to them tells them more about themselves.

We (Tyler and Degoey 1996) further tested this argument by dividing a sample of employees into two groups according to whether they shared the organization's values and whether they said they got their identity from the organization for which they work. These findings suggest that trust is a more important antecedent of the willingness to accept the decisions of authorities when people share the organization's values and when employees get more of their identity from their work. In each case there is a significant relationship between trust and the willingness to accept decisions when there is a strong identity-relevant connection between the individual and the authority or organization, but not when that connection is weaker.

I extended this analysis (Tyler 1997b) by considering two studies that test interactions between value similarity and the impact of the quality of the treatment that people receive from authorities on their willingness to accept the decisions made by those authorities. Each study uses the context of employee interactions with supervisors. In both cases the findings suggest that people care more about the quality of their treatment by authorities if they feel that they share the organization's values. When people share the organization's values, how they are treated by authorities has a stronger influence on their willingness to defer to those authorities.

I have also considered (Tyler 1997b) four studies that explore the degree to which people indicate that they draw their self-identity from work, their family, or their local community. In an analysis that includes interaction terms to reflect variations in the importance of the quality of an individual's treatment, I found that people place significantly more weight on the quality of their treatment when making evaluations of the legitimacy of group authorities if they draw more of their social identity from the group. In the studies, legitimacy is a summary index reflecting the willingness to voluntarily defer to authorities, feelings of obligation to obey authorities, and favorable evaluations of those authorities. The views about the legitimacy of group authorities are more strongly influenced by the quality of their treatment by authorities among those people who define themselves largely by their membership in the group.

Of course, variations in the influence of judgments such as trustworthiness on people's reactions to their experiences with authorities can also reflect differences in resource dependence. If people expect to have a long-term relationship with a group or with the group's authority, they may also be more concerned about the resources they might gain or lose through their long-term relationship with the authority. Hence, it is also important to examine the effect of resource dependence on the influence of trust. If the identity model is correct, variations in resource dependence should not influence the role of trustworthiness in shaping people's reactions to their experiences with authorities.

We have also examined the possible moderating role of resource dependence in shaping the importance of judgments about the quality of one's treatment in shaping deference to authorities (Tyler and Degoey 1996) by exploring the influence of the quality of one's treatment on the willingness to accept decisions among employees who vary in their dependence on their job. A resource-based model predicts that people who are more dependent on their jobs for resources should be more willing to defer based on the quality of their treatment. These findings suggest that quality-of-treatment judgments play an equal role in facilitating deference among those high and low in dependence. Hence, as the identity model predicts, people's dependence on resources does not affect the degree to which they care how they are treated by group authorities.

I extended this dependence analysis (Tyler 1997b) using two samples of employees, each of whom was asked about a recent personal experience with his or her work supervisor. I examined the possible moderating role of six indices of dependence in employees' evaluations of their supervisor. Using each index of dependence, I tested for possible interactions between degree of dependence on one's job and the importance of judgments about the quality of one's treatment in shaping views about the legitimacy of authorities. In this study legitimacy is an overall index that includes the willingness to defer to decisions, feelings of obligation to obey rules, and favorable evaluations of authorities. The results suggest that the role of judgments about the quality of one's treatment in shaping legitimacy does not vary as a consequence of changes in one's dependence on the job.

Group Boundaries

This logic suggests that people should be more strongly affected by the quality of their treatment by others, especially by authorities, when that treatment carries identity-relevant information. The data support the argument that people are more influenced by quality of treatment when they have a social connection with a group or authority.

This idea can also be tested by examining interactions with others that occur within one's own group and across group boundaries. If we extend the argument that has already been outlined to the issue of the influence of group boundaries, our prediction is that people should be more affected by the quality of their treatment by ingroup members or ingroup authorities, since such treatment communicates a message about their status in the group. In contrast, treatment by outsiders does not communicate as much information about one's status within one's group, so it has fewer identity-relevant implications.

My colleagues and I (Tyler, Lind, Ohbuchi, Sugawara, and Huo 1998) tested this idea in two studies. In the first, they considered the willingness of employees in a multicultural workforce to voluntarily accept decisions made by their supervisors. They contrasted two situations. In one, the employee and supervisor shared an ethnic group membership; in the other, they did not. The results of a statistical analysis that included terms to reflect the interaction between group status and the importance placed on judgments about the quality of one's treatment suggest that group status interacted with the importance of judgments about quality of treatment. A separate analysis of within- and between-group conflicts suggests that employees are significantly more strongly affected by the quality of their treatment when their supervisor is an ingroup member.

In a second study, we compared Japanese and Western teachers living in Japan. Each subject describes a dispute within their own national group, and then one with someone from the other national group. Our concern was with the role of judgments about the quality of one's treatment in shaping the willingness to voluntarily defer to decisions reached by a third party about how to resolve the dispute. When the dispute occurs within a single national group, judgments about the quality of one's treatment have a significant influence on willingness to voluntarily accept decisions. When it occurs across groups, judgments about quality of treatment do not influence the willingness to voluntarily accept decisions.

Hence, as in the prior study, concerns about quality of treatment are more important when a dispute occurs within the group. Why? Because within-group members are important to one's sense of identity and self. If the group is not important to one's sense of self, then the relational implications of treatment by the authority should be of less importance. People are less concerned about the trustworthiness of an outsider, or about how that outsider acts toward them.

Similar effects can also be obtained experimentally by manipulating group membership. Smith, Tyler, Huo, Ortiz and Lind (1998) independently manipulated outcome favorability, quality of treatment, and the group affiliation of the authority in a performance task. In the study, a graduate student is responsible for grading a social skills test. That graduate student is presented as either an ingroup member (from the student's university) or an outgroup member (from a rival university). Later the graduate student enters the room and treats the student fairly or unfairly by either carefully or superficially grading the student's work. Independently, the student receives either a favorable outcome (97 percent correct) or an unfavorable outcome (43 percent correct). In the favorable-outcome condition, the high score earns the student a prize, while in the unfavorable-outcome condition the low score is not sufficient to earn a prize.

When the graduate student test grader is an ingroup authority, treatment significantly influences judgments of fairness, while outcome favorability does not influence judgments of fairness. When the authority is an ingroup member, there is a large and significant effect of treatment on overall ratings of fairness. When the authority is an outgroup member, the effect is less; indeed, it is insignificant. On the other hand, when the graduate student test grader is an outgroup authority, outcome favorability significantly influences judgments of overall fairness. When the grader is an ingroup authority, outcome favorability has no significant influence.

In addition to rating fairness, students in the study are asked to volunteer for additional experimental time to help the graduate student. When the test grader is an ingroup member, the willingness to help further is significantly related to fairness of treatment, but not to outcome favorability. If the test grader is an outgroup member, the willingness to help further is significantly related to outcome favorability, but not to the fairness of treatment.

Identification and the Impact of Treatment

If, as I am suggesting, people care more about the quality of the treatment they receive from ingroup authorities because the trustworthiness of ingroup authorities communicates more information about their status and identity, then it would be predicted that the degree to which people identify with a group should also influence the degree to which they care about how they are treated by group authorities. In fact, identification should be a more sensitive measure than group membership, since it reflects the degree to which particular individuals feel attached to groups, not simply whether they are in them. Those who identify more strongly with a group should be expected to be more affected by the quality of their treatment by group authorities.

This argument can be tested using a sample of workers who are asked to voluntarily accept the decisions made by organizational authorities. This is a study of employees at a public-sector institution in California. (The sample is described in Huo, Smith, Tyler, and Lind 1996.) Employees are asked about their trust in the motives of their supervisor and their willingness to voluntarily accept a recent decision by their supervisor. They are also asked about their overall identification with their work organization. An analysis indicates that trust in the motives of the decisionmaking authority generally has an important role in deference. However, the importance of trust interacts with identification with the work organization. That interaction indicates that employees place more weight on trust when they identify more strongly with the organization the supervisor represents.

We have also explored the importance of identification in a regulatory context (Tyler and Degoey 1995) by testing the influence of identification on the importance that citizens attach to the quality of their treatment by a local regulatory authority responsible for allocating water during times of shortage—the water board. Our study was conducted during a water shortage when the water board was making rules to govern water use by community residents. We explored the basis on which people accepted or rejected the rules established by that board. Such rules could be accepted because they were favorable, or because the authorities arrived at them using procedures that conveyed trust and respect.

An overall interaction analysis indicates that people place more weight on quality-of-treatment judgments when they identify more strongly with their community (for details of this analysis, see Tyler 1997b). As predicted by the identity argument, people care more about how they are treated when they identify with the community the authority represents.

We conducted a similar analysis on whites in northern California (Smith and Tyler 1996). We examined the basis on which whites decide whether to endorse congressional policies that redistribute resources to minorities. One basis for supporting or opposing such policies is whether they provide favorable or unfavorable outcomes to advantaged whites. If policies are judged in this manner, the advantaged would generally oppose the redistribution of resources to the disadvantaged. Judging the motives of Congress provides another basis for supporting or opposing such policies. For example, is Congress trying to be fair to all Americans and to consider the views of all groups? In other words, is Congress trustworthy? In this analysis such inferences about trust are linked to the quality of the treatment accorded citizens (respect for rights) and to the neutrality of congressional decisionmaking in forming a general relational factor. The analysis compares the influence of such relational judgments to that of judgments about the favorability of the policies.

The identity argument is that those whites who identify more strongly with being American will evaluate congressional policies in more strongly relational terms. In other words, those who identify with a superordinate group that includes both whites and minorities will react to policies influencing others within that larger group by considering quality-of-treatment issues, not the impact of policies on themselves or their own subgroup.

An interaction analysis supports this suggestion (see Smith and Tyler 1996, 183). Those whites who identify more strongly with being American evaluate redistributive policies significantly more strongly in quality-of-treatment terms. They also place significantly less weight on whether the policies help or hurt them or their ethnic group. Those who identify more with being American care more about the quality-of-treatment aspects of congressional decisionmaking when deciding whether to endorse congressional policies. The identity argument is that, to those who identify with being American, their status in the eyes of group authorities is more central to their sense of self, so they focus more strongly on how they are treated by authorities.

Impact of Treatment on Self-Esteem

Another type of evidence for an identity-based perspective is the link between the quality of the treatment people receive from authorities and their judgments of self-worth and self-esteem. In examining the influence of quality-of-treatment judgments about experiences with authorities in the family, university, and political arenas on people's self-esteem, my colleagues and I (Tyler, Degoey, and Smith 1996) found that in all three settings the quality of people's treatment by group authorities influences their self-esteem. This suggests that people are using the quality of their treatment by authorities to shape their sense of social identity and to evaluate their self-worth.

The impact of quality of treatment by group authorities on self-esteem is also examined in the previously outlined experiment conducted by Smith, Tyler, Huo, Ortiz, and Lind (1998). In that experiment the experimenter is presented as either within or outside of the subject's group. When the authority is an ingroup member, the quality of the treatment received from that person influences judgments of fairness, as already noted, and also directly and indirectly influences self-esteem. On the other hand, when the authority is an outgroup member, treatment has no significant influence on either judgments of fairness or self-esteem. By contrast, outcome favorability influences judgments of fairness when the authority is an outgroup member, as has been noted, but not when the authority is an ingroup member. Quality of treatment matters most strongly when the authority is a member of the subject's group. We are primarily affected by the way we are treated by others within our own group, not by our treatment by outsiders.

Direct Mediation by Identity Judgments

The argument underlying the operation of the relational model is that the way people are treated by authorities changes their behaviors toward the group and their feelings about themselves because it changes their sense of their social status vis-à-vis the group. In other words, group status mediates the impact of the quality of the treatment that people receive from authorities. Two aspects of social status are important: judgments about the status of the organization (pride), and judgments about status within that organization (respect). Each is shaped by people's treatment by authorities.

The mediation argument can be directly tested by an analysis of the mediating role that status judgments play in shaping the impact of quality of treatment on behavior toward the group and feelings about the self. My colleagues and I (Tyler, Degoey, and Smith 1996) did so using four different samples. We subjected each to a two-step procedure. We first examined the impact of quality-of-treatment judgments on the dependent variable. We then entered status judgments into the equation and examined the decline in the strength of the relationship between quality of treatment and status. In this analysis two status judgments—pride and respect—were entered into the equation. If the relationship between quality-of-treatment judgments and compliance with group rules is completely mediated by pride and respect, the initially significant relationship should become insignificant. If the relationship is partially mediated by pride and respect, the initial relationship should diminish in magnitude but remain significant. If the relationship keeps its original strength, that suggests a lack of mediation.

Using compliance with rules as an example, the initial stage-one analysis shows that quality-of-treatment judgments influence compliance with group rules in three of four cases. Of those three cases, the family sample shows complete mediation by pride and respect, the government sample shows partial mediation, and the work sample shows no mediation. Overall, across all the dependent variables, there is substantial evidence across compliance with rules, extra-role behavior, and self-esteem that the impact of quality of treatment on group-related behavior and self-esteem is mediated by status judgments about pride and respect. Such judgments completely mediate impact in four cases and partially mediate impact in three cases. Only one case shows no evidence of mediation.

These findings suggest that the quality of the treatment received from group authorities influences people because it shapes their sense of their social status. That sense of social status, in turn, shapes both their behavior toward the group and their sense of themselves. Hence, as argued by the identity-based model of social trust, people are concerned about issues of trustworthiness, treatment with respect, and neutrality because believing that authorities are neutral, respectful, benevolent, and caring communicates information about favorable social status. People respond to such information by feeling good about themselves and by acting on behalf of the groups to which they belong.

Summary

I am arguing for a more complex view of the link between trust and deference than is suggested by models of trust that link trust to the predictability of other people's actions. This more complex view includes attention to what I have labeled social trust. The findings outlined provide considerable support for the argument that thinking of trust as simply predictive in character is an inadequate model to account for the findings emerging from trust research.

It is widely acknowledged and demonstrated in research that one important aspect of trust is predicting the behavior of others. To some extent people are concerned about what others will do, and their actions are shaped by their expectations about the probable future behavior of others. The findings outlined in this analysis support this argument by finding influences of this form of trust.

The research outlined here also suggests that there is a second aspect of trust that is more social in character. This aspect of trust develops out of a second motivation that people have for interacting with others: to gain information with which to evaluate their status within groups and, through such evaluations, establish their self-esteem and self-worth.

When people interact with others, how they are treated communicates status-relevant information. This information is communicated through the behavior of authorities and institutions. That behavior produces both a procedural justice effect and an influence of relational judgments about the quality of one's treatment. Of particular importance are the relational elements of procedure: respect from others, neutrality, and evidence of trustworthiness ("quality of treatment").

The motive inferences about trustworthiness that are the focus of this discussion are central relational judgments and summarize the information people gain through observing the neutrality of authorities and whether those authorities treat people with dignity and respect. The dynamic relationship between the elements of quality of treatment is beyond the scope of this discussion (see Tyler and Huo 2000). However, since trustworthiness is a key relational issue, it is not surprising that trustworthiness is consistently found to be central to people's evaluations of social authorities.

If people feel that the authorities with whom they deal are benevolent and caring, they are more likely to feel that they are members of a high-status group (pride) and that they are high-status members of that group (respect). These feelings lead to both a positive social identity and a willingness to defer to group authorities and group rules.

Why Interact with Others?

The importance of resource exchange is well known. This aspect of the connection between people and groups is central to both social exchange theory (Thibaut and Kelley 1959) and realistic group conflict theory (Sherif 1966). These models, by suggesting that people are motivated by the desire to gain resources in exchanges with others, lead to a calculative form of trust, in which people base their behavior on the expected actions of others. They do so with the goal of maximizing their own benefits in exchanges of resources. These concerns involve trust that is based on expectations about the future behavior of others.

Social identity theory suggests that people have a second motivation for interacting with others. People also use the information they gain from others to define their social identity, an important component of their sense of self. Social identity is defined through knowledge of social group boundaries, which place individuals within particular groups. People are also affected by their knowledge of their position within groups.

The findings outlined here support the argument that there is a second form of trust—social trust—that involves more than predictions about the behavior of others. Such social trust is linked to the role of groups in providing people with information about their social identities. It is especially important in situations in which people value identity-relevant information, for example, when they are dealing with others within their group, or with people from groups with which they identify. Under such conditions people regard behavior by others as communicating information about their social status.

To fully understand trust, it is important to recognize that both calculative, predictive trust and social trust are important contributors to any explanation of people's attitudes and behaviors within social groups. Neither form of trust considered alone provides an adequate understanding of the dynamics of trust within individuals. Social trust is likely to be especially important in the context of ongoing groups, in which people have long-term relationships with others (Lewicki and Bunker 1996; Sheppard and Tuchinsky 1996), and in situations in which people strongly identify with groups (Kramer, Brewer, and Hanna 1996).

Institutional Implications

The form of trust found in any given setting has consequences for the relationship between individuals and groups. Social trust is linked to social relationships and rises and falls with those relationships. This has the favorable consequence of freeing authorities from having to gain the cooperation of group members and maintain loyalty by imposing the incentive or sanctioning system of promising them rewards or threatening them with punishments. As already mentioned, such systems of exercising authority are cumbersome and ineffective (see Tyler 1997a), so authorities gain when social trust prevails.

The potential value of social trust suggests that it is important to encourage people to invest themselves in groups, group institutions, and group authorities—and to identify with groups, organizations, or societies. To the extent that people's identities are intertwined with the group, a form of "social capital" is created and facilitates the functioning of the social group. How can such identification be created? Further research is needed on both socialization into groups and organizations and the importance of public rituals in maintaining identification.

It is also important to explore the scope of the groups and organizations with which identification occurs. Social psychologists argue that identification with small groups is natural and more easily maintained because those involved have everyday personal interaction. For example, in a small business people have everyday interaction with their work supervisors. Identification with larger groups, such as nations, is more difficult to establish and maintain. In larger groups people have no personal connection to group authorities, and identification must be maintained through commitment to abstract symbols and institutions with which people may have few contacts. This level of identification requires considerable societal effort to develop and maintain.

Interestingly, in the aftermath of the cold war there is less reason to identify with the larger nation-state, and consequently there is an increasing focus on local government. For the reasons outlined here, such local levels of identification may be easier to sustain. Pushed to an extreme, the decline in the nation-state may lead to "tribalism"— people becoming loyal to particular leaders and groups rather than to the more abstract nation-state. In other words, the scope of social trust may decrease.

It is also possible that the basis of social trust will change. This discussion of social trust has linked it to procedures and authorities and to the institutions of society. However, in other situations it may be the charisma of particular leaders that is important, rather than institutional arrangements. Two questions that clearly need further study are the scope of social trust and the basis for social trust.

It is also important to acknowledge that social trust is not without its problems. Relationships based on social trust may be more vulnerable to disruption when trust is broken. In ongoing social relationships people react especially strongly and emotionally to evidence of "betrayal" (Bies and Tripp 1996). Hence, social trust may be more vulnerable than calculative trust. For example, when people who have a high level of trust for organizational authorities feel that those authorities have not lived up to that trust, their commitment to the organization declines more than that of any other group (Brockner, Tyler, and Schneider 1992). Hence, feelings of betrayal can have very serious organizational costs.

In this respect calculative trust is a more stable basis for interaction with others. Although we may miscalculate the likelihood of cooperation from others, the failure of others to cooperate does not carry the emotional intensity of the feelings of betrayal associated with the violation of social trust. This does not mean that people are indifferent to violations of expectations. They are not. But there is clearly an emotional quality to the "injustice" of being betrayed by a friend that is linked to the existence of a social relationship and social trust and is not calculative in nature.

References

Bies, Robert, and Thomas Tripp. 1996. "Beyond Distrust: 'Getting Even' and the Need for Revenge." In *Trust in Organizations,* edited by Roderick Kramer and Tom R. Tyler. Thousand Oaks, Calif.: Sage Publications.

Braithwaite, Valerie, and Margaret Levi. 1998. *Trust and Governance.* New York: Russell Sage Foundation.

Brann, Peter, and Margaret Foddy. 1988. "Trust and the Consumption of a Deteriorating Common Resource." *Journal of Conflict Resolution* 31(4): 615–30.

Brockner, Joel, Tom R. Tyler, and Rochelle Schneider. 1992. "The Higher They Are, the Harder They Fall: The Effects of Prior Commitment and Procedural Injustice on Subsequent Commitment to Social Institutions." *Administrative Science Quarterly* 37(2): 241–61.

Chemers, Martin M. 1983. "Leadership Theory and Research: A Systems-Process Integration." In *Basic Group Processes,* edited by Paul B. Paulus. New York: Springer-Verlag.

———. 1987. "Leadership Processes: Intrapersonal, Interpersonal, and Societal Influences." In *Review of Personality and Social Psychology*, edited by Clyde Hendrick, vol. 8. Newbury Park, Calif.: Sage Publications.

Dansereau, Fred, George Graen, and William J. Haga. 1975. "A Vertical Dyad Linkage Approach to Leadership Within Formal Organizations: A Longitudinal Investigation of the Role-Making Process." *Organizational Behavior* 13(1): 46–78.

Dawes, Robyn. 1980. "Social Dilemmas." *Annual Review of Psychology* 31(1): 169–93.

Dawes, Robyn, Alphons J. C. van de Kragt, and John M. Orbell. 1990. "Cooperation for the Benefit of Us—Not Me or My Conscience." In *Beyond Self-interest,* edited by Jane Mansbridge. Chicago: University of Chicago Press.

Hogg, Michael A., and Dominic Abrams. 1988. *Social Identifications.* New York: Routledge.

Huo, Yuen J., Heather J. Smith, Tom R. Tyler, and E. Allan Lind. 1996. "Superordinate Identification, Subgroup Identification, and Justice Concerns: Is Separatism the Problem, Is Assimilation the Answer?" *Psychological Science* 7(1): 40–45.

Kramer, Roderick M., Marilynn B. Brewer, and B. A. Hanna. 1996. "Collective Trust and Collective Action: The Decision to Trust as a Social Decision." In *Trust in Organizations,* edited by Roderick Kramer and Tom R. Tyler. Thousand Oaks, Calif.: Sage Publications.

Lewicki, Roy J., and Barbara B. Bunker. 1996. "Developing and Maintaining Trust in Work Relationships." In *Trust in Organizations,* edited by Roderick Kramer and Tom R. Tyler. Thousand Oaks, Calif.: Sage Publications.

Lind, E. Allan, and Tom R. Tyler. 1988. *The Social Psychology of Procedural Justice.* New York: Plenum.

Rotter, Julian. 1966. "Generalized Expectancies for Internal Versus External Control of Reinforcement." *Psychological Monographs* 80(1).

Sheppard, Blair H., and Marla Tuchinsky. 1996. "Micro-OB and the Network Organization." In *Trust in Organizations,* edited by Roderick Kramer and Tom R. Tyler. Thousand Oaks, Calif.: Sage Publications.

Sherif, Muzafer. 1966. *Common Predicament: Social Psychology of Intergroup Conflict and Cooperation.* Boston: Houghton Mifflin.

Smith, Heather J., and Tom R. Tyler. 1996. "Justice and Power." *European Journal of Social Psychology* 26: 171–200.

———. 1997. "Choosing the Right Pond: The Influence of the Status of One's Group and One's Status in That Group on Self-esteem and Group-Oriented Behavior." *Journal of Experimental Social Psychology* 33(2): 146–70.

Smith, Heather J., Tom R. Tyler, Yuen J. Huo, Dan J. Ortiz, and E. Allan Lind. 1998. "The Self-Relevant Implications of the Group-Value Model: Group Membership, Self-Worth, and Procedural Justice. *Journal of Experimental Social Psychology* 34(5): 470–93.

Tajfel, Henri. 1978. *Differentiation Between Social Groups: Studies in the Social Psychology of Intergroup Relations.* London: Academic Press.

Tajfel, Henri, and John C. Turner. 1986. "The Social Identity Theory of Intergroup Behavior." In *Psychology of Intergroup Relations,* edited by Stephen Worchel and William G. Austin. Chicago: Nelson-Hall.

Thibaut, John, and Harold Kelly. 1959. *The Social Psychology of Groups.* New York: Wiley.

Turner, John C., Michael A. Hogg, Penelope J. Oakes, Stephen Reicher, and Margaret S. Wetherell. 1987. *Rediscovering the Social Group: A Self-Categorization Theory.* Oxford: Blackwell.

Tyler, Tom R. 1990. *Why People Obey the Law.* New Haven, Conn.: Yale University Press.

———. 1997a. "Procedural Fairness and Compliance with the Law." *Swiss Journal of Economics and Statistics* 133: 219–40.

———. 1997b. "The Psychology of Legitimacy." *Personality and Social Psychology Review* 1(4): 323–44.

Tyler, Tom R., and Steven Blader. 2000. *Cooperation in Groups: Procedural Justice, Social Identity, and Behavioral Engagement.* Philadelphia: Psychology Press.

Tyler, Tom R., and Robyn Dawes. 1993. "Fairness in Groups: Comparing the Self-interest and Social Identity Perspectives." In *Psychological Perspectives on Justice,* edited by Barbara A. Mellers and Jonathan Baron. Cambridge: Cambridge University Press.

Tyler, Tom R., and Peter Degoey. 1995. "Collective Restraint in a Social Dilemma Situation." *Journal of Personality and Social Psychology* 69: 482–97.

———. 1996. "Trust in Organizational Authorities: The Influence of Motive Attributions on Willingness to Accept Decisions." In *Trust in Organizations,* edited by Roderick Kramer and Tom R. Tyler. Thousand Oaks, Calif.: Sage Publications.

Tyler, Tom R., Peter Degoey, and Heather J. Smith. 1996. "Understanding Why the Justice of Group Procedures Matters." *Journal of Personality and Social Psychology* 70(5): 913–30.

Tyler, Tom R., and Yuen J. Huo. 2000. "Trust and the Rule of Law: A Law-Abidingness Model of Social Regulation." Working paper. New York: Russell Sage Foundation.

Tyler, Tom R., and Roderick Kramer. 1996. *Trust in Organizations*. Thousand Oaks, Calif.: Sage Publications.

Tyler, Tom R., and E. Allan Lind. 1992. "A Relational Model of Authority in Groups." In *Advances in Experimental Social Psychology* (edited by Mark P. Zanna) 25: 115–91.

Tyler, Tom R., E. Allan Lind, Kenichi Ohbuchi, Ikuo Sugawara, and Yuen J. Huo. 1998. "Conflict with Outsiders: Disputing Within and Across Cultural Boundaries." *Personality and Social Psychology Bulletin* 24(2): 137–46.

Vecchio, Robert P., and Bruce C. Gobdel. 1984. "The Vertical Dyad Linkage Model of Leadership: Problems and Prospects." *Organizational Behavior* 34: 5–20.

Williamson, Oliver E. 1993. "Calculativeness, Trust, and Economic Organization." *Journal of Law and Economics* 36: 453–86.

Zelditch, Morris, Jr., and Henry A. Walker. 1984. "Legitimacy and the Stability of Authority." *Advances in Group Processes* 1: 1–25.

Chapter 10

Why Is Trust Necessary in Organizations? The Moral Hazard of Profit Maximization

GARY MILLER

> It is *not* necessarily true that maximum profits are earned by firms whose objective is profit-maximization.
>
> —Vickers (1985, 138)

W HY SHOULD trust be of concern to the managers or employees of an organization? Or why should trust be of interest to social scientists trying to understand behavior in the organization? In a business firm, for example, the purpose of the organization is to generate money that is then divided among various stakeholders subject to the terms of the various contracts; surely the motivations for participation are simply economic, and we need merely understand, in a manner customary to economists, the self-interested behaviors elicited by the incentive systems created by those contracts. If so, then "trust" is either an irrelevancy, or merely a shorthand term for a set of rational expectations on the part of some participants about others' future behavior.

Most of the literature on the economics of organization, indeed, does not use the term "trust." The emphasis, instead, is on the construction of contracts that shape the self-interested behavior of subordinates (agents) to the goals of their superiors (principals). Principals therefore need not trust their agents, because the appropriate incentive contract guides their own self-interest to serve the ends of the principals.

In the case of the business firm, the normal mode of analysis has been to presume that the purpose of the firm is to maximize value for its

307

shareholder owners, and that the incentives for managers and employees are designed with that goal in mind (Milgrom and Roberts 1992, 40). The "principal's problem" is to construct an incentive system that induces the agent to pursue the principal's interests at the same time the agent is pursuing his own self-interest. For most papers in principal-agency theory, the calculation of the "optimal contract"—the one that best solves the principal's problem—is the end of the analysis.

A perfect solution to the principal-agency problem eliminates the need for trust by the superior. The organization becomes a machine that can run by itself. And this is the lesson of principal-agency theory that has been applied over and over again. Barry Weingast (1984, 148–50), for example, uses this lesson to explain why regulatory agencies seem to be so independent of Congress. While public administrationists presume that the relative absence of congressional oversight and monitoring implies a free hand for "runaway bureaucracies," Weingast points out that an absence of overt monitoring could simply denote an effective solution to the principal-agency problem. "I draw on principal agent theory to suggest how the congressional system aligns bureaucratic interests with those of the oversight committees in Congress."

Nor is the employee's "trust" in the employer essential. The normal principal-agency problem exactly satisfies the individual's rationality constraint; that is, the agent expects to earn just enough to keep her from walking off the job for her next best activity, and no more. Once again, rational self-interest replaces trust: the employer would be foolish to offer the agent less than she could get elsewhere, and the agent would be foolish to expect more.

This chapter argues, however, that there is a good reason to take the concept of trust more seriously. There are inescapable reasons why individuals try to establish relationships in which each party looks to the other party to do more for each other than their own self-interest would dictate. Although this non-self-interested behavior may be rationalized by conceptualizing the relationship as a repeated game, the repeated game analysis begs the question of how a particular equilibrium (involving "trust") is realized instead of other perfectly feasible equilibria (that do not involve "trust"). Therefore, it is important to understand why superiors and subordinates are able to bridge their hierarchical differences as a result of mutual expectations of self-denying behavior.

Productivity and Incentives in Interactive Teams

> By introducing a third party to break the budget-balancing constraint, one also gives him the clear incentive to engage in morally hazardous behavior.
>
> —Eswaran and Kotwal (1984, 581)

The economic approach to organizations is best typified by Armen Alchian and Harold Demsetz's classic (1972) article. They observe that the reason for any group of people to come together is the fact that they can produce more as a team than they can working separately as individuals. In this analysis "team" production means that each individual's marginal productivity is itself a function of other people's efforts. That is, one individual can contribute more to the group's productivity when others are themselves working harder.

However, Alchian and Demsetz observe that this creates a classic N-person prisoners' dilemma problem. Effort is costly to the individual, while it is rewarding for the group as a whole. As with consumption externalities, the rational individual equates her individual marginal cost of effort with her individual return, thus ignoring the social return of that individual effort. Thus, everyone would be better off if everyone worked harder than they have any individual reason to work.

Alchian and Demsetz's solution to this is the imposition of hierarchical control on the team production process. Because the nonhierarchical team is so inefficient, the team members themselves may well agree to subordination to a monitor who watches individual effort levels and has the power to reward effort or punish non-effort. Under such a system everyone may have an incentive to work harder than they would work when they are given the opportunity to free-ride on each other, and the true benefits of team production are realized. Individual team members are paid enough to keep them on the job, and the residual profits may go to the monitor as a reward for her contribution to the improved productivity of the team. The horizontal team is replaced by a vertically differentiated firm.

Thus, for Alchian and Demsetz, an essential feature of the firm is that the owner (who accepts the residual profits after employees have been paid) must play an active role in the management of the firm. It is the ownership of the residual profits that serves as the motivation for effective monitoring of employees. Although some of the day-to-day responsibility for monitoring and oversight can be delegated to managers who are themselves paid agents, the owner must be at the top of the chain of accountability, writing contracts, monitoring outcomes, and sanctioning subordinates. The firm, then, is best organized hierarchically, and at the top of the hierarchy is the owner, actively using the hierarchy as a means of controlling actions throughout the firm.

Holmstrom and the Passive Owner

Bengt Holmstrom's (1982, 325) classic analysis of "Moral Hazard in Teams" begins by pointing out flaws in Alchian and Demsetz's explanation of hierarchical firms: "My first point will be that the principal's role is not essentially one of monitoring." Monitoring is, after all, potentially a very expensive operation. Developing a technology for reliably discovering which member of a large team is not pulling a rope with full effort, or which member of an advertising team is daydreaming rather than brainstorming, would be costly, if not impossible.

Holmstrom, like Alchian and Demsetz, assumes that teams generate revenues by the interdependent actions of a variety of employees. Interdependence makes it difficult to determine the actual contribution of any one team member. The individual effort levels are not observable, or at least not verifiable, and therefore cannot be contracted on. However, the overall revenue output is jointly observable and may be contracted on.

The immediate problem is how to divide the earnings generated by the team among the members of the team. Again, the team consists of everyone whose efforts contribute to the earnings; if the team is organized hierarchically as a firm, the actions of management help determine the revenue, and managers are considered team members. We would like to divide the team's revenues so that the sum of individual allocations exactly equals the amount to be divided, with no deficit and no unused surplus. Holmstrom calls this the *budget-balancing requirement*. For Alchian and Demsetz, the budget-balancing requirement is met because the owner accepts all of the revenue that is not distributed among the other team members.

In addition, we should recognize that the rules for dividing the revenue constitute an incentive scheme for the employees; an individual acts in equilibrium in such a way that her marginal cost of effort equals her marginal return under the incentive scheme. For example, if a worker receives exactly one-third of the revenue generated, then in equilibrium her marginal cost of effort equals one-third of her marginal productivity, given the effort levels of other team members. A *Nash equilibrium* is defined as an outcome in which every person has done the best for herself that she can, given the actions of all others. In an economic context, this means that each individual has equalized marginal cost and individual marginal return, given the actions of others. Given increasing marginal costs, if the individual's marginal cost is greater than her individual marginal return, she could cut back effort and, in doing so, decrease her costs more than her revenue. Similarly, if her marginal cost is less than her individual marginal return, then her next unit of effort would yield *more* return than cost. Only when her marginal cost equals her marginal return has she maximized her net benefit, given the actions of others.

Finally, we would like to have the ultimate outcome be *Pareto-optimal*. Pareto-optimality, of course, is a minimal definition of efficiency. It means that there is no other possible outcome, consisting of effort levels and distributions of revenue, that everyone would prefer to the one in question.

Holmstrom's result is simple and profound. It states simply that *there is no way to allocate the earnings of the team that is simultaneously budget-*

balancing, Pareto-optimal, and a Nash equilibrium. To put it another way, every budget-balancing incentive scheme must induce a Nash equilibrium that is Pareto-suboptimal.

This can be demonstrated by showing that the conditions of Nash equilibrium and Pareto-optimality are inconsistent as long as budget-balancing is required. Pareto-optimality requires that team members take actions for which the marginal cost is less than the marginal return to the team. For example, if an employee can generate an extra dollar of profit for the firm by taking an action that costs him only seventy-five cents, it is an efficient action. Pareto-optimality requires that marginal revenue equal marginal cost for each member of the team, and it would require the employee to provide additional units of effort until an extra dollar's worth of effort brings in an extra dollar of revenue for the firm.

Nash equilibrium, however, assumes that each team member equalizes marginal cost with marginal revenue *discounted* by the share of the marginal revenue that the team member receives herself. If an employee contemplates an action that will bring the team one dollar and cost himself only seventy-five cents, then he will not take the action if he is to receive less than 75 percent of that dollar. To induce each employee to work until an extra dollar's worth of effort brings in exactly one dollar of revenue for the firm, the firm must let *every* member of the team receive *all* of the last dollar that their interactive efforts produce. But this is mathematically impossible as long as budget-balancing is required.

Holmstrom's Group Penalty Solution: The Owner as Sponge

Thus, there inevitably is some incentive for shirking in a team as long as budget-balancing is required. This implies that self-interest in the team is at war with efficiency; budget-balancing makes every team production problem an N-person prisoners' dilemma game.

However, Holmstrom notes that the prisoners' dilemma can be escaped if budget-balancing is sacrificed. The revenues created by the team must *not* equal the revenues distributed among the productive team members. Someone with *no active role in the team's production efforts* must absorb residual costs and benefits.

As long as the incentives to the team members are not exactly equal to the benefits created by the team, then it is possible to imagine an incentive contract that creates a Pareto-optimal Nash equilibrium. The difference—the residual profits or losses after fulfilling the incentive contracts to the productive team members—must be metaphorically thrown away. As Holmstrom reports (1982, 325), schemes that eliminate shirking in teams "require penalties that waste output or bonuses that exceed output. In both cases the principal is needed, either to enforce the penalties or to finance the bonuses. Thus, the principal's primary role is to break the budget-balancing constraint."

As Holmstrom notes, this is what happens in a modern firm. A firm is *not* budget-balancing, in this use of the word, because the shareholders exist to absorb the residual profits after subtracting wages and incentives to productive members of the firm. For Holmstrom, the "thrown-away" residual goes to the shareholders.

Holmstrom provides an example of an incentive contract, called a group penalty contract, that satisfies the requirements of Pareto-optimality and Nash equilibrium while breaking the budget-balancing constraint. The efficient level of earnings for the team as a whole is observable; the group penalty contract states that every team member will receive a payoff equal to or greater than his opportunity costs as long as the efficient overall level of earnings is observed. If the efficient level of output is not achieved, then no one will be paid anything.

The noncooperative Nash equilibrium under this scheme is Pareto-optimal. Since the efficient level of earnings can be achieved only if every individual works at a given level of effort consistent with the outcome, then no team member has an incentive to be the first to shirk.

The group punishment scheme is not the only possible incentive scheme that will result in an efficient Nash equilibrium. In fact, there is a family of such schemes in which each active team member gets at least his opportunity cost and the sum of the payments is less than or equal to the revenue generated by the team. But in any of these schemes, if one or more team players shirk, then no team member is paid and the "owner" gets the entire surplus. Every possible such scheme has a passive owner whose job is to absorb any residual generated by the team. As Holmstrom correctly observes (1982, 328), "My point is therefore not that group punishments are the only effective scheme, but rather that budget breaking is the essential instrument in neutralizing externalities from joint production."

Holmstrom argues (1982, 328) that this problem illustrates deficiencies in partnerships:

> The reason capitalistic firms enjoy an advantage over partnerships in controlling incentives is that they can (and will) *independently of the level of internal monitoring* employ schemes that are infeasible in closed (budget-balancing) organizations. There is little to suggest that either of the two forms of organization would stand at a comparative advantage when it comes to monitoring alone.

In other words, the true advantage of the modern firm is that, by separating ownership from control, it violates the budget-balancing constraint. The owner can generate efficiency without wasting resources on monitoring, but simply by passively absorbing residual profits or losses—much like the traditional view of shareholders in a modern American corporation.

Holmstrom is emphatic that the advantage of separating ownership and control has nothing to do with active monitoring. Indeed, the case is stronger than that. It is not the case that the residual owners *need* not monitor the members of the firm, shareholders *cannot* engage in active monitoring—because any active role for the owners is inconsistent with their role as budget-breaker.

The Necessary Passivity of the Residual Owner

Holmstrom writes (1982, 328): "Note that it is important that the principal not provide any (unobservable) productive inputs." The reason for this is that the principal as residual-owner must have incentives that are contrary to efficiency; any actions on behalf of the shareholders' interests must therefore be suspect.

In fact, the owner cannot even be allowed to *choose* incentive schemes because, given a choice, she will subvert Holmstrom's efficient group penalty incentive scheme in favor of another that generates more earnings but inefficient outcomes. This is revealed in a brilliant commentary on Holmstrom by Mukesh Eswaran and Ashok Kotwal (1984).

Remember that in the group penalty plan proposed by Holmstrom the owner can expect to get nothing, because in equilibrium team members do not shirk and everyone is paid their share of the revenues. However, the owner will not have to pay *any wages* if just one team member shirks slightly, keeping the team as a whole from meeting its goal. A bribe to one team member would result in a slightly smaller level of team revenue, but a much smaller set of wages to subtract from the earnings. Therefore, the owner cannot be trusted to create incentives for the firm.

The conflict between the residual-owners' interests and those of employees can even undermine the efficiency of Holmstrom's group penalty scheme. Eswaran and Kotwal point out that the employees must be aware that none of them will be paid if the owners bribe any one of the employees to shirk. Anticipating that this will happen, none of the employees have any incentive to work themselves. As long as the incentives of the owner are common knowledge, the Nash equilibrium under any version of Holmstrom's group incentive scheme is zero effort and zero output. As long as the incentive scheme is "enforced by a self-interested principal [owner]," even budget-breaking is insufficient to generate efficient effort (Eswaran and Kotwal 1984, 580).

It is clear that employees must have some assurance or trust that they will not be cheated. If they are not assured that the owner-as-sponge is credibly constrained from bribing one of their coworkers, then they will have to worry that their wage will be denied them as a result of the bribe.

In game-theoretic terms, not only must the owner-as-sponge be constrained from managing the firm, it must be *common knowledge* that the owner is so constrained. Otherwise, Holmstrom's scheme does not motivate efficient levels of effort by employees. In fact, lacking that common knowledge, there is no reason for employees to accept Holmstrom's scheme, when offered.

The bribe offered by an owner constitutes a different incentive scheme; though preferred by the owner because it increases profits, it is Pareto-inefficient. And Eswaran and Kotwal show that the problem is general: for every efficient incentive scheme, there is an inefficient scheme that generates more profits for the residual owner. The incentive scheme that maximizes the profit residual for the owner cannot be one that is Pareto-optimal for the firm as a whole. The owner will always prefer an incentive scheme that sacrifices Pareto-optimality for a larger profit residual.

To see this, remember that an efficient scheme may be defined as one in which none of the N productive team members has an incentive to shirk. However, the N team members plus the residual owner constitute a closed, budget-balancing system of N + 1 actors (Eswaran and Kotwal 1984, 581). But Holmstrom's impossibility result says that in any budget-balanced equilibrium *some* actor must have an incentive to behave inefficiently. Consequently, one of the N + 1 actors must have an incentive to shirk; since by construction it is not the original N team members who are motivated toward inefficiency, then it must be the owner. In other words, an "efficient" scheme relocates moral hazard with the owner.

As Eswaran and Kotwal (1984, 581) point out, "If the monitor is a rational, self-seeking individual or entity, the problem of moral hazard takes a different form but remains unsolved." Thus, under any incentive scheme that motivates efficient actions on the part of the employees of the firm, the owner must necessarily have an incentive to create inefficiency, in order to increase profits. Separation of ownership and control is essential precisely because the residual-absorbing owner *has taken on the moral hazard in team production.* Trust is necessary because moral hazard may be relocated, but never eliminated.

Rational Suspicions

Although the problem as articulated by Holmstrom may seem abstract, the implications of the argument may be seen working themselves out in the management of real firms. In these cases, the profit-maximizing incentive may be seen to work against the efficiency of the firm by inculcating a harmful mistrust in the employees.

For example, piece-rate incentive systems are instituted on the assumption that they motivate high levels of effort by employees.

However, in most piece-rate firms high take-home wages by employees are the occasion for a downward adjustment in piece-rates, in an attempt to reclaim excess wages as profits. Employees are fully aware of this and counsel each other against maximal effort under a beneficial piece-rate, for fear of this downward adjustment (Whyte 1955). The piece-rate system, in other words, is an occasion for gaming over earnings that typically results in severe limitations on efficiency.

Furthermore, at most piece-rate plants hard work and productivity increases result in built-up inventories and layoffs. A rational concern about layoffs therefore limits the productivity of employees. Technical suggestions from employees that could increase productivity are not forthcoming. Employees withhold productive ideas and activities because they suspect that greater productivity will result in larger, earlier layoffs.

Employees regard both a downward adjustment in piece-rates and layoffs during recessions as opportunistic profit-seeking by owners. They respond in ways that limit employee productivity. As a one-shot game, the equilibrium is Pareto-suboptimal; both owners and employees could be made better off if employees worked harder than they have any reason to do, given the incentive scheme, while managers bore the risk associated with macro-economic cycles (Miller 1992).

In other words, if employees trusted employers not to reset piece-rates after employees' effort levels revealed something about the effort costs of a task, then both employers and employees could be made better off.

Note that the solution to this problem is not as simple as having an employer recognize the advantages of being trustworthy. The employer may recognize the advantage of being trustworthy without being able to elicit trust from the employees. As identified by Michael Bacharach and Diego Gambetta in this volume, the problem is for trustworthy employers to be able to identify themselves as such among employees.

Trust and Incentives in Firms

> How can one commit himself in advance to an act that he would in fact prefer not to carry out in the event?
>
> —Schelling (1960, 36)

What would it take to induce a more efficient outcome? It is necessary for employees to trust their employers not to take advantage of greater effort by lowered piece-rates and higher chances of layoffs. This would allow employees to maximize their earnings net of effort levels without having to discount for long-term risks.

The founder of Lincoln Electric, James Lincoln, responded to these concerns in a way that is relatively unique among piece-rate plants. He made a lasting commitment never to lower piece-rates, and never to fire employees during recessions. Lincoln had a bedrock system of values that included honesty with employees. He said (1951, 151–52):

> The cutting of piecework prices when a man earns more than a certain amount is done on the theory that the price is a mistake and was set too high. Cutting such a price does not disturb the boss, as he thinks it is honest to correct a mistake. The production worker knows differently, however. He has been cheated of his honest earnings and he knows it. . . . If there is to be successful incentive management, the wage earner absolutely must regard the boss as a trusted, reliable co-worker on and for the team. The boss can win this acceptance in only one way. He must deserve it. He must hold himself under sterner discipline.

Note that James Lincoln, like many other successful managers, perceived this as a problem of morality. He perceived that there would always be a short-term payoff in profits for lowering the piece-rates of employees who revealed themselves to be capable of hard work and laying off employees when the workforce had built up inventories. But Lincoln felt himself constrained by what David Messick and Roderick Kramer (this volume) would call "shallow morality," or ordinary ethical rules.

This form of morality constraint can be effective as long as employees perceive it to be a real constraint on the behavior of the owner. How was this perception of a morality constraint created in the workers at Lincoln Electric? The factors mentioned by both Toshio Yamagishi and Tom Tyler (this volume) no doubt played a role. James Lincoln was, by all accounts, a blunt, outspoken person who had a reputation for saying exactly what he thought. This reputation no doubt enhanced the ability of his employees to distinguish him from other employers as a trustworthy one. And Lincoln Electric has enhanced this reputation through the years by paying attention to social identity, as argued by Tyler. The firm has generally hired managers from the ranks of its own employees, avoiding the temptation to bring in high-powered MBAs from Harvard and other top business schools. As a result, a notable degree of group identification unites, rather than separates, employees and managers at Lincoln.

The Lincoln Electric commitments to piece-rates and to a policy of no layoffs during recessions were not only made but made in such a way as to be believed by employees. Both of these commitments fly in the face of profit maximization. The firm typically pays take-home wages that are out of line with those of other firms in similar industries. And Lincoln Electric has to make work for employees during recessions, when the bottom drops out of market demand for its products. Nevertheless, while owners suffer smaller profits in any given year than would be available if Lincoln violated its commitments, the strategy has been a winner in the

Figure 10.1   Trust-Honor Game

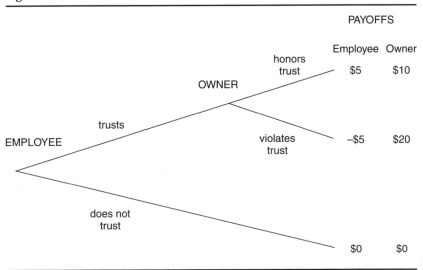

Source: Modified from Kreps 1990.

long run. Lincoln Electric has typically seen large productivity increases, swamped its opposition, and kept out potential entrants.

This is possible at Lincoln Electric because the firm regularly ignores intense short-term pressures to realign wages and to lay off employees during difficult periods. This is a luxury that is out of reach for many other firms where owners exert more pressure to maximize short-term profits. At Lincoln Electric an efficient long-run solution to the trust-honor game has been achieved, owing to a corporate culture that constrains short-run profit maximization.

The Trust-Honor Game

The difference between Lincoln Electric and other piece-rate firms is precisely that Lincoln's employees feel assured that the rules of the game will not be suddenly changed in order to boost profits. They feel free to make productivity-improving innovations, learn firm-specific skills, and provide maximal effort without worrying about producing themselves out of a job.

The Lincoln Electric story is clearly an example of what David Kreps (1990) examines as the "trust-honor game" (see Messick and Kramer, this volume). In one interpretation (see figure 10.1), imagine that an employee can make a relationship-specific investment in training that will improve his productivity. If he does not, they both get a payoff of zero dollars. If he makes the investment, at an effort cost of five dollars, then additional earnings of twenty dollars are generated. The owner may choose to keep the entire twenty dollars, so that the employee is out five dollars. Or the owner may split the twenty dollars equally, so that the employee has a net payoff of five dollars (ten dollars minus five). Making the investment constitutes "trust" by the employee, and the owner's sharing of the earnings constitutes "honoring the trust."

The unique subgame-perfect Nash equilibrium is for the owner to choose to violate the trust if given the chance, while the employee chooses not to give the owner that chance. The equilibrium outcome, then, is Pareto-suboptimal, since both could be better off with the trust-honor outcome. To the extent that employees feel vulnerable to expropriation of the earnings that they help produce, they do not undertake those relationship-specific investments that would leave them vulnerable to exploitation by the owner.

The problem for the modern firm, then, is to create safeguards that allow employees to take those productivity-enhancing actions that put them at risk. The solutions to the trust-honor game may be thought of as commitment devices—making trust a reasonable choice for the employee.

Repeated Games

Although there is but one equilibrium solution to the one-shot trust-honor game, there are many possible equilibrium outcomes to the infinitely repeated trust-honor game, assuming both players have sufficiently high discount factors. One such equilibrium is one in which employees trust, and owners honor trust, as long as the other reciprocates; if employees ever fail to trust and owners ever fail to honor the trust, the other side punishes from that time forward. This is an equilibrium because the owner would prefer to pass up the short-term gain of violating the trust in anticipation of the long-term benefits of cooperation, as long as the owner values future benefits highly enough.

However, this benign long-term equilibrium is not the only equilibrium to the repeated game. Unfortunately, there are an infinite number of equilibria to the repeated game, with distinct distributional implications. For example, another equilibrium is for the owner to honor the trust nine times out of ten as long as the employee always trusts, with a commitment to always violate the trust if the employee ever fails to trust. The employee's best response to this strategy is to always trust the owner, as long as he does not violate the trust more often than one time out of ten. In fact, as the Folk Theorem for repeated games tells us, there are an infinite number of such possible equilibria, with quite different distributional implications for the owner and the employee (Miller 1992).

Because there are multiple equilibria, the problem is coordinating on a particular Nash equilibrium, in particular one that is Pareto-superior to the "never trust/never honor" game. Both owner and employee must expect that the other will play the strategy that is consistent with the one that he himself expects to play, and both must know that the other knows that, and so on. These expectations are especially important because there are self-serving distributional advantages to one equilibrium or another. Why should an employee trust an employer to be committed to one equilibrium of the trust-honor game when another equilibrium is clearly preferable for the owner?

And uncertainty is the enemy of these Pareto-optimal equilibria of the repeated game. If the employee is not *highly certain* that the owner is playing an honorable strategy in the repeated game, then he must always be concerned about the short-run advantages to the owner of violating his trust. Even if the owner has honored his trust in the past, the next period may be different because of external economic conditions that make the payoff to violating that trust look especially inviting to the owner.

For example, is the next recession going to be the one in which Lincoln Electric decides to make massive layoffs? If so, then it is not rational for the employee to invest in relationship-specific human capital, to make a particularly valuable productivity-improving suggestion, or to put in any nonmonitorable effort.

Kreps suggests that what we call "corporate culture" consists of the uncertainty-reducing social reinforcement for a given way of playing the repeated trust-honor game. A strong corporate culture implies that employees and owner have consistently strong beliefs about how everyone else will play the game in the next period. A weak corporate culture implies a great deal of uncertainty; in the presence of that uncertainty, the "never trust/never honor" outcome will be perpetually appealing. Interpreting Kreps in the light of Eswaran and Kotwal, the effect of a positive corporate culture is to signal a commitment on the part of owners not to maximize short-term residual profits.

A classic example of an efficient long-run solution to the trust-honor game is Southwest Airlines, led by Herbert Kelleher. Besides developing a clever and consistent business strategy, Kelleher has developed intense loyalty on the part of the ninety-five hundred Southwest Airlines employees. He spends one day each business quarter loading luggage, working the ticket counter, or dispensing tickets. He spends more time at company social events, where he has appeared as Elvis Presley and Roy Orbison, singing "Jailhouse Rock" and "Pretty Woman." One Halloween night he turned up at Southwest's hangar in drag, as Corporal Klinger from *M*A*S*H*, to thank mechanics for working overtime (Welles 1992, 45). These efforts are supported by concrete trust-instilling measures: employees have a high level of job and wage security. The average pay is among the highest in the airline industry.

With a leader they trust, employees provide enormous levels of non-monitorable, noncompensated effort. Flight attendants sing songs for customers and greet regular customers by name. Ground crews generate turnaround times that are half the industry average—much less than those of competitors. One gate agent takes the place of the standard three. Turnover is the lowest in the industry. The cost per available-sea-mile was the industry's lowest at 6.5 percent (Welles 1992, 47). And despite the high wages, the owners benefit as well: Southwest is the most consistently profitable airline in the nation.

Delegation as a Shortcut to Trust

> To dispel the fear of breach on the part of stakeholders, shareholders find it value maximizing to *seek out* or *train* individuals who are capable of commitment to stakeholders, *elevate* them to management, and *entrench* them.
> —Shleifer and Summers (1988, 40)

There are, of course, several long-term obstacles to owners building a long-term reputation for trustworthiness, as at Hewlett-Packard or Southwest Airlines. Trust is primarily attached by employees to individuals they have come to know personally. Indeed, one is struck, in reading about these firms, how much time and effort the leaders spend projecting themselves to their employees.

In most American firms ownership is too diffuse, anonymous, and short-term to allow a relationship of long-term trust between employees and owners. In these firms delegation of many key decisions from owners to managers may provide an easier path to the kind of constraint on residual profit maximization that is necessary for employees to regard it as worthwhile to make the human capital and commitment decisions necessary for maximum efficiency. And contrary to advice from business journals, the key element in using delegation as a commitment device is *insulating* the manager from the profit-maximizing drive of shareholders, not binding the manager to the interests of shareholders.

Profit Maximization Versus Efficiency in Deferred Compensation

A much-studied manifestation of this kind of tension is the deferred compensation scheme. Labor economists (Lazear 1979) have noticed that labor contracts do not seem to offer employees a wage that is equivalent to their individual marginal products. Rather, employees evidently are paid less than their marginal products early in their careers. Later in their careers their compensation increases more sharply than would seem to be attributable to increased productivity alone.

The standard interpretation of this is that employees are in effect bonding themselves as diligent workers: they accept the low wage early in their careers for a long enough time that their true effort can be discerned by the firm. The firm then rewards them with sharp increases later in their careers. This has efficiency benefits with regard to both adverse selection and the moral hazard of shirking within large teams. Both as an initial hire and as a member of working groups throughout his career, it may be difficult or impossible to tell whether an individual is shirking or not. But over an entire career the probability of discerning that individual's true commitment to the firm is much easier and can be rewarded at the end.

The point, of course, is that this pattern of deferred compensation makes possible significant efficiency improvements. The worker works harder and invests more of his human capital in the firm than he has any short-term incentive to do given the firm's ability to monitor and reward behavior at a given point in time, and the firm responds by generously rewarding him at the end of his career.

A growing body of empirical research supports this hypothesis. In one of the best documented cases, Casey Ichniowski and her colleagues (1997) show that productivity in steel finishing lines is associated with a set of human resource management practices that encourage employees' sense of long-term commitment—for instance, employment security, training, and cooperative teams. John Delery and Harold Doty (1996, 820) find an analogous relationship in a white-collar setting: "The greater the employment security given to loan officers, the greater the returns to banks."

Andrei Shleifer and Lawrence Summers (1988) argue that many employees and suppliers make efficiency-enhancing, transaction-specific investments only because they expect an entrenched management team to persist in a relationship long enough to reward those investments. But, as implied by the Holmstrom paradox, if the deferred compensation scheme creates incentives for efficient behavior by subordinates, it must not be profit-maximizing. Rather, it offers a temptation to the owners: they can let employees work at low wages early in their careers in the expectation of deferred compensation and then either fire them or simply refuse to pay the career-ending bonuses. Consequently employees must be willing to trust the owners not to renege on an implicit contract—one that is not enforceable in courts.

What kinds of firms are employees willing to trust in this way? Since short-term profit maximization is precisely the incentive that could lead the firm to renege, the firm that is dominated by shareholder interests is the firm that would be least trustworthy and therefore least likely to receive the efficiency benefits of the deferred compensation scheme.

And this is precisely the result that Gerald Garvey and Noel Gaston (1991) find in their empirical analysis of Australian firms. Those firms characterized by ownership concentration and incentive pay for the CEO are the ones in which owners' interests are most emphatically served. But these are also the firms that are least characterized by deferred compensation. As Garvey and Gaston (1991, 105) write: "Managers who are not 'forced' to serve shareholder interests are in fact inclined to fulfill implicit contracts." In Garvey and Gaston's interpretation of their data, firms that are committed to serving shareholder interests are not able to offer a credible deferred compensation scheme. Employees are rationally suspicious of a firm's commitment to profit maximization and make no attempt to achieve the efficiency benefits of deferred compensation.

Of course, the intervening decade has demonstrated the rationality of this employee suspicion. A good many firms that historically did rely on schemes of deferred compensation, such as General Electric and AT&T, were forced to renege on those implicit contracts by wage cutbacks and layoffs of employees who had fully expected to reap the rewards of their efforts at the end of their careers.

Delegation as a Commitment Device

As Thomas Schelling (1960, 29) notes, commitments can be made more credible by delegating decision authority to someone whose interests are *known to be different from one's own.* In negotiating to sell a car worth eight thousand dollars to you, it may be worthwhile to hire a negotiator who will not be paid if the car sells for less than ten thousand dollars—even though that rules out a range of profitable outcomes.

Similarly, the trust-honor game may be resolved by committing to hire a manager—but the key is to make sure that the manager's preferences do not replicate those of the profit-maximizer. Suppose that the first step in the game is a decision by the owner: she may openly and completely delegate to a "manager" the choice of honoring or violating the employee's trust in making the relationship-specific investment(see figure 10.2). If not, the game is the same as in figure 10.1. If she does delegate, the manager is paid $5 if and only if he honors the employee's trust.

The managers would have reason to honor the employee's trust, and the employee would have reason to trust the manager. By backwards induction, the owner would be better off delegating to the manager. The equilibrium is therefore the "delegate, trust, honor trust" outcome. However, the owner had time inconsistent preferences, and would like for a delegated manager to violate the employee's trust at the final stage. This illustrates that the success of the scheme depends on constraint of the owner's interests via delegation to the manager.

Thus, in firms in which there is a payoff for employees making firm-specific investments, a person who can convey trustworthiness would be worth hiring. It should be noted that the value of the manager exists *only* as long as he is so "entrenched" that he cannot be threatened or cajoled

Figure 10.2   Trust-Honor Game with Delegation

			PAYOFFS		
			Owner	Employee	Manager
		honors			
EMPLOYEE	OWNER		$10	$5	$0
does not delegate	trusts violates		$20	–$5	$0
	distrusts		$0	$0	$0
	MANAGER honors		$5	$5	$5
EMPLOYEE delegates	trusts violates		$20	–$5	$0
	distrusts		$0	$0	$0

Source: Author's compilation.

into appropriating the rents generated by employee human capital investments (Shleifer and Summers 1988). Indeed, given a choice of hiring such a manager or not at the beginning of the trust-honor game, the owner would prefer to hire such a manager rather than do without and rely on the irrational trust of the employee.

In this illustrative game, backward induction indicates that the manager honors the trust, the employee trusts the manager, and the owner hires the manager. As argued by Schelling, the owner is better off letting someone not interested in profits make decisions for her. And as demonstrated by Eswaran and Kotwal, this is not an accidental feature characteristic only of some firms—it is an inevitable feature of team production.

The Advantages of Managerial Delegation in Interdependent Markets

John Vickers (1985, 138) points out that constraining the profit-maximizing behavior of owners provides advantages that generalize beyond the important one of managing deferred compensation:

> If control of my decisions is in the hands of an agent whose preferences are different from my own, I may nevertheless prefer the results to those that would come about if I took my own decisions. This has some interesting implications for the theory of the firm. For example, in markets where firms are interdependent, it is *not* necessarily true that maximum profits are earned by firms whose objective is profit-maximization.

Vickers makes a general argument, but his most extended example is of the classic Cournot problem. In this game, if one producer can credibly commit himself to a production level before the other producers, he can earn excess profits. This requires a credible commitment, because after the other producers have revealed their production levels he would prefer to adjust his own production level. This adjustment, however, would cause another round of adjustments, which would finally result in the Cournot equilibrium. The only way the Stackelberg profits can be maintained is by credibly committing to a level of output that is higher than the Cournot equilibrium. Vickers shows that this credible commitment can be made by delegating the production decision to a manager who is paid as a function of sales as well as profits. By inducing the correct sensitivity to sales in the agent, the outcome of the game will give the non-profit-maximizing firm an extraordinary profit bonus. "This shows rather vividly the extent to which non-profit-maximisers can surpass profit-maximisers in terms of profits. Indeed, here the non-profit-maximizer earns greater profits than those of his rivals added together, no matter how many rivals there are" (Vickers 1985, 142).

This advantage can be mimicked, of course, by other profit-maximizing firms, which have the option of creating managers who are similarly insensitive to profits. Vickers shows that owners must play a game with each other in setting the payoff functions for their agents. Furthermore, he shows that, in the Nash equilibrium of this payoff-setting game, *each* profit-maximizing owner makes her agent responsive to sales and profits rather than to profits alone. Thus, a status quo of profit-maximizing owners is unstable; they will race to an equilibrium in which each owner has delegated decisionmaking to an imperfect, sales-sensitive agent.

Chaim Fershtman and Kenneth Judd (1987) make a similar argument regarding the chain store paradox. Because the threat to engage in predatory pricing is not credible for a weak firm, it does not deter entry. However, rewarding managers based on market share rather than profits is a way of committing the firm to an incredible threat. Once again, aligning managerial interests with those of profit-maximizing owners is a mistake for the firm—and ultimately for the owners themselves.

Nor are the Cournot or chain store examples special cases. As Vickers shows, hiring an agent is equivalent to revealing your preferences. Hiring an agent with identical preferences to your own is equivalent to revealing your preferences accurately. Whenever a principal has a reason to misreveal his preferences, he can also benefit by hiring an agent whose incentive structure replicates his own incentives. But the literature on incentive compatibility has demonstrated that, in general, it is only under highly restrictive conditions that every actor would have reason to reveal preferences accurately (Gibbard 1973; Satterthwaite 1975).

Consequently in interactive markets there must always be reasons for firms to rely on managers who do not act as perfect agents for owners.

Corporate Law

Corporate law is one source of potentially beneficial constitutional constraint on owners. Gordon (1991, 351) wonders why there is no power of shareholder initiative.

> Thus for the large public corporation the pattern of delegation gives management virtually unbounded decisionmaking authority over business matters and agenda control over significant changes in the management-shareholder relationship. The shareholders' power consists almost exclusively of the power to revoke the delegation through a control contest.

Gordon's explanation for this is that shareholder initiatives would be subject to inefficiencies in preference aggregation as manifested in voting cycles. This chapter provides an alternative efficiency-based explanation for constraints on shareholder initiative: even with perfect aggregation, shareholder preferences are better divorced from the day-to-day management of the corporation, as argued by Vickers and by Garvey and Gaston. Shareholder initiatives would prohibit effective delegation to managers.

Other features of corporate law, documented by Margaret Blair and Lynn Stout (1997, 290–91), also serve to tie the owners' hands. Corporate directors "are not subject to direct control or supervision by *anyone,* including the firm's shareholders. Moreover, this fundamental principle of directorial discretion cannot be explained away as a legal response to the practical difficulties associated with shareholder voting." Shareholders may under restricted circumstances step in for the directors and sue on behalf of the firm, but *"Corporate law only permits shareholders to bring successful derivative claims against directors in circumstances where bringing such claim benefits not only shareholders, but other stakeholders in the coalition as well"* (23, emphasis in original). Through the business judgment rule and other features of corporate law, say Blair and Stout, "modern corporate law does not adhere to the norm of shareholder primacy. To the contrary, case law interpreting the business judgment rule explicitly authorizes directors to sacrifice shareholders' interests for other constituencies" (27).

An example of the importance that directors may place on long-term efficiency is Delta, a firm that has historically been known for maintaining a "family-style" culture, remaining largely union-free, and achieving high customer satisfaction. Ronald Allen became chairman of Delta Airline in 1987. In 1994 he sharply reduced operating costs, in part by slashing twelve thousand jobs from a workforce of sixty-nine thousand. He accepted lowered employee morale with the oft-quoted phrase,

"So be it." After years of heavy losses in the early part of the decade, Delta had eight consecutive quarters of record profits (Brannigan and White 1997, A1).

While profits increased, customer baggage complaints went up as well and on-time performance and customer service satisfaction plummeted. Employee morale was low, and unionization efforts greatly increased. Directors felt that these costs were too high a price to pay for the short-term gain in profits and that Allen's combative style had become a liability. Instead of rewarding Allen, Delta's board fired him in May 1997. The directors announced that they intended to look for a new CEO who would place "a high value on Delta's culture of respect, unity and deep regard for our heritage. They intend to select a person as our next leader who will work well within this culture we all value so highly" (Brannigan and White 1997, A1). Corporate law insulates the directors who choose to sacrifice short-term profits at the cost of alienating other stakeholders vital to the long-run success of the firm. This insulation would not be economically rationalizable if profit maximization and efficiency were always consistent in a firm. But this kind of insulation is exactly what Holmstrom argues is necessary for effective budget-breaking.

The Growth of Mistrust and Its Consequences

> As the incumbent managers are removed after the takeover, control reverts to the bidder, who is not committed to upholding the implicit contracts with stakeholders. Hostile takeovers thus enable shareholders to redistribute wealth from stakeholders to themselves.
> —Shleifer and Summers 1988, 41

Although delegation to managers *may* serve as a useful commitment by lessening employee mistrust of the profit-maximizing motivations of managers, the last fifteen years have certainly seen a reduction of this commitment device—and just as certainly, an increase in employee mistrust.

The primary motif for the analysis of corporate governance in the past decades has been that of inducing firms to act uncompromisingly on behalf of their owners. The theme of this chapter is that this overlooks a logical problem developed by Eswaran and Kotwal's analysis of Holmstrom's impossibility theorem: the active maximization of the owner's residual profits is inconsistent with efficiency. The owner cannot be trusted with the management of the firm.

Obviously there are paradoxes within paradoxes. If the purpose of the firm is articulated to be something other than profit maximization, why should shareholders make their capital available to the firm?

The largest implications of Holmstrom have been ignored by a decade of financial commentators who have urged ever-tighter responsiveness of corporations and their managers to shareholders and shareholder value maximization. The corporate raider T. Boone Pickens Jr. (1986) defended his role in forcing managers to be more responsive to the interests of owners. The Council of Institutional Investors supported the creation of more active boards of directors and the tying of managers' compensation more closely to shareholder value as a way of committing the firm to acting in the interests of the owners.

Academics too picked up the theme that shareholder wealth should be the sole motivation for managerial decisionmaking. Michael Jensen (1988), a leading expert on corporate governance and financial markets, applauded the active market for corporate control for binding managers to shareholders' interests. He complained (1989, 64) that the board of directors could do little to advance the interests of shareholders: "The idea that outside directors with little or no equity stake in the company could effectively monitor and discipline the managers who selected them has proven hollow at best."

Of course, Jensen's claim is in sharp conflict with Holmstrom's argument that owner monitoring is inconsistent with the owners' true role of budget-breaking. But Jensen supported leveraged buyouts precisely because they eliminated the distance between owners and managers, thereby putting the owners back in the driver's seat.

Incentives and Downsizing

As a result of more independent boards, more active shareholders, and a more competitive market for corporate control, managers are disciplined as never before to act in the interests of owners. As one of the leading executive compensation consultants recently observed, "Almost every executive-compensation package is oriented toward maximizing the shareholders' position" (Baker 1995, 1). Managers have become much more aggressive about costs than they were during an earlier period of corporate welfare.

The predictable result is downsizing. Thousands of individuals have been laid off by the most visible American firms, including firms that have historically made long-term commitments to their employees in return for loyalty. The figures are by now familiar: Sears Roebuck CEO Edward Brennan laid off 50,000 employees in the period from 1991 to 1994 and received compensation of more than $3 million for 1993 alone. Robert Allen at AT&T laid off 83,500 employees in the same time and received compensation in 1993 of $2.5 million. John Reed's CITICORP laid off 13,000 employees, and he received $4.15 million for that year (Baker 1995, 1). In 1993 corporate job cutbacks in American firms totaled more than 615,000 (Chilton 1994, 7).

Has downsizing had the efficiency effects it seemed to promise? It is clear that the stock market tends to respond positively to downsizing—and why not? It is a palpable sign that the short-run interests of shareholders are being served. As Shleifer and Summers point out (1988, 43), "Just as it would be inappropriate to gauge the benefit of banning monopoly by the willingness of consumers to pay for the ban, it is wrong to measure efficiency gains from takeovers by share price increases on the announcement of the deal." The reason is that there are redistributional effects in both measurements. Similarly, there are redistributional effects in the share price increases that accompany layoffs.

Downsizing should have had a clear positive effect on productivity ratios, by decreasing the denominator. However, a survey of 531 large companies found that only 34 percent had experienced a productivity increase in a two-year period following downsizing (Chilton 1994, 9). The American Management Association said that 43 percent of a sample of about 1,000 firms had downsized in two or more years between 1987 and 1992. Most of these reported a drop in morale and no increase in efficiency, and half also saw no improvements in profits (10).

Overall, by 1996 there was increasing doubt that the downsizings of 1993 and 1994 had had the unambiguously beneficial effects expected. Revised Commerce Department figures showed that, with GDP based on a chain-weighted calculation, output per worker was about 1.4 percent, instead of the 2.2 percent previously reported. These figures indicated that "economic growth in 1993 and 1994 was considerably slower than previously reported, casting grave doubt on the view that the wrenching process of corporate downsizing has been paying off in big gains in efficiency" (Passell 1996, 17). Richard Lester (1997) concludes that there is no evidence that the layoffs have improved productivity.

Downsizing poses a danger based not in the decreased size of the work force but in the incentive effects on the employees left behind. The net effect has been to reduce markedly the security of most employees in their jobs, and the sense of loyalty of those retained as well as of those removed. After in-depth studies with individuals of different generations in the computer industry, John Clancy (1996, 258) concludes that "trust in management has substantially eroded in the last twenty to twenty-five years."

It is a truism in modern technology that every firm requires its employees to take actions that cannot be coerced—quality-improving suggestions, transaction cost-decreasing cooperation with other employees, personally costly training in firm-specific human capital, personally costly investments in firm-specific human capital, customer-pleasing friendliness. These actions, by their very nature, cannot be guaranteed by any short-term incentive system but may be induced by rational agents who see themselves in a long-term game of cooperation with management and owners. The danger of downsizing is simply that these efficiency-enhancing, long-term "deals" will be called off by employees who lose trust in a management committed solely to the maximization of profits for shareholders. This is exactly the kind of tension between profit and Pareto-optimality to which Holmstrom's theorem alerts us.

Conclusion

> Trust and similar values, loyalty or truth telling . . . have real, practical, economic value; they increase the efficiency of the system, enable you to produce more goods.
>
> —Arrow (1974, 23)

While principal-agency theory has focused on the inefficiencies generated by agents' opportunism, Holmstrom's impossibility result has supplied an alternative vision of opportunism—opportunism on the part of owners themselves. It is an opportunism that follows from their ownership of residual profits, and it paradoxically puts them at odds with the overall efficiency of the firm.

An interdependent technology requires cooperation by a variety of stakeholders—cooperation that is inhibited by the unilateral commitment of the firm to shareholder profits. Maximization of shareholder influence is inadequate as a guide to the constitutional development of the firm.

In the interest of overall efficiency, firms should and sometimes do devise constitutional checks and balances that constrain, rather than unleash, shareholder profit maximization as a motive for the firm. Delegation to managers who have a reputation for trustworthiness and have been charged with the negotiation of efficient long-term contracts with vital stakeholders is one such commitment device. As Vickers shows, this delegation is essential for firm strategy in any interdependent market. It is also essential for the development of the long-term human capital that is vital to the success of most firms in the information age.

The primary significance of the Holmstrom argument is its insight into the fundamentally political nature of social groupings, including firms. Given an interactive team of individuals producing value, imagine that the Holmstrom result did not apply. Then a budget-balancing scheme that satisfied Nash equilibrium and Pareto-optimality could be implemented, ending conflicts between self-interest and group well-being forever. Under this ideal scheme individuals would consult their self-interest and act in socially responsible ways. There would be no need to construct hierarchies, to create and delegate authority, or to hold people responsible for their actions. Constitutions would be irrelevant, and politics as well.

But Holmstrom's impossibility result holds, and because it does, we know that there is no neat, mechanical solution to collective action. Construct your sharing mechanism as you will, you may only relocate the incentives for inefficient action. There is an inevitable tension between social efficiency and the distribution of the surplus of social effort. The distribution of that surplus inevitably raises the central constitutional questions that Holmstrom hoped to bypass by means of his joint forcing contract: who will monitor the distribution of the surplus, and who will monitor the monitors? In the long run the most effective firms, like the most effective states, will address the issue of opportunism by means of constitutional commitment, in order to enhance the trust of those stakeholders whose long-term investments are essential for social success.

I was supported by the Research School of Social Sciences at the Australian National University in Canberra while working on this paper and would like to thank Geoffrey Brennan, its director at that time, for comments on an early draft. I would also like to thank Margaret Blair, Randall Calvert, Bruce Chapman, Kenneth Chilton, Dino Falaschetti, Robert Frank, Robert Gibbons, Thomas Hammond, Eric Helland, Margaret Levi, Jackson Nickerson, Paul Thomas, Robert Thompson, Andrew Whitford, Stanley Winer, and Todd Zenger for comments and discussion leading to this paper. Errors are my own responsibility.

References

Alchian, Armen, and Harold Demsetz. 1972. "Production, Information Costs, and Economic Organization." *American Economic Review* 62(5): 777–95.

Arrow, Kenneth. 1974. *The Limits of Organization.* New York: Oxford University Press.

Baker, Molly. 1995. "I Feel Your Pain?" *Wall Street Journal,* April 13, 1.

Blair, Margaret, and Lynn Stout. 1997. "A Team Production Theory of Corporate Law." *Virginia Law Review* 85(March): 247–328.

Brannigan, Martha, and Joseph B. White. 1997. "'So Be It': Why Delta Airlines Decided It Was Time for CEO to Take Off." *Wall Street Journal,* May 30, A1.

Chilton, Kenneth. 1994. *A New Social Contract for the American Workplace: From Paternalism to Partnering.* Policy Study 123. St. Louis: Washington University, Center for the Study of American Business.

Clancy, John J. 1996. "The Old Dispensation: Loyalty in Business." Ph.D. diss., Washington University.

Delery, John, and D. Harold Doty. 1996. "Modes of Theorizing in Strategic Human Resource Management." *Academy of Management Journal* 39(4): 810–30.

Eswaran, Mukesh, and Ashok Kotwal. 1984. "The Moral Hazard of Budget Breaking." *Rand Journal of Economics* 15: 578–81.

Fershtman, Chaim, and Kenneth Judd. 1987. "Equilibrium Incentives in Oligopoly." *American Economic Review* 77(5): 927–40.

Garvey, Gerald, and Noel Gaston. 1991. "Delegation, the Role of Managerial Discretion as a Bonding Device, and the Enforcement of Implicit Contracts." *Advances in Econometrics* (JAI Press) 9: 879–119.

Gibbard, Alan. 1973. "Manipulation of Voting Schemes." *Econometrica* 41(4): 587–602.

Gordon, Jeffrey. 1991. "Shareholder Initiative: A Social Choice and Game Theoretic Approach to Corporate Law." *University of Cincinnati Law Review* 60 (Fall): 347–85.

Holmstrom, Bengt. 1982. "Moral Hazard in Teams." *Bell Journal of Economics* 13: 324–40.

Ichniowski, Casey, Kathryn Shaw, and Giovanna Prennushi. 1997. "The Effects of Human Resource Management Practices on Productivity: A Study of Steel Finishing Lines." *American Economic Review* 87(3): 291–313.

Jensen, Michael C. 1988. "Takeovers: Their Causes and Consequences." *Journal of Economic Perspectives* 2(1): 21–48.

———. 1989. "The Eclipse of the Public Corporation." *Harvard Business Review* 67(5): 61–74.

Kreps, David M. 1990. "Corporate Culture and Economic Theory." In *Perspectives on Positive Political Economy*, edited by James Alt and Kenneth Shepsle. Cambridge: Cambridge University Press.

Lazear, Edward. 1979. "Why Is There Mandatory Retirement?" *Journal of Political Economy* 87(6): 1261–84.

Lester, Richard. 1997. *The Productive Edge: How U.S. Industries Are Pointing the Way to a New Era of Economic Growth*. New York: Norton.

Lincoln, James M. 1951. *Incentive Management*. Cleveland, Ohio: Lincoln Electric Co.

Milgrom, Paul, and John Roberts. 1992. *Economics, Organization and Management*. Englewood Cliffs, N.J.: Prentice-Hall.

Miller, Gary J. 1992. *Managerial Dilemmas: The Political Economy of Hierarchy*. Cambridge: Cambridge University Press.

Passell, Peter. 1996. "Maybe It Wasn't the Economy, After All." *New York Times*, January 22, 17–18.

Pickens, T. Boone, Jr. 1986. "Professions of a Short-Termer." *Harvard Business Review* 64: 75–79.

Satterthwaite, Mark A. 1975. "Strategy-Proofness and Arrow's Conditions." *Journal of Economic Theory* 10(April): 187–217.

Schelling, Thomas. 1960. *The Strategy of Conflict*. Oxford: Oxford University Press.

Shliefer, Andrei, and Lawrence Summers. 1988. "Hostile Takeovers as Breaches of Trust." In *Corporate Takeovers: Causes and Consequences*, edited by Alan Auerbach. Chicago: University of Chicago Press.

Vickers, John. 1985. "Delegation and the Theory of the Firm." *Economic Journal* 95: 138–47.

Weingast, Barry R. 1984. "The Congressional-Bureaucratic System: A Principal-Agent Perspective with Applications to the SEC." *Public Choice* 44: 147–91.

Welles, Edward O. 1992. "Captain Marvel." *Inc.* 14(1): 44–47.

Whyte, William F. 1955. *Money and Motivation*. Westport, Conn.: Greenwood Press.

Chapter 11

Trust in Social Structures: Hobbes and Coase Meet Repeated Games

ROBERT GIBBONS

I N ONE OF the classic passages in social science, Thomas Hobbes argues that without a state, life would be "solitary, poor, nasty, brutish and short," so people should create a state powerful enough to punish malefactors (Hobbes 1991, 89). Three centuries later Ronald Coase (1937) makes a similar claim, arguing that where the price system performs poorly enough, transactions should be conducted inside firms, so that bosses (rather than prices) can direct workers' actions. Both Hobbes and Coase advocate horse races: comparative analyses of alternative institutions in a given environment.

For Hobbes the environment is the "state of nature," now often modeled as a group of people playing two-person prisoners' dilemmas with each other. Although Hobbes argues that Leviathan is always the best institution for this environment, others have since suggested that anarchy (the absence of a ruler) need not produce the "war of all against all." Instead, institutions other than a state may produce "order without law" in Hobbes's environment, and such institutions may be preferable to a state.

For Coase the environment is an economic transaction between buyer and seller. Unlike Hobbes, Coase makes a contingent prescription: markets as optimal governance structures for some transactions but firms as optimal governance structures for others. Coase's market is the anonymous price system of neoclassical economics; others have since suggested that different institutions, such as "networks" and "relational contracts," are feasible in Coase's environment and may be preferable to both the anonymous price system and firms.

Large literatures are devoted to each of these institutions—states, firms, networks, and so on. There are also small literatures focused on the Hobbesian and Coasean horse races—explicit comparisons of two or more institutions in a given environment. Recently repeated-game models have emerged in all these literatures, often with the observation that repeated games allow economists (and methodological fellow-travelers) to analyze self-enforcing institutions. In this essay I first introduce the theory of repeated games and then sketch some of these recent repeated-game models.

I am not the first to cast Hobbes and Coase in something like these terms. For example, Mark Granovetter (1985, 490) offers two reasons why social relations may discourage malfeasance:

> Individuals with whom one has a continuing relation have an economic motivation to be trustworthy, so as not to discourage future transactions; and departing from pure economic motives, continuing economic relations often become overlaid with social content that carries strong expectations of trust and abstention from opportunism.

I focus only on "pure economic motives," but I am evidently not alone in thinking that such motives are at least part of the story. Indeed, such calculative accounts of trust appear frequently in this book, starting with the opening paragraph, on *The Brothers Karamazov,* of Hardin's chapter.

In fact, Granovetter's paper closely parallels this essay. He correctly criticizes Oliver Williamson's (1975) conception of a market for being "undersocialized" (atomized and anonymous, and therefore without any prospect of supporting cooperation through social relations) and Williamson's conception of a hierarchy for being "oversocialized" (the hierarchical superior settles disputes by fiat but never abuses his powers). But economics has made some progress since 1975, and in Granovetter's direction: the more recent repeated-game models summarized in the second section begin to explore both social relations in markets and abuse of power in firms. Granovetter also makes analogous criticisms of Hobbes, noting the "undersocialized" nature of his conception of anarchy and the "oversocialized" nature of his conception of Leviathan. But the recent repeated-game models summarized in the third section again make progress toward embedding trust and social relations in models of anarchies and states.

An Introduction to Repeated Games

Game theory is rampant in economics.[1] Having long ago invaded industrial organization, game-theoretic modeling is now commonplace in international, labor, macro, and public finance and is gathering steam in development and economic history. Nor is economics alone: accounting, finance, law, marketing, political science, and sociology are beginning similar experiences.

Why is this? Broadly speaking, two views are possible: fads and fundamentals. Although I believe that fads are partly to blame for the current enthusiasm for game theory, I also believe that fundamentals are an important part of the story. Simply put, many modelers use game theory because it allows them to think like economists when price theory does not apply. Examples abound: small numbers, hidden information, hidden actions, and incomplete contracts can turn markets into games; and in other settings markets are at most peripheral—such as the relationship between a regulator and a firm, a boss and a worker, and so on. Thus, where markets have become games, and where transactions do not occur in markets, game theory allows economists to study the implications of rationality, self-interest, and equilibrium when price theory would not.

When people interact over time, threats and promises concerning future behavior may influence current behavior. Repeated games capture this fact of life and hence have been applied more broadly than any other game-theoretic model (by my armchair citation count)—not only in virtually every field of economics but also in finance, law, marketing, political science, and sociology. In this section I describe first a one-shot interaction between two parties (which works out badly) and then an ongoing sequence of such interactions (which work out well because of the parties' concerns for their reputations).

The One-Shot Interaction

Suppose that late last night an exciting new project occurred to you. The project would be highly profitable but is outside your area of expertise, so you would need help in completing it. Furthermore, it would take significant work on your part just to explain the project to someone with the needed expertise. Finally, if you do explain the project to the relevant other, that person could steal your ideas, representing them as substantially his own.

It is not hard to imagine this scenario unfolding in an organization: you work in marketing, and the project is a new product, but you need assistance from someone in engineering, who could later take all (or at least too much of) the credit. To decide whether to pursue the project it would help to know something about the "trustworthiness" of a particular engineer you could approach. But if you have been buried deep inside marketing, you may not have much information about any of the engineers. In this case you would be forced to rely either on the average

Figure 11.1   The Trust Game

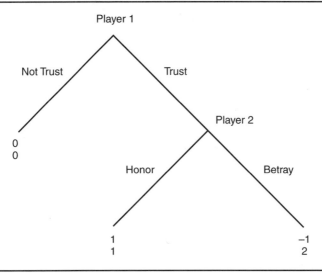

Source: Author's compilation.

sense of human decency among engineers or on your organization's culture: "how we do things around here" (Schein 1992, 9). If the culture emphasizes teamwork over individual accomplishments, for example, you
may have more confidence in approaching an unfamiliar member of the
engineering group.

David Kreps (1990) captures these issues in the Trust Game shown in
figure 11.1. (See also Miller's discussion in this volume of this game in the
context of Lincoln Electric.) The game begins with a decision node for
player 1, who can choose either to trust or not trust player 2. If player 1
chooses trust, then the game reaches a decision node for player 2, who can
choose either to honor or betray player 1's trust. If player 1 chooses not-
trust, then the game ends—effectively, player 1 terminates the relationship. At the end of each branch of the game tree player 1's payoff appears
above player 2's. If player 1 chooses to end the relationship, then both
players' payoffs are zero. If player 1 chooses to trust player 2, however,
then both players' payoffs are one if player 2 honors 1's trust, but player
1 receives minus-one and player 2 receives two if player 2 betrays 1's trust.

We solve the Trust Game by backward induction—that is, by working
backward through the game tree, one node at a time. If player 2 gets to
move (that is, if player 1 chooses to trust player 2), then player 2 can receive either a payoff of one by honoring player 1's trust or a payoff of two
by betraying player 1's trust. Since two exceeds one, player 2 will betray
player 1's trust if given the move. Knowing this, player 1's initial choice

amounts to either ending the relationship (and so receiving a payoff of zero) or trusting player 2 (and so receiving a payoff of minus-one, after player 2 betrays 1's trust). Since zero exceeds minus-one, player 1 should end the relationship.

The Repeated Game

Instead of a one-shot interaction, suppose that you and a *particular* engineer play the Trust Game repeatedly, with all previous outcomes observed by both players before the next period's Trust Game is played. The analysis of this repeated game differs dramatically from the one-shot interaction: the engineer's actions today may affect your expectation of her actions tomorrow; that expectation may affect your actions tomorrow, and your actions tomorrow may affect her payoffs then. Thus, actions not in the engineer's short-run self-interest (as defined by today's payoffs) may be consistent with her overall self-interest (as defined by the total payoff over time).

I do not mean to imply that this logic is surprising or complicated. To the contrary, I think it is close to ubiquitous. (As Hardin notes, Dostoevski clearly understood it.) In this subsection I describe the simplest possible formalization of this logic. Formally we analyze an infinitely repeated game: the game never ends, but both players face an interest rate r per period in discounting their payoffs across periods. (For example, when r is high, a dollar to be received next period is not worth much today— $1/(1 + r)$, to be exact.) We can interpret this "infinitely" repeated game somewhat more realistically by saying that the game ends at a random date. Under this interpretation, the interest rate r reflects not only the time value of money but also the probability that the players will never meet again after the current period. (A dollar to be received next period provided that we are still interacting is not worth much if today's interaction is likely to be our last.) Under either interpretation, the present value of a dollar to be received every period starting tomorrow can be shown to be $1/r$.

Mostly for analytical simplicity (but to some extent for behavioral realism), we consider the following "trigger" strategies in the infinitely repeated game:

Player 1: In the first period, play trust. Thereafter, if all moves in all previous periods have been trust and honor, play trust; otherwise, play not-trust.

Player 2: If given the move this period, play honor if all moves in all previous periods have been trust and honor; otherwise, play betray.

These strategies are not forgiving, like Tit-for-Tat. Rather, under the trigger strategies, if cooperation breaks down at any point, then it is finished for the rest of the game, replaced by the dictates of short-run self-interest. In most games reverting to short-run self-interest after a breakdown in cooperation is a middle ground between two plausible alternatives: forgiveness (that is, an attempt to resuscitate cooperation) and spite (going against short-run self-interest in order to punish the other player). Both forgiveness and spite deserve analytical attention, but I focus on the trigger strategies (with their reversion to short-run self-interest after a breakdown of cooperation) as a tractable compromise.[2]

We analyze whether these trigger strategies are an equilibrium of the infinitely repeated game. That is, given that player 1 is playing her trigger strategy, is it in player 2's interest to play his? We find that the trigger strategies are an equilibrium of the infinitely repeated game provided that player 2 is sufficiently patient (that is, provided that the interest rate r is sufficiently small).

Suppose that player 1 follows his trigger strategy and chooses trust in the first period. Player 2 then faces a dilemma. As in the one-shot interaction, player 2's one-period payoff is maximized by choosing to betray. But in the repeated game, if player 1 is playing the trigger strategy, then such a betrayal by player 2 leads player 1 to choose not-trust forever after, producing a payoff of zero for player 2 in each subsequent period. Thus, the key question is how player 2 trades off the short-run temptation (a payoff of two instead of one now) against the long-run cost (a payoff of zero instead of one forever after). The answer depends on the interest rate: if r is sufficiently low, then the long-run consideration dominates and player 2 prefers to forgo the short-run temptation.

The general point is that cooperation is prone to defection (otherwise we should call cooperation something else—such as a happy alignment of the players' self-interests), but in some circumstances defection can be met with punishment. A potential defector therefore must weigh the present value of continued cooperation against the short-term gain from defection followed by the long-term loss from punishment. If a player's payoffs (per period) are C from cooperation, D from defection, and P from punishment (where $D > C > P$), then this decision amounts to evaluating two time-paths of payoffs: $(C, C, C, \ldots)$ versus $(D, P, P, P, \ldots)$, as shown in figure 11.2.

Because the present value of \$1 received every period starting tomorrow is \$1/r, the time-path of payoffs $(C, C, C, \ldots)$ yields a higher present value than the time-path $(D, P, P, P, \ldots)$ if

$$(*) \quad \left\{1 + \frac{1}{r}\right\} C > D + \frac{1}{r} P$$

Rearranging the inequality (*) yields $r < (C - P)/(D - C)$. In the repeated-game literature, this result is often restated as follows: if the players are sufficiently patient (if r is sufficiently close to zero), then it

Figure 11.2   Incentives in a Repeated Game

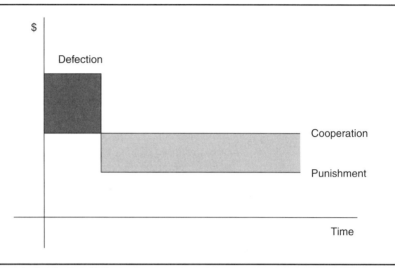

Source: Author's compilation.

is optimal to cooperate, forgoing the short-run temptation (D – C now) for the long-term gain (C – P forever after). For purposes of this essay, however, it is more useful to recall that the interest rate r reflects not only the time value of money but also the probability that the players will never meet again after the current period. If this probability is high, then r is high. Thus, the result that cooperation is optimal if r is sufficiently close to zero can be interpreted in terms of something like social structure: provided the time value of money is not too high, cooperation is optimal today if the players' relationship is sufficiently likely to continue in the future.

The model described here is excessively tidy: cooperation either works perfectly or doesn't work at all, depending on the interest rate. It is natural to ask what happens when the players are not "sufficiently patient." In brief, all is not lost, because it may be possible to achieve partial rather than full cooperation.[3] It is also natural to ask why there are never any fights or misunderstandings in this equilibrium. Edward Green and Robert Porter (1984) have developed a model in which the players' actions are not perfectly observable and cooperation breaks down periodically (but for a finite time, after which it begins again). Adding such imperfect observability, and its resulting temporary breakdowns of cooperation, would be a step toward realism in many of the settings considered in the next two sections.

It is also natural to ask whether cooperation is the inevitable outcome of this repeated game, even when the players are sufficiently patient.

The answer is that it is not: there are a great many other equilibria of the repeated game. Gary Miller (this volume) sketches the range of such equilibria, from perfect cooperation to its polar opposite (perpetual defection); elsewhere (Miller 1992) he says more about this plethora of equilibria and, importantly, about the potential role of leadership in creating and sustaining equilibria in repeated games. These latter issues—creating and sustaining equilibria—are at the forefront of research on repeated games and deserve substantial attention in the near future. But my guess is that such research will enrich the current theory, not overturn its basic insights (such as figure 11.2 and condition [*]). I therefore turn next to applications of the existing theory of repeated games to the problems posed by Coase and Hobbes.

Coase (and Williamson) Meet Repeated Games

Coase argues that firms would not need to exist if markets were perfect.[4] Williamson (1975) makes important progress toward explaining why markets may perform poorly—roughly, because formal contracts are typically incomplete. And as a second prong of his argument, Williamson also suggests why firms may perform better—roughly, because firms may use relational contracts (defined below), as envisioned in Herbert Simon's (1951) theory of the employment relationship.

The second prong of Williamson's argument is clearly correct: firms are riddled with relational contracts—informal agreements, unwritten codes of conduct, and norms that powerfully affect the behaviors of individuals in firms. Virtually every collegial and hierarchical relationship in organizations involves important relational contracts, including informal quid pro quos between coworkers and unwritten understandings between bosses and subordinates about task assignment, promotion, and termination decisions. Many earlier observers also emphasized the importance of such informal agreements in organizations.[5] Even ostensibly formal processes such as compensation, transfer pricing, internal auditing, and capital budgeting often cannot be understood without consideration of their associated informal agreements.[6]

But business relationships are also riddled with relational contracts. Many transactions do not occur in a pure spot market between buyers and sellers who pass (goods) in the night. Instead, supply chains often involve long-run, hand-in-glove supplier relationships through which the parties reach accommodations when unforeseen or uncontracted-for events occur.[7] Similar relationships also exist horizontally, as in the networks of firms in the fashion industry or the diamond trade.[8] Whether vertical or horizontal, these relational contracts influence the behaviors of parties across firm boundaries. Thus, Williamson's (1975) argument seems incomplete: formal contracts may well be incomplete, but relational contracts seem roughly as important between firms as within.

In a recent paper my colleagues and I (Baker, Gibbons, and Murphy 2000) revisit the Coase-Williamson comparison of markets versus firms, taking into account the ubiquity of relational contracts in both domains. Both within and between organizations, relational contracts can help circumvent difficulties in formal contracting. For example, a formal contract must be specified ex ante in terms that can be verified ex post by a third party (such as a court), while a relational contract can be based on outcomes that cannot be verified ex post, and also on outcomes that are prohibitively costly to specify ex ante. A relational contract thus allows the parties to utilize their detailed knowledge of their specific situation and to adapt to new information as it becomes available. For the same reasons, however, these relational contracts cannot be enforced by a third party. Instead, relational contracts must be designed to be self-enforcing: each party's reputation must be sufficiently valuable, relative to the payoffs from reneging on the relational contract, that neither party wishes to lose his reputation by reneging.

What I have called a relational contract seems similar to Carol Heimer's (this volume) "trust relation," with its emphasis on "uncertainty and vulnerability." Following Simon (1951) and Williamson (1975), I have tried to emphasize the important role of uncertainty in making relational contracts potentially valuable: in the presence of uncertainty, the parties want to be able to respond to events after they occur. Furthermore, the (necessarily) self-enforcing nature of relational contracts emphasizes at least one kind of vulnerability: even if condition (*) holds (where C is the payoff from abiding by the relational contract, D is the payoff from reneging on the relational contract, and P is the payoff after losing one's reputation for abiding by relational contracts), the prospect that one party could renege on the relational contract makes the other party vulnerable.

Baker, Murphy, and I have developed a model in which an upstream party uses an asset to produce a good that can be used in a downstream party's production process. We follow Sanford Grossman and Oliver Hart's (1986) terminology: when the upstream party owns the asset, we call the transaction non-integrated (the upstream party is an independent contractor, working with an asset she owns); when the downstream party owns the asset, we call the transaction integrated (the upstream party is an employee, working with an asset owned by the firm). We assume that ownership of the asset conveys ownership of the good. (In fact, the asset could simply be the legal title to the good.) Thus, if the upstream party owns the asset, then the downstream party cannot use the good without buying it from the upstream party, whereas if the downstream party owns the asset, then he already owns the good.

Under either ownership structure, the downstream party would like the upstream party to take actions that improve the value of the good in the downstream production process. Relational contracts can encourage these actions: for example, the downstream party can promise to pay the upstream party a bonus if she produces a good of high (but noncontractible) value. Because this promise is based on observable but noncontractible outcomes, it provides incentives to the upstream party only if it is self-enforcing. (That is, the short-run value of reneging must be less than the long-run value of the relationship.)

The key question in our analysis is whether a particular promise is more likely to be self-enforcing under integration or non-integration. Under vertical integration, if the downstream party reneges on the bonus, he nonetheless owns the good. But under non-integration, if the downstream party reneges on the bonus, he cannot use the good without buying it. In this sense, non-integration gives the upstream party more recourse should the downstream party renege on the promised bonus. But non-integration has a drawback: it creates an incentive for the upstream party to take actions that improve her bargaining position with the downstream party. These two conflicting effects (recourse and bargaining position) produce our main result: integration affects the parties' temptations to renege on a relational contract, and hence affects the best relational contract the parties can sustain. That is, a major factor in the vertical-integration decision is whether integration or non-integration facilitates the superior relational contract. In short, integration is an instrument in the service of the parties' relationship.

So far, I hope to have supported three assertions: there are many relational contracts that have important influences on behavior, both within and between firms; repeated-game models can capture some of the important features and tensions of these relational contracts; and the economic incentive to renege on a given relational contract depends on whether the parties are integrated. The last of these assertions begins to suggest how social structure affects relational contracts, but we can say more. As in the previous section, social structure enters the model through the interest rate r, which reflects not only the time value of money but also the probability that the parties' relationship will continue in the future. One can imagine two polar cases: a "spot" social structure, in which the parties will never see each other again after their current interaction, and a "relational" social structure, in which the parties will continue to interact for the foreseeable future.

These two polar social structures (spot and relational) can be combined with the two possibilities for asset ownership described earlier (integrated or not), producing the four governance regimes summarized in figure 11.3. Consistent with common usage, one can call the integrated case "employment" (where the upstream party is an employee,

Figure 11.3   Four Governance Regimes

	Asset Ownership	
Social Structure	Non-Integrated	Integrated
Spot	Spot outsourcing	Spot employment
Relational	Relational outsourcing	Relational employment

Source: Author's compilation.

working with an asset owned by the firm) and the non-integrated case "outsourcing" (where the upstream party is an independent contractor, working with an asset she owns). The four governance regimes are then spot and relational outsourcing and spot and relational employment.

Baker, Murphy, and I analyze the efficiency of each of these governance regimes. In fact, we consider all possible values of the interest rate r, and hence consider all the social structures between the spot and relational polar cases defined here. For any given value of r, we compute whether integration or non-integration is more efficient. That is, for any given probability that the parties' relationship will continue in the future, we conduct a formal version of the Coase-Williamson horse race between markets and firms, taking relational contracts into account in both domains.

Many of the classic contributions to organizational economics can also be described using figure 11.3. For example, static analyses of integration in the absence of relational contracting (for example, Grossman and Hart 1986) are analogous to our comparison of spot outsourcing to spot employment (the top row in the figure). Similarly, repeated-game analyses of relationships within firms (for example, Kreps 1990) are analogous to our comparison of spot employment to relational employment (the right column), and repeated-game analyses of relationships between firms (for example, Klein and Leffler 1981) are analogous to our comparison of spot outsourcing to relational outsourcing (the left column). Finally, Williamson's (1975) argument that the advantage of firms over markets lies in the firm's ability to enforce relational contracts is analogous to our comparison of spot outsourcing to relational employment (the main diagonal), and Williamson's (1996, ch. 4) argument that important relational contracts exist between firms as well as within them is analogous to our comparison of relational outsourcing to relational employment (the bottom row).[9]

I now hope to have supported a fourth assertion, in addition to the three set out earlier: repeated-game models can be used to run the Coase-Williamson horse race between markets and firms, taking relational contracts into account in both domains. The result is a new perspective on vertical integration, in which the make-or-buy decision is seen as an instrument in the service of the parties' relationship. Baker, Murphy, and I also suggest how this approach can be enriched in future work to analyze specific relational contracts within organizations (such as transfer pricing and capital allocation) as well as the roles of relational contracts in specific multi-organizational forms (such as networks and joint ventures). In short, I think one can see on the horizon an economic theory of trust and social relations within and between firms.

Hobbes (and Axelrod)
Meet Repeated Games

The problem of social order—of creating and maintaining the security of persons and property—is central to political economy.[10] Without social order, people find themselves in the Hobbesian "war of all against all," where life is "solitary, poor, nasty, brutish and short." With social order—that is, when rights are enforced—people can use markets, contracts, and other economic institutions to reap gains from cooperation. Thus, the provision of social order is crucial for prosperity and growth.

Recently economists and others have used the theory of repeated games to analyze institutions that support social order. This emerging literature revisits Plato's question, "Who will guard the guardians?" The answer is that, in a world of self-interest, there is no disinterested third party to enforce society's rules, so some of those rules must be self-enforcing. Put more formally, institutions—that is, the formal and informal "rules of the game" (North 1990, 3)—must be equilibria: they must provide everyone, including enforcers, with an incentive to behave appropriately. Using this approach, Greif (1989, 1993, 1994), Greif, Milgrom, and Weingast (1994), and Milgrom, North, and Weingast (1990) have examined the role of private judges, merchant guilds, and other institutions in the revival of long-distance trade in medieval Europe. Similarly, Robert Ellickson (1991), Gary Libecap (1989), and Elinor Ostrom (1990) have examined the role of institutions in resolving contemporary commons problems in cattle ranching, oil-drilling, fishing, and related industries.

Ironically, these equilibrium institutionalists have so far neglected the most prominent source of social order in the modern world: the state. This neglect stands in stark contrast to the large literature in political economy that takes the state as its central focus. Beginning with Hobbes, Locke, and Madison, this classic line of inquiry has recently developed into three distinct approaches to modeling the state: the rational-predator school, the constitutional economists, and the neo-Hobbesians. Although each of these schools has made important progress, each reveals a weakness in the others, as follows.

The rational-predator school of Yoram Barzel (1992), Robert Bates (1981), Margaret Levi (1988), Douglass North (1981) and Mancur Olson (1993) treats the ruler as a self-interested sovereign with a monopoly on violence but argues that such a ruler is typically not a pure predator: she finds it optimal to provide some services to her subjects. Their reasoning is simple (and akin to the logic of the Laffer curve). For the ruler, subjects are capital goods that provide a flow of income over time. Under a wide range of circumstances, the ruler can expand her tax base by protecting her subjects from each other *and from herself.* Thus, the pursuit of self-interest may induce the ruler to provide a legal system or even representative government.

The rational-predator school shows that even the most powerful predator may want to provide services like those envisioned in the Hobbesian conception of a social contract. In reaching this conclusion, however, these scholars ignore another aspect of the social contract—the constraints it places on the ruler. This omission is remedied by a second approach to models of limited government, that of the constitutional economists (for example, see Brennan and Buchanan 1985; Buchanan and Bush 1974; and Buchanan and Tullock 1962). These theorists analyze the effect of constitutional rules on an otherwise self-interested ruler. That is, they model constitutional rules as shaping politicians' incentives and opportunities, and then ask how political decisions vary with changes in those rules. Because they are interested in policy choice, their models simply assume the ex post enforcement of the rules—for the constitutional economists, the social contract is an exogenously imposed constraint.

A third approach—that of the neo-Hobbesians such as Jean Hampton (1986), Russell Hardin (1990), and Douglas Heckathorn and Steven Maser (1987)—endogenizes the social contract by modeling its choice. They begin with citizens in a state of nature (sometimes modeled as a prisoners' dilemma). Like Hobbes, they then argue that, to avoid the inefficiency of mutual defection, people come together to create a government to enforce private contracts. The neo-Hobbesians model the process of creating a government as a coordination game, in which citizens can escape the state of nature only if they agree on one of many possible social contracts. In these models different contracts distribute the benefits of society differently, but all Pareto-dominate the state of nature. From this Pareto-dominance, the neo-Hobbesians conclude that once the citizens have made their choice, the social contract will be self-enforcing. That is, they ignore the possibility that the ruler's misbehavior can destroy social order. Indeed (and ironically, given their debt to Hobbes), their models include no ruler.

In the rest of this section I first sketch some of the recent repeated-game models of self-enforcing institutions other than the state. I then turn to an analogous model of the state, Gibbons and Rutten (2000), which attempts to integrate the strengths of the three prominent theories of the state just summarized. But in this section I discuss only individual horses; as far as I know, a formal analysis of the Hobbesian horse race between the state and anarchy does not yet exist.

Anarchy: Order Without Law?

Suppose that the state of nature is a group of N people playing two-person prisoners' dilemmas (PDs) with each other. In anticipation of the eventual introduction of a state into the analysis, call the players citizens. Each period, each citizen plays a prisoners' dilemma. There is a matching rule specifying who plays whom each period; for simplicity, suppose it is random.[11] In equilibrium, two citizens playing a PD one time (and then vanishing from the population) would both defect.

This modeling strategy is very abstract, but it is also widely accepted because it captures an important feature of the games of daily life: people are engaged in transactions that they would like to govern by a contract specifying that both cooperate.[12] Following Hobbes, the role of the state in this environment is to enforce such contracts. But as has been noted with increasing frequency in economics, law, political science, and sociology, citizens need not suffer the war of all against all, even if no Hobbesian Leviathan exists to punish defectors. That is, anarchy (literally, the absence of a ruler) does not preclude cooperation.[13]

Perhaps the simplest mechanism for sustaining cooperation under anarchy is bilateral reputation. That is, citizen n keeps a record of her past dealings with citizen m, and if n is ever paired with m again, she consults this record and plays as dictated by some strategy (perhaps Tit-for-Tat), given the recorded history between n and m. In this case, the N-citizen dynamic game can be thought of as a collection of two-player repeated games, although meetings between the two players do not happen every period. If the population is large, however, then the expected time between meetings of a given pair of citizens may be quite long, in which case bilateral-reputation incentives cannot be strong.

More optimistically, one might suppose that all information about other citizens' experiences is publicly available, so that citizen n would know the full history of citizen m's play (with n and with all others) before playing m in a given period. In this public-information case, the N-citizen dynamic game can be thought of as a two-player repeated game, where meetings between the two players occur every period. Cooperation can be sustained in equilibrium if the players are sufficiently patient (that is, the interest rate r is sufficiently small, as derived earlier in the chapter), but remember that this simple analysis applies only in the unlikely case in which all information about all other citizens' experiences is publicly available.

Rather than explore the implications of exogenous information structures, one can endogenize the flow of information that sustains reputation mechanisms. Such analyses begin from an exogenous but impoverished information structure (such as the own-history information structure from the bilateral-reputation case), then define the opportunities for and costs of communication, and finally determine whether a richer information structure (such as the extreme case of public information) can be sustained in equilibrium, together with a level of cooperation consistent with that richer information structure. Michihiro Kandori (1992) and Randall Calvert (1994) provide two such models in abstract settings; the papers cited earlier by (various combinations of) Greif, Milgrom, North, and Weingast build similar applied models to interpret evidence on the development of trade since the eleventh century.

Equilibrium information structures, together with the cooperative behavior they sustain (and threats of punishment following defections), can be interpreted as self-enforcing social institutions—that is, as endogenous rules of the game. A complete analysis must resolve several questions, however, including, "Why the institution was needed, what sanctions were to be used to deter undesirable behavior, who was to apply the sanctions, how the sanctioners learned or decided what sanctions to apply, why they did not shirk from their duty, and why the offender did not flee to avoid the sanction" (Greif, Milgrom, and Weingast 1994, 746). It is important to note that in these equilibrium models two behaviors are endogenous: not only interaction in the PDs but also communication. Thus, all the issues related to sanctioning apply not only to departures from prescribed interaction but also to departures from prescribed communication.

As the applied models of Greif, Milgrom, North, and Weingast illustrate, this equilibrium approach to communication and interaction can be used to interpret real institutions. Furthermore, both decentralized and centralized institutions are within the scope of the theory: Calvert (1994), for example, compares a decentralized mechanism (in which everyone talks to everyone else every period) to a centralized mechanism (in which everyone reports to a center at the end of one period and then asks the center about the next partner's history before play begins in the next period). Unless communication costs are assumed to be zero, however, all these institutions are costly to operate. Furthermore, these costs grow as the size of the population increases. Such communication costs motivate the search for alternative institutions: rules of the game that produce social order but avoid the costs of communication (and the costs of inducing communication) that are an inevitable part of the reputation mechanisms that promise order without law. One possibility is a state.

Hierarchy: Law Without Order?

Rutten and I (Gibbons and Rutten 2000) have developed a repeated-game model of the state that parallels the equilibrium analyses of social institutions that produce cooperation under anarchy. The main points are as follows. First, the state is modeled as an equilibrium institution. Thus, the state's actions in the model (enforcement of contracts between citizens, limited taxation, and provision of a public good) must be in its long-run self-interest.

Second, there are many equilibria. In our basic model they range from a maximum tax rate (above which the citizens prefer anarchy and so will revolt) to a minimum tax rate (below which it is in the state's interest to confiscate all the citizens' wealth in one period, even if this means losing power forever after). The problem of selecting one of these equilibria is precisely the neo-Hobbesians' coordination game in which citizens choose a social contract.

Third, the payoffs in the state's "game of politics" with its citizens are derived from the underlying "games of daily life" among citizens (namely, the same two-person prisoners' dilemmas just studied under anarchy). This embedding of the game of politics in the games of daily life exposes a connection between the social benefits from the state's provision of social order and the state's incentive to abuse its power. Furthermore, rooting the analysis of the state in the same environment used to analyze anarchy is a necessary condition for a subsequent formal model of the Hobbesian horse race between state and anarchy.

Fourth, after developing our basic model of the state as the provider of social order, we enrich the model to allow a second role for the state: providing a public good (as suggested by Hume, Rousseau, and others) as well as social order. We find that having a single actor provide both social order and public goods may create economies of scope: the state can provide public goods more efficiently if it also is charged with providing social order.[14]

Finally, in every equilibrium the state is both a contractor (providing social order, as envisioned by Hobbes) and a predator (extracting resources, as feared by Locke). At one extreme (maximal predation) the ruler takes most of the gains from trade; as long as she leaves the citizens better off than in the state of nature, they will not rebel. At the other extreme (maximal contracting) the citizens keep most of the gains; as long as they do not tempt the ruler too greatly, she will not abuse her power. In all the intermediate equilibria, the state exhibits a mix of predation and contracting. Indeed, even maximal predation includes some contracting, and maximal contracting some predation.

This predatory-contractor model of the state meshes comfortably with the three prominent theories of the state summarized earlier. Like the rational-predator school, we let our ruler extract resources from her subjects; unlike them, we assume that the ruler has only a temporary monopoly over violence, which the citizens may subsequently revoke. Like the constitutional economists, we treat the social contract as a constraint on self-interested politicians; unlike them, we require that the social contract be self-enforcing. Like the neo-Hobbesians, we treat the social contract as a coordination game, distinct from the prisoners' dilemmas facing ordinary citizens; unlike them, we explicitly link the two—in our model the payoffs from the social contract derive from the underlying games between the citizens.

In sum, Rutten and I offer a stick-figure rendering of the grand ideas of Hobbes and Locke. In the stationary and spare world we model, our simple state solves the classical problem of providing social order that inspired its creation. But real constitutions set only the basic rules of the political-economic game: they create other institutions (such as the legislature and the courts) that fill in some of the gaps in the social contract. We envision a rich class of equilibrium models of the state, corresponding to the variety of government structures observed in the world. We hope our model lays the foundation for such a literature on the theory of the state, parallel to the emerging literature on order without law. Further development of these two literatures will make it possible to conduct a formal version of the Hobbesian horse race between state and anarchy, with both modeled as equilibrium institutions in a single environment.

Conclusion

Repeated-game models focus on the role of long-run self-interest in overcoming short-term temptation. I have tried to argue that such models can shed light on relational contracts within and between firms and on the self-enforcing institutions of political economy.

According to the repeated-game approach, if you understand my long-run self-interest, you may "trust" me not to yield to certain short-run temptations. As Hardin (this volume) documents, there has been much debate over whether this calculative conception of trust is all there is to that slippery term. I am inclined to believe that there is more to trust than calculation, but I have tried to argue here that calculative trust is important in the world and that repeated-game models can help us understand it.

But saying that social structure can help create trust leaves open the question of whether we can trust in social structure. That is, there is abundant evidence that relational contracts often hurt rather than improve organizational performance (see Roethlisberger and Dickson 1939; Roy 1952; and many others). As noted earlier, this indeterminacy appears in the economic model as the existence of multiple equilibria in the repeated game. Like Miller (1992), I believe that an economic theory of leadership can and should be developed around the idea that leaders try to create and change equilibria. Such a theory will grope toward ideas such as building and utilizing trust, but even sketching the outlines of this theory must await another essay.

My exposure to many of these issues began in an endogenous discussion group on "Power and Politics in Governance Structures" at the Center for Advanced Study in the Behavioral Sciences, where my fellowship was supported by NSF grant SBR-9022192 and Cornell's Johnson School. Neil Fligstein, Tom Romer, and Neil Smelser are especially guilty of broadening my horizons during that year. Since then, I have pursued these issues in work with George Baker and Kevin J. Murphy and with Andy Rutten; anything coherent I say here has benefited greatly from long discussion with them.

Notes

1. This section draws heavily on Gibbons (1997). Readers familiar with the theory of repeated games—such as condition (*) below—can skip this section.

2. In the Trust Game, unlike most, reverting to short-run self-interest is identical to spite: it achieves the harshest possible punishment of player 2.

3. To see how this may work, examine (*). Note that reducing the payoff from cooperation from C to some lower level is no help at all, in and of itself. That is, holding the payoff from defection (D) constant, reducing C makes it harder to satisfy (*). The trick is that reducing C may also reduce D: making do with partial cooperation may also limit the players' opportunities for profitable deviations. If D falls more than C, then (*) may hold.

4. This section draws heavily on Baker, Gibbons, and Murphy (2000).

5. See Barnard (1938) and Simon (1947), as well as the case studies by Blau (1955), Gouldner (1954), and Selznick (1949), which inspired American sociology's departure from Weber's emphasis on formal organizational structures and processes. Granovetter (1985, 502) offers a more recent assessment: "The distinction between the 'formal' and the 'informal' organization of the firm is one of the oldest in the literature, and it hardly needs repeating that observers who assume firms to be structured in fact by the official organization chart are sociological babes in the woods."

6. See Lawler (1990) on compensation, Eccles (1985) on transfer pricing, Dalton (1959) on internal auditing, and Bower (1970) on capital budgeting. See also Blumenstein and Stern (1996) on the important gaps in the 1,700-page contract between General Motors and the United Auto Workers that are covered by informal agreements.

7. Stewart Macaulay (1963) emphasizes the importance of such "noncontractual relations" in various businesses. Bruce Kogut, Weigian Shan, and Gordon Walker (1992) suggest the prominence of such relationships by

relabeling the make-or-buy decision as "the make-or-cooperate decision." Robert Eccles (1981) describes "quasifirms" in the construction industry—long-run relationships between general contractors and independent, specialized subcontractors.

8. In "Neither Market nor Hierarchy: Network Forms of Organization," Walter Powell (1990) describes a variety of other examples and emphasizes their differences from spot markets and firms. See Podolny and Page (1998) for a summary and critique of this growing literature.

9. Williamson (1985, 83) also emphasizes relational contracts between firms but construes them as lying on a continuum between markets and hierarchies. Table 11.3 suggests that the set of alternative governance regimes is two-dimensional, so it is not possible to locate all governance structures on a line between markets and hierarchies. Compared to Williamson's first book, the second shows much greater concern for limits on the effectiveness of firms and the importance of relational contracts between firms. But it includes little analysis of how relational contracts between firms might differ from those within, and Williamson limits his discussion of alternative organizational forms to brief mention of "hybrid transactions (franchising, joint ventures, and other forms of nonstandard contracting)" (83).

10. This section draws heavily on Gibbons and Rutten (2000). Any statements that reveal more than passing acquaintance with the political economy literature were greatly influenced by Andy Rutten, while any gross errors are surely mine.

11. Note that random matching every period in a large population is very different from Robert Axelrod's (1984) tournaments, in which two players play each other repeatedly over a long horizon. As a result, the institutions that support cooperation in large, decentralized populations (described later in the chapter) are often very different from the Tit-for-Tat strategies that Axelrod emphasizes.

12. See Taylor (1976), Kavka (1986), and Hampton (1986) for discussions of the extent to which Hobbes's state of nature is well modeled by a population playing two-person PDs.

13. Hence Taylor's (1976) title, "Anarchy and Cooperation," and Hirshleifer's (1995), "Anarchy and Its Breakdown."

14. The interaction between these two roles of the state in our model may be a cousin of another interaction suggested by Hardin (1990), in which a leader first emerges to solve a coordination problem, then finds power in such a leadership role, and finally uses this power to solve social dilemmas.

References

Axelrod, Robert. 1984. *The Evolution of Cooperation*. New York: Basic Books.

Baker, George, Robert Gibbons, and Kevin J. Murphy. 2000. "Relational Contracts and the Theory of the Firm." Unpublished paper. Massachusetts Institute of Technology, Sloan School.

Barnard, Chester. 1938. *The Functions of the Executive.* Cambridge, Mass.: Harvard University Press.

Barzel, Yoram. 1992. "Confiscation by the Ruler: The Rise and Fall of Jewish Lending in the Middle Ages." *Journal of Law and Economics* 35: 1–13.

Bates, Robert. 1981. *Markets and States in Tropical Africa: The Political Basis of Agricultural Policies.* Berkeley: University of California Press.

Blau, Peter. 1955. *The Dynamics of Bureaucracy: A Study of Interpersonal Relations in Two Government Agencies.* Chicago: University of Chicago Press.

Blumenstein, Rebecca, and Gabriella Stern. 1996. "UAW, Auto Makers Find Some Things Better Left Unsaid." *Wall Street Journal,* November 25, A1.

Bower, Joseph. 1970. *Managing the Resource Allocation Process: A Study of Corporate Planning and Investment.* Boston: Harvard Business School Press.

Brennan, Geoffrey, and James Buchanan. 1985. *The Reason of Rules: Constitutional Political Economy.* New York: Cambridge University Press.

Buchanan, James, and W. Bush. 1974. "Political Constraints on Contractual Redistribution." *American Economic Review* 64(2): 153–57.

Buchanan, James, and Gordon Tullock. 1962. *The Calculus of Consent: Logical Foundations of Constitutional Democracy.* Ann Arbor: University of Michigan Press.

Calvert, Randall. 1994. "Rational Actors, Equilibrium, and Social Institutions." In *Explaining Social Institutions,* edited by Jack Knight and Itai Sened. Ann Arbor: University of Michigan Press.

Coase, Ronald. 1937. "The Nature of the Firm." *Economica* 4: 386–405.

Dalton, Melville. 1959. *Men Who Manage.* New York: Wiley.

Eccles, Robert. 1981. "The Quasifirm in the Construction Industry." *Journal of Economic Behavior and Organization* 2: 335–57.

———. 1985. *The Transfer Pricing Problem: A Theory for Practice.* Lexington, Mass.: Heath.

Ellickson, Robert. 1991. *Order Without Law: How Neighbors Resolve Disputes.* Cambridge, Mass.: Harvard University Press.

Gibbons, Robert. 1997. "An Introduction to Game Theory for Applied Economists." *Journal of Economic Perspectives* 11: 127–49.

Gibbons, Robert, and Andrew Rutten. 2000. "Hierarchical Dilemmas: Social Contract with Self-interested Rulers." Unpublished paper. Massachusetts Institute of Technology, Sloan School.

Gouldner, Alvin. 1954. *Patterns of Industrial Bureaucracy.* New York: Free Press.

Granovetter, Mark. 1985. "Economic Action and Social Structure: The Problem of Embeddedness." *American Journal of Sociology* 91(3): 481–510.

Green, Edward, and Robert Porter. 1984. "Noncooperative Collusion Under Imperfect Price Information." *Econometrica* 52(1): 87–100.

Greif, Avner. 1989. "Reputation and Coalitions in Medieval Trade: Evidence on the Maghribi Traders." *Journal of Economic History* 49(4): 857–82.

———. 1993. "Contract Enforceability and Economic Institutions in Early Trade: The Maghribi Traders' Coalition." *American Economic Review* 83(3): 525–48.

———. 1994. "Cultural Beliefs and the Organization of Society: A Historical and Theoretical Reflection on Collectivist and Individualist Societies." *Journal of Political Economy* 102(5): 912–50.

Greif, Avner, Paul Milgrom, and Barry Weingast. 1994. "Coordination, Commitment, and Enforcement: The Case of the Merchant Guild." *Journal of Political Economy* 102(4): 745–76.

Grossman, Sanford, and Oliver Hart. 1986. "The Costs and Benefits of Ownership: A Theory of Vertical and Lateral Ownership." *Journal of Political Economy* 94(4): 691–719.

Hampton, Jean. 1986. *Hobbes and the Social Contract Tradition.* New York: Cambridge University Press.

Hardin, Russell. 1990. "The Social Evolution of Cooperation." In *The Limits of Rationality,* edited by Karen Cook and Margaret Levi. Chicago: University of Chicago Press.

Heckathorn, Douglas, and Steven Maser. 1987. "Bargaining and Constitutional Contracts." *American Journal of Political Science* 31(1): 142–68.

Hirshleifer, Jack. 1995. "Anarchy and Its Breakdown." *Journal of Political Economy* 103: 26–52.

Hobbes, Thomas. 1991. *Leviathan.* Richard Tuck (ed.). New York: Cambridge University Press.

Kandori, Michihiro. 1992. "Social Norms and Community Enforcement." *Review of Economic Studies* 59(1): 63–80.

Kavka, Gregory. 1986. *Hobbesian Moral and Political Theory.* Princeton, N.J.: Princeton University Press.

Klein, Benjamin, and Keith Leffler. 1981. "The Role of Market Forces in Assuring Contractual Performance." *Journal of Political Economy* 89(4): 615–41.

Kogut, Bruce, Weigian Shan, and Gordon Walker. 1992. "The Make-or-Cooperate Decision in the Context of an Industry Network." In *Networks and Organizations: Structure, Form, and Action,* edited by Nitin Nohria and Robert Eccles. Boston: Harvard Business School Press.

Kreps, David. 1990. "Corporate Culture and Economic Theory." In *Perspectives on Positive Political Economy,* edited by James Alt and Kenneth Shepsle. Cambridge: Cambridge University Press.

Lawler, Edward. 1990. *Strategic Pay: Aligning Organizational Strategies and Pay Systems.* San Francisco: Jossey-Bass.

Levi, Margaret. 1988. *Of Rule and Revenue.* Berkeley: University of California Press.

Libecap, Gary. 1989. *Contracting for Property Rights.* New York: Cambridge University Press.

Macaulay, Stewart. 1963. "Noncontractual Relations in Business: A Preliminary Study." *American Sociological Review* 28(1): 55–67.

Milgrom, Paul, Douglass North, and Barry Weingast. 1990. "The Role of Institutions in the Revival of Trade: The Law Merchant, Private Judges, and the Champagne Fairs." *Economics and Politics* 2: 1–23.

Miller, Gary. 1992. *Managerial Dilemmas: The Political Economy of Hierarchy.* New York: Cambridge University Press.

North, Douglass. 1981. *Structure and Change in Economic History.* New York: Norton.

———. 1990. *Institutions, Institutional Change, and Economic Performance.* New York: Cambridge University Press.

Olson, Mancur. 1993. "Dictatorship, Democracy, and Development." *American Political Science Review* 87(3): 567–76.

Ostrom, Elinor. 1990. *Governing the Commons: The Evolution of Institutions for Collective Action.* New York: Cambridge University Press.

Podolny, Joel, and Karen Page. 1998. "Network Forms of Organization." *Annual Review of Sociology* 24: 57–76.

Powell, Walter. 1990. "Neither Market nor Hierarchy: Network Forms of Organization." *Research in Organizational Behavior* 12: 295–336.

Roethlisberger, Fritz, and William Dickson. 1939. *Management and the Worker: An Account of a Research Program Conducted by the Western Electric Company, Hawthorne Works, Chicago.* Cambridge, Mass.: Harvard University Press.

Roy, Donald. 1952. "Quota Restriction and Goldbricking in a Machine Shop." *American Journal of Sociology* 57(5): 477–42.

Schein, Edgar. 1992. *Organizational Culture and Leadership.* San Francisco: Jossey-Bass.

Selznick, Philip. 1949. *TVA and the Grass Roots: A Study of Politics and Organization.* Berkeley: University of California Press.

Simon, Herbert. 1947. *Administrative Behavior: A Study of Decision-Making Processes in Administrative Organizations.* New York: Free Press.

———. 1951. "A Formal Theory Model of the Employment Relationship." *Econometrica* 19: 293–305.

Taylor, Michael. 1976. *Anarchy and Cooperation.* London: Wiley.

Williamson, Oliver. 1975. *Markets and Hierarchies: Analysis and Antitrust Implications.* New York: Free Press.

———. 1985. *The Economic Institutions of Capitalism: Firms, Markets, Relational Contracting.* New York: Free Press.

———. 1996. *The Mechanisms of Governance.* New York: Oxford University Press.

Chapter 12

Social Norms and the Rule of Law: Fostering Trust in a Socially Diverse Society

Jack Knight

S OMETIMES alone, sometimes with the related concepts of social capital and community, trust is regularly invoked to explain various forms of social cooperation in political and economic life. Although, as with many such ideas, those who invoke it do not all share the same meaning of the concept, they do, with few exceptions, posit trust as an unquestioned good, a necessary condition for a healthy and productive society. Russell Hardin's contribution to this volume systematically sets out the array of conceptions of trust to be found in the recent debates. In this chapter I focus on one such conception, a general sense of trust in the other members of one's society. This is the form of trust most closely related to other concepts like social capital or community. Its most important features are that it is interpersonal in nature, generalized across the members of a group, and not tied to the reputation of particular individuals.

My substantive concern here relates to a potential challenge to the emergence and maintenance of generalized trust in many modern societies. The challenge is raised by a fundamental, and increasingly prevalent, fact of contemporary social life: social diversity. Many who have studied social cooperation and order raise doubts about the efficacy of phenomena such as trust under conditions of social diversity. Some pose the issue in terms of the challenge that multiculturalism raises for traditional conceptions of a broad and encompassing sense of national community (see, for example, Etzioni 1993). Others put the challenge in the boldest terms when they argue that social diversity is the primary source of conflict and thus the basic challenge to social order in modern society (see, for example, Lukes 1991).

Here I organize the analysis around the following question: under what conditions is generalized trust most likely to develop and be maintained in a socially diverse society? I address this question in two ways. First, I consider whether generalized trust can emerge and be maintained spontaneously through informal interactions. Second, I consider whether generalized trust can be fostered by formal institutional means, more specifically, through the rule of law. Prior to addressing the substantive issues I set out in the next section an account of the micro foundations of generalized trust. This requires a brief review of the relevant literature on trust to clarify the causal mechanisms embedded in prevailing accounts of how trust emerges and how it facilitates cooperation.

These questions raise a complex set of issues, and my goal here is a rather modest one: to clarify the basic logic of the relationship between trust and social institutions (both informal ones like social norms and formal ones like the rule of law) and to suggest what the relevant issues are for assessing the role of social institutions in developing and maintaining trust in socially diverse societies.[1] This is a preliminary effort; I try to identify a set of factors and related tendencies that should be addressed in future analyses. To the extent that I offer empirical evidence in support of this argument, it is merely intended to be suggestive of the types of evidence that I think would be relevant to resolving these questions.

The Micro Foundations of Generalized Trust

The most influential accounts of the importance of generalized trust and the related concept of social capital have been offered by Robert Putnam and James Coleman. Putnam (1993, 167) puts the case for social capital as follows:

> Voluntary cooperation is easier in a community that has inherited a substantial stock of social capital, in the form of norms of reciprocity and networks of civic engagement. Social capital here refers to features of social organizations, such as trust, norms and networks that can improve the efficiency of society by facilitating coordinated action.

In this passage Putnam combines several factors that are relevant to this analysis: social capital, trust, norms, cooperation. He highlights two primary sources of social capital: "Social trust in complex modern settings can arise from two related sources—norms of reciprocity and networks of civic engagement" (171).

On the effects of norms, Putnam offers a standard functional account: "Norms such as those that undergird social trust evolve because they lower transaction costs and facilitate cooperation" (172). As with most functionalist explanations, he redefines the effect but does not elaborate a mechanism that would actually explain it. On the effects of the networks of civic engagement, Putnam emphasizes the positive effects of generalized reciprocity. He lists four reasons why the generalized reciprocity characteristic of these networks enhances cooperation: it increases the costs of defection; it fosters robust norms of reciprocity; it facilitates communication and improves information flows; and it embodies past success at collaboration and provides a blueprint for future cooperation (172).

In a related way Coleman conceives of trust as a factor in certain types of social interactions characterized by risk: "They are situations in which the risk one takes depends on the performance of the other actor" (91). Here the problem that trust helps to resolve is the problem of social cooperation, a situation of interdependent action for mutual benefit. The difficulty that arises from the time lapse between actions is basically the same as the difficulty faced by two actors who have to make simultaneous, but unobserved, choices. Coleman (1990, 306–10) equates mutual trust with social capital and defines it in the functional terms of the reduction of transaction costs in these risky social interactions.

The functionalist logic of both Putnam and Coleman is in part a product of the primarily macro-level focus of their analyses. To address adequately the questions about the relationship between social diversity and generalized trust, we need an account of how trust works at the level of individual social interactions. John Brehm and Wendy Rahn (1997, 1016) extend the analysis to the individual level in their study of the relationship between membership in voluntary associations and social capital. In identifying a strong positive correlation between participation in voluntary associations and generalized trust, they highlight the importance of both personal experience and contextual factors at the individual level:

> Put together, the picture that emerges is that levels of interpersonal trust are very much influenced by real experiences. The coefficients for age cohort, the GINI index, and unemployment also imply that social capital is affected by characteristics of the community, not just individual experiences, including the socialization of children, economic performance, and the distribution of society's resources.

Building on the insights of Brehm and Rahn, we can begin to connect both experience and context to the causal mechanisms of generalized trust by providing a closer interpretation of the reasons why Putnam focuses on networks of civic engagement. Each of these reasons relates to the expectations and beliefs of the actors in the society. Each provides an individual with information about the behavior of those with whom she interacts in her everyday affairs. The existence of high costs of defection reinforces her beliefs that others will cooperate. The existence of avenues of communication increases her knowledge of the interests and beliefs of the other actors. The existence of past success may be the most important reason, because it provides both information about past cooperation and a focal point for the type of behavior that can produce mutual benefits in the future.[2] In this way the concepts of social capital and trust come to be understood in terms of the expectations and beliefs of social actors.

In terms of the specific concept of trust, accounts by Diego Gambetta and Barbara Misztal can better clarify what is at stake in this analysis. Gambetta (1988, 217) defines trust as

> a particular level of subjective probability with which an agent assesses that another agent or group of agents will perform a particular action, both before he can monitor such action (or independently of his capacity ever to be able to monitor it) and in a context in which it affects his own action.

Misztal (1996, 9) offers a similar definition with one significant addition: "To trust is to believe that the results of somebody's intended action will be appropriate from our point of view." Note that while both definitions relate to the actor's confidence in the correctness of his beliefs about the actions of others, only Misztal's definition puts constraints on the nature and content of those beliefs. She includes the requirement that the beliefs "be appropriate from our point of view." Gambetta emphasizes the importance of predictability, but Misztal rightly emphasizes that only certain types of beliefs constitute what we mean by trust in another person.

Thus, the type of trust that would resolve the problems raised by Coleman's analysis of risk is a set of beliefs and expectations that the actions of others will interrelate with my own actions in such a way as to achieve a cooperative and mutually beneficial outcome. Such a conception also captures another important feature of trust as a mechanism of social cooperation: the beliefs must be shared by the participants. As Gambetta (1988, 216) notes: "It is necessary not only to trust others before acting cooperatively, but also to believe that one is trusted by others." This latter belief is necessary to reinforce the idea that both actors' expectations have converged on cooperative behavior.[3]

Here it is important to distinguish two different senses of "sharing" social beliefs, for they support distinct causal accounts of social cooperation. Consider Talcott Parsons's (1937, 76) explanation of basic social order. On his account social order is the product of common obedience to shared social rules; order is a function of "patterns which are, by the actors and other members of the same collectivity, deemed desirable." Parsons means "shared" in an evaluative sense: the members of society share the same values that are instantiated in the rules. Not only do the actors share a common knowledge of the rules, they also share the same values and the same attitude toward the rules. For Parsons social order is contingent on a social consensus on normative values.

We can distinguish this sense of sharing from sharing merely in a cognitive sense. In this latter sense the members of a society share the knowledge of the existence of and the content of the rules, but they need not have the same evaluative attitude toward them. As many have shown (see, for example, Taylor 1982), basic social order is possible on this thin conception of shared beliefs through the realization of each individual's self-interest. On this account cooperative predictable behavior is guaranteed by the existence of mechanisms that converge expectations toward actions that satisfy the requirements of mutual benefit. Cooperation is based on sharing in the cognitive sense: the members of the society share the right kind of cooperative expectations. As long as they share the knowledge that they can individually benefit from following the same pattern of behavior, cooperation can in principle be sustained even though they do not value the pattern of behavior to the same degree or in the same way.

There are no principled reasons of which I am aware for rejecting the possibility that the causal effect of trust might work through either shared values or shared expectations. Here the question is always whether the social conditions exist for either of the two mechanisms to obtain. But for the rest of this chapter I restrict the analysis to the cognitive conception of shared beliefs as common expectations. I do so for two reasons. First, my own view is that the likelihood that the members of a society share the same set of values is quite small except in the most homogeneous of communities. Second, the exposition of the argument about the causal effect of shared beliefs is clearer in the case of common expectations.

If we accept the idea that phenomena such as generalized trust are best conceptualized as certain types of social expectations and beliefs, we must still consider a further feature of these arguments that is fundamental to the claim that this type of trust is of general importance in a society. Put in terms of social expectations, theories of social capital and generalized trust must provide an account of how these expectations extend beyond the instances of interactions with those whom we actually know to a more general expectation of cooperation about the members of a society. This requires an explanation of how the individual members of a society acquire these shared beliefs. For each individual in a society there are two primary sources of expectations and beliefs: individual past experience and cultural factors (the most important of which are social norms and conventions, the informal rules that structure social life). Although past experience is a major source of belief formation for each individual, the diversity of experiences makes it an unlikely primary source of socially shared factors. This leaves cultural factors such as social norms as the probable source of these expectations.

Social norms instantiate commonly held beliefs about the behavior of others.[4] By knowing the content of social norms, social actors can establish stable expectations about how others are going to act in common social situations. When the content of the norms dictates cooperative behavior, social actors can use this information to develop expectations about the likelihood that others will cooperate, and then make a decision to act accordingly. Recent work in cultural anthropology lends substantial support to this idea, offering detailed explorations of the ways in which cultural factors like social norms affect cognition and decision-making (see, for example, D'Andrade 1995; Hutchins 1995; and Shore 1996).[5] Note that this is the case with either possible sense of shared beliefs. On the shared expectations account, social norms instantiate the information that converges expectations on the behavior that produces mutually beneficial outcomes; on the common values account, social norms instantiate the behavior that is valued under the social consensus. In this way social norms generalize expectations beyond those of the actors whom we know personally.

To complete this account of how social norms affect generalized trust we need to maintain two important distinctions: between the general social beliefs that constitute trust and the social beliefs specific to any particular social norm, and between the cooperation inherent in norm compliance and the cooperation that we want to explain through the use of the concept of trust. By maintaining these two distinctions we can support the following plausible account of how social norms affect trust and how trust then affects social cooperation: cooperation through compliance with social norms affects an actor's general beliefs about the propensity of others to cooperate, and that belief about others affects her willingness to cooperate at some subsequent point in time or in some other context.

This helps us to make sense of Putnam's (1993, 169) somewhat ambiguous claim that social capital is similar to Hirschman's concept of "moral resources": "resources whose supply increases rather than decreases through use and which become depleted if *not* used." Although at first blush this idea conjures up confused images of social capital as a tangible phenomenon that can be accumulated and exchanged, thinking about this as certain types of social beliefs clarifies the analogy. Certain beliefs (generalized trust) are necessary to achieve social cooperation; these beliefs can be reinforced and strengthened through cooperation (compliance with prevailing social norms); and these beliefs become less firm and reliable if cooperation is not maintained. In short, the best way to conceptualize Putnam's idea of the benefits of social capital is as an account of the effects of certain types of expectations and beliefs on social cooperation.

On this account generalized trust is in important ways a function of everyday compliance with the prevailing social norms in a community. That is, general beliefs about the willingness of others to cooperate in mutually beneficial ways are in large part a function of our specific expectations about the willingness of others to comply with the prevailing social norms. To the extent to which this relationship between general and specific beliefs holds, the existence of such phenomena as trust and social capital is a product of everyday norm compliance. This is, I think, an instance of what Hardin (this volume) means when he says that "trustworthiness commonly begets trust." The trustworthiness created by norm compliance can lead to generalized trust in the community. The virtue of this account is that it offers a precise way of answering the question of the likelihood that generalized trust will emerge and be maintained in a society: to understand the emergence and maintenance of certain beneficial social beliefs is to understand the emergence and maintenance of certain types of social norms.

Social Norms and the Maintenance of Trust

The key to understanding the effects of social norms is to understand their content, the substantive rules of behavior that they instantiate. Informal social rules can induce various types of behavior, some cooperative and some noncooperative. Thus, we need to know the conditions under which cooperative social rules emerge. Furthermore, there may be a number of different ways of cooperating in any social situation. One important implication of this fact is that social norms can make differing demands on the various members of society. Because of these potential differences, we need to know why social rules that induce one form of cooperative behavior emerge as opposed to a rule that would induce a different form of cooperation. Such differences in the demands of norm compliance may be especially relevant to the ongoing stability of these social rules.

Elsewhere (Knight 1992, 1995) I have analyzed three distinct accounts of the decentralized emergence of social institutions: a theory of the evolutionary emergence of social conventions, a market-based theory of exchange and selection through competition, and a bargaining theory that explains the emergence of institutions in terms of the asymmetries of power in a society. Each of these theories builds its explanation from the micro level, arguing that informal social institutions emerge from repeated interactions between small numbers of social actors. On each of these accounts these informal institutions resolve the strategic problems inherent in social interactions characterized by multiple equilibria: each of the equilibria could serve as the resolution of the social interaction, but the actors need to identify a common equilibrium to pursue. In subsequent work (Knight and Epstein 1996; Ensminger and Knight 1997; Knight and Ensminger 1998) I have applied these theories directly to the question of the emergence and maintenance of social norms. The major advantage of these theories for the present discussion is that they clearly specify the social conditions under which each of the three processes is most likely to be the cause of the emergence of social norms. And each offers a characterization of the types of social norms produced by the different processes.

In this way the theories allow us to correlate social conditions and the defining characteristics of the dominant social norms in a society. If the account of the relationship between compliance with prevailing norms and generalized trust is accurate, then the analysis of dominant social norms should provide insights into the possibility for widespread trust in a community. More specifically, to use this analysis to address the question of the possibility of generalized trust in a socially diverse society we need a sense of how diversity might affect the social conditions relevant to the emergence of social norms.

In his work on the related concept of community Amitai Etzioni (1993, 217) articulates an oft-stated concern about the effects of cultural pluralism on modern society:

> there are two kinds of pluralism: the kind that is unbounded and unwholesome, and pluralism-within-unity. In the former, each group is out to gain all it can, with little concern for the shared needs of the community. In the latter, groups vie with one another yet voluntarily limit themselves when they impinge on common interests. Our pluralism has been—and there is reason to believe it has become increasingly—mainly of the unbounded kind, severely stressing the political system entrusted with crafting policies in the common interest.

His concern suggests that social diversity can have the effect of undermining the constraining effects of community on the democratic process. Steven Lukes (1991) puts the implications more boldly when he argues that the primary source of conflict, and thus the basic challenge to social order itself, is social diversity. His reasoning is helpful in clarifying what is at issue in assessing the effects of social diversity on the mechanisms of trust.

Traditional formulations of the problem of social order are grounded in the tension between the interests of individuals and the collective good of society. This leads to the standard problems of free-riding and the failure to reap the mutual benefits of social cooperation. But analyses of the logic of collective action have shown that under the proper conditions this tension can be reconciled and social order and cooperation can be achieved (Hardin 1982; Axelrod 1985). Implicit in these accounts, as interpreted by Lukes, is that the members of the society share a common notion of a collective good even if it is not a sufficient motivation to ensure social order. The fact of social diversity, however, creates a tension at a more fundamental level. In a society characterized by different cultural groups, the tension is not only at the level of conflicting interests but also at the level of different conceptions of the collective good. On this account the pressure on order is situated both within groups and between groups. Thus, Lukes situates the challenge to social order in the greater diversity of the ends characteristic of socially diverse societies.

We may agree or disagree with Lukes's assertion that the traditional formulation of the problem of order is based on an implicit assumption of a shared conception of the good. To agree with this assertion seems to require us to accept the idea that each social group's culture is characterized by a common conception of collective ends. But one could find the conception of the unity of collective ends unacceptable and still find plausible the weaker claim that there is a close relationship between cultural factors and the definition of collective ends. From this it would follow that, although there may be conflict over the definition of the common good within a given social group, the variation within a social group is not as great as the variation across social groups, assuming, as I do, that there are distinguishable cultural differences across various social groups. Even if we accept only the weaker formulation of the culture-collective ends relationship, we can acknowledge the basis for Lukes's argument about the challenge of social diversity.

There are at least three differences between social groups that may be relevant to an analysis of trust in a culturally diverse society: differences in interests, differences in the definition of basic ends, and differences in social expectations and beliefs (as manifest in different sets of intragroup social norms). The most important relationship for my purposes here is the one between the degree of conflict of interests between the members of a group and the types of social norms that emerge. It is easy to state this relationship in terms of two related tendencies. First, the greater the conflict of substantive interests between the members of a group, the greater the conflict of interest over the content of the social norms. Second, the greater the differences in the distribution of important resources in a group, the more the resultant social norms are characterized by distributional asymmetries that favor some social actors over others. Obviously, the prevalence of both of these conditions, interest conflict and resource asymmetries, involves empirical questions whose answers will vary across societies, but there is considerable evidence from studies of socially heterogeneous societies that both conditions hold.

Consider, as examples of the types of relevant evidence that would support this account, two recent analyses of the effects of social heterogeneity. Charles Tilly (1998, 7–8) recently notes in his analysis of such societies that

> large, significant inequalities in advantages among human beings correspond mainly to categorical differences . . . rather than to individual differences in attributes, propensities, or performances. . . . Durable inequality among categories arises because people who control access to value-producing resources solve pressing organizational problems by means of categorical distinctions. Inadvertently or otherwise, those people set up systems of social closure, exclusion, and control.

The categorical differences to which Tilly refers are generally defined in terms "such as female/male, aristocrat/plebian, citizen/foreigner, and more complex classifications based on religious affiliation, ethnic origin, or race" (6). These differences are, for the most part, the types of intergroup distinctions that diversity allows. Similarly, in his recent review of comparative-historical research on social order, Dennis Wrong (1994, 159) observes that "group conflict in overt or covert form is endemic to societies characterized by social heterogeneity, a high degree of internal differentiation, and social inequalities among large groups or social aggregates."

Evidence such as this suggests that social conditions exist such that the types of norms that emerge in a modern, culturally diverse society are norms that favor dominant social groups by giving their members the advantage in the distribution of the substantive benefits of cooperative behavior and imitating their intragroup cultural traits. The question is: what are the implications of the emergence of such norms for our question about trust in the face of social diversity?

There are two reasons for concluding that trust cannot be informally sustained in a culturally diverse society. They are both related to the effect of the nature and content of social norms on the likelihood that people will comply with them. First, asymmetrical social norms can have a negative effect on general beliefs about the willingness of others to cooperate. This basic belief may be undermined by social norms that dictate differential behavior across social groups. Research on compliance with social and legal norms shows that there are multiple reasons why people comply with social rules (Tyler 1990, this volume; Tyler et al. 1997). One important reason, of course, is the incentive effect of the rule: the costs and benefits of compliance. A second important reason is the belief that the rule is fair. Fairness captures a set of related ideas about how a rule and its application treat the different members of a society. Here fairness can have two related effects. On the one hand, the perception of unfairness may directly affect the compliance levels of disfavored groups. On the other hand, disfavored groups may draw negative inferences about the attitudes of favored groups: the greater the asymmetry of interests reflected in the norm, the more the disfavored groups perceive unfairness, and thus the less they feel that the favored groups are generally willing to cooperate in ways that further the disfavored groups' interests. Both of these effects of fairness undermine trust between members of different social groups.

This last point rests on the assumption that individuals are motivated in part by fairness in their decisions about compliance with social rules. This assumption runs counter to a basic assumption of the rational self-interest accounts of trust and social cooperation (such as those offered by Taylor 1982, and Hardin 1982). On these accounts, as long as the net benefits of compliance exceed the net benefits of noncompliance, the rational self-interested decision is to comply and cooperate regardless of the degree of distributional asymmetries. This suggests that trust may be maintained in the face of significant asymmetries. But there is a second reason for thinking that cooperation and trust are undermined even when individuals are acting merely on their rational self-interest. It relates to a set of factors that may affect the *expected* value of compliance with the prevailing social norms. Here I can merely list this set of factors and suggest how they may affect the strategic calculus at the core of norm compliance in particular and social cooperation in general.

The first three factors involve the compliance of the disfavored members of the society. First, the greater the distributional bias instantiated in the norms, the greater the incentive of the disfavored members of society to disrupt the existing set of rules. Second, the greater the distributional bias, the greater the incentive of the disfavored members to avoid social interactions with members of the dominant group. Third, the greater the distributional bias, the lower the probability that non-instrumental motivations will affect the decisions of disfavored social actors to comply with social norms. Each of these tendencies works to lower the frequency of norm compliance by members of disfavored groups.

This increase in the frequency with which disfavored actors fail to comply with existing norms also creates factors that lower the likelihood that members of the dominant group will support these norms. Fourth, as uncertainty about the compliance of other actors increases, instrumentally motivated compliance declines owing to its lower expected value. From the perspective of an individual actor, noncompliance affects whatever confidence she may have that the prevailing norms accurately predict the behavior of those with whom she interacts. Her confidence in the accuracy of the social norms affects the probability that she places on the likelihood that others will cooperate. The lower her confidence in the information she infers from the norm, the lower the probability she attaches to the likelihood that others will cooperate. This has the effect of lowering the expected value of her own compliance. Finally, as noncompliance becomes more frequent, the costs of informal sanctioning, borne primarily by members of the dominant group, increase, further undermining the expected value of the existing norms. In the end, because of the cumulative effect of these various factors, the ability of the prevailing social norms to induce compliance declines and thus the possibilities for generalized trust in a socially diverse society decrease as well.

Trust and the Rule of Law

The argument in the previous section suggests that under certain social conditions prevalent in many contemporary societies, generalized trust is not sustained by informal mechanisms like social norms. Therefore, if trust is such an important factor in the success of political and economic performance, we must ask: can it be fostered by formal legal means? Many people, from quite different theoretical perspectives, doubt it. For example, Lon Fuller (1981, 77), one of the leading proponents of the view that the moral dimension is essential for social order, concludes that "legal rules are not an effective device for directing human energies to those places where they can be most creatively and effectively applied." Similarly, Michael Taylor (1982, 57), who places greater emphasis on rational self-interest, argues that "the state tends to undermine the conditions which make [stateless social order] workable, and in this way makes itself more desirable. It does this by weakening or destroying *community*." Such doubts are grounded in a conception of law and legal decisionmaking as highly impersonal and routinized.

On this conception, best elaborated by Max Weber (1978), the primary effects of formal legal institutions are to increase the dependence on impersonal formal mechanisms and to undermine the informal resources that foster creative and productive social interaction. Any effort to develop generalized trust in a society that lacks it would involve designing legal institutions that on balance avoid the negative effects of the Weberian conception. The task would be to construct a conception of the rule of law in a socially diverse society that satisfies the requirements of social order and cooperation and, as a *possible* by-product, creates the conditions for the emergence and maintenance of informal mechanisms like trust. It is possible to sketch the characteristics of a set of legal institutions that would be most likely to accomplish such a task, but it is an open question whether such an effort would be successful.

Fostering generalized trust in a society entails a process of changing social beliefs. To better clarify the process I have in mind it might be helpful to distinguish my focus here from the important research agenda reflected in Tyler's contribution to this volume. Tyler's research

on the effects of legal institutions and other organizations on trust in socially diverse environments has concentrated primarily on the attitudes
and beliefs that people have toward authority figures. For example,
Tyler and Belliveau (1996) investigate the effects of two important
mechanisms, procedural justice and superordinate identification, on
the ability of authorities to encourage compliance with group goals in
the face of internal interest conflict. Similarly, Tyler's essay in this volume focuses on the effects of social identity on "social trust," defined
as deference to authority in various group settings. Thus, while Tyler
is mainly interested in the formal institutional effects on what we might
call vertical beliefs (beliefs of group members about the trustworthiness
of their leaders), I am interested here in the possibility of formal institutional effects on horizontal beliefs (beliefs of group members about
the trustworthiness of members of their own and other social groups).

One of the central insights of Tyler's research is that the effectiveness of formal legal institutions at inducing social cooperation and
order among the members of differing social groups is in significant
part a function of their capacity to foster such vertical beliefs. But the
arguments of those who emphasize the importance of social capital
and generalized trust rest on similar claims about the independent
benefits of horizontal beliefs. As a way of considering how formal legal
institutions may foster these horizontal beliefs in socially diverse societies, we can focus briefly on the research on the contact hypothesis.
This research is especially relevant to this discussion because it focuses
on the effects of social interactions between members of different social groups on their beliefs and attitudes about other groups. We can
use the evidence drawn from this research to gain a better sense of the
types of conditions most likely to cause positive changes in the relevant
social beliefs.

H. D. Forbes (1997, ix) offers this formulation of the hypothesis,
which is generally attributed to Gordon Allport (1954): "The idea is that
more contact between individuals belonging to antagonistic social
groups (defined by customs, language, beliefs, nationality, or identity)
tends to undermine negative stereotypes and reduce prejudice, thus
improving intergroup relations by making people more willing to deal
with each other as equals." Although the hypothesis is cast in positive
terms, the results of the research based on it are rather mixed. This research has generally established the sets of conditions under which
contact can produce both positive and negative effects on social beliefs.

A number of similar statements about the types of conditions relevant
to everyday intergroup interactions have been developed. Stewart Cook
(1978) sets out five conditions: "(1) the degree of proximity between the
groups provided by the situation, (2) the direction and strength of the
norms of one's own group within the situation with regard to intergroup

association, (3) the direction and strength of the expectations with regard to intergroup association believed to characterize authority figures in the situation, (4) the relative status within the situation, and (5) the interdependence requirements of the contact situation in terms of competition and cooperation" (restated in Forbes 1997, 23). Each of these conditions is relevant to the analysis of the emergence of trust across social groups. Condition 1 is self-evident; without significant interaction across social groups, the emergence of intergroup norms does not occur. Condition 2 is relevant to the issue of the potential conflicts of interests between members of different social groups. Condition 3 relates to the goals and beliefs of the elites in the various social groups. Condition 4 measures the degree of inequality among the groups. Condition 5 treats the underlying structure of the interaction, measuring both the possibility of mutual benefit and the extent of potential conflicts of interest between the parties to the interaction.

The research results emphasize the primary importance of the degree of inequality, the level of real conflicts of interests, and the attitudes of elites. Thomas Pettigrew (1971, 275), in his research on interracial contact, emphasizes an important feature of intergroup contact: "Increasing interaction, whether of groups or individuals, intensifies and magnifies processes already underway. Hence, more interracial contact can lead either to greater prejudice and rejection or to greater respect and acceptance, depending upon the situation in which it occurs." He found that contact had positive effects on interracial attitudes and beliefs when "the two groups (1) possess equal status, (2) seek common goals, (3) are cooperatively dependent upon each other, and (4) interact with the positive support of authorities, laws, or customs." More generally, the research on contact suggests that the negative effects of interaction on social beliefs increase as the degree of inequality between the groups increases, as the degree of conflict of interest increases, and as the level of support for positive interactions between authorities and other elites declines (Forbes 1997).

This research identifies the procedures that would need to be incorporated into the design of legal institutions in order to foster positive change in horizontal beliefs: ones that increase equality of status, decrease conflicts of substantive and cultural interest, and reinforce the encouragement of elites. The conception of the rule of law that would have the best chance of satisfying these goals would be one organized on principles of pragmatism. Pragmatism has been the subject of a great deal of recent work that I cannot review here.[6] But two points in support of the pragmatic approach are in order.

First, pragmatism serves for many as the default option when it comes to law and legal decisionmaking. Analyses of the judicial process offer overwhelming evidence of the political nature of judicial decisionmaking (Epstein and Knight 1997). This has both normative and practical implications. The normative implication is that the numerous attempts to ground law in some general principle of jurisprudence have failed and will continue to do so. The practical implication is that the image of an impersonal and routinized legal system is undermined by the evidence of widespread discretion in the legal decisionmaking process. This sets the primary task of any efforts to institutionalize the rule of law to be that of structuring this discretion in socially productive ways. Second, pragmatism offers an attractive approach to such a task, especially for socially diverse societies. It emphasizes the fundamental importance of the participation of diverse interests and of the benefits of a focus on social problem-solving (Knight and Johnson 1996).

A legal system must satisfy various functions in any society. At a minimum these functions include: the proscription of certain negative actions, the coordination of mutually beneficial interactions, the regulation of lawmaking, and the resolution of legal conflict. In regard to the first function, H. L. A. Hart (1994, 189–95) argues that there is a certain set of proscribed actions, what he calls the "core of good sense" in the doctrine of natural law, that is common to all norm systems. Based on an assumption that survival is the minimum purpose "which men have in associating with each other" (193), Hart concludes that there are "minimum forces of protection for persons, property and promise which are similarly indispensable features of . . . law" (199). Beyond this set of basic protections, pragmatism implies certain guidelines that shape how these functions should be institutionalized in order to enhance the possibility of fostering informal mechanisms like trust.

First, both the content of the laws and the procedures of application and interpretation should, whenever possible, reflect the common features found in the cultures of the different social groups. As Justice Holmes (1881, 36) says in a famous passage: "The first requirement of a sound body of law is that it should correspond with the actual feelings and demands of the community, whether right or wrong." Part of this is common sense: the rules and procedures shared by all of the groups are generally the ones preferred as the societywide standards. But another reason is specifically related to compliance. To the extent that there is a correlation between the formal and informal rules in a society, then individual actors have greater confidence that the rules accurately predict the behavior of those with whom they interact. Given the fact that the question of whether compliance is instrumentally rational is in part a function of one's expectations about other actors, greater confidence in those expectations enhances the sense of the rationality of compliance.

Second, the rule of law should be flexible enough to accommodate the diversity of problems characteristic of a modern, socially heterogeneous society. To meet this requirement, the rule of law must encompass an array of institutional mechanisms. Among scholars of the rule of law, Lon Fuller is noted for his sustained attention to the relative appropriateness of legal processes for various types of problems and social situations. Much of Fuller's work focuses on the circumstances under which various mechanisms (adjudication, mediation, managerial discretion, contract, and legislation) best resolve common legal problems. The primary insight of Fuller's (1969, 185) analysis is the importance of communication: "I believe that if we were forced to select the principle that supports and infuses all human association we would find it in the objective of maintaining communication with our fellows." Fuller's basic maxim is an appropriate guide for how we should institutionalize the rule of law: "Open up, maintain and preserve the integrity of the channels of communication by which men convey to one another what they perceive, feel or desire" (186). Among other things, this reasoning implies a greater role for non-adversarial mechanisms (for example, mediation and collective dispute resolution procedures) as part of the legal process. Legal disputes should be treated as social problems that require socially beneficial solutions.

This relates to a third important principle of pragmatism: the processes of applying legal rules must take account of the full range of relevant interests in a socially diverse society. This has implications both for the terms of participation in the decisionmaking process and for the criteria for what constitutes a legitimate decision. To see this consider the implications for legal interpretation. In a socially diverse society legal interpretation involves resolving conflicts over different understandings of the behavioral dictates of a rule, where the understandings may derive from different cultural groups. In resolving these conflicts pragmatism suggests that a decision should satisfy a condition of equal respect and treatment of the members of the different social groups and produce the best consequences for the society (Knight and Johnson 1996).

Consider two ways of satisfying these conditions. One focuses on the nature of participation: a collegial court consisting of representatives of the different groups who have the responsibility of arriving at a free and uncoerced group decision. The second focuses on the constraints on the nature of the justification of the decision: judges should either ground their decisions on a reason common to the different groups or make a decision that can be justified by some reason available from each group. In the latter instance, the decision is justified by reason to each group, but not by the same reason for all groups.[7] If this is not possible, then judges should make the best decision for the society as a whole and assume that the legitimacy of the decision derives from the long-term success of the process. On this last point it should be noted that the legitimacy of the adjudication process will be challenged over time if adjudication cannot be justified according to these principles.

These three principles capture some of the fundamental features of a pragmatic conception of the rule of law. And together they create a context for social interactions that might have a positive effect on social beliefs. Two categories of an individual's beliefs are relevant here: beliefs that compliance with the rule of law will further her individual self-interest, and beliefs that others with whom she interacts (especially the members of other social groups) will cooperate with her in mutually beneficial ways. Without the first type of belief, formal institutional mechanisms like the rule of law will fail to foster social order across social groups. Each of the pragmatic principles discussed here—common features, flexibility in problem-solving, and guarantees about the participation of diverse interests—enhances the probability that any individual's interests will be reflected in the application of legal rules.[8] By fostering the belief that the rule of law is an effective means of achieving individual interests, we can sustain social order in a socially diverse society.

The second type of belief, that the members of diverse social groups cooperate in mutually beneficial ways in informal settings, is at the core of the question as to whether the rule of law can produce, as a by-product, informal mechanisms of social cooperation. The conditions that this pragmatic conception of the rule of law places on the institutionalization of legal and judicial institutions seem to be those that best incorporate the findings of the social scientific research on attitudes across conflicting social groups. For example, a major strength of the pragmatic conception of the rule of law is that the principles that encourage formal cooperation are also the principles that are most likely to encourage the types of interactions endorsed by the contact hypothesis. Especially important here is the analogy between interactions involving formal legal rules and the role of social norms in informal social interactions. On this conception of the rule of law individuals work together at problem-solving over the proper application of formal rules. This process provides the opportunity for communication between members of different social groups as to how formal rules should structure their common interactions. By analogy these actors can translate their experiences in the legal sphere to their informal social interactions. If they do so, then the beneficial effects of their formal social interactions can influence the ongoing process by which social norms emerge and change.

It is important to note, in conclusion, that this by-product scenario represents only a possibility. Even Fuller, the advocate of conceptualizing legal processes as communication mechanisms, offers a skeptic's perspective. Fuller distinguishes two basic principles of human association, shared commitment and legal principle. These roughly approximate the informal and formal mechanisms that I have analyzed here. In his later writings Fuller (1981, 76) warns against the negative effects of "creeping legalism":

As a matter of sociological observation we may therefore assert that as an association becomes increasingly dominated by the legal principle, the element of shared commitment—thought tacitly operative—tends to sink out of sight; any attempt to secure recognition for its role is likely to stir anxieties and meet with strong resistance. This reaction will extend, not simply to what may be called the element of shared substantive commitment, but to that minimum commitment essential to make the legal system itself function properly.

There are obviously no guarantees that reliance on legal institutions can be prevented from having such an effect. But the pragmatic conception of the rule of law seems to offer the best institutional means of offsetting such a result. The task is to maintain formal procedures that enhance participation and interest representation in the legal process and thus establish the conditions that increase the *possibility* that effective intergroup social norms will emerge. But it is merely a possibility. For most societies the willingness to institutionalize such conditions would involve a balancing of conflicting principles and hard political choices. But this analysis suggests that if generalized trust is a desired goal in a world increasingly characterized by social diversity, these are the types of choices that must be made.

Notes

1. I develop ideas here that I briefly addressed in Knight (1998). In that essay I identify commonalities between the research on such phenomena as trust, social capital, and community and the research program often labeled the "new institutionalism." While, with a few notable exceptions (see, for example, Levi 1997), there is usually only passing reference to one body of research in the work of the other, the guiding interests of the two research programs are remarkably similar.

2. For the best discussion of the importance of focal points as a mechanism of social cooperation, see Schelling (1960).

3. Gambetta (1988, 234) identifies an additional feature of trust that is similar to the relationship between social capital and cooperation: "Trust can be easily destroyed since it is . . . a belief predicated on the lack of *contrary* evidence." Just as social capital is depleted by lack of cooperation, trust is undermined by lack of cooperation.

4. See Knight (1992, ch. 3) for a more developed account of the effects of social institutions (including social norms) on social expectations and beliefs. See Knight and North (1997) for an analysis of the implications of this account for explanations of economic performance and change.

5. For an excellent discussion of the conceptual issues related to this approach to cognition, see Clark (1997).

6. See Menand (1997) and Dickstein (1998) for accessible introductions to both the classical and the contemporary work on pragmatism.

7. One recent effort to justify a similar approach to judicial decisionmaking is offered by Cass Sunstein (1999).

8. A common challenge to pragmatic conceptions of law is that the emphasis on future consequences undermines the predictability of the rule of law, a predictability that is necessary for stable social order. Space prevents me from addressing this argument here. See Posner (1990) for an effective counter to this challenge.

References

Allport, Gordon. 1954. *The Nature of Prejudice.* Reading, Mass.: Addison-Wesley.

Axelrod, Robert. 1985. *The Evolution of Cooperation.* New York: Basic Books.

Brehm, John, and Wendy Rahn. 1997. "Individual-Level Evidence for the Causes and Consequences of Social Capital." *American Journal of Political Science* 41(3): 999–1023.

Clark, Andy. 1997. *Being There: Putting Brain, Body, and World Together Again.* Cambridge, Mass.: MIT Press.

Coleman, James. 1990. *The Foundations of Social Theory.* Cambridge, Mass.: Harvard University Press.

Cook, Stewart W. 1978. "Interpersonal and Attitudinal Outcomes in Cooperating Interracial Groups." *Journal of Research and Development in Education* 12(1): 97–113.

D'Andrade, Roy. 1995. *The Development of Cognitive Anthropology.* Cambridge: Cambridge University Press.

Dickstein, Morris. 1998. *The Revival of Pragmatism: New Essays on Social Thought, Law, and Culture.* Durham, N.C.: Duke University Press.

Ensminger, Jean, and Jack Knight. 1997. "Changing Social Norms." *Current Anthropology* 38(1): 1–24.

Epstein, Lee, and Jack Knight. 1997. *The Choices Justices Make.* Washington, D.C.: CQ Press.

Etzioni, Amitai. 1993. *The Spirit of Community.* New York: Touchstone.

———. 1996. *The New Golden Rule.* New York: Basic Books.

Forbes, H. D. 1997. *Ethnic Conflict: Commerce, Culture, and the Contact Hypothesis.* New Haven, Conn.: Yale University Press.

Fuller, Lon. 1969. *The Morality of Law.* 2d ed. New Haven, Conn.: Yale University Press.

———. 1981. *The Problem of Social Order.* Durham, N.C.: Duke University Press.

Gambetta, Diego. 1988. *Trust: Making and Breaking Cooperative Relations.* Oxford: Blackwell.

Hardin, Russell. 1982. *Collective Action.* Baltimore, Md: Johns Hopkins University Press.

Hart, H. L. A. 1994. *The Concept of Law.* 2d ed. Oxford: Clarendon Press.

Holmes, Oliver Wendell. 1881. *The Common Law.* New York: Little Brown.

Hutchins, Edwin. 1995. *Cognition in the Wild.* Cambridge, Mass.: MIT Press.

Knight, Jack. 1992. *Institutions and Social Conflict.* Cambridge: Cambridge University Press.

————. 1995. "Models, Interpretations, and Theories: Constructing Explanations of Institutional Emergence and Change." In *Explaining Social Institutions*, edited by Jack Knight and Itai Sened. Ann Arbor: University of Michigan Press.

————. 1998. "The Bases of Social Cooperation: Social Norms and the Rule of Law." *Journal of Institutional and Theoretical Economics* 154(4): 754–63.

Knight, Jack, and Jean Ensminger. 1998. "Conflict over Changing Social Norms." In *The New Institutionalism in Economic Sociology*, edited by Victor Nee and Mary Brinton. New York: Russell Sage Foundation.

Knight, Jack, and Lee Epstein. 1996. "On the Struggle for Judicial Supremacy." *Law and Society Review* 30(1): 87–120.

Knight, Jack, and James Johnson. 1996. "The Political Consequences of Pragmatism." *Political Theory* 24(1): 68–96.

Knight, Jack, and Douglass North. 1997. "Explaining Economic Change: The Interplay Between Cognition and Institutions." *Legal Theory* 3: 211–26.

Levi, Margaret. 1997. *Consent, Dissent, and Patriotism*. Cambridge: Cambridge University Press.

Lukes, Steven. 1991. "The Rationality of Norms." *Archives Européennes de Sociologie* 32: 142–49.

Menand, Louis. 1997. *Pragmatism: A Reader*. New York: Vintage Books.

Misztal, Barbara. 1996. *Trust in Modern Societies*. Cambridge: Polity Press.

Parsons, Talcott. 1937. *The Structure of Social Action*. New York: McGraw-Hill.

Pettigrew, Thomas. 1971. *Racially Separate or Together?* New York: McGraw-Hill.

Posner, Richard. 1990. *The Problems of Jurisprudence*. Cambridge, Mass.: Harvard University Press.

Putnam, Robert. 1993. *Making Democracy Work*. Princeton, N.J.: Princeton University Press.

Schelling, Thomas. 1960. *The Strategy of Conflict*. Cambridge, Mass.: Harvard University Press.

Shore, Bradd. 1996. *Culture in Mind: Cognition, Culture, and the Problem of Meaning*. Oxford: Oxford University Press.

Sunstein, Cass. 1999. *One Case at a Time: Judicial Minimalism on the Supreme Court*. Cambridge, Mass.: Harvard University Press.

Taylor, Michael. 1982. *Community, Anarchy, and Liberty*. Cambridge: Cambridge University Press.

Tilly, Charles. 1998. *Durable Inequality*. Berkeley: University of California Press.

Tyler, Tom. 1990. *Why People Obey the Law*. New Haven, Conn.: Yale University Press.

Tyler, Tom, and Maura A. Belliveau. 1996. "Managing Work Force Diversity: Ethical Concerns and Intergroup Relations." In *Codes of Conduct: Behavioral Research into Business Ethics*, edited by David M. Messick and Ann E. Tenbrunsel. New York: Russell Sage Foundation.

Tyler, Tom, Robert J. Boeckmann, Heather J. Smith, and Yuen J. Huo. 1997. *Social Justice in a Diverse Society*. Boulder, Colo.: Westview Press.

Weber, Max. 1978. *Economy and Society*. Berkeley: University of California Press.

Wrong, Dennis. 1994. *The Problem of Order*. Cambridge: Cambridge University Press.

Chapter 13

Trust in Ethnic Ties: Social Capital and Immigrants

VICTOR NEE AND JIMY SANDERS

T HE UNITED STATES is experiencing a revival of mass immigration on a scale that approaches the migration from Europe of the late nineteenth and early twentieth centuries. The new immigrants come overwhelmingly from Asia and Latin America. As in the earlier high-volume immigration from Europe, today's immigrants rely heavily on ethnic ties to organize chain migration that links distant towns and villages to immigrant enclaves in the United States and to firms in the enclave economy and beyond in the open economy. Ethnic ties assume such a central role in the incorporation of immigrants that this form of social capital is often more important than human and financial capital in shaping the trajectory of adaptation for many immigrants. Indeed, the more immigrants come to depend on ethnic-based social capital to secure scarce resources, the greater the incentive to invest in this form of capital. At the community level, however, dependence on ethnic-based social capital can tend to reinforce a segmented trajectory of adaptation, as we shall see. By contrast, immigrants whose job mobility stems from investments in human capital are more likely to assimilate into the economic and social mainstream.

Why do many immigrants rely so heavily on ethnic-based social capital, especially at the outset of migration and during the period of settling in? A network of ethnic connections between home communities and receiving societies substantially reduces the risks associated with international migration by providing a conduit of useful and timely information relevant to the decision to move (Massey et al. 1987; Massey, Goldring, and Durant 1994; Moretti 1999; Tilly 1978). Newly arrived immigrants confront a host of immediate needs and practical problems for which trust in the readiness of direct assistance and in the reliability of information is critical to successful accommodation. Immigrants typically turn to friends, acquaintances, and relatives in the immigrant community during the initial period of transition (Boyd 1989). Through these ties, new arrivals learn about job opportunities, find affordable housing, and master the informal and formal rules of the game as they adapt to the host society.

Trust in ethnic ties is the default position of many immigrants when they must choose between those who are familiar and speak the same language and strangers who are not and do not. Transposed to this arena, Hardin's (this volume) encapsulated-interest hypothesis suggests that trust among co-ethnics involves the same criterion as trusting relationships in general: it depends on whether the co-ethnic with whom you have a relationship has an incentive to fulfill your trust. Typically, friends, acquaintances, and relatives are more likely to have an interest in being trustworthy than strangers. Sanctions intrinsic to ongoing personal relationships reduce the payoff to opportunism and guile (Nee and Ingram 1998, 24–30). In other words, the betrayal of trust must incur costs not only for the truster but also for the trusted party. As James Coleman (1988, S107–8) argues, within closed networks—that is, in families and among friends—the enhanced monitoring and sanctioning capacity renders obligations and expectations more trustworthy. Alejandro Portes and Julia Sensenbrenner (1993) make essentially the same point in emphasizing the informal monitoring and sanctioning capacity of socially isolated immigrant enclaves in securing trust through ethnic ties. If the outside society appears to immigrants as unfriendly and even hostile, this tends to generate the social closure that enhances the effectiveness of community-level sanctioning.

But just as ethnic ties constitute the social bases of trust in immigrant communities, so are they a source of apprehension. Entrapment by way of dependence on ethnic ties in workaday lives of virtual servitude is not uncommon in immigrant communities. As an immigrant worker revealed to us:

> My relatives and friends all told me, try not to work in Chinese circles anymore. Once you plunge yourself into it, you cannot free yourself, because you always face Chinese and never have the chance to speak English. . . . And Chinese people, if they are boss, they are more likely to squeeze all your labor. And people share this feeling and saying.

The lesson our informant has learned from his friends and relatives is this: beware—those who appear trustworthy may entrap you in a suboptimal outcome, which you may apprehend only when it is too late to escape. Consequently, trust in ethnic ties cannot be separated entirely from distrust stemming from the possibility of guile by opportunists who use ethnic ties instrumentally to gain advantages not otherwise possible in the open economy. Although ethnic entrepreneurs risk incurring reputational costs of social disapproval should they transgress norms of appropriate conduct, the encapsulated-interest hypothesis does not necessarily predict a trustworthy relationship, given the entrepreneur's interest in securing cheap and pliable labor. Even good intentions gone awry may yield the same suboptimal results. Uncertainty ex ante about the consequence of social action based on trust can give rise to mixed sentiments toward the trusted party. Consequently, trust and distrust—experienced as apprehension or misgiving—often are inseparable and intertwined in the same relationship. Thus, although immigrants frequently rely on ethnic ties to secure resources and learn about job opportunities, they may remain apprehensive about the consequences of doing so.

In this chapter we illustrate the use of ethnic-based social capital with quotes from life-course interviews we conducted with a sample of Asian immigrants. Then we examine the consequences of reliance on ethnic-based social capital in finding jobs. We compare the quality of jobs found through reliance on ethnic ties to that of jobs obtained by immigrants who could rely instead on investments in human capital and who brought with them financial capital. We demonstrate that reliance on ethnic-based social capital increases the risk of segmented assimilation and incorporation into low-quality jobs. In contrast, we show that immigrants who rely on their stock of human capital are more likely to move into higher-quality jobs. From these analyses we can observe that the mixed sentiments of trust and distrust (that is, misgiving, suspicion, apprehension) of ethnic ties are grounded in fact. Among immigrant workers in the enclave economy runs a justifiable undercurrent of worry of entrapment and concern about the long-term consequences of social action based on trust in ethnic ties.

Ethnic-Based Social Capital

Social capital, accumulated through repeated social exchange, is reflected in the sentiments of obligation and solidarity. Like financial capital, social capital is an asset, yielding profit in economic action or in social rewards like approval and status. Immigrants draw on social capital when they ask a relative or friend for an affidavit of support; when they initially live with relatives who immigrated earlier; when family labor is utilized in a family business; when they use tips or direct assistance provided by friends, acquaintances, or relatives to find work and housing; and when they draw on the experiences of others in learning how to deal with American institutions so as to obtain a driver's license, start telephone service, open a bank account, establish creditworthiness, and pursue any number of other social actions.

The utility of ethnic-based social capital is revealed in interviews with informants in our sample of Asian immigrants. They illustrate just how important friends, acquaintances, and relatives are in obtaining timely information about hiring practices and labor market conditions. Through ethnic ties immigrants receive advice about appropriate etiquette for job interviews and tips about the reputation of local firms. In some cases the help can be quite direct, as when a relative accompanies the immigrant to her place of work and introduces him to the employer or foreman. How useful ethnic ties can be to immigrants in their job searches is evident in these remarks:

> I had a friend who was working at a factory. Originally, she wanted to introduce her sister to that factory. But her sister did not want to go. She had already told her boss that she would introduce a friend to the factory, and she was afraid that the boss would complain [if she didn't refer someone], so she called me. I said that I could try it, but I did not know English and also I knew nothing about the job. But when I went there he hired me. (*Hong Kong immigrant*)

> Because my family members all attend that church, when I came, I went to this church too. The church gave me a lot of help, I got my job in a Korean clinic because of the relations in the church. I arrived on Saturday, and on Monday, I went to work. (*Korean immigrant*)

> A Korean I met on the plane introduced me to the company chairman. The chairman told me that the positions for mechanics were filled, but they needed someone to work in the warehouse. So I took the job. (*Korean immigrant*)

> [How did you find your first job?]: It was through a friend's introduction. Because I had two friends who lived in Washington. Later they went to Texas to work. They were on good terms with their boss, so at that time they needed a hand, and they talked to the boss about me, and he called me. I went to Texas immediately, and the next day I went to work. (*Chinese-Vietnamese immigrant*)

Relatives often recruit newly arrived immigrants for jobs in their own firms:

> My older sister sponsored me here as needed labor, so I first worked in the kitchen as a helper in her restaurant. (*Chinese immigrant*)

> When I first came, I lived in my sister's house so she helped me find my first job. She went to the restaurant and talked with the boss, who told her that a waitress quit so he wanted me to work there. I got a job working in the kitchen, washing dishes, cutting vegetables, washing rice. (*Taiwanese immigrant*)

My sister-in-law was a manager in a sewing factory in Beverly Hills. She asked me if I wanted to work, so I said yes. There, I made jeans, doing cutting work. (*Korean immigrant*)

In all of these accounts, informants trust the other party sufficiently to follow up on tips and leads and to accept direct assistance in finding their first job. We see just how natural it is for them to entrust their job searches to ethnic relationships. Even though knowing nothing about the job proposed by the friend, the immigrant nonetheless took it. The alternative to reliance on ethnic ties is to search for jobs through the employment agencies common in immigrant enclaves or in the classifieds section of ethnic newspapers. In our sample of Asian immigrants, the first job was rarely found through an impersonal job search, although immigrants often turned to impersonal means in subsequent job searches (Nee, Sanders, and Sernau 1994).

Not only did informants attest to the usefulness of ethnic ties in finding their first jobs, but their accounts reveal that they rely on the same ethnic connections for assistance with housing and other needs:

When I first came to America I lived with my sister. She went to the airport to meet me. I stayed in her house for about one and a half months, and then she introduced me to work in a restaurant. (*Hong Kong immigrant*)

When we lived in our relatives' house, they didn't want us to pay the living expense. And they also helped us find a house. My sister's friend runs a store in Chinatown, so she asked me to work there. (*Chinese immigrant*)

In the first half year of our immigration, we lived in his aunt's home. We paid nothing there, such as food, room, utility, children's tuition, and children's clothes. She helped us a lot. During that time we got jobs. Because she did not ask us to return the money, we saved it. When we moved out, she gave us furniture, bedclothes, etc. She really helped us a lot. (*Korean immigrant*)

My landlord is a Chinese Cambodian, and when he came here, his economic situation was not very good. They never increased our rent because they wanted to help us. Sometimes they visited us. They told us to go to adult education school. (*Chinese immigrant*)

In the settling-in period, new arrivals eagerly seek from such ethnic connections good advice, useful tips, and direct assistance in finding a place to live, negotiating the purchase of a first car, learning about available public services and helping agencies, and an array of other practical activities:

His mother [the speaker's mother-in-law] paid rent for us. She also paid our living expenses. She always gave us some money or bought some food for us. Sometimes she bought clothes for us. His mother is an attentive woman. Sometimes she brought us to the market because we did not know what we needed to buy. She bought us many things, and her friends gave us some clothes and bedcovers. (*Chinese immigrant*)

I met some Chinese people here when I was in English school. I heard from them about how to apply for social welfare. They also told me how to report my tax. (*Chinese immigrant*)

My friend taught us to drive a car. He also gave us some advice about how to look for a job. (*Taiwanese immigrant*)

A friend I met in the army helped me to get a driver's license, my church pastor signed my affidavit for a green card, and Cal Center [the firm he worked for] made the appointment with the driving school. (*Korean immigrant*)

We got all of our information from my husband's friend, who is the principal of the Korean Language School in Orange County. (*Korean immigrant*)

We met some Chinese people with good intentions when we first arrived here. For example, we lived in an apartment, and the manager named Lee showed his concern for us. He showed us how to turn on the gas, how to get our telephone connected, and how to get to the bus stop. (*Chinese immigrant*)

Initially, immigrants view their co-ethnic employers in the context of trusting in ethnic ties, but the ethnic entrepreneur's interest in securing cheap and pliable labor often comes into conflict with the immigrant workers' interests (Waldinger 1986).

The [Chinese] boss set the price [of each garment] at her will. At the beginning I worked slowly because I was not familiar with the job, so I made less money. But I became more skilled and thus expected to make a little more money. But instead, she lowered the price. If I could speak English, I would prefer working with a Mexican boss. Since I can't speak English, I chose a Chinese boss because it is convenient for me to talk with the boss when I have some problems. (*Chinese immigrant*)

Chinese bosses are very strict. They ask you to work long hours at low pay. The boss wants you to work without resting and he treats you like a working machine. (*Chinese immigrant*)

Compared to Americans, I was paid lower. I was paid fifteen dollars per patient, but Americans would have been paid forty dollars a patient. Thus they wanted to hire me. I chose the [Chinese] company because they trusted me. I felt lucky to be making that much money as a newcomer, and I was satisfied with my earnings, so I never complained. (*Taiwanese immigrant*)

My brother introduced me to his friend who was a doctor. Because he is a friend of my brother, I didn't bargain with him about my salary. I felt funny about my work. (*Taiwanese immigrant*)

The last two informants reveal the implicit cost of receiving assistance in finding a job through ethnic ties. Such help implicitly obliges the immigrant to accept a lower structure of wages. From the employers' perspective, workers who never complain are difficult to find in the open labor market, and therefore their use of ethnic ties to recruit workers is very much to their advantage.

Forms of Capital and Modes of Incorporation

Immigrants arrive with varying amounts of social, financial, and human capital. The mix of these forms of capital in their families significantly affects the shape of their trajectory of incorporation. Many elite and middle-class immigrants bring with them varying amounts of financial capital and useful human capital, which includes the cultural competence needed to succeed in an English-speaking society. (Hereafter we refer to our expanded view of this form of capital as *human-cultural capital*.) Immigrant families with considerable financial capital have little reason to rely on ethnically controlled resources, which are more limited in comparison to resources in the open economy and majority society. Whereas personal savings for middle-class immigrants may be quickly expended in the transition period, the human-cultural capital that immigrant families bring with them or invest in after coming to their new country provides an enduring and replenishable source of profit. These are potent resources; through them elite and middle-class immigrants often replicate or exceed the lifestyles to which their class status entitled them in their homeland. Those who attend college in the United States, whether at the undergraduate or graduate level, are especially likely to accumulate sufficient human-cultural capital to enter into the social networks that provide access to mainstream institutions (Bourdieu 1983; DiMaggio and Mohr 1985).[1] By contrast, working-class immigrants typically bring less of the financial capital and human-cultural capital that is useful in the majority society, and therefore they may rely more on ethnic-based social capital for needed resources and opportunities.

In our view, the mode of immigrant incorporation is largely a function of the stock of social, financial, and human capital of immigrant families and how individuals within and apart from ethnic institutions use these resources (Nee and Sanders, forthcoming). In the quantitative analysis that follows, our aim is to examine the consequences of trust in ethnic ties for the quality of jobs that immigrants find. We compare the jobs found by immigrants who mainly relied on ethnic-based social capital with the jobs found by immigrants who brought with them financial capital and/or could rely on human-cultural capital as a strategy of accommodation.

Data

During the summers of 1989 and 1990 a multi-ethnic research team conducted 134 face-to-face interviews with Chinese, Filipino, and Korean immigrants in greater Los Angeles. Interviews were typically conducted over two days and lasted three to five hours in the preferred language of the respondent. When possible, the interviews included not only householders but also spouses and other live-in adults, such as in-laws. The interviews had two foci: job histories in the United States and residential histories in the United States. The interviews explored how these were influenced by the financial resources that immigrants brought to this country or continue to hold in the home country, by the adaptive strategies that families (nuclear and extended) have conceived and carried out, by participation in ethnic institutions and social networks, and by various background characteristics such as educational attainment, occupation, and English-language skills. A total of 171 job histories were recorded from adult breadwinners. Details of the sampling strategies and of the sample are provided in Nee, Sanders, and Sernau (1994). Because of the limited sample size, our findings should be considered as preliminary until comparable analyses can be conducted on larger samples.

Modeling Job Transitions

We use event history procedures to analyze the job transitions (job changes) of immigrants. Transition rates into four employment states are considered. Two of these states involve working in the ethnic domain of the labor market, and two states capture employment throughout the labor market. First, we estimate the rate of transition into jobs wherein the employer and employee are members of the same ethnic group. There are 157 of these transitions. Second, we model transitions into jobs that fall into the "enclave economy," as defined by Portes and Bach (1985)—that is, the combination of employment under a co-ethnic boss and self-employment. This second analysis adds 76 transitions into self-employment to the 157 transitions into employment under a co-ethnic boss, resulting in 233 transitions into the enclave economy. Given the limited number of transitions, we do not directly model moves into self-employment, but any differences in the findings of these two analyses are attributable to the presence of the self-employed in the latter analysis and their absence in the former. The third outcome we consider is the transition into semi- or low-skilled factory jobs and low-paid service positions. There are 218 such transitions. The fourth type of transition is into skilled professional, managerial, or technical positions. There are 240 of these transitions. The third and fourth types of transitions include employment under bosses of any ethnicity.

The data contain all jobs in the employment history of these immigrants since coming to the United States. When two jobs partially overlap in time, the ordering of jobs is based on the date that each job began. Proportional hazard models are utilized to carry out the event history analyses. Jobs are the unit of analysis and duration in the origin job is measured in months. The censoring events are coded 1 for cases characterized by the specific type of transition being modeled (the four destination states described here) and 0 otherwise (including the right censored cases).

Each type of job transition is modeled with a common set of independent variables. The measures include controls for social capital, human-cultural capital, financial–pre-immigration class advantage, and demographic control variables. The values of the independent variables are allowed to vary across an immigrant's job history.

The Forms of Capital: Factor Analytic Methods

According to our arguments, three forms of "capital" predict transitions into various states of employment. These forms of capital may be conceived of as latent variables. We specify a confirmatory factor analysis for each form of capital and use the resulting factor scores as independent variables in the event history analyses of job transitions. Table 13.1 reports the specification and results of the factor analytic procedures.

The factor analyses are conducted in two ways. First, the factor scores are derived from a Pearson product-moment correlation matrix. Because several of the observed variables are dummy-coded, we also carried out the factor analyses with what is, in principle, a more appropriate correlation matrix—a polychoric correlation matrix that includes the appropriate biserial and tetrachoric correlations. Both sets of factor analyses are reported in table 13.1. Both analyses yield essentially the same factor loading pattern.

The social capital factor is specified with three observable indicators of social connections to the ethnic community at the time of the origin job (the job immediately prior to the transition event). These are dummy variables that indicate: (1) the use of ethnic-based social ties in seeking employment (for example, family members or acquaintances giving

Table 13.1   Factor Loadings of the Three Forms of Capital

	Factor Loadings Derived from Pearson Product-Moment Correlations	Factor Loadings Derived from Biserial and Tetrachoric Correlations
Ethnic-based social capital		
Used ethnic-based social ties in seeking employment (for example, family members or acquaintances giving advice on where to apply for jobs, arranging introductions to prospective employers, vouching for the prospective employee)	.737	.774
Participation in at least one ethnic social association such as an alumni group, a rotating credit association, or a church	.319	.336
Employment (origin job) under a co-ethnic	.736	.771
Human-cultural capital		
Number of post-immigration jobs held prior to the transition event	.294	.244
Strong English skills	.680	.796
No education in the United States	−.820	−.931
At least a four-year college degree from a U.S. institution	.805	.980
Financial capital–pre-immigration class advantage		
Arrived in the United States with so few liquid assets (less than $2,000 in 1989 dollars) as to be unable to provide for own housing and other essential needs	−.789	−.856
Retaining valuable assets back home (for example, savings, stocks, property), the cash value of which could be transferred to the United States, or having relatives in the United States from whom loans may be obtained or with whom joint investments can be undertaken	.674	.739
At least a four-year college degree from a non-U.S. institution	.517	.545

Source: Authors' compilation.

advice on where to apply for jobs, arranging introductions to prospective employers, vouching for the prospective employee); (2) participation in at least one ethnic social association, such as an alumni group, a rotating credit association, or a church; and (3) employment under a co-ethnic. As shown in the top panel of table 13.1, the first and third indicators load most heavily. With respect to the specification of social capital as an independent variable in the subsequent event history analyses of job transitions, the factor loadings imply that the larger (positive) the factor score for individual immigrants, the greater their involvement in ethnic-based social capital.

The human-cultural capital factor is modeled with four observable variables. One variable controls for an important aspect of accumulated job experience in the United States—the number of post-immigration jobs held prior to the transition event. The second indicator is a dummy variable that distinguishes immigrants with strong English-language skills. The third and fourth observable indicators are dummy variables that distinguish those with no education in the United States and those with at least a four-year college degree earned in the United States. The factor analysis estimates reported in the second panel of table 13.1 indicate that education and competence in the English language load most heavily on the human-cultural capital factor. As for the resulting factor scores to be used in the analysis of job transitions, positive values imply greater human-cultural capital and negative values imply weaker human-cultural capital.

The final latent factor, financial capital–pre-immigration class advantage, is specified with three dummy variables. The first indicator variable identifies immigrants who arrived in the United States with so few liquid assets (less than $2,000 in 1989 dollars) as to be unable to provide for their own housing and other essential needs. The second variable controls for whether they retain valuable assets back home (such as savings, stocks, or real estate), the cash value of which could be transferred to the United States, or whether they have relatives in the United States who could extend loans to them or with whom joint investments could be undertaken. The third observable variable distinguishes people who obtained at least a four-year college degree in their home country prior to immigration. The bottom panel of table 13.1 shows that each of the factor loadings is reasonably strong, with positive values representing advantages in financial capital–pre-immigration class advantage.

Our arguments imply that the ethnic-based social capital factor should associate positively with moves into the first three employment states under examination: jobs wherein the employer and employee are members of the same ethnic group; the combination of employment under a co-ethnic boss and self-employment; and semi- or low-skilled

Table 13.2   Predicted Associations Between the Three Forms of Capital and Types of Job Transitions

	1 Employed by a Co-ethnic Boss	2 Employed in the Enclave Economy	3 Employed in a Semi- or Low-skilled Factory Job or Low-Paid Service Position	4 Employed in a Skilled Professional, Managerial, or Technical Position
Ethnic-based social capital	Pos.	Pos.	Pos.	Neg.
Human-cultural capital	Neg.	Neg.	Neg.	Pos.
Financial capital–pre-immigration class advantage	Neg.	Neg.	Neg.	Pos.

Source: Authors' compilation.

factory jobs and low-paid service positions. By contrast, it should relate negatively to moves into the more prestigious fourth employment state, which includes skilled professional, managerial, and technical positions. The predictions that pertain to the human-cultural capital factor and the financial capital–pre-immigration class advantage factor are the opposite for those for the ethnic-based social capital factor. These predictions are summarized in table 13.2.

Control Variables

The number of years of residence in the United States, age at the start of a job, and dummy variables for married cohabitation, sex, and ethnicity are specified as control variables. Chinese from the mainland and a few from Hong Kong who originally came from the mainland are the reference group in our sample. We distinguish the Taiwanese from other Chinese immigrants to control for the advantages in education, financial resources, and familiarity with Western customs enjoyed by the Taiwanese. It would be desirable to estimate separate models for each ethnic group, but the limited sample size makes such a strategy impossible. Because economic conditions influence the job market, we also specify the state unemployment rate at the time of a job transition. This helps to control for the strength of the regional economy.

Findings

Estimates obtained from the event history analyses are reported in table 13.3.[2] Transition rates into jobs under a co-ethnic boss are reported in column 1 of table 13.3. Reliance on ethnic-based social capital is strongly related to transitions into co-ethnic employment. The relationships pertaining to human-cultural capital and to financial capital–pre-immigration class advantage are not statistically significant, although the signs of these estimates are consistent with our arguments.

Cohabiting married immigrants and those who have been in the United States for several years tend to have low transition rates into co-ethnic employment. The former finding is consistent with Nee, Sanders, and Sernau (1994), who report that single immigrants, and those with few or no family connections to draw on, are the most likely to be embedded as employees in the ethnic labor market.[3] The finding involving length of time since immigration was expected insofar as the rate of job change tends to slow the longer an immigrant has been in the United States. This reflects a *settling-in* effect: the longer the period of residence, the more stable life becomes and the less frequently major transitions such as job changes occur.[4]

The second column in table 13.3 models transitions into the immigrant enclave economy (as defined by Portes and Bach 1985)—co-ethnic employment and self-employment. Hence, the only difference between columns 1 and 2 is in the treatment of the self-employed. As in column 1, reliance on ethnic-based social capital appears to be related to transitions into the enclave economy. Scores on the human-cultural capital factor are inversely related to job transitions into the enclave economy. The greater the human-cultural capital of immigrants, the lower their odds of a transition into the immigrant ethnic economy. Financial capital–pre-immigration class advantage is not significantly related to transitions into the enclave economy, but as in column 1, the sign of the coefficient is in the expected direction. No differences obtain between columns 1 and 2 with respect to the control variables.

Thus far, the analysis of transition rates into co-ethnic employment, or more generally, into the immigrant enclave economy, reveals the importance of ethnic-based social capital. As we predicted, reliance on this form of capital encourages job moves that are embedded in the ethnic labor market. It is in the ethnic domain of the labor market that ethnic-based social capital would be expected to carry the greatest weight. But to what extent can immigrants draw on this form of capital to find jobs beyond the ethnic economy? Columns 3 and 4 enable us to address this question. We have also seen that immigrants who possess a high stock of human-cultural capital have low transitions into the immigrant enclave economy. According to our arguments, this finding is due to the ability of immigrants who are well endowed in human-cultural capital to use that capital to obtain skilled and prestigious jobs in the mainstream economy where, because of the advantages of scale, opportunities for good jobs are greater than in the ethnic economy. We expected similar findings with regard to financial capital–pre-immigration class advantage, but we have found this form of capital to be unrelated to job transitions in the ethnic domain of the economy. Do these forms of capital facilitate transitions into good jobs and reduce transitions into poor jobs throughout the economy? Column 3 reports transition rates for moves into low- and semi-skilled blue-collar manufacturing jobs and low-paid service positions. None of these positions include self-employed workers, and the ethnicity of the employer is allowed to vary. The findings indicate that reliance on ethnic-based social capital increases the rate of transition into these low-quality jobs. This means that this form of capital is useful in assisting immigrants to find new jobs, regardless of the ethnicity of the new employer. Ethnic-based social capital appears to be a powerful resource for immigrants who are seeking a new job. Of course, the transitions estimated with column 3 pertain only to low-quality jobs, but notwithstanding, the findings imply that reliance on ethnic-based social capital is important for the job-seeking behavior of immigrants well beyond the ethnic economy.

Human-cultural capital is negatively related to transitions into the low-quality jobs examined with column 3. The relationship involving financial capital–pre-immigration class advantage is negative, as predicted, but the estimate is not statistically significant. These findings are consistent with the argument that human-cultural capital enables immigrants to avoid poor jobs. But such an interpretation implies that this form of capital must also help immigrants find good jobs. This issue is addressed with column 4,[5] which models transitions into skilled professional, managerial, or technical jobs. Reliance on ethnic social capital appears to be unhelpful in facilitating transitions into these jobs, but the remaining forms of capital do facilitate such moves. Both human-cultural capital and financial capital–pre-immigration class advantage are related to increased transitions into skilled professional, managerial, and technical jobs.[6]

In sum, we have found that ethnic-based social capital encourages employment moves in the ethnic domain of the economy and into low-skilled jobs throughout the economy. Such capital, however, does not facilitate moves into skilled professional, managerial, and technical jobs in the open economy. Human-cultural capital appears to lower job transitions into the ethnic domain of the economy and into low-skilled jobs throughout the economy. Both human-cultural capital and financial capital–pre-immigration class advantage appear to increase transitions into high-skilled jobs throughout the economy.

(Text continues on p. 390.)

Table 13.3 Event History Analysis: Proportional Hazards Estimates of Types of Job Transitions

	1 Employed by a Co-ethnic Boss	2 Employed in the Enclave Economy	3 Employed in a Semi- or Low-skilled Factory Job or Low-Paid Service Position	4 Employed in a Skilled Professional, Managerial, or Technical Position
Independent variables				
Forms of capital				
Ethnic-based social capital	.16[+] (.07)	.10[+] (.06)	.15[++] (.06)	-.06 (.06)
Human-cultural capital	-.07 (.15)	-.09[+] (.04)	-.20[++] (.05)	.10[++] (.03)
Financial capital or pre-immigration class advantage	-.09 (.07)	-.07 (.06)	-.09 (.06)	.10[+] (.06)
Controls				
Married, living with spouse	-.89** (.20)	-.55** (.17)	-.57** (.17)	-.02 (.16)
Years since immigrating	-.12** (.02)	-.07** (.02)	-.05** (.02)	-.07** (.02)

	(1)	(2)	(3)	(4)
Age	.02	.01	-.00	-.02*
	(.01)	(.01)	(.01)	(.01)
Sex (female = 0, male = 1)	.25	.25	.28	.06
	(.18)	(.15)	(.16)	(.14)
Unemployment rate	-.01	-.06	.01	.08
	(.06)	(.05)	(.05)	(.04)
Korean	-.16	.18	.10	.48
	(.24)	(.20)	(.20)	(.34)
Filipino	-1.56**	-1.23**	-.56	1.25**
	(.39)	(.32)	(.29)	(.34)
Taiwanese	-.41	-.20	-.55*	.69*
	(.28)	(.23)	(.26)	(.34)
Model chi-square	118(DF = 11)	103(DF = 11)	116(DF = 11)	113(DF = 11)
	p < .001	p < .001	p < .001	p < .001
N	614	614	614	614
N experiencing a transition	157	233	218	240

Forms of capital hypotheses	⁺⁺p < .01 (one-tail)	⁺p < .05 (one-tail)
Control variables	**p < .01 (two-tail)	*p < .05 (two-tail)

Source: Authors' compilation.

Note: Standard errors in parentheses, probability levels based on Wald chi-square statistics.

Conclusion

For contemporary immigrants who have insufficient financial and human-cultural capital, social capital—embodied in intrafamily, kinship, and ethnic ties—serves as an important form of capital. Unlike financial and human-cultural capital, social capital is available to all classes of immigrants. It is a form of capital that is spontaneously produced and reproduced within the institution of the family and extended family group, and through recurrent social exchanges within the immigrant community.

Our event history analysis of job histories of immigrants examines the effect of ethnic-based social capital compared to other forms of capital—human-cultural and financial capital—on the type and quality of jobs that immigrants find. Immigrants with high stocks of ethnic-based social capital are more likely to find jobs located in the immigrant enclave economy. However, reliance on ethnic-based social capital increases the risk of getting low-skilled and low-paid jobs. Although the ethnic firm may provide a more informal work environment, the small size of the ethnic firm rules out internal labor markets and benefit programs (Light and Karageorgis 1994). Moreover, on-the-job training is often minimal, since ethnic jobs typically are low-skilled, low-wage positions. Paternalism in the workplace may make workers reluctant to demand better working conditions and higher wages.

Ethnic ties constitute a form of capital that is readily accessible to even the poorest immigrants. As the immigrant informants testify, the assistance gained through ethnic ties meets the immediate practical needs of immigrants, especially in the early period of accommodation to workaday lives in the United States. Yet reliance on ethnic ties does not come without cost. Immigrants become obligated to the trusted party who provides the assistance. The feeling of obligation binds immigrant workers to jobs in ethnic firms that provide lower returns to investments in human capital than a comparable job in the open economy (Sanders and Nee 1987; Nee, Sanders, and Sernau 1994). Immigrant workers employed in the ethnic economy generally have few social relationships outside their kinship and ethnic groups. Social life is confined primarily to the family household and the community of fellow immigrants. For these immigrant workers, the continuity of social and cultural practices with their previous life is striking (Light and Bonacich 1988). The immigrant community may provide a feeling of security and an ease of communication that helps to compensate for the lower wage structure of the ethnic economy. But many immigrant workers we interviewed were discontented with their jobs in the ethnic economy. For immigrant workers who had hoped for more in their quest to establish a new life in America, being locked into low-skilled and low-paid jobs in the ethnic economy is likely to foster distrust as well as trust in ethnic ties.

Notes

1. Friends and acquaintances made in college constitute investments in social capital that enable immigrants to profit from non-ethnic social connections. Highly fungible human-cultural capital such as attendance at a major university, foreign language fluency, and cosmopolitan cultural tastes facilitates interactions with the middle class of the receiving society.

2. The three forms of capital specified as factor scores are based on the factor analyses of the biserial and tetrachoric correlations. The findings of the event history analyses reported in this section of the chapter replicate when we use the factor scores derived from the Pearson product-moment correlations.

3. In effect, marital status is an indicator of the degree to which immigrants are in a position to draw on family resources in their employment efforts. From this perspective, marital status can be viewed as a crude measure of family capital, a resource that may help immigrants to avoid jobs of the lowest quality.

4. Filipinos have lower transitions into co-ethnic employment than the other groups, a finding that is consistent with the comparatively low rate of business ownership among their fellow Filipinos.

5. As for the control variables, the ethnic group that is most advantaged in socioeconomic circumstances (the Taiwanese), cohabiting married immigrants, and those who have resided in the United States the longest tend to have the weakest transitions into low-quality jobs.

6. The two most advantaged ethnic groups, Filipinos and Taiwanese, experience relatively high rates of transitions into skilled professional, managerial, and technical jobs. Such transitions tend to be lower for older immigrants and for those who have been in the United States the greatest number of years. The latter effect reflects the same settling-in process we see in the earlier equations.

References

Bourdieu, Pierre. 1983. "Forms of Capital." In *Handbook of Theory and Research for the Sociology of Education,* edited by John C. Richardson. New York: Greenwood.

Boyd, Monica. 1989. "Family and Personal Networks in International Migration: Recent Development and New Agendas." *International Migration Review* 23(3): 638–70.

Coleman, James C. 1988. "Social Capital in the Creation of Human Capital." *American Journal of Sociology* 94: S95-S120.

DiMaggio, Paul, and John Mohr. 1985. "Cultural Capital, Educational Attainment, and Marital Selection." *American Journal of Sociology* 90(6): 1231–61.

Light, Ivan, and Edna Bonacich. 1988. *Immigrant Entrepreneurs: Koreans in Los Angeles, 1965–1982.* Berkeley: University of California Press.

Light, Ivan, and Stavros Karageorgis. 1994. "The Ethnic Economy." In *Handbook of Economic Sociology,* edited by Neil Smelser and Richard Swedberg. Princeton, N.J.: Princeton University Press and Russell Sage Foundation.

Massey, Douglas, Rafael Alarcon, Jorge Durand, and Humberto Gonzalez. 1987. *Return to Aztlan: The Social Process of International Migration from Western Mexico.* Berkeley: University of California Press.

Massey, Douglas, Luin Goldring, and Jorge Durand. 1994. "Continuities in Transnational Migration: An Analysis of Nineteen Mexican Communities." *American Journal of Sociology* 99(6): 1492–1534.

Moretti, Enrico. 1999. "Social Networks and Migration: Italy 1876–1913." *International Migration Review* 33(3): 640–57.

Nee, Victor, and Paul Ingram. 1998. "Embeddedness and Beyond: Institutions, Exchange, and Social Structure." In *The New Institutionalism in Sociology,* edited by Mary C. Brinton and Victor Nee. New York: Russell Sage Foundation.

Nee, Victor, and Jimy Sanders. Forthcoming. "Understanding the Diversity of Immigrant Incorporation." *Ethnic and Racial Studies.*

Nee, Victor, Jimy M. Sanders, and Scott Sernau. 1994. "Job Transitions in an Immigrant Metropolis: Ethnic Boundaries and Mixed Economy." *American Sociological Review* 59(6): 849–72.

Portes, Alejandro, and Robert Bach. 1985. *Latin Journey: Cuban and Mexican Immigrants in the United States.* Berkeley: University of California Press.

Portes, Alejandro, and Julia Sensenbrenner. 1993. "Embeddedness and Immigration: Notes on the Social Determinants of Economic Action." *American Journal of Sociology* 98(6): 1320–50.

Sanders, Jimy M., and Victor Nee. 1987. "Limits of Ethnic Solidarity in the Enclave Economy." *American Sociological Review* 52(6): 745–67.

Tilly, Charles. 1978. "Migration in Modern European History." In *Human Migration,* edited by William H. McNeil and Ruth S. Adams. Bloomington: Indiana University Press.

Waldinger, Roger. 1986. *Through the Eye of the Needle: Immigrants and Enterprise in New York's Garment Trades.* New York: New York University Press.

Index

Numbers in **boldface** refer to figures and tables.